# Lecture Notes in Computer Science 12541

Sihem Ben Sassi · Stéphane Ducasse ·
Hafedh Mili (Eds.)

# Reuse in Emerging Software Engineering Practices

19th International Conference on Software
and Systems Reuse, ICSR 2020
Hammamet, Tunisia, December 2–4, 2020
Proceedings

 Springer

*Editors*
Sihem Ben Sassi (iD)
Manouba University
Tunis, Tunisia

Taibah University
Medina, Saudi Arabia

Hafedh Mili (iD)
Université du Québec à Montréal
Montréal, QC, Canada

Stéphane Ducasse (iD)
University of Lille, Inria, CNRS
Lille, France

ISSN 0302-9743  ISSN 1611-3349  (electronic)
Lecture Notes in Computer Science
ISBN 978-3-030-64693-6  ISBN 978-3-030-64694-3  (eBook)
https://doi.org/10.1007/978-3-030-64694-3

LNCS Sublibrary: SL2 – Programming and Software Engineering

This Springer imprint is published by the registered company Springer Nature Switzerland AG
The registered company address is: Gewerbestrasse 11, 6330 Cham, Switzerland

# Preface

This volume contains the proceedings of the 19th edition of the International Conference on Software and Systems Reuse (ICSR 2020), initially planned to be held during November 9–11, 2020, in the beautiful seafront city of Hammamet, Tunisia, considered by many as the 'Tunisian Riviera'. Due to the COVID-19 pandemic, ICSR 2020 was delayed by 22 days, and was held as a fully virtual event, during December 2–4, 2020.

ICSR is the premier international event in the software reuse community, and starting from last year, Systems was added to the name of the conference to emphasise the role of systems engineering in reuse. It highlights the relevance of reuse to embedded systems, cyber physical systems, socio-technical systems, and systems of systems. The main goal of ICSR is to present the most recent advances in the area of software and systems reuse and to promote an exchange of ideas and best practices among researchers and practitioners.

The 19th edition's guiding theme was "Reuse in emerging software engineering practices". Recent advances in software engineering include agile software development, cloud computing, the IoT, and the increasing reliance on black box AI components to implement critical system functionalities. The impact of these technologies on the theory and practice of software and system reuse is not yet clear, and sometimes appears to be contradictory. For example, while agile development pleads against development for reuse, agile teams increasingly rely on ecosystems of reusable software components developed by quintessential reuse organizations open source developer communities. Similarly, cloud computing and container technologies have revolutionized software architectures reuse at the architectural level now embodied as reusable services on cloud platforms. We solicited papers that explored these, and more traditional software reuse themes.

We adopted a two-phase submission process, with abstracts first, and full papers two weeks later. We received a record of 84 abstracts, which yielded after some pre-review filtering, 60 full, in-scope submissions, from 19 countries and all continents with the exception of antarctica. We adopted a double-blind review process, and all papers received a minimum of 3 reviews; 15 papers received 4 or more reviews, including a handful with 5 reviews, and 1 with 6 reviews, as we kept seeking fourth, fifth, and sixth opinions to settle differences between reviewers! Based on the reviews, we accepted 16 submissions as full-length research papers (26% acceptance rate), and 2 papers, where a consensus was difficult to obtain, as short papers.

We take this opportunity to extend our sincerest thanks, first to the authors who submitted their great work to the conference, making it a success, despite incredible circumstances. We also extend our sincerest thanks to the Program Committee members, and the external reviewers they recruited, for the quality of their reviews, and for remaining fully engaged during the discussion period. Last, but not least, we would like to thank Rafael Capilla, the ICSR Steering Committee chair, who provided us with much timely and useful guidance as we navigated the various phases of the organization of the conference, and the pandemic!

Finally, we thank Lamia Labed Jilani (Université de Tunis, Tunisia) the workshops and tutorials chair, and Chouki Tibermacine (Université de Montpellier, France) the publicity and doctoral symposium chair, for helping make the conference a logistical success.

ICSR 2020 benefited from the logistical and financial support of the LATECE Research Lab (www.latece.uqam.ca) of the Université du Québec a Montréal, Canada, the RIADI Research Lab (http://www.riadi.rnu.tn) of the École Nationale des Sciences de l'Informatique, Tunisia, and the Cristal research team (UMR9189) of the University of Lille, France (https://www.cristal.univ-lille.fr).

October 2020

Sihem Ben Sassi
Stéphane Ducasse
Hafedh Mili

# Organization

## General Chair

Hafedh Mili                   Université du Québec, Canada

## Program Committee Chairs

Stéphane Ducasse         University of Lille, Inria, CNRS, France
Sihem Ben Sassi           Manouba University, Tunisia
                                  Taibah University, Saudi Arabia

## Workshops and Tutorials Chair

Lamia Labed Jilani        Université de Tunis, Tunisia

## Doctoral Symposium and Publicity Chairs

Mohamed Wiem Mkaouer   Rochester Institute of Technology, NY, USA
Ali Ouni                    Higher technology institute, Montréal, Canada
Chouki Tibermacine       Université de Montpellier, France

## Local Chair

Anja Habacha              Manouba University, Tunisia

## Steering Committee

Eduardo Almeida         Federal University of Bahia, Brazil
Goetz Botterweck        Lero, University of Limerick, Ireland
Rafael Capilla            Rey Juan Carlos University, Spain
John Favaro               Trust-IT, Italy
William B. Frakes        IEEE TCSE, USA
George Angelos         University of Cyprus, Cyprus
   Papadopoulos
Claudia Werner          Federal University of Rio de Janeiro, Brazil

## Program Committee

Eduardo Almeida         Federal University of Bahia, Brazil
Apostolos Ampatzoglou    University of Macedonia, Greece
Francesca Arcelli Fontana   University of Milano-Bicocca, Italy
Claudia P. Ayala          Universitat Politècnica de Catalunya, Spain

# Additional Reviewers

Ali Parsai
Nicolas Anquetil
Anis Boubaker
John Businge
Steven Costiou
Sabrine Edded
Diana El-Masri
Zeinab (Azadeh) Kermansaravi
Ilaria Lunesu

Carolina Hernandez Phillips
Henrique Rocha
Fatima Sabir
Andrés Paz
Marco Ortu
Andrea Pinna
Cristiano Politowski

# Contents

**Modelling**

Semantic Software Capability Profile Based on Enterprise Architecture
for Software Reuse . . . . . . . . . . . . . . . . . . . . . . . . . . . . . . . . . . . . . . . . 3
  *Abdelhadi Belfadel, Jannik Laval, Chantal Bonner Cherifi,
  and Nejib Moalla*

Safety Patterns for SysML: What Does OMG Specify? . . . . . . . . . . . . . . . 19
  *Nan Niu, Logan Johnson, and Christopher Diltz*

A Hybrid Approach Based on Reuse Techniques for Autonomic Adaptation
of Business Processes . . . . . . . . . . . . . . . . . . . . . . . . . . . . . . . . . . . . . . 35
  *Jamila Oukharijane, Mohamed Amine Chaâbane, Imen Ben Said,
  Eric Andonoff, and Rafik Bouaziz*

Reusable Formal Models for Threat Specification, Detection, and Treatment . . . 52
  *Quentin Rouland, Brahim Hamid, and Jason Jaskolka*

Dynamic Reconfiguration of Cloud Composite Services Using Event-B . . . . . 69
  *Aida Lahouij, Lazhar Hamel, and Mohamed Graiet*

**Reuse in Practice**

15 Years of Reuse Experience in Evolutionary Prototyping for the
Defense Industry . . . . . . . . . . . . . . . . . . . . . . . . . . . . . . . . . . . . . . . . . . 87
  *Pierre Laborde, Steven Costiou, Éric Le Pors, and Alain Plantec*

CxDev: A Case Study in Domain Engineering for Customer eXperience
Management . . . . . . . . . . . . . . . . . . . . . . . . . . . . . . . . . . . . . . . . . . . . . 100
  *Imen Benzarti, Hafedh Mili, and Abderrahmane Leshob*

**Reengineering**

Modular Moose: A New Generation of Software Reverse
Engineering Platform . . . . . . . . . . . . . . . . . . . . . . . . . . . . . . . . . . . . . . . 119
  *Nicolas Anquetil, Anne Etien, Mahugnon H. Houekpetodji,
  Benoit Verhaeghe, Stéphane Ducasse, Clotilde Toullec,
  Fatiha Djareddir, Jerôme Sudich, and Moustapha Derras*

DeepClone: Modeling Clones to Generate Code Predictions . . . . . . . . . . . . 135
  *Muhammad Hammad, Önder Babur, Hamid Abdul Basit,
  and Mark van den Brand*

Analysing Microsoft Access Projects: Building a Model in a Partially
Observable Domain. . . . . . . . . . . . . . . . . . . . . . . . . . . . . . . . . . . . . . .    152
   *Santiago Bragagnolo, Nicolas Anquetil, Stephane Ducasse,*
   *Seriai Abderrahmane, and Mustapha Derras*

**Recommendation**

Automated Reuse Recommendation of Product Line Assets Based
on Natural Language Requirements. . . . . . . . . . . . . . . . . . . . . . . . . . . . . .    173
   *Muhammad Abbas, Mehrdad Saadatmand, Eduard Enoiu,*
   *Daniel Sundamark, and Claes Lindskog*

Learning to Recommend Trigger-Action Rules for End-User Development:
A Knowledge Graph Based Approach . . . . . . . . . . . . . . . . . . . . . . . . . . . .    190
   *Qinyue Wu, Beijun Shen, and Yuting Chen*

AndroLib: Third-Party Software Library Recommendation
for Android Applications . . . . . . . . . . . . . . . . . . . . . . . . . . . . . . . . . . . .    208
   *Moataz Chouchen, Ali Ouni, and Mohamed Wiem Mkaouer*

**Empirical Analysis**

Investigating the Impact of Functional Size Measurement on Predicting
Software Enhancement Effort Using Correlation-Based Feature Selection
Algorithm and SVR Method. . . . . . . . . . . . . . . . . . . . . . . . . . . . . . . . . . .    229
   *Zaineb Sakhrawi, Asma Sellami, and Nadia Bouassida*

How Does Library Migration Impact Software Quality
and Comprehension? An Empirical Study . . . . . . . . . . . . . . . . . . . . . . . .    245
   *Hussein Alrubaye, Deema Alshoaibi, Eman Alomar,*
   *Mohamed Wiem Mkaouer, and Ali Ouni*

How Do Developers Refactor Code to Improve Code Reusability? . . . . . . . .    261
   *Eman Abdullah AlOmar, Philip T. Rodriguez, Jordan Bowman, Tianjia*
   *Wang, Benjamin Adepoju, Kevin Lopez, Christian Newman, Ali Ouni,*
   *and Mohamed Wiem Mkaouer*

**Short Papers**

Analyzing the Impact of Refactoring Variants on Feature Location . . . . . . . .    279
   *Amine Benmerzoug, Lamia Yessad, and Tewfik Ziadi*

An Exploratory Study on How Software Reuse is Discussed
in Stack Overflow. . . . . . . . . . . . . . . . . . . . . . . . . . . . . . . . . . . . . . . . . .    292
   *Eman Abdullah AlOmar, Diego Barinas, Jiaqian Liu,*
   *Mohamed Wiem Mkaouer, Ali Ouni, and Christian Newman*

**Author Index** . . . . . . . . . . . . . . . . . . . . . . . . . . . . . . . . . . . . . . . . . . .    305

# Modelling

# Semantic Software Capability Profile Based on Enterprise Architecture for Software Reuse

Abdelhadi Belfadel$^{(\boxtimes)}$ ⓘ, Jannik Laval, Chantal Bonner Cherifi, and Nejib Moalla

University Lumière Lyon 2, DISP Laboratory, Lyon, France
`abdelhadi.belfadel@univ-lyon2.fr`

**Abstract.** Open source and software reuse become more and more challenging for companies to save time and development cost. Collecting existing service-oriented solutions and qualifying them helps to reuse them directly or via orchestration. Our objective in this research work targets the consolidation of an advanced service repository able to be directly mapped to end-user requirements for new business application development. In this perspective, we define a model-based capability profile based on Enterprise Architecture offering a wider view qualification for service-oriented software. We propose a meta-model to gather architecture artifacts used to guide the development of existing solutions. The generated capability profiles help to create a repository of software capabilities. Furthermore, an ontology is proposed to exploit the resulted capability profiles to guide the future business needs to reuse the qualified software in an efficient way. This contribution aims to upgrade research on dynamic services consumption and orchestration to the level of end-users' requirements mapped with advanced service assets as an enabler for accelerating business application development.

**Keywords:** Capability profile · Enterprise architecture · Service reuse · Requirements specification · Service oriented architecture · Ontology

## 1 Introduction

Information systems and technology are revolutionizing and transforming organization business. They are essential components of implementing any company's strategy to achieve its goals. Organisation's business activities related to business processes define how specific business tasks are performed and it can be assisted by software tools and enterprise applications whose objective is the automation of the exchanges in the business environment. In addition, these business processes need to be adapted as a response to evolutions in external or internal environments that become more and more complex such as variations in stakeholders' needs or business domain [1]. However, companies are facing problems to

© Springer Nature Switzerland AG 2020
S. Ben Sassi et al. (Eds.): ICSR 2020, LNCS 12541, pp. 3–18, 2020.
https://doi.org/10.1007/978-3-030-64694-3_1

implement new ICT solutions, finding challenges both from IT vendors' expensive integrated digital solutions and from a myriad of disparate highly focused technological open source solutions for specific functions. Besides the benefits of open source software reuse such as the independence from vendors, or the availability of source code, the complexity of the external software ecosystem leads to difficulties in searching, evaluating and retrieving technical components to reuse [2]. Factors such as lack of documentation, uncertainty on the quality of the technical components, and the difficulty in searching and retrieving these components are the most important factors preventing reuse [2].

Describing capabilities of software as capability profile and share or exchanging the information of software capability through capability profile is an interesting and valuable way to find and select adequate software components which fit the requirement [3]. Several contributions and research works ([4–6] or [7]) proposed solutions to describe the capability of services by specifying non-functional attributes as Quality of Service, or adding semantics to functional attributes enabling to realize ontology matching between requirements and services as in [4] or [5]. Nevertheless, existing description or qualification works as mentioned lack a wider view coverage for software capabilities, by taking into consideration the business, operational and technical views of software and their related services. As for example consideration of the constraints specification, technology platform and execution environment regarding the software exposing the services, or the requirements that assisted the realization and development of those solutions.

To leverage internal and external solutions for companies, several approaches might be considered. A component view with a concise evaluation model of software components allow having a big picture of existing solutions, and facilitate the discovery, selection and reuse decision. Also, an organization of the different artifacts resulting from this qualification model, enables to facilitate decision making when choosing the suitable solution that fit the requirements. In addition, focusing on service-oriented solutions, many opportunities for reuse of functionality will arise, resulting in more efficient use of existing resources.

With regard to this context, we are targeting to (i) define a Capability Profile for Software that describes components' capabilities of software from technological, technical, functional and organizational viewpoints along with its associated quality and constraints; (ii) establish a common foundation for managing and sharing the capability profiles and stakeholder concerns produced during the evaluation or qualification process.

The expected results from this work are (i) An ISO and TOGAF-based metamodel for Software Capability Profile that offers higher-level of functional representations and covers the qualification of software components from the organizational, business, operational and technical aspects; (ii) An ontology that provides a standard vocabulary for the produced knowledge preventing semantical problems, and establish a common foundation for sharing produced capability profiles among different stakeholders. However, to attend these objectives, some problems have been identified. The first one is how to capture the architectural knowledge that guided the development of existing solutions for the evaluation and reuse of software components? The second problem is how to consume architectural artifacts to improve software reuse?

To respond to this research problem, this paper is organized as follows: Sect. 2 focuses on the related work. We focus afterward on the principal building blocks of the proposed solution in Sect. 3 and present the proposed Enterprise Architecture Capability Profile meta-model and an example of its derived model. Section 4 presents an implementation of the derived ontology from the proposed meta-model. Section 5 discusses our work and finally a conclusion is drawn in Sect. 6.

## 2   Related Work

Based on the systematic analysis of relevant research works published between 2012 and 2019 regarding component or service description with consideration of our needs, Table 1 classifies the related software and API description works according to the following criteria:

- C1) Functional and technical description of the service interfaces, including the business functions and their related inputs and outputs
- C2) Semantic annotations that defines the concepts
- C3) QoS description and the overall performance of a service
- C4) Description of the combinations of technology needed to achieve a particular technology stack
- C5) Organizational impact with a description of the business problems, stakeholders, objectives and goals
- C6) Implementation or architecture specification stating measurable criteria that should be met during the implementation of the architecture. The typical content of these architectural requirements contains the implementation guidelines, implementation specifications, implementation standards, and Interoperability requirements
- C7) Constraints specification that guided the development of the services as business, technical, standard, technology or interoperability constraints
- C8) Reasoning capabilities to deduce logical consequences from a set of axioms

Out of Table 1, the related work based on OWL-S and WSMO have a wide coverage for describing services regarding the needed criteria to achieve a wider view coverage for service capabilities. However, very few works have considered the constraints specification, technology platform and execution environment regarding the software exposing the services, nor the organizational impact that the service has on the organization where it is used.

To maximize and enable the reuse of the exposed features, we should go beyond current research and service descriptions as depicted in Table 1. A representation of a high-level view of IT systems and enterprises business processes consuming the services is needed to provide a wider view qualification, by taking into consideration the business, operational and technical views of software and their related services. This can be realized by considering an Enterprise Architecture-based methodology for describing and classifying different artifacts produced during previous projects to be available as building blocks for reuse in future projects.

**Table 1.** Software and service description works

| Software/service capability description | C1 | C2 | C3 | C4 | C5 | C6 | C7 | C8 |
|---|---|---|---|---|---|---|---|---|
| Haniewicz et al. 2012 [8], Verborgh et al. 2013 [9], Bravo et al. 2014 [10], Alarcon et al. 2015 [11] | + | + | | | | | | |
| Barros et al. 2012 [12], Ghazouani et al. 2017 [13] | + | | + | | | | | |
| Mezni et al. 2012 [14], Keppeler et al. 2014 [15] | + | | + | | | | | |
| Matsuda et al. 2012 [3] | + | | | + | | | + | |
| Pedrinaci et al. 2014 [16] | + | + | + | | | | | |
| Narock et al. 2014 [7] | + | + | + | | | + | | + |
| Wei et al. 2014 [17], Roman et al. 2015 [18], Chhun et al. 2016 [19], Ghazouani et al. 2017 [20], Ben Sassi 2016 [21], Yanes et al. 2017 [22], | + | + | + | | | | | + |
| De et al. 2017 [23], Khodadadi et al. 2015 [24] | + | | | | | | | |
| Benfenatki et al. 2017 [25] | + | + | + | + | | | | |
| Khanfir et al. 2015 [6] | + | + | + | | + | | | + |

## 3    Enterprise Architecture Capability Profile for Software Reuse

Our goal is to maximize the reuse of an organization's internal and external software by improving the capability description of existing solutions, and by describing the functional and non-functional properties of existing solutions with their related constraints. For this purpose, we propose the Enterprise Architecture Capability Profile (EACP) which is based on TOGAF Framework [26] and its Architecture Development Method (ADM). This proposed meta-model offers high-level of functional representations and covers the qualification of software from the organizational, business, operational and technical aspects.

## 3.1  EACP Meta-Model

The proposed EACP Capability Profile is depicted in Fig. 1 and is inspired mainly from TOGAF [26], ISO 16100 [27], ISO 25010 [28] and Microsoft®Application Architecture Guide [29]. It gathers functional and non-functional specifications; organizational impact and connects business services to their associated physical components to offer a broader view qualification. The proposed meta-model is composed of 6 packages:

1. Organization package outlines the organizational unit with its associated business goals and objectives that led to the development of the software.
2. Architecture Building Blocks (ABBs) package is built based on the construction life-cycle of the architecture building blocks of the ADM method. This package outlines the business problem for what this component was developed for, the chosen standards, stakeholders concerns and implementation specification. It gathers other details for instance the operational vision of the component, the business function, its attributes and constraints, application and data interoperability requirements and design time quality attributes based on best practices and guidelines from ISO 25010 [28] and Microsoft®Application Architecture Guide [29]. An example of the derived ABB model is depicted in Fig. 2.
3. Solution Building Blocks package (SBB) represent the physical counterpart of ABBs. The SBB is related to the exposed service or API (e.g. REST-based API). It is described by the URI, the HTTP method needed to reach the resource, the related parameters and the serialisation used in communication (e.g. JSON). Moreover, it defines run time quality metrics and transversal attributes (e.g. security setup such as authentication or authorization parameters).
4. Application package gathers technical requirements of the service-oriented software in general with its exposed components. It gathers also the execution environments on which the application is running (e.g. Platform class).
5. Business Process package is composed of the activities that compose the targeted business application, the actors, roles, and the event that triggers the process. This package will be used in the exploitation phase and represents the "to-be" business application to realize.
6. Requirements package gathers requirements produced during an elicitation process, helping to guide the developer or the architect during the engineering lifecycle. This package will be used during the exploitation phase.

In case of services or Web APIs, QoS parameters such as availability, response time and reliability are among the most important ones [30]. However, the design of services is influenced by the environment, the context and other decisions made by service designers [31], and this may lead to violations of quality principles known as antipatterns [31]. Thus, to guide an organization in a future exploitation and reuse of any solution, whether it's an internal or external company's solution, we aligned different metrics from ISO 25010 [28] recommended technical indicators, extended with best practices from Microsoft®Application

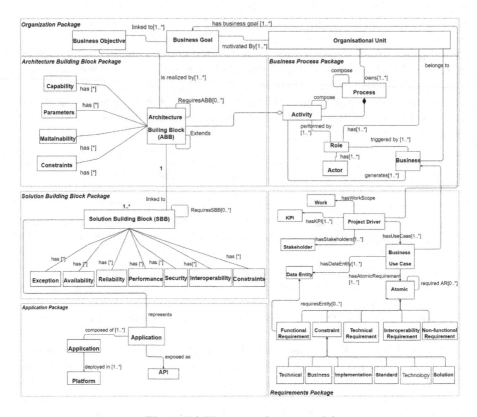

**Fig. 1.** EACP proposed meta-model

Architecture Guide [29] and TOGAF Technical Reference Model [26] which is universally applicable used to build any system architecture. Obviously, the proposed meta-model may be enhanced with new indicators if necessary.

To facilitate the discovery and reuse of the qualified solutions based on the proposed EACP Capability Profile, we present in the next Sect. 4 the implementation work to design an Enterprise Architecture Knowledge Repository (EAKR) that will gather the defined capability profiles. This latter is based on a specific ontology that offers a standard vocabulary, and a formal language to reason about software semantic annotation tags and infer new knowledge to answer to future business needs.

## 4   Implementation and Validation of the EACP

We present in this subsection the different steps that we followed to design the Enterprise Architecture Capability Profile Ontology. We considered the Uschold and King's methodology presented in [32] for two main reasons: based on the literature review this methodology is one of the most cited methodologies and

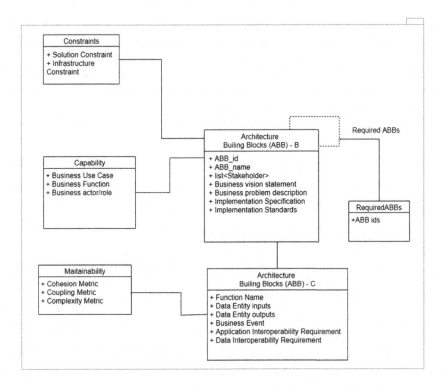

**Fig. 2.** Proposed model for ABBs

it explains in details all the steps required in the ontology development process. Here, we present the different steps that we followed.

First, we define the scope of the targeted ontology by exposing some competency questions (CQs). We analyze the relevant entities such as individuals, classes, and their relationships, and we examine their important characteristics, for instance, the transitivity of a relation or subsumption between two entities to document the domain knowledge. We note that the competency questions cited below are not representative of all expected or intended usages of this ontology.

- CQ1: Retrieve Business Objectives related to business goals
- CQ2: Retrieve the list of ABBs from end-users' requirements based on business function definition and related data entities
- CQ3: Retrieve SBBs related to selected ABBs

Second, we identified from state-of-the-art solutions some existing ontologies that enable to cover some of our needs such as Basic Formal Ontology (BFO) which is a top-level ontology and four domain ontologies, namely Ontology Web Language for Services (OWL-S) [33], The Open Group Architecture Framework ontology (TOGAF-Ontology) [34] and Information Artifact Ontology (IAO). These ontologies are well-defined, consistent and reused in other projects. We have followed a modular architecture, that consist of the main ontology importing several modules. The main motivation for this design choice was the possibility to easily extract entities from already existing ontologies. [35].

Third, we managed the selected foundational and domain ontologies, by integrating and extending in a coherent way the different ontologies into the targeted EACP ontology using the Protégé Ontology Editor.

Finally, we evaluated the consistency and inferences of the resulted model using the Fact++ reasoner.

In the following subsections, the *"Italic"* form is used to designate semantic classes and ontology relationships. Regarding the latter, labels such as BFO, OWL-S or TOGAF are used instead of the Internationalized Resource Identifier (IRI) for the stake of legibility.

### 4.1 Construction Steps of the EACP Ontology

We depict in this section the construction steps of the EACP ontology from the meta-model presented in Sect. 3.1 with regards to the main steps of our ontology building approach.

**Step 1: identification of existing ontologies** In the proposed semantic model, we have described all entities of the meta-model. The resulted ontology contains 230 classes, 78 object properties, and 30 data properties.

The targeted modular EACP ontology defines its entities and relations under the BFO framework. This latter is designed to support information analysis, retrieval and integration from different semantic resources [36]. To map EACP entities to BFO, we realized the alignment based on the methodology described in [36].

We choose to reuse the BFO based ontology, namely IAO ontology, to model information artifacts of the meta-model (e.g., conditional specification, objective specification, and goal specification). In terms of implementation, IAO is easy to integrate given that it is already based on the foundational ontology BFO. Moreover, we chose to reuse TOGAF 9 ontology for three main reasons: first, TOGAF 9 ontology, developed in Knowledge-Projects[1], is the most suitable terminological model that represents meta-data of TOGAF 9 artifacts. Second, it has been used in other research works in [37] and [38], to semantically manage and share enterprise architecture information and third, TOGAF 9 ontology meets some of main modeling needs that are expressed in the meta-model as the description of entities that describe Business Architecture Component (e.g., actor, organizational unit, objective, goal, and event). In this work, we used the OWL formal language in the specification of the Terminological Box (TBox) and in the generation of Resource Description Framework (RDF) [39] triples.

---

[1] https://sites.google.com/site/ontologyprojects/home.

**Step 2: Integration of Existing Ontologies into the BFO Ontology (classes and Relations)** To achieve semantic compatibility within our resulted domain ontology, we link candidate domain ontologies to the BFO ontology. The basic pattern of the main classes in the EACP ontology is illustrated in Fig. 3 and the followed steps of the alignment task are detailed below.

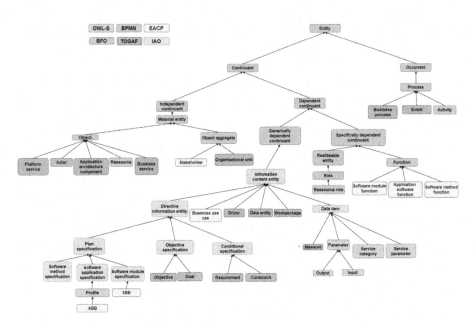

**Fig. 3.** Alignment of top-level domain classes (IAO, TOGAF, EACP, OWL-S and BPMN) under the BFO ontology

To build this OWL ontology, we first analyzed the class hierarchy of our semantic modules (namely, TOGAF, BPMN, IAO and OWL-S). Then, we aligned existing ontologies' classes to the BFO class hierarchy according to the BFO principles. By doing this alignment work, we improved the definition of key concepts of the TOGAF ontology by making them explicit. For example the class *"TOGAF:core content"* regroups heterogeneous sub-classes as *"TOGAF:function"*, *"TOGAF:process"*, *"TOGAF:capability"*, *"TOGAF:role"* and *"TOGAF:organization unit"*. As we can notice, the meaning of the *"TOGAF:core content"* class as it is defined within the TOGAF ontology is confusing and ambiguous regarding the description of the kind of data that it covers. In order to remove this confusion and inconsistency, we first defined the class *"TOGAF:content classification"* as a *"BFO:entity"*, and then we defined the classes like *"TOGAF:function"*, *"TOGAF:role"*, *"TOGAF:capability"* as sub classes of *"TOGAF:core content"* and *"BFO:specifically dependent continuant"* given that they describe a continuant that inheres in or is borne by other entities. As consequence, the meanings of theses sub-classes are more explicit and clear under the BFO framework. An overview of top-level domain classes mapping into the BFO ontology is shown in Fig. 3.

After describing classes, we aligned the object properties of existing ontologies to the BFO relationship hierarchy in order to ensure the integrity of our ontology. Table 2 summarizes the BFO object properties that we used in the resulted ontology in order to semantically describe the relationships of the meta-model. We introduced data properties in the ontology as the data property "*EACP:hasDescription*" to specify a textual description of artifacts. This data property can be use for example to link a "*TOGAF:goal*" to its value, for instance "efficiency in business operation to increase productivity".

**Table 2.** Top-level relationship mappings to cover the upper-level relations of the meta-model

| Meta-model relation | Direct relation in EACP ontology | Parent relation in EACP ontology |
| --- | --- | --- |
| Has (between continuant entities) | BFO:hasContinuantPart | BFO:topObjectProperty |
| | BFO:hasFunction | RO:bearerOf |
| | BFO:hasSpecifiedInput | BFO:hasParticipant |
| Has (between occurrent entities) | BFO:hasOccurrentPart | BFO:topObjectProperty |
| Represents, describes | IAO:isQualityMeasurementOf | IAO:isAbout |
| | IAO:denotes | IAO:isAbout |

**Step 3: Extension of Existing Ontologies** New 30 additional classes are inserted in the EACP ontology based on the proposed meta-model. For example, we introduced the "*EACP:ABB service category*" class as a direct subclass of "*IAO:data item*" and an indirect subclass of "*BFO:generically dependent continuant*". Therefore, "*EACP:ABB service category*" is assumed to be a superconcept of the classes "*EACP:maintainability*", "*EACP:security*", "*EACP:capability*" and "*EACP:interoperability*". We adopted the following naming convention: for classes borrowed from existing ontologies in general, we kept existing IRIs, as well as existing annotations (e.g. "*RDFS:label*", "*RDFS:prefLabel*"). For new EACP classes, we assigned new IRIs (based on English labels) as well as "*RDFS:prefLabel*" in English.

The ontology is enriched with semantic axioms in order to define in a concise way classes and relations and to improve the ontology with reasoning capabilities. In what follows, we explain how we semantically describe the ABB class and link this entity to others EA associated entities (e.g., SBB, business activity, and business objectives).

We defined the class *"EACP:architecture building blocks"* as a subclass of the *"TOGAF:business service"* class, and by using the necessary conditions (i.e., existential restrictions) listed below:

- *"BFO:hasContinuantPart"* some *"EACP:solution building blocks"*,
- *"BFO:hasContinuantPart"* some *"TOGAF:parameter"*,
- *"BFO:hasContinuantPart"* some *"OWL-S:service category"*,
- *"IAO:isAbout"* some *"EACP:software function"*,
- *"BFO:realizedBy"* some *"TOGAF:process"*.

To complete the definition of the class *"EACP:architecture building blocks"* we directly state that this class is disjoint with the class *"EACP:solution Building Blocks"*. And given that, *"EACP:architecture building blocks"* isA *"TOGAF:business service"* as consequence it is disjoint with all the subclasses of the class *"TOGAF:business architecture component"* (i.e., actor, service quality, event, process, or organizational unit).

In TOGAF ontology the concept *"TOGAF:business service"* is A subconcept of the concept *"TOGAF:business architecture component"*. The class *"TOGAF:business architecture"* is defined using an equivalent class property: *[equivalentClass]* *"TOGAF:architecture"* and (*"BFO:continuant PartAtSomeTime"* only *"TOGAF:business architecture component"*). We note that a necessary and sufficient condition are called Equivalent classes in OWL.

We made some modeling decisions about the description of some unclear TOGAF aspects: we interrelate classes using a min number of relationships than those proposed in TOGAF ontology. This will improve the reasoning performance of the EACP ontology. In TOAGF, there is a mix between class hierarchy and necessary conditions for example, the *"TOGAF:business architecture"* is defined as *"TOGAF:architecture"* and (*"BFO:hasContinuantPart"* some *"TOGAF:business architecture component"*). We modified the some OWL restriction with a some necessary condition as explained above. This correction is valid for all the kind of business architecture component of the TOGAF ontology.

Finally, we completed the definition of the EACP ontology with textual annotations that aim to give the users more details about our ontology components; in this annotation task we based our textual definitions on the documentation of TOGAF 9.

**Step 4: Evaluation of the Consistency** To check the validity and the correctness of the designed ontology, we first populated the ontology manually, then used the Fact++ reasoner. The classification result is presented in the left side of Fig. 4. Inferred assertions are presented based on the axioms described in step 3 of Sect. 4.1. No errors are found and all classes and relations are correctly classified.

**Step 5: EACP-Onto Based Qualification Example** We illustrate in Fig. 5 an excerpt in RDF format of an Architecture Building Block which is the pivotal instance in this graph, and annotated with "Abb 3DScan 3Dobject". It represents a REST API which is titled "Get 3D Object".

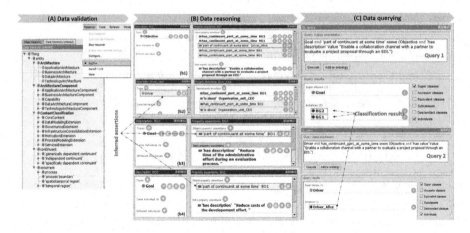

**Fig. 4.** Data validation, reasoning and querying result on the EAKR repository using the FACT++ reasoner, Protégé Ontology Editor

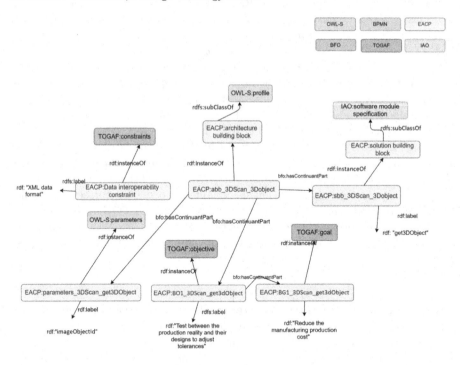

**Fig. 5.** An excerpt in RDF format of an architecture building block. Gray boxes refer to classes of the ECAP-Onto. Instance level relations are modeled with arcs.

The value of this ABB is included in the capability profile of the exposed API. We leveraged the object property "BFO:hasContinuantPart" to describe the composition between two instances. Regarding the data property

"RDFS:label", it enables to define the textual content of an instance, for example "EACP:3DScan Get 3D Object" has as label the following value "Reduce the manufacturing production cost".

This kind of annotation work enables to formalize and classify service capability profiles through several requests, for example the selection or retrieval of ABBs from user requirements that is based on business objectives or goals.

## 5    Discussion

In this work, we proposed a semantic Enterprise Architecture Capability Profile specifically designed to describe the properties, design constraints, and capabilities of service-oriented software. This helps to offer a wider view qualification process that deals with business and technical perspectives of software services. The business perspective brings value-in-use of the qualified feature for an organization that is interested into reuse, and the technical perspective along with a quality of service describe the feature encapsulated by the software service.

The use of a semantic approach helped us in the formalization of the content of the proposed meta-model through the use of OWL language that explicitly specifies the meaning of EA meta-model entities and relations. Added to this, the proposed semantic model called EACP ontology supports advanced reasoning and querying requests on the Enterprise Architecture Knowledge Repository that facilitates the discovery, comprehension and reuse of service-oriented software meta-data (capabilities, parameters, requirements, etc.). We note that the automatic content-based data management cannot be achieved in existing EA meta-models that do not use semantic markup. We adopted a semantic approach to describe EA information and we presented the different steps that we followed to design the EACP ontology.

Unlike existing EA ontologies mainly TOGAF first, the developed ontology is based on a foundational ontology namely BFO. Second, it is based on existing well-defined ontologies to cover all the meta-model components (functional, operational and technical). Third, the EACP ontology is modular, thus it can be easily extended by future users. Finally, the EACP ontology defines a data properties hierarchy to specify concrete values of concepts use cases.

The use of BFO has facilitated the integration of heterogeneous knowledge from different ontologies into a unique coherent semantic model. In most cases the alignment was not a trivial task for us for two main reasons: the complexity of the meta-model on one hand, and on another hand the ambiguity of TOGAF OWL concepts and object relations.

The usage of an ontology for designing the model-based capability profile enables to achieve the targeted objectives and address the major challenges, namely create a software capability profile that is modular, flexible, and extensible with a standard vocabulary to qualify existing solutions with semantic annotations. This helps either to capitalize on existing knowledge produced during a software development lifecycle and infer new knowledge to answer future business needs.

As future work, we intend to exploit this model-based semantic repository for the discovery and reuse of the qualified solutions based on a requirements engineering and an entreprise architecture approach. This to support developers or architects for requirements elicitation during the engineering life-cycle. Furthermore, we intend to capitalize on artifacts produced during the engineering cycle of the projects to offer more visibility and sustainability to software for accelerating future business application development.

## 6 Conclusion

The objective of this work is to create a profile for describing software capabilities. This will allow us to discover and reuse suitable software and related services for the design and implementation of new business applications. A meta-model is proposed and based on an Enterprise Architecture Framework (TOGAF). This later is combined with dynamic quality metrics needed for services selection. This meta-model offers a wider view qualification for software and its related services covering business, technical and organizational aspects. A detailed model is proposed for every aspect in order to design the repository gathering the qualifications. This helps to support software discovery during the engineering lifecycle of new business needs.

**Acknowledgment.** This paper presents work developed in the scope of the project vf-OS. This project has received funding from the European Union's Horizon 2020 research and innovation programme under grant agreement no. 723710. The content of this paper does not reflect the official opinion of the European Union. Responsibility for the information and views expressed in this paper lies entirely with the authors.

## References

1. Valenca, G., Alves, C., Alves, V., Niu, N.: A systematic mapping study on business process variability. Int. J. Comput. Sci. Inf. Technol. **5**(1), 1 (2013)
2. Kakarontzas, G., Katsaros, P., Stamelos, I.: Component certification as a prerequisite for widespread OSS reuse. In: Electronic Communications of the EASST, vol. 33 (2010)
3. Matsuda, M.: Manufacturing software interoperability services which ISO 16100 brings about. In: van Sinderen, M., Johnson, P., Xu, X., Doumeingts, G. (eds.) IWEI 2012. LNBIP, vol. 122, pp. 60–70. Springer, Heidelberg (2012). https://doi.org/10.1007/978-3-642-33068-1_7
4. Chhun, S., Cherifi, C., Moalla, N., Ouzrout, Y.: A multi-criteria service selection algorithm for business process requirements. CoRR, vol. abs/1505.03998 (2015)
5. Boissel-Dallier, N., Benaben, F., Lorré, J.-P., Pingaud, H.: Mediation information system engineering based on hybrid service composition mechanism. J. Syst. Softw. **108**, 39–59 (2015)
6. Khanfir, E., Djmeaa, R.B., Amous, I.: Quality and context awareness intention web service ontology. In: 2015 IEEE World Congress on Services, pp. 121–125. IEEE (2015)

7. Narock, T., Yoon, V., March, S.: A provenance-based approach to semantic web service description and discovery. Decis. Support Syst. **64**, 90–99 (2014)
8. Haniewicz, K.: Local controlled vocabulary for modern web service description. In: Rutkowski, L., Korytkowski, M., Scherer, R., Tadeusiewicz, R., Zadeh, L.A., Zurada, J.M. (eds.) ICAISC 2012. LNCS (LNAI), vol. 7267, pp. 639–646. Springer, Heidelberg (2012). https://doi.org/10.1007/978-3-642-29347-4_74
9. Verborgh, R., Steiner, T., Van Deursen, D., De Roo, J., Van de Walle, R., Vallés, J.G.: Capturing the functionality of web services with functional descriptions. Multimedia Tools Appl. **64**(2), 365–387 (2013)
10. Oliveira, B.C., Huf, A., Salvadori, I.L., Siqueira, F.: Ontogenesis: an architecture for automatic semantic enhancement of data services. Int. J. Web Inf. Syst. **15**(1), 2–27 (2019)
11. Alarcon, R., Saffie, R., Bravo, N., Cabello, J.: REST web service description for graph-based service discovery. In: Cimiano, P., Frasincar, F., Houben, G.-J., Schwabe, D. (eds.) ICWE 2015. LNCS, vol. 9114, pp. 461–478. Springer, Cham (2015). https://doi.org/10.1007/978-3-319-19890-3_30
12. Birkmeier, D.Q., Overhage, S., Schlauderer, S., Turowski, K.: How complete is the USDL? In: Barros, A., Oberle, D. (eds.) Handbook of Service Description, pp. 521–538. Springer, Boston, MA (2012). https://doi.org/10.1007/978-1-4614-1864-1_21
13. Ghazouani, S., Slimani, Y.: A survey on cloud service description. J. Network Comput. Appl. **91**, 61–74 (2017)
14. Mezni, H., Chainbi, W., Ghedira, K.: Aws-policy: an extension for autonomic web service description. Procedia Comput. Sci. **10**, 915–920 (2012)
15. Jonas, P.B., Gewald, H.: A description and retrieval model for web services including extended semantic and commercial attributes. In: 2014 IEEE 8th International Symposium on Service Oriented System Engineering, pp. 258–265. IEEE (2014)
16. Pedrinaci, C., Cardoso, J., Leidig, T.: Linked USDL: a vocabulary for web-scale service trading. In: Presutti, V., d'Amato, C., Gandon, F., d'Aquin, M., Staab, S., Tordai, A. (eds.) ESWC 2014. LNCS, vol. 8465, pp. 68–82. Springer, Cham (2014). https://doi.org/10.1007/978-3-319-07443-6_6
17. Wei-bing, M., Wen-guang, W., Yi-fan, Z., Fa-yi, Y.: Semantic web services description based on command and control interaction user context. In: 2014 IEEE 7th Joint International Information Technology and Artificial Intelligence Conference, pp. 541–544. IEEE (2014)
18. Roman, D., Kopeckỳ, J., Vitvar, T., Domingue, J., Fensel, D.: WSMO-lite and hRESTS: lightweight semantic annotations for web services and restful APIs. J. Web Semant. **31**, 39–58 (2015)
19. Chhun, S., Moalla, N., Ouzrout, Y.: QoS ontology for service selection and reuse. J. Intell. Manuf. **27**(1), 187–199 (2016)
20. Ghazouani, S., Slimani, Y.: Towards a standardized cloud service description based on USDL. J. Syst. Softw. **132**, 1–20 (2017)
21. Ben Sassi, S.: Towards a semantic search engine for open source software. In: Kapitsaki, G.M., Santana de Almeida, E. (eds.) ICSR 2016. LNCS, vol. 9679, pp. 300–314. Springer, Cham (2016). https://doi.org/10.1007/978-3-319-35122-3_20
22. Yanes, N., Sassi, S.B., Ghezala, H.H.B.: Ontology-based recommender system for cots components. J. Syst. Softw. **132**, 283–297 (2017)
23. De, B.: API management. API Management, pp. 15–28. Apress, Berkeley, CA (2017). https://doi.org/10.1007/978-1-4842-1305-6_2

24. Khodadadi, F., Dastjerdi, A.V., Buyya, R.: Simurgh: a framework for effective discovery, programming, and integration of services exposed in IoT. In: 2015 International Conference on Recent Advances in Internet of Things (RIoT), pp. 1–6. IEEE (2015)
25. Benfenatki, H., Da Silva, C.F., Benharkat, A.-N., Ghodous, P., Maamar, Z.: Linked USDL extension for describing business services and users' requirements in a cloud context. Int. J. Syst. Serv.-Orient. Eng. (IJSSOE) **7**(3), 15–31 (2017)
26. T. O. Group: The Open Group Architecture Framework TOGAF$^{TM}$ Version 9. Basharat Hussain (2009)
27. ISO 16100–1:2009 industrial automation systems and integration - manufacturing software capability profiling for interoperability - part 1: Framework (2009)
28. ISO/IEC 25010:2011 systems and software engineering - systems and software quality requirements and evaluation (square) - system and software quality models (2011)
29. Patterns, M., P. Team: Microsoft® Application Architecture Guide, 2nd Edition (Patterns and Practices). Microsoft Press (2009)
30. Al-Masri, E., Mahmoud, Q.H.: QoS-based discovery and ranking of web services. In: 2007 16th International Conference on Computer Communications and Networks, pp. 529–534. IEEE (2007)
31. Ouni, A., Kessentini, M., Inoue, K., Cinnéide, M.O.: Search-based web service antipatterns detection. IEEE Trans. Serv. Comput. **10**(4), 603–617 (2015)
32. Uschold, M., King, M.: Towards a methodology for building ontologies (1995)
33. Martin, D., et al.: Bringing semantics to web services: the OWL-S approach. In: Cardoso, J., Sheth, A. (eds.) SWSWPC 2004. LNCS, vol. 3387, pp. 26–42. Springer, Heidelberg (2005). https://doi.org/10.1007/978-3-540-30581-1_4
34. Gerber, A., Kotzé, P., Van der Merwe, A.: Towards the formalisation of the TOGAF content metamodel using ontologies (2010)
35. Ceusters, W.: An information artifact ontology perspective on data collections and associated representational artifacts. In: MIE, pp. 68–72 (2012)
36. Arp, R., Smith, B., Spear, A.D.: Building Ontologies with Basic Formal Ontology. MIT Press, Cambridge (2015)
37. Czarnecki, A., Orłowski, C.: Ontology as a tool for the it management standards support. In: Jędrzejowicz, P., Nguyen, N.T., Howlet, R.J., Jain, L.C. (eds.) KES-AMSTA 2010. LNCS (LNAI), vol. 6071, pp. 330–339. Springer, Heidelberg (2010). https://doi.org/10.1007/978-3-642-13541-5_34
38. Chen, W., Hess, C., Langermeier, M., von Stülpnagel, J., Diefenthaler, P.: Semantic enterprise architecture management. ICEIS **3**, 318–325 (2013)
39. Lassila, O., Swick, R.R., et al.: Resource description framework (RDF) model and syntax specification (1998)

# Safety Patterns for SysML: What Does OMG Specify?

Nan Niu[1](✉)(iD), Logan Johnson[1], and Christopher Diltz[2]

[1] University of Cincinnati, Cincinnati, OH 45221, USA
nan.niu@uc.edu, johns6lo@mail.uc.edu
[2] Edaptive Computing, Inc., Dayton, OH 45458, USA
c.diltz@edaptive.com

**Abstract.** The Systems Modeling Language (SysML) represents a significant and increasing segment of industrial support for building critical systems. The Object Management Group (OMG) has been releasing and revising the formal specification of SysML since 2007, with version 1.6 recently formalized in November 2019. However, little is known about what OMG specifies and how the official specification influences model-driven engineering (MDE). To fill the gap, we present a new way of analyzing the OMG SysML specification (version 1.6) to uncover reusable guidelines and constraints for safe MDE practice. We illustrate our approach with the discovery of the recurring "Asset Leakage" safety pattern and the development of a semantic-role-based theory to support practitioners' identification, formulation, and verification of critical properties in their modeling contexts.

**Keywords:** Systems Modeling Language (SysML) · Systems reuse · Specification patterns · Temporal constraints · Semantic roles · Grounded theory

## 1 Introduction

The Systems Modeling Language (SysML), first adopted by the Object Management Group (OMG) in 2006, is a general-purpose, visual modeling language for systems engineering [32]. It builds on UML as its foundation and provides additional extensions to facilitate the communication and collaboration among various stakeholders who participate in the model-driven engineering (MDE) activities. SysML is designed to equip MDE practitioners with simple but powerful constructs for modeling a wide range of problems in different application domains, including aerospace, automotive, energy, healthcare, manufacturing, and telecommunications.

In safety-critical domains, crucial properties—such as "a vehicle's revolutions per minute (RPM) shall never exceed 4,000"—must be checked. The MDE

DISTRIBUTION STATEMENT A: Approved for public release: distribution unlimited. Approval ID: 88ABW-2020-1390.

literature distinguishes two modes of checking: offline verification and online monitoring. In offline settings, techniques like model checking [11] are employed to formally examine whether the models satisfy a given property, e.g., the LTL formula "[ ]!(RPM > 4000)" expresses the aforementioned safety requirement. In contrast, online monitoring deploys techniques like observer automata [31] to detect property violations for models at runtime [6]. A key difference is that runtime monitoring focuses on the current run of the deployed models, whereas model checking analyzes all the runs [8].

Researchers have addressed reusability and scalability issues in order for these property-checking mechanisms to be readily adopted in practice. For instance, Dou *et al.* [18] proposed a model-driven approach to generating diagnostic information for temporal properties, and further used synthesized data with millions of events to show that the approach grew linearly with respect to the size of the events logging the execution of a system. Besnard and colleagues [8] developed the observer automata in the same language as the models (i.e., by using UML), and their simulation on a STM32 discovery board showed that the runtime overhead of the monitoring based on observer automata was 6.5% for the embedded target.

Despite these advances, an inherent challenge facing MDE practitioners is to specify the critical properties, e.g., those related to safety, security, and dependability [39]. Not only is expertise required to identify important concerns in a specific domain, but the concerns also have to be formulated in ways amenable to the particular machinery (e.g., TemPsy temporal formulas [18] or UML state invariants [8]). The engineers are left with many questions: which properties to begin with, how to assess the validity of the properties, and realistically speaking, how others specify properties in their work.

In their seminal work, Dwyer and his colleagues [19] surveyed 555 temporal logic specifications and showed that an overwhelming majority (92%) fell into eight highly reusable patterns: Response, Universality, Absence, etc. While we review Dwyer *et al.*'s work in more detail in the next section, their patterns have had extensive influence in software and systems engineering: querying model histories [17], developing a UML interpreter [7], debugging declarative models [26], discovering latent behavior of UML models [20], model-based testing from UML/OCL [15], to name a few. However, like Dwyer *et al.*'s patterns, the MDE extensions stay mainly at a syntactic level. Take "[ ]!(RPM > 4000)" as an example, although it is an instance of the globally-scoped Absence pattern ([ ](!$P$)) [19], the modeler has to semantically map $P$ without much guidance.

If the RPM case seems too straightforward, consider the requirement of a cruise control system: "When the system is engaged, the cruise speed should be defined [8]." Here, should $P$ in [ ](!$P$) be instantiated with "systemEngaged & unknownCruiseSpeed", or with "systemEngaged $\rightarrow$ unknownCruiseSpeed"? Or should a completely different pattern, namely Response ([ ]($Q \rightarrow <>R$)) [19], be applied where $Q$ = "systemEngaged" and $R$= "! unknownCruiseSpeed"? Unfortunately, syntactic patterns offer little help.

In this paper, we propose to reduce the semantic gap by taking a fresh look at what OMG specifies. In particular, we manually analyze the OMG specification [33] to search for recurring and reusable patterns that guide SysML-based software and systems engineering practices. We pay special attention to the parts of the specification where the integrity of SysML is discussed. We therefore call our results *safety patterns* to indicate the risk or danger of violating them. We further codify the *semantic roles* of each pattern to ease the mapping of syntactic structures in the modeler's MDE contexts.

The contributions of our work lie in the analysis of the OMG SysML specification as a new way to guide MDE practices. Our work is particularly valuable for the practitioners who are required or recommended to adhere to OMG specifications, and our results on safety patterns offer concrete insights into the kind of critical properties subject to be verified in all SysML models. The remainder of the paper is organized as follows: Sect. 2 provides background information and discusses related work, Sect. 3 presents our research methodology for analyzing the OMG SysML specification, Sect. 4 describes our results by detailing the "Asset Leakage" pattern, Sect. 5 elaborates our vision about semantics-enriched support for MDE and systems reuse, and finally, Sect. 6 concludes the paper.

## 2 Background and Related Work

### 2.1 Property Patterns in MDE

The seminal work by Dwyer *et al.* [19] tackled the challenge concerning practitioners' unfamiliarity with temporal logic notations. They developed a pattern-based approach to ease the specification of informal requirements into temporal logic formulas. Eight reusable patterns were reported in [19]: Absence, Bounded Existence, Chain Precedence, Chain Response, Existence, Precedence, Response, and Universality. Figure 1 organizes these patterns based on occurrence and order. A survey of 555 specifications from over 35 sources showed that 92% were instances of the eight patterns shown in Fig. 1, with the top three accounted for 80% of the sample: Response ($\frac{245}{555} = 44\%$), Universality ($\frac{119}{555} = 21\%$), and Absence ($\frac{85}{555} = 15\%$) [19]. The results provided empirical evidence of human specifiers' use and reuse of common formalisms to express behavioral aspects of their subject systems.

Inspired by these patterns, MDE extensions are made. An important task of offline checking is trace diagnostics, i.e., providing the modeler with the relevant information in case a property fails to hold. When checking the logged events of a system's execution, some tools pinpoint the last log entry (i.e., the last event) read before detecting the property violation. However, the usefulness of the traces truncated in this manner is limited, because a property can be violated in different ways and the last read event may not necessarily be the event responsible for the violation. To provide relevant diagnostic information, Dou *et al.* [18] developed algorithms and their development was guided directly by Dwyer *et al.*'s work [19]. As shown in the left column of Table 1, six patterns were presented to classify the violation of a property: two on occurrence and four on

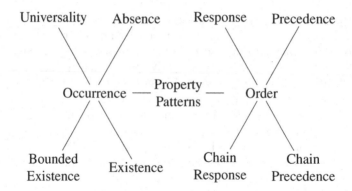

**Fig. 1.** Temporal property patterns by Dwyer *et al.* [19] (*figure adopted from* [17]).

**Table 1.** Illustrating the MDE Extensions of Dwyer *et al.*'s Reusable Patterns [19]

| Property violations [18] | Model histories [17] (# of OCL operations) |
|---|---|
| (1) unexpected occurrence | (i) basic version traversal (7) |
| (2) no-show occurrence | (ii) temporal assertions (5) |
| (3) no-show order | (iii) predicate-based version scoping (3) |
| (4) wrong temporal order | |
| (5) wrong temporal chain | (iv) context-based version scoping (2) |
| (6) wrong temporal order and chain | (v) version unscoping (1) |

order [18]. The trace diagnostics algorithms were then informed by the patterns, two of which (diagnostic information of Existence and that of Precedence) were explained in detail in [18].

Another extension was made by García-Domínguez *et al.* [17] to allow a model's histories to be queried online. Five groups of querying [17] are listed in the right column of Table 1. In each group, one or more OCL operations are defined to instrument the temporal assertions. For example, to check model $x$'s property $p$ within predicate-based version scoping, three operations are added: one for the versions since $p$ ( $x.since(v\,|\,p)$, $x.after(v\,|\,p)$ ), the second until $p$ ( $x.until(v\,|\,p)$, $x.before(v\,|\,p)$ ), and the third with the matching of $p$ ( $x.when(v\,|\,p)$ ). García-Domínguez *et al.* [17] showed that all the order patterns and all the five scopes (i.e., globally, before $Q$, after $R$, between $R$ and $Q$, and after $R$ until $Q$) by Dwyer *et al.* [19] were mapped to one or more of the 18 OCL operations.

The patterns of property violation [18] and time-aware querying [17] illustrate the MDE extensions of Dwyer *et al.*'s work [19]. These patterns offer much syntactic help, as the chief intent is to assist practitioners in understanding the scope of temporal logic modalities encapsulated in each pattern's generalized description of permissible state/event sequences [19]. Having only syntactic support can be limited, e.g., the main query of the remote data mirroring case study in [17] was a composition of ten OCL primitives and two OCL operations involving four syntactic structures, i.e., (i), (iii), (iv), and (v) of Table 1. Semantic support bridging the syntactic structures and the practical modeling concerns can be complementary and lead to enhanced benefit. Next we describe the major source from which we derive the semantic knowledge.

## 2.2  OMG SysML Specification

The OMG SysML specification, like all other OMG specifications (e.g., UML and CORBA), addresses vertical (application domain independent) practices to promote interoperability, portability, and reusability. Because SysML reuses a subset of UML, the specification facilitates systems engineers modeling with SysML and software engineers modeling with UML to be able to collaborate on models of software-intensive systems [3]. In addition, OMG specifies the language so that modeling tool vendors can implement and support SysML [5, 40].

Being a standards consortium, OMG has an open process allowing all the specifications to undergo continuous review and improvement. There is no exception for the SysML specification [33]. Version 1.0 of the formal specification was adopted in September 2007. Since then, OMG has made six revisions, each taking an average of 24.3 months to be released. The most recent version—released in November 2019—is the formal SysML specification version 1.6 [34] which we use in our study. Throughout this paper, we simply refer to [34] as the "OMG SysML specification".

This specification is a 398-page PDF document containing 17 sections and 7 annexes [34]. The main contents can be divided into general principles (e.g., conformance and language formalisms), model elements (covering both structural and behavioral constructs), and crosscutting topics (e.g., extending metamodel via stereotypes). While the contents of such an international standard are expected to evolve in an incremental and stable fashion, we next present the strategies for analyzing the OMG SysML specification.

# 3  Research Methodology

Our goal is to discover useful and reusable pattern-oriented knowledge from the OMG SysML specification so as to ease the MDE practitioners' identification and formulation of critical properties. To that end, we develop a research methodology based on grounded theory [37]. Figure 2 overviews the process of our approach. Our underlying research question is to explore commonly occurring guidelines and constraints from the OMG SysML specification. We rely on the specification descriptions, but also go beyond the syntactic layer to uncover semantic patterns to inform the MDE practices. While our approach of Fig. 2 takes the OMG SysML specification as the input, the output is a theory providing new ways of formulating critical properties in the modeling contexts that

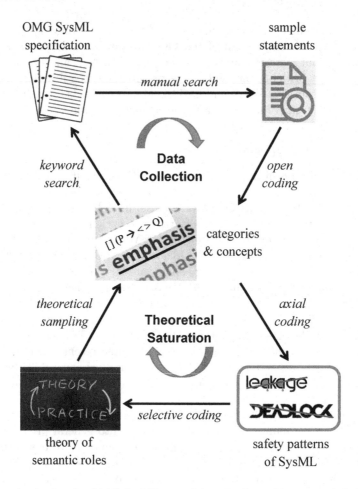

**Fig. 2.** Analyzing the OMG SysML specification informed by grounded theory.

can be reused across different domains (e.g., automotive, energy, manufacturing, etc.).

The process of Fig. 2 consists of two cycles. The first cycle is concerned with data collection. Initially, we manually search the OMG SysML specification for the statements that express rules of thumb or impose limiting powers in modeling. For example, one of the statement samples is:

"... *control can only enable actions to start. SysML extends control to support disabling of actions that are already executing. This is accomplished by providing a model library with a type for control values that are treated like data*" (§11.1.1 "Control as Data" *page 155* [34])

We then apply open coding [37] to explicitly annotate the categories and concepts from the sample statements. For the above example, the category "Activities" (as a diagram element) and the concepts "disabling" and "executing" are coded. The open coding results are fed back to the specification to enrich the data collection. Here, keyword search based on "disabling", "executing", and their lexical variants like "disable" and "disables" is performed, and more focused manual search of §11 on "Activities" is conducted. As a result, the following statement, among others, is selected and coded:

> "... when an activity invokes other activities, they can be associated by a composition association, with the invoking activity on the whole end, and the invoked activity on the part end. If an execution of an activity on the whole end is terminated, then the executions of the activities on the part end are also terminated" (§11.3.1 "Diagram Extensions" page 164 [34])

When no new categories or concepts are generated, our data collection comes to a fixed point and we proceed to the second cycle of Fig. 2. This cycle first involves axial coding [37] where the categories and concepts are related and possibly combined. This allows us to synthesize the core variable. In our study, for instance, an essential dependency emerges from the codes of the above two statements: "data depends on control" and "part depends on whole". Any SysML modeling that violates this class of dependencies is then unsafe. Such dependencies form what we call a safety pattern of SysML, which we further apply selective coding [37] to build a theory. In selective coding where the tentative core has already been established, we deliberately code data without bothering about concepts with little importance to the safety patterns. If necessary, selective coding leads us to go back to the OMG specification, further improving our data collection. Once our codified semantic roles of each safety pattern are able to incorporate most selective coding results, theoretical saturation is reached and our theory shall be put into use.

## 4  Results and Analysis

We share the analysis results by first describing our effort level, followed by a detailed account of the top safety pattern from our work ("Asset Leakage"). We then demonstrate our application of the "Asset Leakage" pattern to a SysML model, and conclude this section by discussing the threats to validity affecting our results.

**Effort.** Three researchers spent a total of about 40 h in analyzing the OMG SysML specification [34]. The data collection phase of our process, as shown in the top cycle of Fig. 2, involved two researchers working independently to identify sample statements and to code categories and concepts. These individual sessions totaled approximately 30 h.

A two-hour meeting was held among the three researchers to merge the collected data, perform axial coding, formulate safety patterns, and build a theory to offer semantic support for SysML-based MDE. This was followed by selective coding done individually, occasionally collecting more data from the

OMG specification. The entire theory building cycle of Fig. 2 took around 10 h in total. Although our manual analysis effort was not negligible, we expect this cost would be amortized over the application of our theory to all SysML models and potential reuse of our results in other MDE tasks (e.g., trace diagnostics [18], requirements discovery [9,21], visual analytics [29,35], obstacle and mistake analysis [2,4], and so on).

**Asset Leakage.** Our most prominent result is what we call the "Asset Leakage" pattern. Table 2 provides the details of this safety pattern. We express the pattern in LTL as: "$[] ((p \rightarrow q) \text{ U } !q)$", which is interpreted as: "it is always the case that if $p$ is running/executing, then (it is because that) $q$ is running/executing, and this will hold until $q$ stops running/executing". In this pattern, $p$ can be thought of as an asset which is guarded by $q$, and if the specified property fails to hold, then asset leakage occurs. Although the pattern positively prevents the asset from leaking, we negatively name the pattern to alert what will go wrong if SysML is unsafely practiced. Our naming convention is in line with such terms as "segmentation fault" and "buffer overflow" [42].

We were able to identify ten instances of "Asset Leakage" from the OMG specification. Table 2 lists the ten statements resulted from our axial coding, as well as the categories and concepts of each statement. The keywords underlying the concepts show strong connections with $p$ and/or $q$'s creation (e.g., "start") and termination (e.g., "destroying"). In addition, the dependency between the two are important (e.g., "invokes"). Some keywords like "dependency" return many automatically searched results, which suggests weighting the keywords may be more effective to automate data collection. Some statements, such as #9 and #10 in Table 2, do not contain any keyword, which implies that manual search is indispensable.

Table 2 sorts the ten statements based on their page numbers, and the category column of the table shows that six "Asset Leakage" instances appear in the OMG specification's behavioral constructs (§11—§14), one in the structural constructs (§7—§10), one in the crosscutting constructs (§15—§17), and two in the annexes. Unsurprisingly, more than half of the statements tie directly to the behavioral aspects of SysML as "Asset Leakage" concerns more about functions and responses; however, structural integrity like #1 shall not be ignored. Although §C defines SysML elements that are deprecated, statements #9 and #10 are of relevance when modelers or tool vendors face backward compatibility issues.

As our overarching goal is to support MDE practice, we are building a theory that not only raises the modelers' awareness of SysML safety patterns, but also shields them from the complexity of the formal notations like "$[] ((p \rightarrow q) \text{ U } !q)$". We thus develop a theory of semantic roles to guide practice and promote reuse in systems engineering. Our idea is inspired by *frame semantics* [16] arguing that one cannot understand a word's meaning without access to all the essential knowledge that relates to that word. Better understanding is gained once a frame of semantic knowledge which the word evokes is teased out.

**Table 2.** "Asset Leakage" safety pattern grounded in the statements of the OMG SysML specification [34]

| No. | Statement (concepts are underline) | Category (enclosing section & page #) | Instantiation of [] ( (p → q) U !q) |
|---|---|---|---|
| 1 | *"If the general ports had binding connectors to internal parts, then the full specialization would be invalid."* | "Proxy and Full Ports" (§9.4.4 & page 139) | [] ( (fullSpecialization → ! bindingConnector) U bindingConnector ) |
| 2 | *"...control can only enable actions to start. SysML extends control to support disabling of actions that are already executing. This is accomplished by providing a model library with a type for control values that are treated like data"* | "Control as Data" (§11.1.1 & page 155) | [] ( (dataActive → controlActive) U ! controlActive ) |
| 3 | *"Destroying an instance of an activity terminates the corresponding execution ..."* | "Diagram Extensions" (§11.3.1.1.1 & page 164) | [] ( (activity → execution) U ! execution ) |
| 4 | *"Terminating an execution also terminates the execution of any other activities that it invoked synchronously ..."* | "Diagram Extensions" (§11.3.1.1.1 & page 164) | [] ( (sub-exec → main-exec) U ! main-exec ) |
| 5 | *"Composition means that destroying an instance at the whole end destroys instances at the part end."* | "Diagram Extensions" (§11.3.1.1.1 & page 164) | [] ( (composedPart → whole) U ! whole ) |
| 6 | *"...when an activity invokes other activities, they can be associated by a composition association, with the invoking activity on the whole end, and the invoked activity on the part end. If an execution of an activity on the whole end is terminated, then the executions of the activities on the part end are also terminated"* | "Diagram Extensions" (§11.3.1.1.1 & page 164) | [] ( (composedPart → whole) U ! whole ) |
| 7 | *"if an instance of Operating Car is destroyed, terminating the execution, the executions it owns are also terminated."* | "Usage Examples" (§11.4 & page 176) | [] ( (sub-exec → main-exec) U ! main-exec ) |
| 8 | *"When a Copy dependency exists between two requirements, the requirement text of the client requirement is a read-only copy of the requirement text of the requirement at the supplier end of the dependency."* | "Stereotypes" (§16.3.2.2 & page 217) | [] ( (clientReqReadOnly → supplierReqCopied) U ! supplierReqCopied ) |
| 9 | *"The isConjugated attribute inherited from UML port is interpreted in the following way: ... if the direction of every flow property specified in the flow specification is reversed (IN becomes OUT and vice versa). If set to True, then all the directions of the flow properties specified by the flow specification that types a nonatomic flow port are relayed in the opposite direction ..."* | "FlowPort" (§C.3.2.2 & page 260) | [] ( (nonatomicFlowReversed → isConjugated) U ! isConjugated ) |
| 10 | *"If a flow port is not connected to an internal part, then isBehavior shall be set to true."* | "Semantic Variation Point" (§C.3.2.3 & page 261) | [] ( (! isBehavior → flowPortConnected) U ! flowPortConnected ) |

We made an initial attempt to build a semantic frame for the "Asset Leakage" pattern. Table 3 shows our results where the three "semantic roles" (or three pairs of roles) are what we believe to best guide reusable MDE practice. To understand and apply each role-pair, "key relationship" and "action trigger" provide further hints, as they are evoked by the given roles. Table 3 also links each role-pair to the OMG specification's statements listed in Table 2. We elaborate the semantic roles as follows.

**Table 3.** Semantic Roles of "Asset Leakage"

| Semantic Roles (p–q) | Key Relationship | Action Trigger | Examples (cf. Table 2) |
|---|---|---|---|
| delegate-constituency | invoked execution | terminate | #2, #3, #4, #7 |
| part–whole | composite binding | destruction | #5, #6, #8 |
| value–condition | special configuration | setup | #1, #9, #10 |

**delegate–constituency** captures a dynamic relationship driven by constituency's invocation of delegate's execution, e.g., main invokes sub, or control enables data. The safety concern here is triggered by constituency's termination of the delegate, and if delegate's execution is not properly halted, then the asset leaks.

**part–whole** binds a composition or a client-supplier relationship. Once the whole or the supplier is destructed, the part or the provided service must follow the same course; otherwise, the binding is breached.

**value–condition** allows special setup and configuration to be defined. This pair of roles can be used to enforce prohibitions (#1), behaviors (#9), and default values (#10).

**Demo.** We illustrate how our theory of semantic roles might be applied in practice via a state machine model adopted from the cruise control system (CCS) study presented in [8]. As SysML reuses UML's state machine diagram, the model shown in Fig. 3 is syntactically sound in SysML. Figure 3 models how the cruise speed manager (CCM) and the pedals manager (PM) set, reset, increase, or decrease the cruise speed (CS).

In this safety-critical scenario, our "Asset Leakage" pattern is readily applicable. The SysML modeler can be prompted with the three pairs of semantic roles of Table 3 to identify whether any would apply to the state machine diagram. Suppose "Lock" is recognized by the modeler as the "delegate" to stabilize the CS. Then, the formulation and the model checking of the property, $[]$ (("Lock" $\rightarrow$ "Engaged") U ! "Engaged"), can be done automatically without the modeler's input. The result—in this case, a failed model checking and a counterexample—can be presented to the modeler for further investigation. With the assistance of our semantic roles in Table 3, the modeler notices an important value-condition constraint (i.e., "Lock" is enabled upon "Pause") and adds it to the delegate-constituency relationship. The property is automatically updated to, $[]$ (("Lock" $\rightarrow$ ("Engaged" | "Pause") U ! ("Engaged" | "Pause")), and this time, model checking successfully verifies that the state machine of Fig. 3 has no "Asset Leakage".

**Threats to Validity.** We followed grounded theory [37] to design and execute our research, driven by the question seeking for recurring themes from the OMG SysML specification to guide safe MDE practice. A threat to construct validity hinges on our integrity-focused, and admittedly temporal-property-biased, interpretation of safety, exemplified by the "Asset Leakage" pattern. Safe SysML practice may also be explained from a more structural point of view; however, our study focuses more on the model behaviors.

We mitigate threats to internal validity by explicitly defining our overall process (cf. Fig. 2) as well as protocols to the concrete qualitative data analysis: open, axial, and selective coding. We also made sure that each phase and activity of our study were carried out jointly rather than by a single researcher. Neither of these steps removes researcher bias entirely; only replications (including the theoretical ones [23,28]) can address this issue. An important threat to external

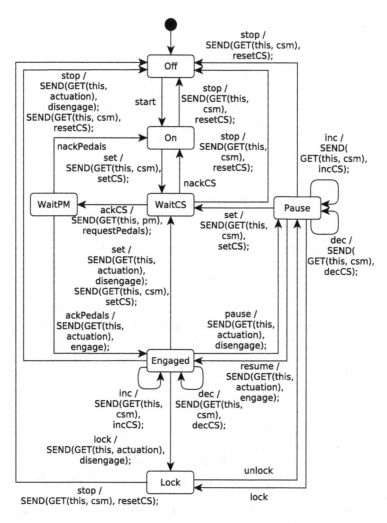

**Fig. 3.** State machine of the cruise control system (CCS) example (*figure adopted from* [8]).

validity is that our results may not generalize beyond the OMG SysML specification. While this is a comprehensive document, it is the only data source of our study. Therefore, it is not clear how generalizable our safety patterns and semantic roles are if additional sources are considered (e.g., the OMG UML specification).

## 5   Discussion

**Inadequacies in the State-of-the-Art.** Our work addresses two major gaps in the literature. For systems engineers, SysML has become a *de facto* choice [1, 36]. As more industries and organizations adopt SysML, rigorous MDE that is capable of handling safety, security, and other dependability concerns will be of crucial significance. As pointed out by Dou *et al.* [18]: "*... our industrial partner, which uses a software development methodology that requires all solutions to adhere to OMG specifications.*" To our surprise, researchers have not attempted to analyze arguably the most authoritative documentation: the OMG SysML specification [33]. Our work therefore fills a much-needed gap.

Secondly, the contemporary support for MDE practitioners to formulate critical properties mainly stays at a syntactic level. While syntactic patterns like those pioneered by Dwyer *et al.* [19] offer insights into how often the modal operators have been used, we take a step toward codifying what $p$ and $q$ mean in the syntactic structures. With our semantic layer of support, not only can the complexity of syntactic notations be hidden from the modelers, but the support can better relate to their modeling concerns. We thus hypothesize that semantic-enriched support like ours could shorten practitioner's cognitive distance toward critical requirements formalization thereby improving reusability. We posit this closer distance is manifested in both term acquaintance (e.g., "Asset Leakage" sounds more familiar than "Universality") and application closeness (e.g., "Asset Leakage" tends to encapsulate domain characteristics at a proper level of abstraction). We plan to build upon the recent literature [12–14] to further test our hypothesis empirically.

**Pertinence and Correctness.** Three strands of work help establish the pertinence of our development of a semantic-role-based theory. Liaskos *et al.* [24] applied frame semantics to identify variability from natural language documents and then to incorporate the semantically framed variability as OR-decompositions into requirements goal modeling. Niu and Easterbrook [27] used semantic frames to characterize the functional requirements in software product lines [38]. Breaux *et al.* [10] reported their experience of deriving generalizable natural language patterns to aid engineers in mapping frequently recurring requirements phrases from policy and regulatory descriptions, and showed that these patterns' reuse level was above 50% when Internet privacy policies and the U.S. HIPAA Privacy Rules were analyzed.

Correctness can be backed up by the negative results. For example, we were tempted to create semantic roles for what we call the "Deadlock" safety pattern. We had already formalized the LTL expression as: "[] ( $(p$ & $q)$ → <> $r$ )", and found a couple of instances from the OMG SysML specification. Due to this, "Deadlock" was part of our axial coding results as illustrated in Fig. 2. However, we were unable to find more instances during selective coding, leading us to put a hold on this particular tentative core at the moment. Because our theory, especially the development of our theory, is refutable, correctness of our results can be evaluated on more solid grounds.

**Potential Impacts.** We discuss our work's impacts from three angles. For MDE practitioners, the theory of semantic roles, exemplified by "Asset Leakage", offers practical and reusable guidance to uncover important modeling concerns without them being bogged down in the syntactic complexity or formal methods unfamiliarity. For SysML tool builders, recognizing the semantic roles and associated frames allows more effective and robust configurations to be set up, and more pertinent properties to be verified offline or monitored online. For researchers, our study illustrates grounded theory in action, encouraging more effort to understand and analyze MDE assets like the OMG specifications in a principled way.

## 6    Conclusions

In MDE, critical concerns such as safety and security must be ensured. SysML represents a significant and increasing segment of industrial support for building critical systems that are interdisciplinary, complex, and constantly evolving. We have presented in this paper a new way of analyzing the OMG SysML specification in order to support the identification, formulation, and verification of critical properties, which are codified in reusable safety patterns like "Asset Leakage" and further encapsulated via semantic roles, such as delegate–constituency, part–whole, and value–condition.

Our future work includes expanding the data sources to include the relevant documentation like the OMG UML specification or industry-specific standards, e.g., functional safety for road vehicles (ISO 26262 [22]). Our current safety patterns and their semantic roles are likely to be updated by the vertical or horizontal expansions. In light of the possible expansions, we are also interested in keyword weighting mechanisms for potentially speeding up the search and data collection over natural language documents [25,30,41]. Finally, we want to explore synergies of our patterns and the syntactic ones like "Bounded Existence" by Dwyer *et al.* [19]. We anticipate such synergies as: "access to the asset shall be bounded to $n$ times without any leakage" would offer a wider range of guidance and assistance to the MDE practitioners.

**Acknowledgments.** We thank Raj Desai and Mounifah Alenazi from the University of Cincinnati for their assistances during data collection and analysis.

## References

1. Alenazi, M., Niu, N., Savolainen, J.: A novel approach to tracing safety requirements and state-based design models. In: International Conference on Software Engineering, pp. 848–860 (2020)
2. Alenazi, M., Niu, N., Savolainen, J.: SysML modeling mistakes and their impacts on requirements. In: International Model-Driven Requirements Engineering Workshop, pp. 14–23 (2019)
3. Alenazi, M., Niu, N., Wang, W., Gupta, A.: Traceability for automated production systems: a position paper. In: International Model-Driven Requirements Engineering Workshop, pp. 51–55 (2017)

4.  Alenazi, M., Niu, N., Wang, W., Savolainen, J.: Using obstacle analysis to support SysML-based model testing for cyber physical systems. In: International Model-Driven Requirements Engineering Workshop, pp. 46–55 (2018)

5.  Alenazi, M., Reddy, D., Niu, N.: Assuring virtual PLC in the context of SysML models. In: International Conference on Software Reuse, pp. 121–136 (2018)

6.  Bencomo, N., Götz, S., Song, H.: Models@run.time: a guided tour of the state of the art and research challenges. Software Syst. Model. **18**(5), 3049–3082 (2019)

7.  Besnard, V., Brun, M., Jouault, F., Teodorov, C., Dhauss, P.: Unified LTL verification and embedded execution of UML models. In: International Conference on Model Driven Engineering Languages and Systems, pp. 112–122 (2018)

8.  Besnard, V., Teodorov, C., Jouault, F., Brun, M., Dhaussy, P.: Verifying and monitoring UML models with observer automata: a transformation-free approach. In: International Conference on Model Driven Engineering Languages and Systems, pp. 161–171 (2019)

9.  Bhowmik, T., Niu, N., Savolainen, J., Mahmoud, A.: Leveraging topic modeling and part-of-speech tagging to support combinational creativity in requirements engineering. Requirements Eng. **20**(3), 253–280 (2015). https://doi.org/10.1007/s00766-015-0226-2

10. Breaux, T.D., Antón, A.I., Doyle, J.: Semantic parameterization: a process for modeling domain descriptions. ACM Trans. Software Eng. Methodol. **18**(2), 5:1–5:27 (2008)

11. Clarke, E.M., Grumberg, O., Peled, D.A.: Model Checking. MIT Press, Cambridge (2001)

12. Czepa, C., Amiri, A., Ntentos, E., Zdun, U.: Modeling compliance specifications in linear temporal logic, event processing language and property specification patterns: a controlled experiment on understandability. Software Syst. Model. **18**(6), 3331–3371 (2019)

13. Czepa, C., Zdun, U.: How understandable are pattern-based behavioral constraints for novice software designers? ACM Trans. Softw. Eng. Methodol. **28**(2), 11:1–11:38 (2019)

14. Czepa, C., Zdun, U.: On the understandability of temporal properties formalized in linear temporal logic, property specification patterns and event processing language. IEEE Trans. Software Eng. **46**(1), 100–112 (2020)

15. Dadeau, F., Fourneret, E., Bouchelaghem, A.: Temporal property patterns for model-based testing from UML/OCL. Softw. Syst. Model. **18**(2), 865–888 (2017). https://doi.org/10.1007/s10270-017-0635-4

16. Fillmore, C.J., Baker, C.F.: Frame semantics for text understanding. In: WordNet and Other Lexical Resources Workshop (2001)

17. García-Domínguez, A., Bencomo, N., Ullauri, J.M.P., Paucar, L.H.G.: Querying and annotating model histories with time-aware patterns. In: International Conference on Model Driven Engineering Languages and Systems, pp. 194–204 (2019)

18. Dou, W., Bianculli, D., Briand, L.C.: Model-driven trace diagnostics for pattern-based temporal specifications. In: International Conference on Model Driven Engineering Languages and Systems, pp. 278–288 (2018)

19. Dwyer, M.B., Avrunin, G.S., Corbett, J.C.: Patterns in property specifications for finite-state verification. In: International Conference on Software Engineering, pp. 411–420 (1999)

20. Goldsby, H., Cheng, B.: Automatically discovering properties that specify the latent behavior of UML models. In: International Conference on Model Driven Engineering Languages and Systems, pp. 316–330 (2010)

21. Guo, J., Wang, Y., Zhang, Z., Nummenmaa, J., Niu, N.: Model-driven approach to developing domain functional requirements in software product lines. IET Software **6**(4), 391–401 (2012)
22. International Organization for Standardization. Road Vehicles – Functional Safety (ISO 26262). https://www.iso.org/standard/68383.html. Accessed October 2020
23. Khatwani, C., Jin, X., Niu, N., Koshoffer, A., Newman, L., Savolainen, J.: Advancing viewpoint merging in requirements engineering: A theoretical replication and explanatory study. Requirements Eng. **22**(3), 317–338 (2017)
24. Liaskos, S., Lapouchnian, A., Yu, Y., Yu, E., Mylopoulos, J.: On goal-based variability acquisition and analysis. In: International Requirements Engineering Conference, pp. 76–85 (2006)
25. Mahmoud, A., Niu, N.: Supporting requirements to code traceability through refactoring. Requirements Eng. **19**(3), 309–329 (2013). https://doi.org/10.1007/s00766-013-0197-0
26. Montaghami, V., Rayside, D.: Pattern-based debugging of declarative models. In: International Conference on Model Driven Engineering Languages and Systems, pp. 322–327 (2015)
27. Niu, N., Easterbrook, S.: Extracting and modeling product line functional requirements. In: International Requirements Engineering Conference, pp. 155–164 (2008)
28. Niu, N., Koshoffer, A., Newman, L., Khatwani, C., Samarasinghe, C., Savolainen, J.: Advancing repeated research in requirements engineering: a theoretical replication of viewpoint merging. In: International Requirements Engineering Conference, pp. 186–195 (2016)
29. Niu, N., Reddivari, S., Chen, Z.: Keeping requirements on track via visual analytics. In: International Requirements Engineering Conference, pp. 205–214 (2013)
30. Niu, N., Wang, W., Gupta, A.: Gray links in the use of requirements traceability. In: International Symposium on Foundations of Software Engineering, pp. 384–395 (2016)
31. Ober, I., Graf, S., Ober, I.: Validating timed UML models by simulation and verification. Int. J. Softw. Tools Technol. Transfer **8**(2), 128–145 (2006)
32. Object Management Group. Systems Modeling Language (SysML). http://www.omgsysml.org. Accessed Oct 2020
33. Object Management Group. Systems Modeling Language (SysML) Specification. https://www.omg.org/spec/SysML/. Accessed Oct 2020
34. Object Management Group. Systems Modeling Language (SysML) Specification (Version 1.6). https://www.omg.org/spec/SysML/1.6/PDF. Accessed Oct 2020
35. Reddivari, S., Chen, Z., Niu, N.: ReCVisu: a tool for clustering-based visual exploration of requirements. In: International Requirements Engineering Conference, pp. 327–328 (2012)
36. Schäfer, W., Wehrheim, H.: The challenges of building advanced mechatronic systems. In: International Conference on the Future of Software Engineering, pp. 72–84 (2007)
37. Strauss, A.L., Corbin, J.: Grounded Theory in Practice. Sage Publications, Thousand Oaks (1997)
38. Vale, T., Santana de Almeida, E., Alves, V., Kulesza, U., Niu, N., de Lima, R.: Software product lines traceability: a systematic mapping study. Inf. Softw. Technol. **84**, 1–18 (2017)
39. Wang, W., Gupta, A., Niu, N., Xu, L.D., Cheng, J.-R.C., Niu, Z.: Automatically tracing dependability requirements via term-based relevance feedback. IEEE Trans. Industr. Inf. **14**(1), 342–349 (2018)

40. Wang, W., Niu, N., Alenazi, M., Xu, L.D.: In-place traceability for automated production systems: a survey of PLC and SysML tools. IEEE Trans. Industr. Inf. **15**(6), 3155–3162 (2019)
41. Wang, W., Niu, N., Liu, H., Niu, Z.: Enhancing automated requirements traceability by resolving polysemy. In: International Requirements Engineering Conference, pp. 40–51 (2018)
42. Westland, T., Niu, N., Jha, R., Kapp, D., Kebede, T.: Relating the empirical foundations of attack generation and vulnerability discovery. In: International Conference on Information Reuse and Integration, pp. 37–44 (2020)

# A Hybrid Approach Based on Reuse Techniques for Autonomic Adaptation of Business Processes

Jamila Oukharijane[1]([✉])[ID], Mohamed Amine Chaâbane[1], Imen Ben Said[1],
Eric Andonoff[2], and Rafik Bouaziz[1]

[1] University of Sfax, MIRACL, Route de L'Aéroport,, BP 1088, 3018 Sfax, Tunisia
`jamila.oukharijane@fsegs.u-sfax.tn`
[2] IRIT, University Toulouse 1-Capitole, 2 Rue du Doyen Gabriel Marty,
31042 Toulouse Cedex, France

**Abstract.** Complexity of highly dynamic environments in which processes operate makes their adaptation difficult to perform. However, adaptation of an in-progress process is an essential requirement for any Business Process Management System (BPMS). So, several contributions have recommended the use of the MAPE-K (Monitor, Analyze, Plan, Execute - Knowledge) control loop from the autonomic computing as a solution to tackle this issue, thus bringing BPMS with self-adaptation capabilities. However, in these contributions, a comprehensive overview of the generic process self-adaptation has been missing. Moreover, faced with the high cost and the difficulty of self-adapting processes, the idea of capitalizing on previous adaptation solutions by implementing reuse techniques is appealing. In this paper, we recommend a hybrid approach to adapt running processes using versions, previous adaptation cases and rules as reuse techniques. Our solution is implemented as an adaptation engine that instantiates the MAPE-K control loop and that can be connected to any BPMN-based BPMS using appropriate adapters. Our adaptation engine is therefore reusable. Finally, we demonstrate the advantages and feasibility of the recommended approach with an example from the crisis domain.

**Keywords:** Self-adaptation · MAPE-K · Context · Version ·
Adaptation case · Rule

## 1 Introduction

The growing complexity and dynamicity of the operating environment of processes emphasizes the need for developing autonomic Business Process Management Systems (BPMS). With the autonomic adaptation of process, it indeed becomes possible to achieve changes occurring in the operating environment of this process with minimal human intervention, cost reduction for performing required adaptation and real-time responsiveness [1]. This is a key advantage for

© Springer Nature Switzerland AG 2020
S. Ben Sassi et al. (Eds.): ICSR 2020, LNCS 12541, pp. 35–51, 2020.
https://doi.org/10.1007/978-3-030-64694-3_3

companies that need to quickly and efficiently manage changes to remain competitive. Basically, a fully autonomic BPMS supports an autonomous reasoning to detect needs for adaptation and eventually resolve them. This reasoning is based on the analysis of the current situation of the operating environment and the use conditions of running processes. Autonomic adaptation of running processes is usually achieved using a MAPE-K control loop [2], which is an efficient solution for self-adaptation of systems in autonomic computing. This loop advocates the use of the four components: (i) *Monitor (M)*, which collects data on the managed system and its operating environment, filter the data and aggregates them into symptoms, (ii) *Analyze (A)*, which analyzes the symptoms to detect if changes are required, (iii) *Plan (P)*, which defines the adaptation operations needed to resolve detected changes and (iv) *Execute (E)*, which performs the defined operations to adapt the behavior of the managed system. These components (MAPE) share *Knowledge (K)* between them. The latter involves repositories that contain the necessary information to detect the adaptation needs and resolve them. As this paper deals with the adaptation need resolution issue, it focuses on the *Plan* component.

Process adaptation issue has been highly investigated in recent past. On the one hand, several taxonomies to characterize process adaptation have been proposed in literature. The most suitable one is given in [3]. This taxonomy has identified the following adaptation needs for processes: (i) *adaptation by variability* for handling different models of processes, called variants, each of which is to be used in a specific situation, (ii) *adaptation by evolution* for handling changes in processes, which require occasional or permanent modifications in their models, (iii) *adaptation by deviation* for handling occasional situations or exceptions, which have not been necessarily foreseen in process models, and (iv) *adaptation by looseness* for handling processes, which have unknown or incompletely known at design-time. In addition to this taxonomy, two main categories of adaptation techniques have been introduced to define how to achieve self-adaptation of processes. The first one, which includes the *goal-based* technique, is based on the definition of a new process fragment based on the current situation of the operating environment and the goal state (desired outputs of the process fragment) when there is an adaptation need. The second one is based on the reuse techniques to be able to adapt a running process by reusing knowledge relating to models or parts of models used in a similar situation. In this paper, we defend the process self-adaptation by reuse techniques because these techniques can reduce the time, cost and effort required to adapt processes, and we have an already such constructed knowledge (*e.g.,* process model versions) in our previous works for adaptation modeling. Generally, there are four reuse techniques proposed in the literature [4]: (i) *rule-based* [5], which reuses a set of pre-defined rules, (ii) *case-based* [6], which enables to reuse historical process adaptation cases (change logs), (iii) *variant-based* [7], which reuses a set of variants of the process components (*i.e.,* the process itself, its sub-processes and its tasks), each variant being convenient to a given context, and (iv) *version-based* [8], which is an extension of the variant-based as it reuses a set of alternative versions (*i.e.*, variants) or consecutive versions (*i.e.*, evolution of variants) of the process. Each technique may be considered as a guide for defining adaptation operations. Generally, these adaptation operations can impact the different dimensions of a process: (i) its *behavioral* dimension to adapt how it is achieved (process activities, including tasks and sub-processes, and their coordination), (ii) its *organizational* dimension to adapt the resources invoked by task execution, and (iii) its *informational* dimension to adapt the used or produced data by task executions.

On the other hand, several contributions (*e.g.*, [9–12]) have been made to address the process self-adaptation based on the MAPE-K control loop. However, these contributions are incomplete for the following reasons. First, the adaptation techniques of these contributions are either variant-based or goal-based, but none of these contributions combine these techniques in order to find out the best adaptation to perform. Second, they do not consider all process dimensions to ensure comprehensive adaptation of running processes: they focus on the adaptation of only one or two dimensions among the behavioral, informational and organizational ones. Finally, they do not address the issue of autonomic adaptation of processes in a comprehensive and global approach taking into account all the four adaptation needs identified in the Reichert and Weber's taxonomy [3]: they only take into account one or two adaptation needs but never all four at the same time.

To overcome these weaknesses, we recommend a MAPE-K based adaptation engine for self-adapting running processes to changes occurring in their operating environment. This adaptation engine is designed separately from the BPMS. This separation makes the adaptation engine reusable for various BPMS. In addition, this adaptation engine has the following features. First, it recommends the use of the three following reuse techniques: version-based, case-based and rule-based to improve process adaptation. Second, it advocates a context-based selection of already defined adaptations. In fact, the context notion is used for representing the use condition in which each adaptation operation has to be executed as well as the current situation of the operating environment that influences the execution of processes. Matching both contexts (*i.e.*, use condition of adaptation operation and current situation) allows (i) the detection of the adaptation needs when the operating environment of running process changes and (ii) retrieving the most suitable solution to be adapted for the current situation.

To sum up, the paper deals with the autonomic adaptation of BPMN processes at run-time and more precisely the resolution of detected adaptation needs. Its contributions are as follows. The first one is the recommended adaptation engine architecture, which instantiates the MAPE-K control loop for self-adaptation of processes. The second contribution is the hybrid approach recommended for the *Plan* component, which is responsible for defining the adaptation operations to be carried out in order to resolve adaptation needs. Finally, the feasibility and applicability of the recommended approach is demonstrated by a case study from the crisis domain.

The remainder of the paper is organized as follows. Section 2 provides the state-of-the-art on self-adaptation of processes using the MAPE-K control loop. Section 3 gives an overview of the adaptation engine recommended for self-adaptation of BPMN processes. Section 4 discusses in detail the hybrid approach proposed for realizing the *Plan* component. Section 5 demonstrates the applicability of the proposed approach on the case study. Finally, Sect. 6 summarizes paper contributions and gives some directions for future researches.

## 2    Related Work

In the literature, there are several works that focus on the self-adaptation of processes. The common point of these works is the use of the MAPE-K control loop for detecting adaptation needs and resolving them at run-time. Due to the specific focus of the paper on the adaptation need resolution, this section only considers contributions that really recommend a concrete approach of the related *Plan* component of the MAPE-K control loop.

Ayora et al. recommended in [9] a solution that allows variability modeling at design-time by describing process variants using three models: (i) the base model to specify process fragments shared by all process variants (*i.e.,* consistent part of processes), (ii) the variation model to specify the replacement fragments that alternatively can be used for the fragments of the base model, and (iii) the resolution model to specify the context conditions that define the use conditions for the replacement fragments. At run-time, the recommended solution provides the completion of each variation point of the base model with the appropriate alternative fragment that satisfies the context of the operating environment.

In [10], the authors defined an approach that enables the modeling of autonomic processes at design-time and managing them at run-time. At design-time, this approach makes it possible to model all the necessary elements that guide the self-adaptation of a process at run-time: which tasks must be monitored, which context changes impact the execution of the process and how to resolve them. At run-time, this approach uses the MAPE-K control loop for managing autonomic processes. More precisely, it checks all the variation points and examines the context of each variant of these variation points to identify adaptation needs. If adaptations are required, it selects and executes the suitable variant for each variation point, *i.e.,* the variant that satisfies the context of the operating environment.

On the other hand, Ferro and Rubira introduced in [11] an adaptation engine for the completion of the loosely parts of ill-defined processes at run-time. This adaptation engine, which is based on the MAPE-K approach, ensures the completion of the loosely part of the process by either (i) selecting existing activities in the process repository or (ii) deriving a new process fragment by analyzing pre-conditions, post-conditions and interdependences between activities.

Finally, Seiger et al. proposed in [12] a framework that enables the self-adaptation of processes in cyber-physical systems. This framework allows monitoring and analysis of consistency between the sensed physical world and the assumed cyber world of each task execution. In case an inconsistency is detected, it replaces the resource involved in the task execution by another resource variant and then executes this task.

Table 1 evaluates the previous contributions with respect to the following criteria defined in [13] and related to process self-adaptation:

- *Supervised component*: it identifies the granularity level of adaptation, which can be the process level, the sub-process level and the task level,
- *Adapted process dimension*: it indicates which process dimensions are considered in the examined contribution, which can be the behavioral, the organizational and/or the informational dimensions,
- *Process adaptation needs*: it indicates which adaptation needs of the taxonomy defined by [3] are taken into account,
- *Adaptation technique*: it indicates the technique used to define the needed adaptation operations.

**Table 1.** Related work evaluation

| Criteria | Ayora et al. [9] | Oliveria et al. [10] | Ferro et Rubira [11] | Seiger et al. [12] |
|---|---|---|---|---|
| Supervised components | sub-process | task | sub-process | task |
| Adapted process dimensions | behavioral | informational organizational | behavioral | organizational |
| Process adaptation needs | variability looseness | variability deviation | looseness | deviation |
| Adaptation technique | variant-based | variant-based | goal-based | variant-based |

The first observation we can make from Table 1 is that all the examined contributions partially consider the self-adaptation of process dimensions: (i) in [9] and in [11], the adaptation may only impact the behavioral dimension; (ii) in [10], it may impact the informational and organizational dimensions of processes, whereas, in [12], only the organizational dimension of processes may be adapted. This is mainly due to the granularity of the supervision. In fact, (i) when the supervised element is a sub-process or a process, its adaptation may impact the coordination of the process (or sub-process) tasks, and thus the behavioral dimension of processes; (ii) when the supervised element is a task, the process adaptation may impact the resources or the data involved in the task execution, and thus the informational and the organizational dimensions of processes. However, in [12], even if the supervised element is a task, only the organizational dimension of processes can be impacted by the adaptation as the contribution deals with malfunction of resources involved in task realization.

Second, we can observe that the adaptation needs of Reichert and Weber's taxonomy [3] are partially considered. *Adaptation by looseness* is supported in [9] and in [11], while *adaptation by deviation* is taken into account in [10] and in [12]. As for *adaptation by variability*, it is supported in [9] and in [10] at design-time. However, none of the examined works has dealt with *adaptation by evolution*. Moreover, the adaptation techniques of the examined contributions are either variant-based as in [9,10,12] or goal-based as in [11], but none of these contributions has recommended the use of more than one technique in order to find out the best adaptation to perform.

To overcome the limitations of the examined contributions, we recommend an adaptation engine that takes up the interesting features of the examined adaptation engines, namely, the fact to be BPMN-compliant, the MAPE-K control loop, and the context-based approach, but which differs from them in the following respects:

- The proposed adaptation engine considers the process self-adaptation at the following abstraction levels: (i) the *process* and the *sub-process* levels, to support adaptation of the behavioral dimension, and (ii) the *task* level to support adaptation of the informational and organizational dimensions. Considering these three abstraction levels makes the self-adaptation of the three dimensions of processes possible.
- It recommends the mixing of reuse techniques, version-based, case-based and rule-based, in order to improve adaptation and support the different types of process adaptation needs defined in [3].

## 3    Adaptation Engine Architecture

Figure 1 below presents the architecture of the adaptation engine we propose to support an instantiation of the MAPE-K control loop. As argued in [2], self-adaptation in the general level encompasses various self-* properties in the major level, including self-configuring, self-healing, self-optimizing and self-protecting. We consider that the approach presented in this paper falls under self-healing category. Self-healing is the capability of the adaptation engine of discovering, diagnosing and reacting to disruptions [14]. Self-healing can be classified into self-diagnosing and self-repairing, where the former concerns itself with identifying adaptation needs, and the latter focuses on the resolution of the identified adaptation needs, namely the definition and the execution of the adaptation operations. The focus of the proposed adaptation engine is to provide an integrated approach for self-diagnosis and self-repairing using context, versions, adaptation cases and rules.

The Knowledge (K) is composed of the *model repository*, the *instance repository*, the *case repository* and the *rule repository*. The model repository stores versions of tasks, sub-processes and processes as well as their use conditions, described as contexts. The instance repository stores the current situation of

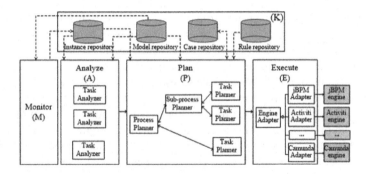

**Fig. 1.** Adaptation engine architecture

the operating environment of running processes, described also as contexts. We characterize the current situation by a set of context parameters defined as pairs (context parameter, value), and the use condition of a version by a set of conditions involving these context parameters. These conditions are defined as triplets (context parameter, operator, value). As for the case repository, it stores a set of all cases representing ad hoc changes defined by the *Plan* component for managing deviations. Each case consists of a past situation that has needed adaptation, described as context and the corresponding solution (*i.e.,* applied adaptation operations). The rule repository stores a set of a priori defined rules by domain experts for managing deviations and dependencies between adaptation operations. Each rule is constructed using *conditions* and *actions* and it has the form: *if* set of conditions *then* execute actions.

The *Monitor* component implements the M of the MAPE-K control loop. It aims at getting an accurate picture of the operating environment of running processes (including their sub-processes and tasks). It receives data from sensors and process engine listeners, filters, aggregates and interprets these data and records them in the *instance repository*.

The *Analyze* component, which implements the A of the MAPE-K control loop, is responsible for the detection of the adaptation needs since it generates several *task analyzers* (as many as activated tasks in the process) to compare the context featuring the current situation, described in the *instance repository*, with the use conditions of the versions of each concerned task, described in the *model repository*. Thus, if an adaptation need is detected, the *Plan* component is triggered. It should be noted that our solution to the *Monitor* and *Analyze* components implementing the self-diagnosing approach is under publication.

The *Plan* component implements the P of the MAPE-K control loop. It receives as input the different adaptation needs (when there is at least one task that has identified a need for adaptation) and produces as output an adapted process instance model that meet these adaptation needs. The *Plan* component is composed of several planners that define needed operations to implement the identified adaptation: one process planner, as many sub-process planners as sub-processes in the supervised process instance and as many task planners as tasks in the supervised process instance. Each planner deals with its own adaptation and defines the operations required to carry it out by reusing defined solutions stored in the *knowledge* base. Thus, a *process planner* has a better global vision of the adaptation needs and defines the adaptation operations for the process and its components (sub-processes, tasks, resources and data), while at the lower level, *i.e.,* a task or a sub-process planner solves a local adaptation need at the concerned activity (task or sub-process) when there is no adaptation operations defined by the process planner. Notifications between planners are visualized in Fig. 1 as thin arrows. More details about the *Plan* component are presented in Sect. 4. It should be noted that the dotted arrows of Fig. 1 visualize the read/write operations in K of the *Monitor, Analyze,* and *Plan* components.

Finally, the *Execute* component implements the E of the MAPE-K control loop. It (i) receives from the *Plan* component the adapted process instance model, (ii) generates the generic operations to be carried out to migrate the considered process instance model to the adapted one, (iii) maps these operations into operations of the target process engine, since each process engine has different operation signatures and ways of performing each same adaptation operation, and (iv) performs them by invoking the process engine by means of a native Application Programming Interface (API). Since each process engine (*e.g.,* Activiti, Camunda, jBPM) has its own specificities, we have defined several engine adapters, such as *jBPM Adapter*. Each engine adapter is suitable for a process engine; it has to map the operations defined by the *Plan* component onto operations that can be understood by this process engine. Ultimately the *Execute* component triggers the execution of these mapped adaptation operations in the target process engine. We do not detail this component implementation in this paper as we adopt the access layer of the academic generic BPMS proposed in [15], that supports communications with the target process engines allowing the realization of the generic operations mapped in concrete ones, and maps the generic operations to operations that conform to the target process engine. For more details about this generic BPMS implementation, the reader can refer to [15].

We detail below the recommended approach for defining adaptation operations required for resolving adaptation needs.

## 4   Detailing the Recommended Approach for Adaptation Definition

This section details the hybrid approach recommended for the definition of adaptation operations by the *Plan* component to resolve process adaptation needs. This approach recommends the use (i) of versions, previous adaptation cases and rules for adaptation achievement and (ii) context-based selection of versions as well as previous adaptation cases. As shown in Fig. 2, once an adaptation need is received from the *Analyze* component, three major steps are possibly performed.

The first step "**Search compliant process model version using contexts**" consists of querying the *model repository*, which contains the process

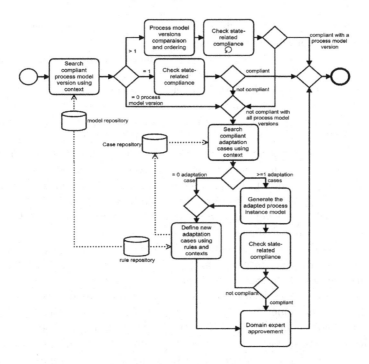

**Fig. 2.** Process instance adaptation definition steps

model versions and their use contexts, with the aim of retrieving the process model version satisfying the current situation of the operating environment. More precisely, it searches the appropriate process model version by comparing the current situation that provokes need for adaptation and that is defined in the *instance repository*, with the use conditions of the versions of this process instance, defined in the *model repository*. More precisely, this step goes through the following actions. The first action is dedicated to the identification of the possible model versions of the considered process. It is implemented as queries on the *model repository*. The second action calculates, for each identified version, the similarity between the current situation and their use condition. Three scenarios can occur:

- **Scenario 1.1**- There is exactly one process model version that satisfies the current situation, *i.e.,* the current situation acquired from the *instance repository* exactly matches the use condition of the returned version. So in this case, the **check state-related compliance** is performed for verifying if the considered process instance is compliant with the returned process model version or it is not compliant. This allows ensuring that the resulting execution states of the considered process instance also remain correct and consistent states in the returned version. The goal of this check is to ensure the correctness of process instance migration to the returned process model version. Moreover, the state-related compliance check is done according to the state compliance conditions proposed in [16], which allow checking if a process instance model version (Si) is compliant with a process model (S'). In case a state-related incompliance is detected, *i.e.*, it is not possible to migrate the running process instance to the returned process model version, the *process planner* searches for a suitable previous adaptation in the *case repository*.

– **Scenario 1.2-** There are many retrieved process model versions satisfying the current situation. In this case, the *process planner* determines the proximity between the process instance model version and each returned process model version using the proximity calculation algorithm proposed in [17]. The goal of this proximity calculation is to order the returned process model versions based on their proximity to the process instance model version. Afterward, the *process planner* checks the state-related compliance of this version with the ordered process model versions, starting with the closer process model version to this instance model version, to find a process model version that satisfies the state-related compliance conditions. When there are no process model versions ensuring the state-related compliance, then the search of suitable adaptation cases in the *case repository* is triggered.

– **Scenario 1.3-** There is no suitable process model version to the current situation. Let us remember that to consider a model version suitable, each condition involved in the use condition of this version must satisfy the current situation. So in this scenario, the step "**Search compliant adaptation cases using contexts**" is performed for reusing previous adaptations used in a similar situation and defined in the case repository.

The second step "**Search compliant adaptation cases using contexts**" is triggered when either (i) there is no process model version satisfying the state-related compliance from the returned ones in the first or the second scenario, or (ii) there is no suitable process model version returned in the third scenario of the first step. In this second step, the *process planner* looks for previously defined adaptation cases in similar situation by the lower level planners (planners of tasks and/or sub-processes), in the *case repository*. More precisely, it searches to retrieve the most relevant adaptation cases from the *case repository* by comparing the current situation of the considered process instance with the situation of the adaptation cases, as well as the process instance model version with the process model versions of the adaptation cases. Two possible scenarios can then occur:

– **Scenario 2.1-** There is no retrieved adaptation case corresponding to the model version of the current process instance and satisfying the current situation of the operating environment. So, in this case, the rule-based adaptation is triggered to define a new solution resolving the need for adaptation.

– **Scenario 2.2-** There is one or more retrieved adaptation cases corresponding to the model version of the current process instance and satisfying the current situation. As indicated in Algorithm 1, these adaptation cases are then examined one by one. For each of them, the defined adaptation operations in the considered adaptation case are applied to the process instance model version in order to adapt it. Then, the **check state-related compliance** is triggered to check the state-related compliance of the process instance model version with the resulting one. When there is no resulting process model version verifying the state-related compliance conditions, the rule-based adaptation is performed to define a new solution resolving the need for adaptation; otherwise, the resulting process model version is to approve by a domain expert.

---

**Algorithm 1.** adaptation Cases Application

---

**Require:** *cases*: set (Adaptation case), *pi*: Process instance model version
**Local**
*c*: Adaptation case; $V'$, $Vtemp$: Process model version
**begin**
$V' \leftarrow pi$
**for** each *c* in *cases* **do**
  $Vtemp \leftarrow$ generateAdaptedmodel $(V', c)$
  $CpRes \leftarrow$ stateComplianceChecks $(pi, Vtemp)$
  **if** $CpRes$ is Compliant **then**
    $V' \leftarrow Vtemp$
  **end if**
**end for**
**if** $V' = pi$ **then**
  Rule-basedAdaptation ()
**else**
  adaptationApprovement $(V')$
**end if**
**end**

---

The third step "**Define new adaptation case using rules and contexts**" is triggered when there is no solution defined as a version and no adaptation case that deals with the adaptation of the considered process instance. This step uses the a priori defined adaptation rules stored in the *rule repository* and the current situation described in the *instance repository* to define a new adaptation case that resolves the identified adaptation needs and accordingly stores it in the *case repository*. Two main types of adaptation rules are supported: (i) the *reactive rules*, which react to a given situation, and (ii) the *dependency rules*, which manage the impact of adaptation operations as indicated in [18]. It should be noted that both types of adaptation rules define adaptation operations using either adaptation patterns or primitives like suspending or redoing a task version. This step is as follows. First, the *process planner* creates a planner per task that has identified a need for adaptation. Each *task planner* deals with the definition of the adaptation operations using reactive rules for resolving the local adaptation need. Once the adaptation operations are defined, they are forwarded to the *planner* of the component in which the considered task is involved, and which is either a *sub-process planner* or a *process planner*. This latter has to analyze the dependency of the defined adaptation operations using dependency rules. After that, the adaptation operations are suggested to a domain expert, who will approve the solution or further adapt it. Finally the solution (*i.e.,* process instance model version, the approved adaptation operations and their situations) will be stored by the *process planner* in the *case repository* as a new adaptation case that can be reused in a situation similar to the current one.

Note that we use the version-based technique at the beginning for the following reasons. First, this technique always guarantees the process model correctness, because all the process model versions are verified and validated by a process designer at design-time. Second, in the version-based technique, the process instance is always compliant to a process model version, which is stored in the *model repository.*

## 5  Case Study: The Flood Management Process

This section illustrates the applicability of the recommended approach through the case study *Flood Management Process* (FMP). First it shows how to model at design-time the required knowledge for flood management process adaptation using versions and rules. Then it uses this case study to demonstrate the execution of a sample adaptation.

### 5.1  Rules and Versions Modeling at Design-Time

This sub-section introduces the FMP case study, which is a simplification of a more complete case study in the context of the flooding of a major French river "the Loire" on the city of Blois, and more particularly on the district of Mareuil, which is protected by a dyke. This district is the object of a very particular attention at the time of floods of the Loire River: a rise in water levels caused by heavy rainfall upstream, or on the affluent of the Loire, may cause important damages on the potentially impacted area.

Like any other process, the FMP might be subject to different operating environment variations that could interrupt its functioning. Indeed, changes relative to the water level, precipitation amount, lack of resources, impacted roads, etc., impose the process to self-adapt to take into account these changes. For this reason, we have defined several versions of the model of this process and of its components, namely several versions of its tasks and sub-processes, one per situation. The first version defines the process of watching over the state of the dike while the second defines the process of lowering the water level of the Loire by opening the Boullie spillway upstream. In addition, the three other versions, which are triggered when the situation is of serious concern, define what to do when an evacuation decision is made. According to the crisis cell, these five process model versions depend upon the following context parameters among others:

- **Water level,** which indicates the level of water rising in the Loire,
- **Impacted area,** which features the size of the population potentially impacted,

- **Road state,** which can be *not flooded, flooded and drivable* or *flooded and blocked.* When the roads are not flooded, so peoples evacuate themselves when the water level is not above 4.5 m; otherwise, when the roads are flooded but still drivable, so the people evacuation is carried out using specific vehicles with help of gendarmes. While, when the roads are blocked because they are highly flooded, people evacuation must be carried out by firefighters with zodiacs.
- **Water growth,** which indicates the rapidity of water rising.

Table 2 shows these different versions and their corresponding use conditions (*i.e.,* in which situation condition the process model version must be used). The different conditions defined in the use condition of each process model version are connected to each other by the logical operator *"and"*.

**Table 2.** Use conditions for flood management process model versions

| Version id | Version use condition | | | |
|---|---|---|---|---|
| | Water level | Impacted area | Road state | Water growth |
| FMP.V1 | < 2 | = "Urbanized" | = "Not flooded" | = "Slow" or = "Moderately fast" |
| FMP.V2 | ≥ 2 and < 3 | = "Urbanized" | = "Not flooded" | = "Slow" or = "Moderately fast" |
| FMP.V3 | ≥ 3 and < 4.5 | = "Urbanized" | = "Not flooded" | = "Slow" or = "Moderately fast" |
| FMP.V4 | ≥ 4.5 | = "Urbanized" | = "Flooded and drivable" | = "Slow" or = "Moderately fast" |
| FMP.V5 | ≥ 4.5 | = "Urbanized" | = "Flooded and blocked" | = "Slow" or = "Moderately fast" |

Due to lack of space, we explain below only the third model version of this process among the five ones. As shown in Fig. 3, this version is triggered in urbanized impacted area when the water level of the river "Loire" in France rises above 3 m and the roads state is not flooded. In response to this event, the crisis cell decides whether or not to evacuate people from the flooded zones by assessing the flooding situation. In case an evacuation is needed, the Prefect emits an evacuation order, then the COD, which is the operational committee set up within the crisis cell, informs the population about the flood. After that the gendarmes proceed to the evacuation of people from the flooded zones using vehicles. Finally, the crisis cell reports on the evacuation, and the Prefect sends the report to the interior ministry. Moreover, we define for each process component (process, sub-process or task) rules, that manage component deviation, and their dependency. We give below two rules related to *People evacuation* task in the form of if-then statements. The first rule is used when the road state is not flooded and the water keeps rising very fast, so there is a risk that the road state will be flooded. In this case, people's evacuation must be carried out by gendarmes with specific vehicles; it adds resources (*i.e.*, gendarmes) to the *People evacuation* task. While the second rule is used to manage dependency of the people evacuation. For instance, when the *People evacuation* task is carried out by gendarmes, then it is necessary to insert the new task *Evacuation supervision* that allows the supervision of peoples during the evacuation. It should be noted that these rules are modeled using Drools rule engine.

FMP.V3

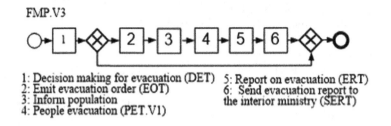

1: Decision making for evacuation (DET)    5: Report on evacuation (ERT)
2: Emit evacuation order (EOT)              6: Send evacuation report to
3: Inform population                            the interior ministry (SERT)
4: People evacuation (PET.V1)

**Fig. 3.** The third model version of the flood management process "FMP.V3"

**R1:** if Watergrowth = "Very fast" Then AddTaskResource (Running process, People evacuation task, gendarme).

**R2:** if AddTaskResource (Running process, People evacuation task, gendarme) Then InsertSerialTask (Running process, Evacuation supervision task, People evacuation task, Report on evacuation).

## 5.2    Process Self-adaptation at Run-Time

The goal of autonomic adaptation of processes is to modify the process instance model version in response to changes in its operating environment. To demonstrate this, we suppose that the third model version of the flood management process (FMP.V3 from Table 2) is running for Mareuil district affected by Loire's floods and that the *people evacuation* task is activated. For this illustration, we refer to the following context parameters and values, which feature the current situation of the operating environment: *Water level* = 4 m and *Impacted area* = "*Urbanized*" and *Road state* = "*Not flooded*" and *water growth* = "*Very fast*". In response to this situation, the *Plan* component, precisely the *process planner* of the running process model version proceeds to the "Search compliant model version using contexts" step. First it identifies the corresponding model versions and their use conditions, second it calculates, for each of these model versions, the similarity between the model version use condition and the current situation. The result of this step is that there is no existing version that deals with the current situation. Given that there is no solution modeled as a model version, the *process planner* performs the "Search compliant adaptation cases using contexts" step, which also returns that there is no stored adaptation case that addressed the current situation. So in this case, the *task planner* of the *People evacuation* task is triggered to search rules that match with the current situation. The result of this search is the rule R1, which allocates gendarmes to the activated model version of the *People evacuation* task. Then the *process planner* is triggered to manage dependency of this change using rule R2. The final result of this adaptation is illustrated in Fig. 4.

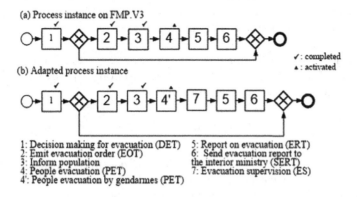

**Fig. 4.** Adapted process instance

# 6   Conclusion and Future Work

Adapting processes to the frequent changes of their operating environment remains a challenging and complex task. To tackle this issue, this paper recommends an Adaptation Engine based on the MAPE-K approach of autonomic computing so that supervised processes self-adapt to changes occurring in their operating environment. More precisely, the paper focuses on the definition of the adaptation operations required to resolve adaptation needs using contexts and reuse techniques: version-based, case-based and rule-based. Benefits of our solution are as follows. First the recommended solution benefits from the MAPE-K control loop advantages. This loop from the autonomic computing field makes possible the implementation of adaptation for monitored processes with minimal human intervention. Second, the separation between the adaptation engine and the process engine with which it interacts makes the adaptation engine reusable for various process engines (BPMS). Third, the combined use of version-based, case-based and rule-based techniques makes possible to take the different adaptation needs identified in Reichert and Weber's taxonomy for well-defined processes into account. Thus our recommended solution supports in a coherent framework the adaptation by deviation, evolution, variability and looseness. Third, adaptation of processes at the three abstraction levels makes the self-adaptation of all the dimensions of processes possible. Finally, the use of several adapters for connecting process engines aims to overcome the drawbacks of embedding the adaptation logic within the process engine, thus it improves the reusability and independency of the adaptation engine.

As future works, we plan to continue improving this adaptation engine in two main directions:

- Improvement by performing an analysis of the impact of the defined adaptations by the *Plan* component before they are transmitted to the *Execute* component. In other words, we need to assess the quality of the adapted process instance model version in terms of comprehensibility and modifiability such as in [19].
- Improvement by considering the collaborative aspects of the adaptation engine, as BPMN allows the definition of collaborative processes within collaboration and choreography diagrams.

# References

1. Oukharijane, J., Ben Said, I., Chaâbane, M.A., Andonoff, E., Bouaziz, R.: Towards a new adaptation engine for self-adaptation of BPMN processes instances. In: 14th International Conference on Evaluation of Novel Approaches to Software Engineering (ENASE), Heraklion, Crete, Greece, pp. 218–225 (2019). https://doi.org/10.5220/0007626602180225
2. IBM: An architectural blueprint for autonomic computing. IBM White Paper 31 (2006)
3. Reichert, M., Weber, B.: Enabling Flexibility in Process-Aware Information Systems: Challenges, Methods, Technologies. Springer, Heidelberg (2012). https://doi.org/10.1007/978-3-642-30409-5
4. Fantinato, M., Toledo, M.B.F.D., Thom, L.H., Gimenes, I.M.D.S., Rocha, R.D.S.R., Garcia, D.Z.G.: A survey on reuse in the business process management domain. Int. J. Bus. Process Integr. Manag. **6**, 52–76 (2012)
5. Müller, R., Greiner, U., Rahm, E.: Agentwork: a workflow system supporting rule-based workflow adaptation. Data Knowl. Eng. **51**(2), 223–256 (2004)
6. Minor, M., Bergmann, R., Görg, S.: Case-based adaptation of workflows. Inf. Syst. **40**, 142–152 (2014)
7. Milani, F., Dumas, M., Ahmed, N., Matulevičius, R.: Modelling families of business process variants: a decomposition driven method. Inf. Syst. **56**, 55–72 (2016)
8. Ben Said, I., Chaâbane, M.A., Andonoff, E., Bouaziz, R.: BPMN4VC-modeller: easy-handling of versions of collaborative processes using adaptation patterns. Int. J. Inf. Syst. Change Manage. **10**(2), 140–189 (2018)
9. Ayora, C., Torres, V., Pelechano, V., Alférez, G.H.: Applying CVL to business process variability management. In: VARiability for You Workshop: Variability Modeling Made Useful for Everyone, pp. 26–31. ACM, Innsbruck, Austria (2012)

10. Oliveira, K., Castro, J., España, S., Pastor, O.: Multi-level autonomic business process management. In: Nurcan, S., Proper, H.A., Soffer, P., Krogstie, J., Schmidt, R., Halpin, T., Bider, I. (eds.) BPMDS/EMMSAD -2013. LNBIP, vol. 147, pp. 184–198. Springer, Heidelberg (2013). https://doi.org/10.1007/978-3-642-38484-4_14
11. Ferro, S., Rubira, C.: An architecture for dynamic self-adaptation in workflows. In: International Conference on Software Engineering Research and Practice (SERP), pp. 35–41 (2015)
12. Seiger, R., Huber, S., Heisig, P., Assmann, U.: Enabling self-adaptive workflows for cyber-physical systems. Softw. Syst. Model. **18**(2), 1117–1134 (2019)
13. Oukharijane, J., Ben Said, I., Chaâbane, M.A., Bouaziz, R., Andonoff, E.: A survey of self-adaptive business processes. In: 32nd International Business Information Management Association (IBIMA), pp. 1388–1403. IBIMA, Seville, Spain (2018)
14. Salehie, M., Tahvildari, L.: Self-adaptive software: landscape and research challenges. ACM Trans. Auton. Adapt. Syst. (TAAS) **4**(2), 1–42 (2009)
15. Delgado, A., Calegari, D.: A generic BPMS user portal for business processes execution interoperability. In: Latin American Computer Conference, vol. 329, pp. 1–10 (2019)
16. Rinderle, S.: Schema evolution in process management systems (2004)
17. Chaâbane, M.A.: De la modélisation á la spécification des processus flexibles: une approche basée sur les versions. Ph.D. thesis, Université Toulouse 1 (2012)
18. Kherbouche, M.O.: Contribution á la gestion de l'évolution des processus métiers. Ph.D. thesis, Université du Littoral Côté d'Opale (2013)
19. Oukharijane, J., Yahya, F., Boukadi, K., Ben-Abdallah, H.: Towards an approach for the evaluation of the quality of business process models. In: 15th International Conference on Computer Systems and Applications, pp. 1–8 (2018)

# Reusable Formal Models for Threat Specification, Detection, and Treatment

Quentin Rouland[1] , Brahim Hamid[1]([∞]) , and Jason Jaskolka[2]

[1] IRIT, University of Toulouse, Toulouse, France
{quentin.rouland,brahim.hamid}@irit.fr
[2] Systems and Computer Engineering, Carleton University, Ottawa, ON, Canada

**Abstract.** One of the main challenges in engineering secure software systems is the formalization of threats for the automation of security architecture threat detection, analysis, and mitigation. On top of that, there is a growing need for the development of reusable security solutions to support secure systems engineering at early stages of development. We address this challenge by proposing an integrated approach for threat specification, detection, and treatment in component-based software architecture models via reusable security threat and requirement formal model libraries. Our solution is based on metamodeling techniques that enable the specification of the software architecture structure and on formal techniques for the purposes of precise specification and verification of security aspects as properties of a modeled system. To validate our work, we explore a set of representative threats from categories based on Microsoft's STRIDE threat classification in the context of secure component-based software architecture development. In addition, we use model-driven engineering techniques for the development of a tool suite to support our approach.

**Keywords:** Engineering secure systems · Software architecture · Threat · Formal methods · Reuse

## 1 Introduction

In recent years, a paradigm shift has occurred in terms of design with the combination of multiple software engineering paradigms. Among them is software reuse [9]. This paradigm shift is changing the way in which systems are currently developed and offers substantial benefits in productivity, quality, and business performance [8]. It can boost the productivity of system development and prevent expensive rework due to the high level of composition-based reuse of dedicated subsystem artifacts that have been pre-engineered to adapt to a specific domain. This situation is more distinct when addressing specific concerns, such as reuse of security solutions.

Most practitioners agree that reuse is not only about code. During system development lifecycles, artifacts may be employed in various forms, such

© Springer Nature Switzerland AG 2020
S. Ben Sassi et al. (Eds.): ICSR 2020, LNCS 12541, pp. 52–68, 2020.
https://doi.org/10.1007/978-3-030-64694-3_4

as domain models, design patterns, component models, code modules, and test and code generators [9]. Our work aims to support system and software engineers in the process of developing reusable formal model libraries that effectively supports reuse for engineering secure systems. Applying reuse at the formal specification level has long been advocated [4,5]. Formal methods generally result in a cleaner architecture, making a system more efficient and more easily maintainable. Furthermore, developing libraries of formally verified components or models can reduce overall development costs and increase confidence in component integrity.

Architecture threat analysis is very useful when it comes to detecting threats at early stages of system development processes. Software threat analysis at the level of the software architecture is a complement to risk assessment because software threats appear due to the level of details of the software architecture. Hence, risks identified by risk assessment are reevaluated and can be treated accordingly. However, the complexity of the discipline of secure systems engineering requires automated tool support where the precise definition and specification of a threat become a prerequisite.

In the context of our work, we propose to use Model Driven Engineering (MDE) abstraction mechanisms [24] to define and handle security threats and requirements through a software architecture metamodel that unifies those concepts. Then, we apply formal techniques to precisely specify and analyze security architecture threats, and to elicit security requirements as properties of a modeled system. To evaluate our approach, we study a set of representative threats based on Microsoft's STRIDE [19] threat classification[1] against the components and the communication links in component-port-connector architecture views [6]. In this work, Eclipse Modeling Framework Technology (EMFT)[2] is used to build the support tools for our approach.

The rest of this paper is organized as follows. Section 2 gives a general overview of our proposed approach. Section 3 describes the software architecture metamodel and an implementation in Alloy. Section 4 presents our reusable security threat and requirements libraries for detecting and treating representative threats from STRIDE categories. Section 5 describes the architecture of the tool suite and presents an example implementation. Section 6 discusses related work. Lastly, Sect. 7 provides some concluding remarks and discusses directions for future work.

## 2   The Proposed Approach

The goals of the proposed approach are to: (1) formalize the security requirements of the system, determined through threat modeling and risk analysis, as desired properties of the system architecture, (2) verify the desired properties, and (3) suggest new security requirements to improve the system design and

---

[1] STRIDE classifies threats into six categories: *Spoofing, Tampering, Repudiation, Information Disclosure, Denial of Service,* and *Elevation of Privilege.*

[2] https://eclipse.org/modeling/emft/.

treat any identified security violations. Below, we outline the overall development process depicted in Fig. 1.

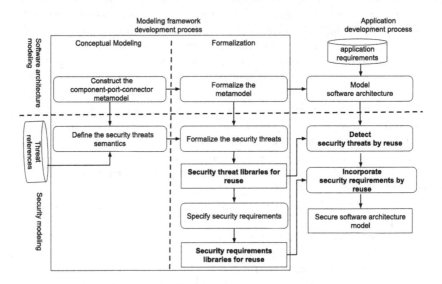

**Fig. 1.** An overview of the proposed development process

**Modeling Framework Development Process.** To support the specification and verification of reusable security solutions for specifying secure software architectures, we consider both the conceptual modeling and formalization activities from both the software architecture and security viewpoints.

*Conceptual Modeling.* We begin by developing a component-port-connector metamodel as high-level concepts of the software architecture. The details of the metamodel are described in Sect. 3.1. We provide a structural model by describing the structural concepts of the metamodel to ensure that software architectures are well-formed. We also provide a behavior model that supports asynchronous message-passing communication through the expression of action occurrences over time. In addition, we develop a property view of the metamodel to describe security threats and requirements. The property view describes the concepts required for building reusable property model libraries.

*Formalization.* After constructing the component-port-connector metamodel, we formally specify the developed model using a suitable language with automated tool support for model checking and verification. By doing so, we obtain a formal architecture metamodel and a formal specification of some representative security threats for each STRIDE threat category. This gives us a set of reusable threat libraries (properties) capable of identifying security threats in a concrete software architecture model and for developing specifications of security solutions to mitigate these threats. The result is a set of abstract formal security solution modules (discussed Sect. 4) that can be easily reused. In this paper, we elect to use Alloy for this formalization due to its the simplicity and straightforward usage of its analyzer to verify properties of the formally specified connectors. This formalization step is required to leverage available tool support used in software and system modeling to enable straightforward instantiation and model checking capabilities to support the elicitation of an appropriate set of security requirements to treat any detected threats.

**Application Development Process.** We build a concrete architecture by instantiating the abstract architecture metamodel into a concrete model for an application-specific distributed software system. Then, using the application-specific system security requirements, we use the security threat libraries to identify potential threats in the system model by checking that it satisfies the desired properties reflecting the security requirements. If we determine that the system model does not satisfy the security requirements, we use our developed libraries to incorporate security solutions to treat those threats in the software architecture model. We then verify the satisfaction of the security requirements in the updated software architecture model. In this way, we iterate over the requirements specification and architecture design to revise and improve the set of security requirements that will help to mitigate the threats. As a result, we converge on a complete set of system security requirements.

# 3   Modeling Framework

## 3.1   Software Architecture and Communication Metamodel

We propose to build a modeling framework to define architectural models that are conceptually close to the industrial practice, i.e., containing a UML-like [20] and UCM-like [21] vocabulary. Figure 2 visualizes a metamodel as a class diagram. The metamodel provides concepts for describing software architectures in terms of different views [16], focusing on the:

1. *Logical view.* To capture the functional architecture of the system in terms of component hardware taking into account the distributed aspects.
2. *Scenario view.* Which builds upon the logical view, describing the behavioral aspects of the architecture elements with respect to the targeted computing model.

In what follows, we detail the principal classes of our metamodel, as described with UML notations in Fig. 2.

- *Component:* A Component is a modeling artifact which represents a piece of software architecture. It has a set of Ports which realize InteractionNature defining how it can interact with other Components.
- *Port.* A Port is the interaction point through which a Component can communicate with its environment.
- *Connector.* A Connector specifies a link that enables communication between Ports by allowing the exchange of communication artifacts (cf. *Scenario view*, CommunicationStyle).

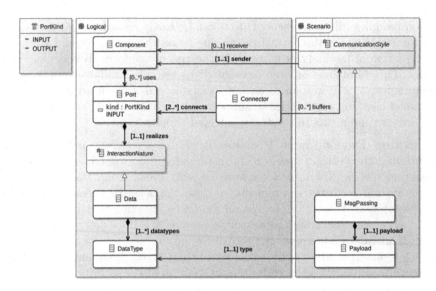

**Fig. 2.** Component-port-connector metamodel

- *InteractionNature.* An InteractionNature defines the nature of an interaction between two Components. This is an abstract concept. In our work, we have focused on defining the following two InteractionNatures:
  - *Data.* A Data defines a data interaction between two Components. Any Component that realizes a Data can be either providing content (data) as a producer where Data is of type OUT, or requiring content (data) as a consumer where Data is of type IN.
- *CommunicationStyle.* A CommunicationStyle represents a specific communication behavior between Components (sender and receiver(s)). This is an abstract concept. In our work, we have focused on defining the following CommunicationStyle:
  - *MsgPassing.* A MsgPassing is the representation of a message exchange from a sender Component that is producing it (i.e., a Component realizes an OUT Data with its corresponding DataType) and a receiver Component that is consuming it (i.e., a Component realizes an IN Data with its corresponding DataType).

The metamodel also includes a *property view* for describing threats and requirements in the form of categories to build property model libraries for reuse, as visualized in Fig. 3. A *PropertyCategory* is a classification for properties. For instance, *Spoofing* and *Tampering* are defined as categories within the STRIDE library. These libraries are then used as external models to type the properties of the components and connectors. In addition, we define *mitigate* as a link between properties to capture relationships between requirements and threats.

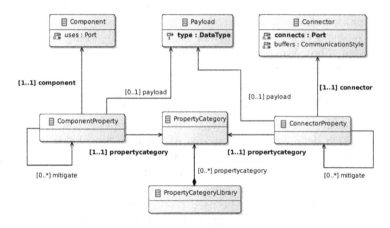

**Fig. 3.** Property metamodel

## 3.2 Software Architecture and Communication Formal Model in Alloy

Next, we present the formalization of the principal concepts of our software architecture metamodel using a suitable language with automated tool support. The metamodel incorporates the concepts of a component-port-connector architecture and involves new concepts to capture the behavioral aspects of a specific message-passing communication model.

**Requirements.** The formal language with tool support should meet the following requirements with respect to the proposed approach:

- Enable the creation of a formal component-port-connector metamodel;
- Enable the creation of a component-port-connector-based system architecture model, describing the target application model according to the metamodel;
- Support the specification and verification of security threats and requirements properties of the system model based upon the component-port-connector architecture as reusable formal model libraries; and
- Support the reuse of the resulting formal model libraries during the creation of a target application model.

While any suitable formal language with tool support that can fulfill these requirements can be used for the realization of the proposed approach, we choose to use Alloy because of the simplicity and the straightforward usage of its analyzer. In our work, the Alloy Analyzer [1] essentially acts as a model checker and counterexample generator. By operating as a counterexample generator, when the Alloy Analyzer identifies the violation of a property, it indicates the existence of a threat. In much the same way, by operating as a model checker, the Alloy Analyzer enables the use of a property as a requirement to indicate the absence of the threat. This enables us to construct models incrementally,

allowing rapid iterations between modeling and analysis when writing a specification. A recent article [14] has further highlighted the strengths of Alloy for
software design. These strengths provide additional motivation and justification
for adopting Alloy in this work.

**An Introduction to Alloy.** Alloy is a lightweight formal modeling language
based on first-order relational logic [13]. An Alloy model is composed of a set
of signatures each defining a set of atoms. Atoms may have fields which define
relations between atoms. In addition, signatures serve as types, and sub-typing
may be defined as signature extension. Constraints in a model can be specified
as *Facts* that should hold at all times, as *Predicates* defined in the form of
parameterized formulas that can be used elsewhere, or as *Assertions* that are
intended to follow from the facts of a model. In some situations, functions in the
form of parameterized expressions may be used as helpers in the specification
and verification processes.

An architect can instruct the Alloy Analyzer to verify whether the property
of the system design holds, which involves exhaustively exploring every model
instance within a specified scope (upper bound). If it does not hold, a counterexample will be generated which can be visualized. The absence of counterexamples
guarantees that the property holds in the modeled system, within the specified
scope. As claimed in [13], most counterexamples are found in a reasonably small
scope.

For the purpose of this paper, we formalize software architecture models and their semantics following some properties to identify the presence of
threats and to provide a set of requirements to treat them. We facilitate this
by providing an architectural metamodel in Alloy and an Alloy implementation of the threats and requirements in the form of reusable libraries. A complete presentation of our Alloy metamodel, the full specification of the other
constructs (e.g., communication primitives, etc.), and the reusable libraries of
threats and requirements are available online via http://www.semcomdt.org/
semco/resources/ThreatModeling_Alloy.zip.

**Structural Model.** A software architecture as visualized in Fig. 2 is formalized in Alloy as follows. The mapping of structural elements is straightforward.
An architectural *Component, Port, Connector, InteractionNature* and *Data* are
mapped to their namesake types in Alloy and are represented as a set of Alloy
signatures as depicted in Listing 1.1. Before two (or more) components can interact, we assume that a connector must be present between them. A component
is connected to a connector through a number of ports.

```
1  sig Component {
2     uses: set Port}
3  sig Port {
4     realizes: one InteractionNature}
5  abstract sig InteractionNature {}
6  abstract sig Connector {
7     // Associate to each port a set of Ticks at which it is connected
```

```
 8       connects: Port -> Tick}
 9   sig DataType {}
10   sig Data extends InteractionNature {
11       datatypes: set DataType
12   }
```

**Listing 1.1.** Software architecture metamodel in Alloy

**Behavioral Model.** To model the behavior of the system, we consider abstract time in the form of a parameter to express instants of occurrences of actions. An execution of a system is a sequence of steps (instants), where a step is determined by two successive time points. We used the *Ordering* module provided within Alloy to express a time in a discrete sense, referred to as *Tick*, where time is explicitly modeled as a set of discrete, ordered *Tick* instances.

To support message passing communication under the connector, we provide the formal specification of the connector as a buffer of messages and define the appropriate communication primitives as depicted in Listing 1.2.

```
 1   abstract sig CommunicationStyle extends Messaging {
 2     sender: one Component, // the component from which the receiver
              believes the communication originates
 3     receiver: Component,
 4     origin_sender:   one Component
 5   }{
 6     to = receiver
 7     from = sender
 8     origin_sender != receiver}
 9   sig Payload {
10     data: one univ,
11     type: one DataType}
12   sig MsgPassing extends CommunicationStyle {
13     sent: one Tick,
14     received: Component -> lone Tick,
15     payload: one Payload
16     }
17   sig ConnectorMPS {
18     buffer : MsgPassing -> Tick}
19   pred Component.send [c:Component,d:Payload, t:Tick] {
20     some m: MsgPassing {
21       m.payload = d
22       m.origin_sender = this
23       m.receiver = c
24       m.sent = t}}
25   pred Component.receive [c:Component,d:Payload,t:Tick] {
26     some m: MsgPassing {
27       m.payload = d
28       m.received[this] = t
29       m.sender = c }}
```

**Listing 1.2.** Message passing communication primitives

Threats can now be defined in terms of a system specification, i.e., in terms of enabled actions, messages, components, and connectors.

## 4  Reusable Security Threat and Requirement Libraries

In the context of our work, threats and security requirements are defined as properties and provided as formal model libraries to support reuse.

## 4.1   Formal Property Models for Reuse

We encode the property view as described in Sect. 3.1 by defining the corresponding concepts *ComponentProperty* and *ConnectorProperty* as abstract signatures in Alloy. For each one, the helper function *holds* is used to easily verify that the property holds in a given model fostering reuse.

```
1  abstract sig ComponentProperty {
2      comp: one Component,
3      payl: one Payload}
4  fun ComponentProperty.holds[c1:one Component,p: one Payload]: set
       ComponentProperty {
5      { m: this { m.comp = c1 and m.payl = p }}}
6  abstract sig ConnectorProperty {
7      conn: one Connector,
8      payl: one Payload
9  }{ comp1 != comp2 }
10 fun ConnectorProperty.comp1 : one Component {{ c:Component | this.
       conn.portI in c.uses}}
11 fun ConnectorProperty.comp2 : one Component {{ c:Component | this.
       conn.portO in c.uses}}
12 fun ConnectorProperty.holds[c1,c2:one Component,p: one Payload]:
       set ConnectorProperty{
13     { m: this { m.comp1 = c1 and m.comp2 = c2 and m.payl = p }}}
```

**Listing 1.3.** Property view concepts in Alloy

Next, we build a set of reusable libraries for threat detection and treatment. To do so, we model threats from the STRIDE categories using constructions such as *Predicate*, *Assertion*, and *Fact*. Threats will be specified as constraints in the model. Each threat category is associated with a representative property such that the violation of the specified property indicates the presence of the threat. Therefore, each threat is associated with a property defined as a predicate in the Alloy model describing the targeted software architecture and communication system (e.g., *NotBeSpoofed*). Then, the presence of a threat, as a result of the violation of the property, is detected by the Alloy Analyzer through an assertion finding a counterexample. As a result, an appropriate security property is defined as a predicate (e.g., *spoofProof*) to codify a security requirement to constrain the operation of the system and to protect against the corresponding threat.

Our intent is to illustrate the approach described in Sect. 2 using representative threats in the context of a component-port-connector architecture model and message passing communication. For reasons of space, we only provide the details of a representative threat from the spoofing STRIDE category such that the violation of the specified property indicates the presence of the spoofing threat. However, in a similar way, we have also specified representative threats and requirements for each of the other STRIDE categories. These property specifications are included as part of the security threat and requirements libraries so that they can be reused in other concrete instantiations of systems built using component-port-connector architectures and message passing communication.

## 4.2   A Representative Spoofing Threat

Spoofing refers to the impersonation of a component in the system for the purpose of misleading other system entities into falsely believing that an attacker is legitimate. Spoofing threats violate the authentication objectives of a system. In the context of message passing communication, spoofing threats take the form of message senders falsely claiming to be other system components, to entice other components to believe that the spoofed component is the originator of the message. Therefore, a spoofing threat can be identified by verifying whether the system ensures that all of the senders of message are authentic, i.e., *the sender of a message is always the originator of the message.*

In a distributed software system components communicate and synchronize by sending and receiving messages through existing connectors. A computation program encodes the local actions that components may perform. The actions of the program include modifying local variables, sending messages, and receiving messages to/from each component in the corresponding system architecture. Let $C$ be a set of components and $M$ be a set of messages. For $c_1, c_2 \in C$, we denote this representative property as $SenderSpoofing(c_1, c_2)$ which is specified for all messages $m \in M$ as:

$$\mathbb{E}_{c_2}(\text{get\_src}(c_2, m, c_1)) \Rightarrow \text{sent\_by}(m, c_1) \tag{1}$$

Here, $\mathbb{E}_{c_2}(\text{get\_src}(c_2, m, c_1))$ is a predicate indicating that component $c_2$ is able to get the declared source $c_1 \in C$ from message $m \in M$ and $\text{sent\_by}(m, c_1)$ is a predicate indicating that at some past point in time, component $c_1 \in C$ sent message $m \in M$.

The Alloy specification of the *SenderSpoofing* threat is shown in Listing 1.4. The *SenderSpoofing* threat is considered within the connector and can be identified by checking whether the communication system provided by the connector ensures that all messages transmitted through the connector have authentic senders.

The *NotBeSpoofed* property is defined in accordance with the logical specification of the *SenderSpoofing* threat (Expression (1)) and the system computing model. The property that every message that is received by a component $c_2$ that it believes was sent by component $c_1$, was actually sent by $c_1$ and not by any other component. In this way, there is no way in which a malicious component can pretend to be the sender of the message.

Note that in Listing 1.4, while the *SenderSpoofing* threat is considered within the connector, we define the *NotBeSpoofed* property (Lines 3–5) with respect to two components (c1 and c2) representing the endpoints of the connector being considered. Note that the *SenderSpoofing* threat specified in Listing 1.4 is an instantiation of the abstract *ConnectorProperty* defined in Listing 1.3. This demonstrates the reuse of the property view model.

```
1   sig SenderSpoofing extends ConnectorProperty {}{
2       not NotBeSpoofed[comp1,comp2,payl]}
3   pred NotBeSpoofed[c1,c2:Component, p:Payload] {
4       all t:Tick | let m={m:MsgPassing | m.payload = p}|
5       E_get_src[c2,m,c1,t] implies sent_by[m,c1,t]}
6   assert MPSCanBeSpoofed {
7       all c1,c2:Component, p:Payload |
8       | no SenderSpoofing.holds[c1,c2,d]}
```

**Listing 1.4.** Detection of spoofing

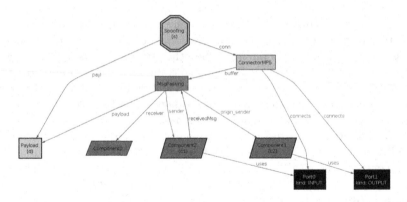

**Fig. 4.** Spoofing counterexample provided by the Alloy Analyzer

The Alloy Analyzer detects a *SenderSpoofing* threat by finding a counterexample, as a violation of the *NotBeSpoofed* property. Figure 4 shows a model where the *SenderSpoofing* threat occurs. We proceed by defining a security requirement as a predicate to protect against the *SenderSpoofing* threat. The idea is to ensure that no component can send a message by pretending to be some other component. The *spoofProof* property is defined as a predicate on the connector to ensure the authenticity of the sender of each message transmitted through this connector (Listing 1.5, Lines 1–4).

```
1  pred ConnectorMPS.spoofProof {
2    all mp:MsgPassing, t:Tick |
3      mp in this.buffer.t implies
4        mp.sender = mp.origin_sender // The sender is authentic}
5  assert MPSCanNotBeSpoofed {
6    (all c:ConnectorMPS | c.spoofProof) implies
7    (all c1,c2:Component, p:Payload |
8      | no SenderSpoofing.holds[c1,c2,d])}
```

**Listing 1.5.** Treatment of spoofing

According to the Alloy Analyzer, no counterexample was found. The satisfaction of the *spoofProof* property allows the fulfillment of the corresponding security requirement to protect against the *SenderSpoofing* threat.

## 5   Tool Support

We have implemented a prototype to support the proposed approach (Sect. 2) as an Eclipse plug-in, using the open-source Eclipse Modeling Framework (EMF) [25], Xtext [3] to develop textual Eclipse editors, and Xtend [3] to allow the implementation of model transformations in Eclipse. Our starting point is the software architecture metamodel presented in Sect. 3.1 as the metamodel for a software architecture Domain Specific Language (DSL). The metamodel describes the abstract syntax of the DSL, by capturing the concepts of the component-port-connector software architecture domain and how the concepts are related.

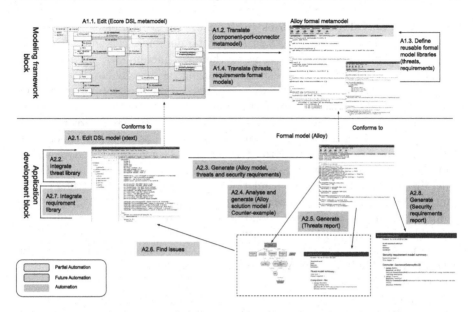

**Fig. 5.** Tool support architecture and artifacts of the approach.eps

The architecture of the tool, as shown in Fig. 5, is composed of two main blocks: (1) Modeling framework block and (2) Application development block. Each block is composed of a set of modules to support the corresponding activities (the numbers in parentheses correspond to the activity numbers in Fig. 5).

**Modeling Framework Block for Reuse.** The first block is dedicated to supporting four activities. (*A1.1*) is responsible for creating the DSL metamodel. The resulting metamodel is used to formally define (in Alloy) the static and behavioral semantics, based upon the DSL metamodel according to the procedure discussed in Sect. 3.2. We name this definition the formal metamodel (*A1.2*). Furthermore, reusable threat model libraries and security requirements model libraries are also defined as Alloy models according to the procedure discussed in Sect. 4 (*A1.3*). We will name this definition the formal model libraries. The last activity (*A1.4*) is the definition of a set of DSL model libraries from the Alloy specification of threats and requirements (formal model libraries), using the *property view* of the DSL metamodel (Fig. 3). Each threat property is associated with a set of security requirements to mitigate it, during *A1.3*. As an example, we use spoofing as an instance of PropertyCategory, senderSpoofing as an instance of the ConnectorProperty within the *StrideThreat* library and spoofProof as an instance of the ConnectorProperty within the *SecurityRequirement* library. Finally, we set up that the spoofProof requirement *mitigates* the senderSpoofing threat. To support these four activities, we used EMF, Xtext to develop the DSL metamodel, and the Alloy Analyzer to encode the corresponding formal metamodel. No further implementation was required.

**Application Development Block by Reuse.** The second block is dedicated to supporting eight activities. (*A2.1*) allows the designer to model a software architecture (DSL model) conforming to the DSL metamodel, where (*A2.2*) allows to integrate the threats specification reusing the already developed threat model libraries (*A1.4*). Then, *A2.3* is the generation of a formal model (in Alloy) from a DSL model, through a transformation engine. The Alloy Analyzer is then invoked, with several iterations, to detect the targeted threat (*A2.4*) and a report on the detected threats may be generated as an HTML document (*A2.5*). The report is then analyzed (*A2.6*) and *A2.7* allows the designer to add the corresponding security requirements to the DSL model reusing the DSL model libraries and the *mitigation* relationship between properties (*A1.4*). The resulting DSL model is then transformed to a formal Alloy model (*A2.3*), where the formal definition of the corresponding security requirements are automatically added in the produced Alloy software architecture model from their DSL definitions. At the end of mitigation (i.e., when no counterexample was found when the Alloy Analyzer is invoked), a security requirements report is generated as an HTML document (*A2.8*).

To support these eight activities, we developed a textual editor to model the architecture of the system using EMF and Xtext. In addition, the textual editor provides auto-completion for the manual integration of the threat library (*A2.2*), proposing the possible threat categories and properties for a software architecture elements, when the designer is typing the elements. We also developed two transformation engines to generate the formal Alloy model (*A2.3*) and the HTML reports using Xtend (*A2.5* and *A2.8*). The transformation process takes advantage of the template feature provided by Xtend and consists of a set of transformation rules that are applied for each concept (using tree traversal) on a DSL model to generate a Alloy formal model. The generation process allows to automatically incorporate the formal definition of the targeted threats from their DSL definition in the produced Alloy software architecture model. Finally, the Alloy Analyzer is used to verify the resulting models and to generate counterexamples.

# 6 Related Work

A taxonomy for the categories to compare different reuse techniques and illustrate some of the fundamental issues in software reuse have been introduced in the seminal paper of Krueger [17] as a five-dimension construct: a.) Build for reuse: (1) Abstraction: Identify units of reusable knowledge and concisely represent them in abstract form; (2) Classification: Store the reusable knowledge into a "knowledge base" that is indexed and classified, b.) Build with reuse: (1) Selection: Query the reusable knowledge into a parameterized form (e.g. function with formal parameters); (2) Specialization: Modify the reusable knowledge to fit new situations (e.g., function with actual parameters); (3) Integration: Combine the reusable knowledge with your project (e.g., invocation and weaving).

In this paper, we focused on the reuse in the context of formal techniques to support the development of secure software architectures, providing support for a.(1), b.(2) and b.(3).

The development of reusable formal libraries has been seen in a number of works. For example, Rivera [23] described a framework called the Object Toolbox which is a library focused on reuse of generic functions. The collection of functions are formally tested, and can be linked together to create a solution that can also be tested via abstraction. The Object Toolbox framework enables developers to reuse a previously designed and formally tested function or component. Khosravi et al. [15] provided a reusable library of Reo channels in Alloy that can be used to create a model of a Reo connector. The model of a connector can be reused as a component for constructing more complex connectors. Similar to our work, properties of the Reo connector expressed as predicates can be verified by automatically by the Alloy Analyzer tool. Periyasamy and Chidambaram [22] described an approach for ensuring structural compatibility of formal specifications (using the Z notation) by describing the structure and behaviour of software components enabling their reuse.

The formalization of threat models and security properties for the verification and validation of system models has been studied in the recent past. Existing formalization attempts for threats include the work in [12] using VDM++ to specify the core components of threat modeling techniques including STRIDE, DREAD[3], and basic confidentiality, integrity, availability, authentication, authorization, and non-repudiation security mechanisms. The work does not describe the whole approach, but rather presents the core ideas and makes a case for the adoption of formal methods in threat modeling and secure system development. Works from authors in [18] used a logic-based representation for describing abstract security properties which were implemented and verified using Coq [2]. Moreover, [11] used Software Cost Reduction (SCR) tables to specify and analyze security properties codifying system requirements.

In general, the output of these methods is a set of recommendations and guidelines to detect, evaluate, and mitigate possible threats. This eases in defining security requirements. However, a global closed-loop process has not been applied to be able to iterate to specify the complete set of requirements. It should be noted that most of these works have limitations in formalizing threats (only a subset of threat categories are considered), in reusing and extending them, and in automating the verification process. With this contribution, we propose to improve the global process and to apply it on a concrete security architecture design. We also propose tool support to facilitate the iteration of the loop. Our focus is to apply formal methods with tool support by determining how to design a secure system with the addition of more formality.

---

[3] DREAD is a risk assessment model for risk rating security threats using five categories: *Damage*, *Reproducibility*, *Exploitability*, *Affected users*, and *Discoverability*.

# 7 Concluding Remarks and Future Works

Security is a quality attribute that is becoming increasingly critical in current software-intensive systems and is thus gaining substantial attention by the research and industrial community. One of the related research issues is the formalization of threats for the automation of security architecture threat analysis by detecting and mitigating existing threats.

In our work, we proposed an approach to threat specification, detection, and treatment in component-based software architecture models via reusable security threat and requirement formal model libraries. The modeling framework we propose takes into account reuse in software engineering considerations in conjunction with the state-of-the-art to specify and design secure software architectures. Our solution is based on metamodeling techniques that enable the specification of the software architecture structure and on formal techniques for the purposes of precise specification and verification of security aspects as properties of a modeled system. The combined formal modeling and MDE to specify threats and develop their targeted system security requirements allows to develop an accurate analysis, for evaluation and/or certification. Furthermore, we walked through an MDE-based prototype to support the proposed approach. An example of this tool suite is constructed using EMFT, Xtext, and Xtend and is currently provided in the form of Eclipse plug-ins. We illustrate the application of the proposed approach and the developed tool to develop a set of reusable security threat and requirement model libraries following the STRIDE categories.

In our future work, we plan to improve the tool support to cover more aspects of the Krueger [17] fundamental reuse issues and for more automation. For instance, we seek to handle the storage and the selection of the reusable models [10] and to add an automatic (or systematic) incorporation the results of analysis (report) into the DSL software architecture model. We would also like to study the integration of our tools with other MDE tools. The objective is to show the process flow and the integration of the tools in the domain tool chains. We will seek new opportunities to apply the proposed approach to other threat models (e.g., the ENISA threat taxonomy [7]). Moreover, a preliminary and promising result in the domain of threat references indicates some interferences between threats that we plan to investigate further in the near future.

# References

1. Alloy Analyzer. http://alloytools.org/. Accessed Apr 2019
2. Bertot, Y., Castéran, P.: Interactive Theorem Proving and Program Development: Coq'Art: The Calculus of Inductive Constructions. Texts in Theoretical Computer Science, An EATCS Series. Springer, Heidelberg (2004). https://doi.org/10.1007/978-3-662-07964-5
3. Bettini, L.: Implementing Domain Specific Languages with Xtext and Xtend, 2nd edn. Packt Publishing, Birmingham (2016)

4. Bowen, J.P., Hinchey, M.G.: Ten commandments of formal methods. Computer **28**(4), 56–63 (1995)
5. Bowen, J.P., Hinchey, M.G.: Ten commandments of formal methods... ten years later. Computer **39**(1), 40–48 (2006)
6. Crnkovic, I.: Component-based software engineering for embedded systems. In: Proceedings of the 27th International Conference on Software Engineering, ICSE 2005, pp. 712–713. ACM (2005)
7. European Union Agency for Network and Information Security (ENISA): Threat Taxonomy (2016). https://www.enisa.europa.eu/topics/threat-risk-management/threats-and-trends/enisa-threat-landscape/threat-taxonomy/view. Accessed Nov 2018
8. Ezran, M., Morisio, M., Tully, C.: Practical Software Reuse. Springer, Heidelberg (2002). https://doi.org/10.1007/978-1-4471-0141-3
9. Frakes, W., Kang, K.: Software reuse research: status and future. IEEE Trans. Softw. Eng. **31**(7), 529–536 (2005)
10. Hamid, B.: A model repository description language - MRDL. In: Kapitsaki, G.M., Santana de Almeida, E. (eds.) ICSR 2016. LNCS, vol. 9679, pp. 350–367. Springer, Cham (2016). https://doi.org/10.1007/978-3-319-35122-3_23
11. Heitmeyer, C.: Applying *practical* formal methods to the specification and analysis of security properties. In: Gorodetski, V.I., Skormin, V.A., Popyack, L.J. (eds.) MMM-ACNS 2001. LNCS, vol. 2052, pp. 84–89. Springer, Heidelberg (2001). https://doi.org/10.1007/3-540-45116-1_11
12. Hussain, S., Erwin, H., Dunne, P.: Threat modeling using formal methods: a new approach to develop secure web applications. In: Proceedings of the 7th International Conference on Emerging Technologies, pp. 1–5 (September 2011)
13. Jackson, D.: Software Abstractions: Logic, Language, and Analysis. The MIT Press, Cambridge (2006)
14. Jackson, D.: Alloy: a language and tool for exploring software designs. Commun. ACM **62**(9), 66–76 (2019). https://doi.org/10.1145/3338843
15. Khosravi, R., Sirjani, M., Asoudeh, N., Sahebi, S., Iravanchi, H.: Modeling and analysis of Reo connectors using alloy. In: Lea, D., Zavattaro, G. (eds.) COORDINATION 2008. LNCS, vol. 5052, pp. 169–183. Springer, Heidelberg (2008). https://doi.org/10.1007/978-3-540-68265-3_11
16. Kruchten, P.: Architectural blueprints - the "4+ 1" view model of software architecture. IEEE Softw. **12**(6), 42–50 (1995)
17. Krueger, C.: Software reuse. ACM Comput. Surv. **24**(2), 131–183 (1992)
18. Mana, A., Pujol, G.: Towards formal specification of abstract security properties. In: Proceedings of the Third International Conference on Availability, Reliability and Security, pp. 80–87 (March 2008)
19. Microsoft: The STRIDE Threat Model. Microsoft Corporation, Redmond (2009)
20. OMG: Unified modeling language (UML), Version 2.5 (2015). https://www.omg.org/spec/UML/2.5. Accessed July 2020
21. OMG: Unified component model for distributed, real-time and embedded systems, Version 1.2 (2020). https://www.omg.org/spec/UCM/1.2. Accessed July 2020
22. Periyasamy, K., Chidambaram, J.: Software reuse using formal specification of requirements. In: Proceedings of the 1996 Conference of the Centre for Advanced Studies on Collaborative Research, CASCON 1996, p. 31. IBM Press (1996)
23. Rivera, J.: Cyber security via formal methods: a framework for implementing formal methods. In: 2017 International Conference on Cyber Conflict (CyCon U.S.), pp. 76–81 (November 2017)

24. Selic, B.: The pragmatics of model-driven development. IEEE Softw. **20**(5), 19–25 (2003)
25. Steinberg, D., Budinsky, F., Paternostro, M., Merks, E.: EMF: Eclipse Modeling Framework 2.0, 2nd edn. Addison-Wesley, Boston (2009)

# Dynamic Reconfiguration of Cloud Composite Services Using Event-B

Aida Lahouij[1(✉)] ⓘ, Lazhar Hamel[2] ⓘ, and Mohamed Graiet[2] ⓘ

[1] ISITCom, Université de Sousse, 4011 Hammam Sousse, Tunisia
aida.lahouij@gmail.com
[2] ISIMM, Université de Monastir, 5000 Monastir, Tunisia
lazhar.hamel@isimm.rnu.tn, mohamed.graiet1@gmail.com

**Abstract.** One of the key characteristics of the Cloud environment is hight dynamicity; constantly new services are added and others are deleted due to unavailability, faulty behaviour or performance degradation. Cloud services can be packaged together and offered as a composite service to overcome the atomic service's shortage or respond to specific user demand. In this context, a faulty component service must be dynamically replaced in order to preserve the functional and non-functional correctness of the composite service. This work presents a formal approach to verify the dynamic behaviour of the Cloud composite service. We mainly focus on the correctional dynamic such as the substitution of faulty or unavailable services and resources. The proposed Event-B approach ensures the preservation of the composite service consistency, reliability and efficiency after the substitution of faulty or unavailable components.

**Keywords:** Cloud environment · Composite service · Faulty behaviour · Dynamic behaviour · Formal approach · Service substitution · Event-B

## 1 Introduction

The Cloud environment [7] is a dynamically changing environment. As time goes on, new services are deployed in the cloud and the existing services may also change or became unavailable. CPUs, storages, network devices and the application context are subject to constant changes or failures in dynamic environments. Cloud providers must respond quickly to these changes.

One of the key concepts in the Cloud environment is reusability. Services can be reused to form a composed service that responds to a more complex business requirement. The obtained service is called composite service and the services composing it are called component services. As many component services are interacting in this context, the failure of one of them affects the execution of the composite service. The failed or unavailable component must be quickly replaced to avoid the failure of the whole composite service. The preservation

© Springer Nature Switzerland AG 2020
S. Ben Sassi et al. (Eds.): ICSR 2020, LNCS 12541, pp. 69–84, 2020.
https://doi.org/10.1007/978-3-030-64694-3_5

of the reliability and consistency of the composite service after the replacement of the faulty component is not a trivial task. The replacement should respect some structural, semantic and behavioural constraints in order to maintain the composite service consistency. This task gets more awkward with the deployment of the composite services in the Cloud, which adds the necessity to consider the Cloud resources allocated to the component services.

As mentioned before, these resources can be turned on and off, or moved from one place to another, or broke down, networks may be congested and packets are dropped, etc. Services running on a failed resource must be moved to another in order to avoid data loss. Resource replacement must be done automatically and quickly. Constraints on the resource capacity and shareability must be considered while replacing the faulty resource by a new one. It is important also to preserve the composite service efficiency. The efficiency requirements are tightly related to a set of quality-of-service (QoS) constraints that are required by customers. The reconfiguration should maintain the level of performance of the composite service or even enhance it. Therefore, in this paper, we check the QoS of the replacing component service/resource. Only component service/resource with an equal QoS or better QoS are selected.

As we can notice, the verification requirements are complex and divided into many levels. Therefore, we opt for the Event-B [5] formal method that facilitates the modelling of complex systems through its refinement capabilities. Formal verification is necessary to preserve the composition behaviour and avoid incorrect reconfigurations. The purpose of this paper is to extend our previous works [13] by presenting a formal reconfiguration approach that maintains the reliability of the composite service. The objective is to select the replacing component and verify its adaptability to the rest of the component services.

The remainder of this paper is organized as follows; in the following section, we give a summary of existing related works. In Sect. 3, we present our motivations. An overview of the Event-B method is given in Sect. 4. Our formal model is introduced in Sect. 5. The verification and validation approach is detailed in Sect. 6. Finally, we conclude and provide insights for future works in Sect. 7.

## 2    Related Work

In this section, we present an overview of existing approaches dealing with the dynamic reconfiguration of Cloud composite services. In [17], authors deal partly with the dynamic reconfiguration of cloud applications. They use the Unifying Theories of Programming (UTP) to provide a formal model for understanding and reasoning about cloud services. However, they do not assess the semantic and behaviour properties during reconfiguration which may affect the correctness of the application. In [1], authors present a novel protocol, which aims at reconfiguring cloud applications. The protocol supports virtual machine failures, and the reconfiguration always terminates successfully even in the presence of a finite number of failures. Compared to this work, our work supports both component services and resource reconfiguration and verify the replacing component consistency on multiple verification levels.

The work, in [9], proposes a service selection method for workflow reconfiguration based on interface operation matching. This method covers both the functional behaviours and non-functional requirements of workflow changes when a service failure occurs. This work is interesting, however, it lacks the reconfiguration of Cloud resources. An approach to data consistency checking for the dynamic replacement of the service process is proposed in [8]. This approach checks the data consistency of a service dynamic replacement by computing the similarity degree between interface data which is not sufficient. In our work, we consider not only the interface data matching but the interacting protocol matching.

In our previous work [11], we deal with component service reconfiguration in the SCA (service component architecture) context. An Event-B based approach is proposed to configure the SCA composition dynamically. This approach checks the structural and behavioural compatibility between the replacing service and the faulty service. The proposed work lacks the semantic verification of the replacement. In [10, 12, 14], we deal with the composite service behaviour verification. Based on the Event-B method the composite service behaviour is verified based on the interacting protocols and communication patterns. The absence of a dynamic reconfiguration method can affect the correctness of the composite service at runtime where unexpected service failures can happen any time.

In this paper, we extend our work in [13] by adding events related to the dynamic reconfiguration of component services and resources. As in the previous work, we perform the verification at design time and runtime and deals with structural, semantic, behavioural and resource allocation requirements of a Cloud composite service, in this work, we perform the reconfiguration on the same basis. As we can notice the existent works generally focus only on one side of the verification. We find those who have neglected the precondition and effects verification despite their increased importance in establishing semantic reliability, especially in the last few years. Other works do not afford any matching technique to check the semantic matching among between the replacing service and the other component services. In the literature, we find also works that deal only with the behaviour requirements. Others were interested only in the resource reconfiguration problem. Compared to these works, our work performs the verification of the dynamic configuration on four levels: structural, semantic, behavioural, and resource allocation.

## 3   Motivations

The Travel booking composite service (see Fig. 1) is constituted of six component services; *Webform request* (WFR): a webform is used to enter travel information such as the departure date, the return date, the departure city, and the arrival city, *Search Flights* (SF): to search for the available flights at the required dates, *Search Hotels* (SH): to search for the available hotels at the required dates, *Booking* (BG): used to book the selected flight and hotel, *Credit card payment* (CP):

the payment service for the booked flight and hotel, *The reservation confirmation* (RC): sends an e-mail to confirm the reservation.

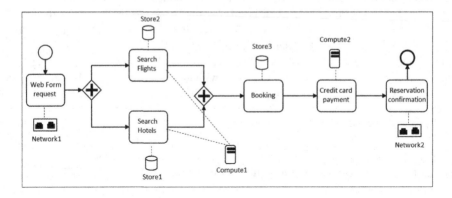

**Fig. 1.** The travel booking composite service

To run the aforementioned component services, Cloud resources are required. First, the execution of the component service *Web form request* needs to communicate its inputs via a virtual networking Cloud resource (*Network1*). The component services *Search Flights* and *Search Hotels* share the virtual machine (*compute1*) with 4 GB of RAM. Moreover, they respectively need the storage resources *Store1* and *Store2*. The component service *Booking* stores its data in the storage resource Store3 which has a capacity of 5 GB of available storage size. The execution of the *Credit card payment* service is performed in the virtual machine (*compute2*) with 2 GB of RAM. Finally, the component service *Reservation confirmation* needs to communicate its outputs via a virtual networking Cloud resource (*Network2*).

However, what to do when a component service is no longer available or when it behaves in a faulty way. For instance, if the $FS$ component service fails, we have to find a new component service ($NFS$) able to search for a flight. Links between the output of the $WFR$ component service and the $NFS$ component service and links between the output of the $NFS$ component service and the input of the $BG$ component service may be invalid. Therefore we have to verify the semantic matching between the new component service and its related component services in the composition. Which is to check the semantic compatibility between the new component service and the dead component service. Adding that the changes resulting from the execution of $WFR$ may contradict the execution conditions of $NFS$ and the changes resulting from the execution of $NFS$ may contradict the execution conditions of $BG$. The execution conditions of service and the changes resulting from its execution denotes respectively the Preconditions and Effects of services. To preserve the composite service consistency, we have to select the replacing component service that is compatible in terms of preconditions and effects with the faulty/unavailable component service.

Checking the behavioural compatibilities between the new component service the dead component service is also necessary in order to preserve the behaviour correctness of the composite service and avoid blocking situations. We have then to ensure that for each message that will be sent/received by the replacing component service, there is a component service that will respectively receive/send that message. Which is to verify that its protocol compatible with the dead component service.

It is important also to manage the resources allocated to the new component service and avoid any deadlock situation related to the resources shareability. Resources can also break down and become unavailable which affects the composite service execution. The replacing resource must be able to handle the component services running on the old resource in terms of capacity and shareability properties. Ensuring the functional correctness of the composite service is not enough, a non-functional verification is also needed to ensure the composite service efficiency. The QoS of a component service/resource can degrade which may affect the composite service execution. Dynamic reconfiguration is required in this case to preserve the QoS of the composite service and the SLA established between the service user and the service provider.

In order to cope with the requirements mentioned above, we propose in this paper a formal approach based on the Event-B method to model the reconfiguration of Cloud composite services. With its formal syntax and semantics, the Event-B specification is able to validate the behaviour of the built models through the execution of several verification properties.

## 4   The Event-B Method

Event-B is an evolution of the B-method also called classical B [2]. Event-B [5] reuses the set-theoretical and logical notations of the B method and provides new notations for expressing abstract systems or simply models based on events [6]. Through sequential refinement, this formal method enables incremental development of software step by step from the abstract level to more detailed levels and possibly to the code level. The complexity of a system is mastered thanks to the refinement concept allowing to gradually introduce the different parts that constitute the system starting from an abstract model to a more concrete one. A stepwise refinement approach produces a correct specification by construction since we prove the different properties of the system at each step. Event-B is supported by the Eclipse-based RODIN platform [4] on which different external tools (e.g. provers, animators, model-checkers) can be plugged in order to animate/validate a formal development.

An Event-B specification is made of two elements: context and machine. A context describes the static part of an Event-B specification. An Event-B context is optional and contains essentially the following clauses: the clause SETS that describes a set of abstract and enumerated types, the clause CONSTANTS that represents the constants of the model and the clause AXIOMS that contains all the properties of the constants and their types. A context can optionally extend another one by adding its name in the clause EXTENDS. A context is referenced by the machine in order to use its sets and constants by adding its name in the clause SEES. An Event-B machine describes the dynamic part of an Event-B specification. It is composed of a set of clauses organized as follow; the clause VARIABLES representing the state variables of the model, the clause INVARIANTS defining the invariant properties of the system that it must allow, at least, the typing of variables declared in the clause VARIABLES and finally the clause EVENTS containing the list of events related to the model. An event is modelled with a guarded substitution and fired when its guards are evaluated to true. The events occurring in an Event-B model affect the state described in the clause VARIABLES. A machine can optionally refine another one by adding its name in the clause REFINES. An event consists of a guard and a body. When the guard is satisfied, the event can be activated. When the guards of several events are satisfied at the same time, the choice of the event to enable is deterministic.

## 5    Formal Reconfiguration Using Event-B

In this section, we present our formal model that supports dynamic composition changes during run-time. Based on the Event-b formal method, our approach consists of defining a couple of events in order to substitute a cloud service or resource.

### 5.1    Modelling the Cloud Composite Service

In our previous works [13], we have paid attention to the verification of the correctness of Cloud composite services. This verification is performed during the component services selection and execution. The designed formal model comprises four abstraction levels to model the structural, semantic, behavioural and resource allocation requirements that must be considered in order to avoid inconsistent composite services. In this section, we give an overview of the presented model that will be extended in this work to consider the dynamic reconfiguration of Cloud composite services. Figure 2 depicts the formalization architecture of the Event-B model denoted by *CloudM*. Our model's abstraction is provided in four levels: *StructM1* sees *StructC1* and models the structural properties of the Cloud composite service. *StructM1* sees *StructC1* and models the structural properties of the Cloud composite service. *BehM1* refines *SemM1* by adding the behavioural properties of the composition. *ResM1* refines *BehM1*, where details about the resource allocation are added.

### 5.2    Modelling the Service Substitution

To substitute a component service by another one, we have to check the compatibility between them. The replacing service must ensure the same functions as the faulty service. It must be semantically and behaviourally compatible with the rest of the component services. There should not be any conflict on the resource allocation. This verification is done on the four abstraction levels previously introduced. A new Event *SubstituteCS* is added in order to substitute faulty and unavailable component services. This event is firstly added in the structural level and then refined in the other abstraction levels.

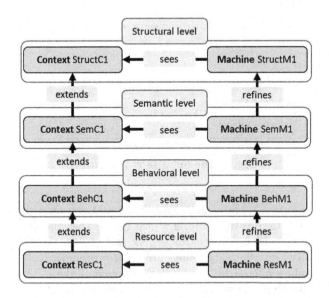

**Fig. 2.** CloudM specification

**Structural Level.** In the structural level, we have defined the *SubstituteCS* (Fig. 3) that has five parameters:

- *c*: the composite service containing a faulty or unavailable component service,
- *OldS*: the faulty or unavailable component service,
- *NewS*: the replacing component service we are searching for,
- *op1*: the operation of the OldS,
- *op2*: the operation of the NewS.

The composite service *c* is running ($c \mapsto running \in St$ (grd2)). The *SubstituteCS* event is triggered when a component service of the running composite service *c* became unavailable or fails to accomplish its expected function. The state of *OldS* is then either *failed* or *unavailable* (grd3). The state of *NewS* is deployed (grd4). The replacing component service must be functionally compatible with the faulty service in order to accomplish the desired tasks. Therefore, in grd5, we require that *NewS* provides the same function of operation as *OldS* ($FctOfOp(op1) = FctOfOp(op2)$).

A non-functional selection is also performed at this level to maintain the QoS level of the composite service. The QoS criteria considered in this paper

Event SubstituteCS ⟨ordinary⟩ ≙

**any**

c OldS NewS op1 op2
**where**

grd1: $OldS \in Components \land c \in dom(SerOf) \land OldS \in dom(OpOfS) \land NewS \in Components$

grd2: $(OldS \in SerOf(c)) \land (c \mapsto running \in St)$

grd3: $OldS \mapsto failed \in St$

grd4: $NewS \mapsto deployed \in St$

grd5: $op1 \in OpOfS(OldS) \land op2 \in OpOfS(NewS) \land NewS \in dom(OpOfS) \land FctOfOp(op1) = FctOfOp(op2)$

grdAv: $Av(NewS) \geq Av(OldS)$

grdRe: $Re(NewS) \geq Re(OldS)$

grdCst: $Cst(NewS) \leq Cst(OldS)$

grdRt: $Rt(NewS) \leq Rt(OldS)$
**then**

act1: $SerOf(c) := (SerOf(c) \setminus \{OldS\}) \cup \{NewS\}$

act2: $St(NewS) := readyToInvoke$
**end**

**Fig. 3.** The *SubstituteCS* event

are availability (Av), reliability (Re), cost (Cst) and response time (Rt). The Av and Re criteria are positive criteria which means that the higher the value is the better the QoS is. In the guards grdAv and grdRe, we require that the *NewS'* availability and reliability values are greater or equal to the availability and reliability values offered by the *OldS* component service. The Cst and Rt criteria are negative criteria which means the lower the value is the better the QoS is. Therefore, in the guards grdCst and grdRt, we require that the *NewS'* cost and response time values are lower or equal to the cost and response time values offered by the faulty/unavailable component service.

After executing the *SubstituteCS* event the component service *OldS* is deleted from the set of component services constituting the composite service *c* and is replaced by *NewS* which is added to this set in the event action *act1*. The set of *NewS* is set to ready to invoke in *act2* in order to enable the execution of this component service.

**Semantic Level.** At this level, we refine the *SubstituteCS* (Fig. 4) event in order to check the semantic compatibility between the faulty/unavailable component service and the replacing component service. The event refinement has the same parameters as in the previous level. The NewS must have the same inputs as the OldS in order to execute and must produce the same outputs as OldS or more. As mentioned in our previous work [13], a component service cannot be executed without its required inputs. *NewS* must preserve the composition consistency in terms of vertical and horizontal matching. This traduced in Event-B in the guards *grd6* and *grd7*. In *grd6*, we require that for each input *i* of the operation *op1* of the component service *Olds*, there exists an *i'* input of *op2*, the operation of *NewS*, such that *i* and *i'* have the same type $(TypeOf(i) = TypeOf(i'))$. In *grd7*, we require that for each output *o* of the operation *op1* of the component service $Olds$, there exists an $o'$ output of $op2$, the operation of $NewS$, such that $o$ and $o'$ have the same type $(TypeOf(o) = TypeOf(o'))$.

---

Event SubstituteCS $\langle$ordinary$\rangle$ $\hat{=}$
extends SubstituteCS

**where**

> grd6: $(\forall i \cdot op1 \in OpOfS(OldS) \wedge OldS \in dom(OpOfS) \wedge op1 \in dom(I) \wedge i \in I(op1) \Rightarrow (\exists i' \cdot op2 \in$
> $OpOfS(NewS) \wedge FctOfOp(op1) = FctOfOp(op2) \wedge NewS \in dom(OpOfS) \wedge op2 \in dom(I) \wedge i' \in$
> $I(op2) \wedge TypeOf(i) = TypeOf(i')))$
>
> grd7: $(\forall o \cdot op1 \in OpOfS(OldS) \wedge OldS \in dom(OpOfS) \wedge op1 \in dom(O) \wedge o \in O(op1) \Rightarrow (\exists o' \cdot op2 \in$
> $OpOfS(NewS) \wedge FctOfOp(op1) = FctOfOp(op2) \wedge NewS \in dom(OpOfS) \wedge op2 \in dom(O) \wedge o' \in$
> $O(op2) \wedge TypeOf(o) = TypeOf(o')))$
>
> grd8: $(\forall pr \cdot op1 \in OpOfS(OldS) \wedge OldS \in dom(OpOfS) \wedge op1 \in dom(precsOp) \wedge pr \in$
> $precsOp(op1) \Rightarrow (\exists pr' \cdot op2 \in OpOfS(NewS) \wedge FctOfOp(op1) = FctOfOp(op2) \wedge NewS \in$
> $dom(OpOfS) \wedge op2 \in dom(precsOp) \wedge pr' \in precsOp(op2) \wedge pr = pr' \wedge finite(precsOp(op1)) \wedge$
> $finite(precsOp(op2)) \wedge card(precsOp(op1)) = card(precsOp(op2))))$
>
> grd9: $(\forall ef \cdot op1 \in OpOfS(OldS) \wedge OldS \in dom(OpOfS) \wedge op1 \in dom(effsOP) \wedge ef \in effsOP(op1) \Rightarrow$
> $(\exists ef' \cdot op2 \in OpOfS(NewS) \wedge FctOfOp(op1) = FctOfOp(op2) \wedge NewS \in dom(OpOfS) \wedge op2 \in$
> $dom(effsOP) \wedge ef' \in effsOP(op2) \wedge ef = ef' \wedge finite(effsOP(op1)) \wedge finite(effsOP(op2)) \wedge$
> $card(effsOP(op1)) = card(effsOP(op2))))$

---

**Fig. 4.** The first refinement of the $SubstituteCS$ event

Preconditions and Effects of services describe the execution conditions of service and the changes resulting from its execution. A service can be executed only if its preconditions are verified. Therefore $NewS$ must have the same preconditions as $OldS$. In $grd8$, we require that for each precondition $pr$ of the operation $op1$ of the component service $Olds$, there exists a $pr'$ precondition of $op2$, the operation of $NewS$, such that $pr$ and $pr'$ are equal predicates. $NewS$ must produce the same effects as $OldS$ in order to preserve the other component services preconditions. In $grd9$, we require that for each output $ef$ of the operation $op1$ of the component service $Olds$, there exists an $ef'$ output of $op2$, the operation of $NewS$, such that $ef$ and $ef'$ are equal predicates.

**Behaviour Level.** This abstraction level refines the $SubstituteCS$ event and check the behavioural compatibilities between the faulty/unavailable component service and the replacing component service. In other words, we have to check that the services interacting protocols are compatibles in order to preserve the composite service behaviour and avoid blocking situations. For instance, we assume that for each message that will be sent/received, there is a component service that will respectively receive/send that message. Such constraints enable us to avoid any blocking situation where for example a component service is waiting to receive a message however none of the other component services is willing to send it, dragging the composite service execution to failure. Therefore, the protocol of $OldS$ and the protocol of $NewS$ must have the same number, type and order of message. This is expressed in Event-B through the guards $grd10$ and $grd11$ (Fig. 5). In $grd10$, we require that the protocol of $OldS$ has the same required messages as the protocol of $NewS$. In $grd11$, we require that the protocol of $NewS$ is willing to send the same set of messages as the protocol of $OldS$.

---

Event SubstituteCS ⟨ordinary⟩ $\widehat{=}$
extends SubstituteCS

  **where**

    grd10: $\quad \forall m \cdot OldS \in dom(ProtOf) \wedge m \in RMsg(ProtOf(OldS)) \Rightarrow (\exists m' \cdot ProtOf(OldS) \in$

        $dom(RMsg) \wedge NewS \in dom(ProtOf) \wedge ProtOf(NewS) \in dom(RMsg) \wedge m' \in$

        $RMsg(ProtOf(NewS)) \wedge Id(m) = Id(m'))$

    grd11: $\quad \forall m \cdot OldS \in dom(ProtOf) \wedge m \in SMsg(ProtOf(OldS)) \Rightarrow (\exists m' \cdot ProtOf(OldS) \in$

        $dom(SMsg) \wedge NewS \in dom(ProtOf) \wedge ProtOf(NewS) \in dom(SMsg) \wedge m' \in$

        $SMsg(ProtOf(NewS)) \wedge Id(m) = Id(m'))$

---

**Fig. 5.** The second refinement of the $SubstituteCS$ event

**The Resource Level.** At this level, we define the Cloud resources and manage their allocation to the component services. The set of resources allocated to $OldS$ are released in the third refinement of the $SubstituteCS$ event (Fig. 6). After its selection, the $AllocateResource$ event will be triggered to allocate resources to the $NewS$ component service. The $AllocateResource$ event is already defined in [13].

---

Event SubstituteCS ⟨ordinary⟩ $\widehat{=}$
extends SubstituteCS

  **where**

  **then** grd12: $r \in dom(AllocTo) \wedge OldS \in AllocTo(r)$

  **end** act3: $AllocTo(r) := AllocTo(r) \setminus \{OldS\}$

---

**Fig. 6.** The third refinement of the $SubstituteCS$ event

### 5.3 Modelling the Resource Substitution

The intention, in this section, turns to the resource reconfiguration. Resources allocated to the component services can also break down or become unavailable. If this situation happens during a component service execution, it will affect the composite service execution and lead to failure. Therefore, we have added a new event to the resource level untitled $SubstituteR$ in order to substitute failed or unavailable resources. To substitute a resource, the replacing resource should have the same capacity or more, the same type, the same shareability properties or less restricted ones. This is expressed in Event-B in the guards of the *SubstituteR* event (Fig. 7). In $grd1$ and $grd2$, the state of the failed/unavailable resource ($OldR$) is equal to $Nav$ and the state of the replacing resource ($NewR$) is available ($av$). In $grd3$, we require $NewR$ to have the same type as $OldR$. In $grd4$, we require that the available capacity of $NewR$ is greater than or equal to the global capacity of $OldS$. In $grd6$, $grd7$ and $grd8$, we require that $NewR$ has the same properties as $OldR$, respectively, in terms of shareability, elasticity, and scalability. A non-functional selection is also performed at this level to select the best in term of QoS. We consider the same QoS criteria as for a component service: availability (AvR), reliability (ReR), cost (CstR) and response time (RtR). The AvR and ReR criteria are positive criteria which means that the higher the value is the better the QoS is. In the guards grd10 and grd11, we require that the $NewR$' availability and reliability values are greater or equal to the availability and reliability values offered by $OldR$. The CstR and RtR criteria are negative criteria which means the lower the value is the better the QoS is. Therefore, in the guards grdCst and grdRt, we require that the $NewR$' cost and response time values are lower or equal to the cost and response time values offered by the faulty/unavailable resource. After the event execution the actions $act1$ and $act2$ are performed. In $act1$, $NewR$ is allocated to the set of services $OldR$ was allocated to. In $act2$, The set of services running on $OldR$ are moved to $NewR$.

---

**Event SubstituteR** ⟨ordinary⟩ $\widehat{=}$

**any**

    OldR NewR

**where**

    grd1: $ResSt(OldR) = Nav$
    grd2: $ResSt(NewR) = av$
    grd3: $TypeOfr(OldR) = TypeOfr(NewR)$
    grd4: $NewR \in dom(ACa) \wedge ACa(NewR) \geq GCa(OldR)$
    grd5: $IsSh(OldR) = IsSh(NewR)$
    grd6: $IsEl(OldR) = IsEl(NewR)$
    grd7: $IsSca(OldR) = IsSca(NewR)$
    grd8: $OldR \in dom(RrunnigSer)$
    grd9: $OldR \in dom(AllocTo)$
    grd10: $AvR(NewR) \geq AvR(OldR)$
    grd11: $ReR(NewR) \geq ReR(OldR)$
    grd12: $CstR(NewR) \leq CstR(OldR)$
    grd13: $RtR(NewR) \leq RtR(OldR)$

**then**

    act1: $AllocTo(NewR) := AllocTo(OldR)$
    act2: $RrunnigSer(NewR) := RrunnigSer(OldR)$

**end**

---

**Fig. 7.** The resource substitution event *SubstituteR*

# 6   Verification and Validation

In this section, we describe the steps followed in order to verify and validate our model. The verification covers the static and dynamic properties of the model. The static properties are expressed through the invariants. The invariants of the model must hold for all states of the model; they must hold at the initial state and must be preserved by each event. Dynamic properties refer to the temporal properties of the system. Such properties could not be expressed through invariants. They express the different states of the system at different animation times. Indeed, the validation consists in observing the specification's behaviour. The Rodin platform[1] provides the plugin ProB [16] for the animation and validation of Event-B specifications. This plugin gives us the possibility to play different scenarios by showing, at each stage, the values of each variable and distinguishing the enabled events from the disabled ones.

## 6.1   Proof-Based Verification

The term proof obligation is mentioned in this section regularly. It is in fact, a theorem that needs to be proved in order to verify the correctness of the model [18]. The proof obligations (POs)[2] are automatically generated by the Proof Obligation Generator tool of the Rodin Platform. The generated proof obligations were of types well-definedness (WD) and Invariant preservation (INV) (for the invariants of the model). The INV POs ensure that each event preserves the invariants. The name of an INV PO is of the form evt/inv/INV where for each event, we have to establish that:

$$\forall S, C, X.(A \wedge G \wedge Inv \Rightarrow [Act]Inv)$$

where the event actions Act must preserve the invariant $Inv$. In other words, INV POs guarantee that:

- The initialization of a machine leads to a state where the invariants are valid.
- Assuming that the machine is in a state where the invariants are preserved, every enabled event leads to a state where the invariants are still preserved.

The well-definedness proof obligation rule (WD) ensures that a potentially ill-defined axiom, theorem, invariant, guard, action, variant, or witness is indeed well-defined [3].

To summarize, 195 proof obligations have been generated: 105 of them are automatically discharged by the automatic prover. It fails to discharge the remaining proofs due to the numerous steps they require and not on account of their difficulty. To finish discharging these proofs, we resorted to the interactive prover and helped it find the right steps and rules to apply. The proof statistics are given in Fig. 8.

---

[1] http://www.event-b.org/.

[2] For more details on proof obligations rules please refer to the B-Book [3] on page 190.

| Element Name | Total | Auto | Man. | Rev. | Und. |
|---|---|---|---|---|---|
| **NewProject** | **195** | **105** | **82** | **0** | **8** |
| BehM1 | 65 | 31 | 26 | 0 | 8 |
| ResM1 | 76 | 40 | 36 | 0 | 0 |
| SemM1 | 21 | 8 | 13 | 0 | 0 |
| StructM1 | 33 | 26 | 7 | 0 | 0 |

**Fig. 8.** Proof statistics

## 6.2   Validation by Animation

For model validation, we use the ProB animation [16]. ProB is an animator, constraint solver and model checker for the B-Method. It allows fully automatic animation of B specifications and can be used to systematically check a specification for a wide range of errors. The constraint-solving capabilities of ProB can also be used for model finding, deadlock checking and test-case generation [15]. We use animation to execute specifications. Thanks to ProB we have played and observed different scenarios in order to check the behaviour of our model. The animation is performed on a concrete Event-B model. For this purpose, we have given values to the carrier sets, constants, and variables of the model. To do so, we have considered the motivating example introduced in Sect. 3. The animation consists of the following steps (Fig. 9):

**Step1.** we start by firing the SETUP-CONTEXT event that gives values to the constants and carrier sets in the context,

**Step2.** we then fire the INITIALISATION event to set the model into its initial state,

**Step3.** we, finally, proceed to the steps of the scenario to check. At each step, the animator computes all guards of all events, and enables the ones with true guards, and shows parameters which make these guards true. After event firing, substitutions are computed and the animator checks if the invariants still hold.

In [13], we have animated the complete behaviour of the composite service as follows:

1. First the *SelectService* event is fired to select the set of required component services.
2. Then, the required resources are allocated to each component service using the *ResourceAllocation* event.
3. The *RunComposite* event is then enabled to run the composite service and the request inputs are sent to the first component service by means of the non-blocking send pattern using the *Non_Blocking_Send* event.
4. The *RunComponent* event is then enabled,
5. The resource capacity is decreased (*DecResCap* event) and the received messages are consumed (*Consume* event).

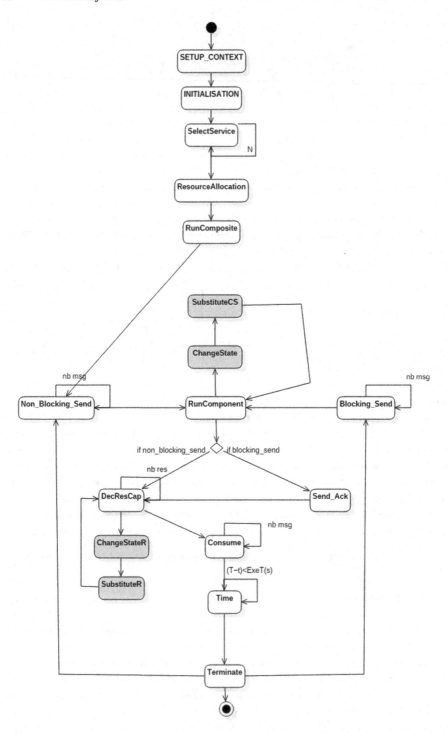

**Fig. 9.** Animation scenario

6. The execution of the component service is terminated ($Terminate$ event) after the completion of its execution time ($Time$ event: (T-t)=ExeT(s)) and the allocated resources are released and the outputs of the component service are sent either using the non-blocking send pattern ($Non\_Blocking\_Send$ event) or the blocking send pattern ($Blocking\_Send$ event), to the next component service.

In this work, we intervene in steps 4 and 5. To mimic the real composite service execution, we declare the existence of a failed or unavailable component service by changing its state in the $ChangeState$ event, which enables the $SubstitueCS$ event. The latter performs the component service substitution according to previously introduced constraints and the animation resumes from step4. The $ChangeStateR$ event changes the state of a resource to failed or unavailable. It can be triggered once the $DecResCap$ event (step5) is enabled. Once triggered, the $SubstitueR$ event is enabled to substitute the failed/unavailable resource. The animation resumes then from step5.

## 7 Conclusion and Future Works

In this work, we have addressed the Cloud composite service dynamic reconfiguration problem. We have presented several constraints that must be considered while replacing a faulty/unavailable component service/resource by a new one. The verification is done on four abstraction levels; the structural, semantic, behavioural, and resource allocation levels. A proof-based approach, coupled with a model animation, is performed in order to verify and validate the proposed model. Thanks to the proposed approach, we succeeded to rigorously perform the reconfiguration of the Cloud composite service.

In the near future, we aim to extend the present work by considering other kinds of dynamic such as adaptive dynamic or evolutionary dynamic. We are also planning to develop an Eclipse plugin to automate the present approach in order to be readily used in practice.

## References

1. Abid, R., Salaün, G., De Palma, N.: Formal design of dynamic reconfiguration protocol for cloud applications. Sci. Comput. Program. **117**, 1–16 (2016). https://doi.org/10.1016/j.scico.2015.12.001. http://www.sciencedirect.com/science/article/pii/S0167642315004128
2. Abrial, J.R.: The B tool (abstract). In: Bloomfield, R.E., Marshall, L.S., Jones, R.B. (eds.) VDM 1988. LNCS, vol. 328, pp. 86–87. Springer, Heidelberg (1988). https://doi.org/10.1007/3-540-50214-9_8
3. Abrial, J.: The B-Book - Assigning Programs to Meanings. Cambridge University Press, Cambridge (2005)
4. Abrial, J.-R., Butler, M., Hallerstede, S., Voisin, L.: An open extensible tool environment for Event-B. In: Liu, Z., He, J. (eds.) ICFEM 2006. LNCS, vol. 4260, pp. 588–605. Springer, Heidelberg (2006). https://doi.org/10.1007/11901433_32

5. Abrial, J.-R., Mussat, L.: Introducing dynamic constraints in B. In: Bert, D. (ed.) B 1998. LNCS, vol. 1393, pp. 83–128. Springer, Heidelberg (1998). https://doi.org/10.1007/BFb0053357

6. Cansell, D., Méry, D.: The Event-B modelling method: concepts and case studies. In: Bjørner, D., Henson, M.C. (eds.) Logics of Specification Languages. MTC-SAES, pp. 47–152. Springer, Heidelberg (2008). https://doi.org/10.1007/978-3-540-74107-7_3

7. Furht, B., Escalante, A.: Handbook of Cloud Computing, 1st edn. Springer, Heidelberg (2010). https://doi.org/10.1007/978-1-4419-6524-0

8. Gao, H., Duan, Y., Miao, H., Yin, Y.: An approach to data consistency checking for the dynamic replacement of service process. IEEE Access **5**, 11700–11711 (2017)

9. Gao, H., Huang, W., Yang, X., Duan, Y., Yin, Y.: Toward service selection for workflow reconfiguration: an interface-based computing solution. Future Gener. Comput. Syst. **87**, 298–311 (2018). https://doi.org/10.1016/j.future.2018.04.064. http://www.sciencedirect.com/science/article/pii/S0167739X17320575

10. Graiet, M., Lahouij, A., Abbassi, I., Hamel, L., Kmimech, M.: Formal behavioral modeling for verifying SCA composition with Event-B. In: 2015 IEEE International Conference on Web Services, ICWS 2015, New York, NY, USA, June 27–July 2, 2015, pp. 17–24 (2015)

11. Lahouij, A., Hamel, L., Graiet, M.: Formal modeling for verifying SCA dynamic composition with Event-B. In: 2015 IEEE 24th International Conference on Enabling Technologies: Infrastructure for Collaborative Enterprises, pp. 29–34 (2015)

12. Lahouij, A., Hamel, L., Graiet, M.: Deadlock-freeness verification of cloud composite services using Event-B. In: On the Move to Meaningful Internet Systems. OTM 2018 Conferences - Confederated International Conferences: CoopIS, C&TC, and ODBASE 2018, Valletta, Malta, October 22–26, 2018, Proceedings, Part I, pp. 604–622 (2018). https://doi.org/10.1007/978-3-030-02610-3_34

13. Lahouij, A., Hamel, L., Graiet, M., el Ayeb, B.: An Event-B based approach for cloud composite services verification. Form. Asp. Comput. 1–33 (2020). https://doi.org/10.1007/s00165-020-00517-0

14. Lahouij, A., Hamel, L., Graiet, M., Malki, M.E.: A formal approach for cloud composite services verification. In: 11th IEEE Conference on Service-Oriented Computing and Applications, SOCA 2018, Paris, France, November 20–22, 2018, pp. 161–168 (2018). https://doi.org/10.1109/SOCA.2018.00031

15. Laili, Y., Tao, F., Zhang, L., Cheng, Y., Luo, Y., Sarker, B.R.: A ranking chaos algorithm for dual scheduling of cloud service and computing resource in private cloud. Comput. Ind. **64**(4), 448–463 (2013). https://doi.org/10.1016/j.compind.2013.02.008. http://www.sciencedirect.com/science/article/pii/S0166361513000365

16. Leuschel, M., Butler, M.: ProB: a model checker for B. In: Araki, K., Gnesi, S., Mandrioli, D. (eds.) FME 2003. LNCS, vol. 2805, pp. 855–874. Springer, Heidelberg (2003). https://doi.org/10.1007/978-3-540-45236-2_46

17. Meng, S., Fu, G.: A formal design model for cloud services, pp. 173–178 (July 2017). https://doi.org/10.18293/SEKE2017-055

18. Padidar, S.: A study in the use of Event-B for system development from a software engineering viewpoint (2011). http://www.ai4fm.org/papers/MSc-Padidar.pdf

# Reuse in Practice

# 15 Years of Reuse Experience in Evolutionary Prototyping for the Defense Industry

Pierre Laborde[1]([⊠]), Steven Costiou[2], Éric Le Pors[1], and Alain Plantec[3]

[1] THALES Defense Mission Systems France - Établissement de Brest,
10 Avenue de la 1ère DFL, 29200 Brest, France
{pierre.laborde,eric.lepors}@fr.thalesgroup.com
[2] Univ. Lille, Inria, CNRS, Centrale Lille, UMR 9189 - CRIStAL, Lille, France
steven.costiou@inria.fr
[3] Univ. Brest, Lab-STICC, CNRS, UMR 6285, 29200 Brest, France
alain.plantec@univ-brest.fr

**Abstract.** At Thales Defense Mission Systems, software products first go through an industrial prototyping phase. We elaborate evolutionary prototypes which implement complete business behavior and fulfill functional requirements. We elaborate and evolve our solutions directly with end-users who act as stake-holders in the products' design. Prototypes also serve as models for the final products development. Because software products in the defense industry are developed over many years, this prototyping phase is crucial. Therefore, reusing software is a high-stakes issue in our activities. Component-oriented development helps us to foster reuse throughout the life cycle of our products. The work presented in this paper stems from 15 years of experience in developing prototypes for the defense industry. We directly reuse component implementations to build new prototypes from existing ones. We reuse component interfaces transparently in multiple prototypes, whatever the underlying implementation solutions. This kind of reuse spans prototypes and final products which are deployed on different execution platforms. We reuse non-component legacy software that we integrate in our component architectures. In this case, we seamlessly augment standard classes with component behavior, while preserving legacy code. In this paper, we present our component programming framework with a focus on component reuse in the context of evolutionary prototyping. We report three scenarios of reuse that we encounter regularly in our prototyping activity.

**Keywords:** Evolutionary prototyping · Component reuse · Traits · Pharo

## 1 Introduction

In the defense industry, software systems are designed, developed and evolved over many years. It is therefore important to evaluate and to adjust systems' design ahead of time before starting long and costly development phases.

© Springer Nature Switzerland AG 2020
S. Ben Sassi et al. (Eds.): ICSR 2020, LNCS 12541, pp. 87–99, 2020.
https://doi.org/10.1007/978-3-030-64694-3_6

At Thales Defense Mission Systems (DMS), the Human-Machine Interface (HMI) industrial prototyping activities are an important part of the software production process. HMI industrial prototyping is the building of software prototypes as close as possible to real products from the HMI point of view (graphics and ergonomics). Using prototypes, we evaluate software HMI design and experiment complete use-cases with end-users. This enables early and strong feedback loops between developers and end-users. Using prototypes, we anticipate architectural needs and problems before development of real products begin. The prototyping activity is followed by an industrialization phase, in which we build final products based on prototypes' evaluations and feedback.

Because we build and rebuild prototypes, we need means to reuse code from existing pieces of software. We need to evolve parts of prototypes without changing how these parts interact with the rest of the software. To foster such modular architectures, Thales use component-oriented programming [11,17]. Component-based architectures bring the necessary modularity to enable reuse and evolution of prototypes.

In this paper, we present our requirements for reusable software in our industrial context. We describe how component-oriented programming helps us fulfill these requirements (Sect. 2). We present how we implement components for modular and reusable software architectures with the *Molecule* component-oriented programming framework (Sect. 3). This framework is today the main tool that we use for evolutionary prototyping, for which we report and discuss 15 years of reuse experience and the difficulties we face today (Sect. 4).

## 2   Reuse in Prototyping for the Defense Industry

Exploring design ideas through Concept prototyping [4,12] is one of the main activities at Thales DMS. Prototypes are developed to help communicate concepts to users, demonstrate the HMI usability and exhibit potential problems. Moreover, prototypes are developed and maintained until they meet users expectations regarding not only the HMI, but also the main business functionalities. Some of our prototypes implement complete business behavior and fulfill functional requirements. Thus, they are also kind of evolutionary prototypes [12]. Thales DMS engineers maintain a lot of them since 15 years.

Maintaining evolutionary prototypes is a very expensive activity and Thales struggled with evolution issues. Building a final product is also an expensive and a tedious task, and engineers must take advantage of the prototyping activity. Furthermore, the prototyping and the final product teams have to fully understand each others' designs. This poses a knowledge sharing issue.

We use component-oriented programming to build and to maintain evolutionary prototypes, and to share knowledge between prototyping and industrialization activities. In this context, this section introduces briefly the component model we use in prototyping, and the overall benefits of component-oriented programming that we observed in our development process.

## 2.1    The Molecule Component Model

Our component model is close to the light-weight CCM [1]. We use Molecule, a Thales open-source implementation[1] of the light-weight CCM.

A Molecule component implements a contract defined by its Type (Fig. 1). A contract consists in a set of services that the component provides, a set of services that the component uses, a set of events that the component may emit, and a set of events that the component is able to consume. The Type implements the services that the component provides and that are callable by other components, and defines the events that the component produces. Other components use its *Provided Services* interface through their *Used Services* interface. Other components listen to the component's *Produced Events* interface through their *Consumed Events* interface. Components subscribe and unsubscribe to event interfaces to start and stop receiving events. Parameters are specific and are not present in the CCM. We use parameters to control components' state, and only once when initializing components.

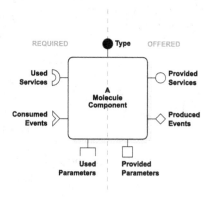

**Fig. 1.** Public view of a Molecule component.

## 2.2    Components as Reusable Modules

At the beginning of a project, we benefit from direct reuse of previous prototypes' components. Through composition of existing components, we reduce the time and efforts to get to the first versions of a new prototype.

Being able to build reusable and homogeneous software architectures was the first motivation for using components. This is particularly true for Graphical User Interfaces (GUI) components that we call Panels. It is well known that GUIs are expensive to implement. Our panels expose a stable public interface and implement a standard contract. We therefore directly reuse our panels in several prototypes (Fig. 2). The reused parts include not only the contract but also its

---

[1] https://github.com/OpenSmock/molecule.

implementation provided by the Type. This kind of reuse is now possible because we capitalized a sufficient quantity of components. After a decade, we benefit from a virtuous cycle where a finished prototype is kept in a prototype repository and some of its component set can be reused later for another prototype. This virtuous cycle tends to minimise the number of prototypes that we need to implement from scratch.

In Fig. 2, we show our prototyping reuse chain. From previous legacy code, we build standardized and reusable components, defined by their contracts. When a component assembly covers a technical or a business requirement, it becomes a sub-system (*e.g.*, a geographic view with layering, filtering, selection...). Prototypes (re)use and deploy instances of sub-systems and/or of single components. Each time we build a new prototype, we identify new functionalities or reusable bricks and we integrate them back into the repository of existing components or sub-systems for future reuse.

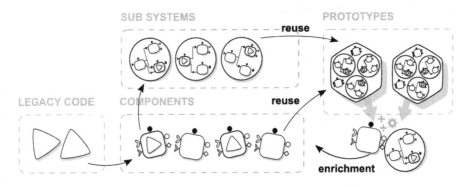

**Fig. 2.** From components to prototypes: a reuse chain.

## 2.3  Components to Ease Evolution

Change and evolution of software is always an issue. Switching to another technology implies modifying the existing software code to integrate that technology. This kind of change hinders our ability to reuse software to evolve our prototypes. For example, GUI technologies are often changed, because they evolve, they become obsolete or they stop being maintained. A new GUI framework will expose different interfaces and trigger different events. This forces developers to rewrite the same GUI in different technologies over the years [8,19].

Without components, this kind of change forces us to change how GUIs interact with legacy or business software. It implies adaptation of such software, which will impact all using projects, or force us to maintain different versions of the adapted code. This is not desirable as, *e.g.*, we have legacy sub-systems in use since a decade by multiple maintained prototypes. Because our prototypes are composed of components, in case of such a change, only a well identified part of the system has to be adapted (Fig. 3). We evolve the related components implementation without changing GUI clients nor legacy and business software.

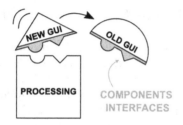

**Fig. 3.** Components to ease evolution, for example: changing GUIs.

## 2.4 Engineering Impact: Design Traceability and Co-working

Thales DMS' design process involves different and specific teams that work together throughout the life cycle of a product. The system engineering team builds systems' design models using dedicated methods like Arcadia [20] and modeling tools like Capella [5]. System engineers model interactions between hardware entities, software entities, users, etc. These models are produced early in the design of a product. The prototyping team develops and evaluate prototypes based on these models. The software engineering team develops final products.

The prototyping team is composed of 5 to 10 engineers. For each product, there are 10 times more system and software engineers working with the prototyping team. The descriptive properties of components models (interfaces, interaction models...) ease communication between different teams working with different technologies (Fig. 4). For example, when building a GUI panel, the system team uses components to specify interactions between end-users and the panel. From these specifications, the prototyping team builds a first version of the panel to evaluate these interactions with end-users. Finally, the software engineering team builds a stable and robust version of the panel, connected to the real product's environment.

Using a common vocabulary also favors reuse, as components can be inserted and (re)used in an architecture solely based on their contract, without having to master implementation details.

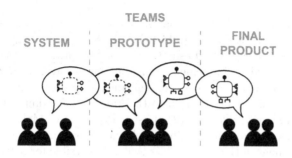

**Fig. 4.** Engineering impact: design traceability and co-working;

## 3    Component-Oriented Programming with Molecule

Since 2005, Thales DMS use Smalltalk for prototyping. The main motivations behind the choice of Smalltalk is the ability to quickly design and program complex prototypes, and the capabilities to lively change a design in the front of customers [9, 15]. Thales adopted component-based development to ease software reuse and separation of concerns. Since 2016, we use Pharo [7] with the Molecule component-oriented programming framework. Thales developed Molecule to capitalize on its experience in component-based development. This section briefly describes how we program components with Molecule.

The Molecule framework relies on Traits [6, 16, 18] to implement component Types. A Trait is an independent set of methods with their implementation and requirements (methods and variables). Classes using a Trait automatically benefit from these methods, and must define that Trait's requirements. A Trait can be composed of multiple other traits. In this case, a class using this composed Trait benefits from all the methods provided by the Traits composition. A Trait provides orthogonal behavior to all classes using that Trait, regardless of their class inheritance hierarchies.

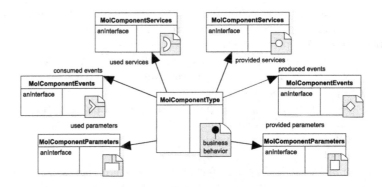

**Fig. 5.** Component contract implementation in Molecule.

In Molecule, we define the elements of a component's contract (services, events, parameters) as a set of Traits (Fig. 5). A component Type aggregates theses traits, and is itself defined as a Trait. Molecule provides a dedicated Trait MolComponentImpl, which implements cross-cutting behavior shared by all components (*e.g.*, components' life-cycle management). Implementing a component consists in defining a class that (1) uses the MolComponentImpl Trait to obtain component shared behavior and (2) uses a Type Trait (MolComponentType) implementing the component's business behavior (Fig. 6).

The direct benefit of this approach is that it is possible for any existing class to become a component. This existing class is then turned as (or augmented as) a component, and becomes usable in a Molecule component application while remaining fully compatible with non-component applications (Fig. 7).

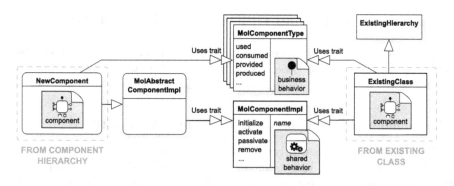

**Fig. 6.** Two ways to implement a component: by inheriting from the Molecule base component implementation (left side), and by extending a class using Molecule component Traits (right side). In both cases, components and extended classes use a component Trait type defining the component's business behavior.

Molecule provides syntactic sugar to directly implement components by inheriting from the MolAbstractComponentImpl class (Fig. 6). In that case, we only need to satisfy (2) by using a Type Trait for our component.

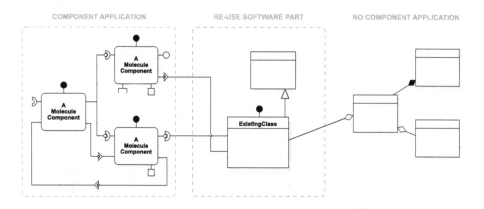

**Fig. 7.** We use augmented classes in component and non-component applications.

The evolution of components is driven by Traits. For example, to provide new services, an augmented class will use additional Traits defining these services. The integration of the Traits implementing the component contract with the original class may require some code adaptation. Typically, when we reuse classes from legacy software as components (*e.g.*, a radar class), we have to adapt how the component's Type (*i.e.*, it's business behavior) interacts with the class API (*e.g.*, by converting the radar's accuracy from feet to meters). This code adaptation ensures that the augmented class provides the correct level of information in regards with the requirements of the connected components.

## 4   Reuse Scenarios and Difficulties at Thales DMS

In this section, we describe three reuse scenarios that we regularly and success-fully deal with during our prototyping activity. While we learnt how to cope with these reuse scenarios, we still encounter many difficulties that we discuss.

### 4.1   Common Reuse Scenarios in the Prototyping Activity

While prototyping, we frequently deal with three reuse scenarios: long-term reuse of legacy code, reuse of non-component frameworks and reuse of component business interfaces. The story of *Prototype X* [2] is a successful illustration of the application of these scenarios. This prototype is an HMI for touch tables with completely new ergonomics and multi-user functionalities, that we built in 2019. We did not have any functional code implementing touch table ergonomics with multiple users at the same time. However, most of the business and tooling behavior already existed in previous prototypes. Overall, the complete proto-type is composed of 674 components and 1704 additional classes, for a total of 47447 methods. We only wrote 22 new components and 35 classes. We reused 603 components and 991 classes from 5 existing sub-systems (Table 1). Reused components represent 89.47% of the prototype's components and reused classes represent 58.16% of the prototype's classes [3]. This use-case is representative of fast-written prototypes we build, with multiple iterations over two years.

**Table 1.** Component and class reuse in a prototype from 2019: 603 reused components (89.47% of the prototype's components) and 991 reused classes (58.16% of the non-component prototype's classes).

| Sub-system (the * means reuse) | Components | % | Classes | % |
|---|---|---|---|---|
| Prototype X (new code) | 22 | 3.26 | 35 | 2.05 |
| Survey mission system* | 37 | 5.49 | 71 | 4.17 |
| Mission technical system* | 332 | 49.26 | 236 | 13.85 |
| Command-control architecture* | 26 | 3.86 | 34 | 2.00 |
| Scenarios and simulation* | 53 | 7.86 | 127 | 7.45 |
| Tactical views and models* | 155 | 23.00 | 523 | 30.69 |
| Prototyping tools & models (framework) | 49 | 7.27 | 678 | 39.79 |
| Total | 674 | 100 | 1704 | 100 |

---

[2] For confidentiality reasons, we cannot give the real name of this prototype.
[3] We do not count the prototyping framework's code as reuse.

**Long-Term Reuse of Legacy Code.** This scenario is the most common case of reuse in our prototyping activity. For each new prototype, we systematically need to reuse functionalities from previous prototypes or from legacy code. Before we based all our architectures on reusable components (2005–2013), we used to reuse code by manually performing copy/paste of hundred of classes from prototype to prototype. Since then, component-based architectures help us to reuse legacy code from previous prototypes in new prototypes.

For example, 10 years ago, we took an old prototype using an old GUI technology. As this prototype was component-based, we were able to redesign the HMI with another technology without modifying the component architecture. The complete business layer of this old prototype continued to work transparently with the new HMI design (as in Fig. 3). Components forming this business layer became particular sub-systems reused in many other prototypes. Today, 10 years later, we continue to reuse and enrich these sub-systems in our new prototypes. Typically, these sub-systems simulate complex hardware and software systems such as radars, sensors, detection and communication equipment, etc.

Another example of frequently reused sub-system is the tactical view[4]. This view is a recurrent requirement throughout our different prototypes. We reuse the same tactical view sub-system from prototype to prototype since 10 years.

**Reuse of Non-component Frameworks in Component Architectures.** In this scenario, we need to reuse non-component code in our component-based architectures. Typically, we rely on open-source frameworks in our prototypes: UI models, graphics engines, visualization engines, etc. These frameworks are object-oriented, so we augment their classes with Molecule to reuse them directly in our component-based prototypes.

We start by inheriting from the framework classes we want to reuse. We then apply the Molecule component Traits to the inherited classes to augment them with component behavior. As illustrated by Fig. 7, these classes become usable transparently by both standard applications and our component systems.

For example, we regularly need to reuse graphical, non-component elements from open-source graphics engine. This happens when we want to extend a component sub-system to support another graphics engine. Therefore, we augment classes of graphical elements (views) as components to directly connect them to our component sub-systems. This allows us to add new graphics technologies as display backends with very few adaptations.

**Reuse of Component Business Interfaces.** In this scenario, we reuse components' business contract to replace component implementations transparently (as in Fig. 5). Interactions between components are expressed through component contracts, which are reusable for different components implementations. Components exposing the same contract are seamlessly interchangeable.

---

[4] Geographical business objects display on a map.

For example, we had a prototype for which we needed to migrate the database system to a new database backend. The database access (*i.e.*, database requests) was implemented in a dedicated component. High-level data access (*i.e.*, data requests) was defined in that component Type (*i.e.*, its Type Traits). Other components communicated with the database through the contract defined by the Type, *i.e.*, to request data without knowing about the database access details.

To change the database, we implemented a new component for a new backend and we reused the Type Traits for high-level data access. We were then able to transparently switch the old component by the new one in the prototype.

## 4.2   Discussion

The example of Table 1 is a nice success story of software reuse. We built a new prototype from existing sub-systems, while developing additional code only for new aspects of this prototype. Software reuse brings direct benefits to our prototyping activity, but there are difficulties that we do not overcome yet.

**Benefits of Reuse for Evolutionary Prototyping.** We apply systematic reuse [13] of software to reduce the time and cost of building, maintaining and evolving prototypes. The ability to reuse (parts of) previous prototypes, legacy software and non-component code within component architectures enables fast building of new prototypes. We can build a base prototype for a new project in a few days. From there, we experiment ideas, enrich that base, then evolve and maintain the resulting prototype over years. Some sub-systems (*e.g.,* the tactical view, or a radar simulator) will not change over many years while being systematically reused in many prototypes. These sub-systems became more stable with time, and today we trust that we can reuse them while maintaining software quality. Typically, we encounter less bugs in older and frequently reused components than in more recent components.

Similar benefits of software reuse in industrial contexts are reported in the literature [2,14]. The most reported benefits are increased quality [2], increased productivity [2,14], reduced development cost and time and a lower defect rate [2]. While reflecting on 15 years of reuse, we observe these same benefits throughout our different prototypes. Another commonly reported benefit of reuse is a shorter time to market [2]. In our case, prototypes are not destined to end up in the market. Rather than a shorter time to market per se, we speak of a shorter time to prototype evolution. The purpose of our prototypes is to live and evolve from end-users feedback and evaluation. Fast prototype evolution is therefore a valuable benefit. Over the years, this benefit has been plebicited by our customers and this encouraged us to push it further this way.

**Smalltalk to Explore Reuse Opportunities.** While building and evolving prototypes, we rely on Smalltalk's live and exploratory nature [9,15] to find and to understand components to reuse.

To select which component to reuse, we lively explore and experiment components from our repository. For a given requirement, we study components' interfaces, we start and connect them, observe how they behave, and dynamically explore how they can be reused. We choose which component to reuse from these experiments, and with time we know from this empirical experience which components fit specific (re)use-cases.

This strategy of components selection seems common in practice [10]. Using Smalltalk provides a live and dynamic perspective, that improves this strategy's output. However after many years, relying on this sole strategy became less effective. We have today too much components and sub-systems: we cannot explore everything lively, and the amount of necessary knowledge to choose the right components is oversized. To overcome this difficulty, we need to study means to filter meaningful components ahead of time, before live experiments.

**Pitfalls of Reusing Everything.** We observe that we tend to reuse everything. The example from Table 1 is a typical illustration of massive reuse, although successful. However, we still lack rigorous means of evaluation to determine if we should reuse a component [10], if we should implement a new component, and in this latter case if we should make this component reusable. Making components reusable has a cost but in practice some of them are never reused. In this case, the cost of systematic reuse exceeds the cost of ad-hoc development.

While applying massive reuse, we do not allow enough time for documenting our prototypes, their components and their sub-systems. We therefore lack the knowledge to choose which component or sub-system to reuse, nor how to reuse them. Typically, building the prototype from Table 1 requires an extensive knowledge of existing sub-systems, how to integrate them into the new prototype architecture and what is missing to realize the new prototype. Consequently, it is difficult to select components and sub-systems for reuse.

In addition, this expertise is shared among developers but mostly depend on a few experts. This is a problem for transmitting knowledge to new people, and a serious concern in the long term. If the few reuse experts leave, knowledge will be lost and reuse possibilities will be jeopardized as well as all its benefits. Knowledge and retrieval of reusable components in the context of a project, while in our case not directly inhibiting reuse [3, 13], are clearly a weakness and a slowdown in our development process.

Finally, some of our sub-systems implementations are too focused on the realization of business behavior, and mix business and technical concerns. To reuse technical parts of such sub-system, we have to reuse the complete sub-system. In this case, we lack perspective while implementing and architecturing components into sub-systems to avoid this pitfall.

## 5 Conclusion

At Thales DMS, we elaborate evolutionary prototypes that we refine until they meet end-users functional and ergonomics requirements. We then evolve and maintain these prototypes for years. Prototypes serve as realistic demonstrators used as the main input when building and evolving final products. This process is expensive, and we heavily reuse software to minimize development costs and to maximize the quality of our prototypes.

To support the reuse of software, we use component-based development. Since 15 years, we develop reusable components using Smalltalk, and we reuse these components in our prototypes. Today, Thales capitalized this experience in Molecule, a component framework built in Pharo Smalltalk, with which we build our new prototypes. We organize our components and sub-systems in a repository. We reuse elements from this repository to build new prototypes, and each time we enrich the repository back with new reusable elements. Building a realistic demonstrator based on these reusable elements is industrially efficient. Our prototyping team builds prototypes with reduced development costs and time, while focusing on functional concepts and ergonomics. Long-time reused elements expose less bugs and are trusted while reused in new prototypes.

We presented our reuse scenarios: long-term reuse of legacy code, reuse of non-component frameworks and reuse of component business interfaces. After 15 years, we can highlight a beneficial rate of component reuse. We also reported our reuse difficulties. We struggle with our too large amount of reusable elements, and the necessary knowledge required to exploit them efficiently. It is more and more difficult to identify reusable elements to build prototypes.

To improve how we select reusable elements, we plan to study how to exploit preliminary systems models to allow for the early identification of reusable elements. We also plan to conduct larger scale empirical studies at Thales to better understand how we applied reuse over the years. This will help us to take a step back and to reflect more on our reuse processes in order to improve our prototyping activity and to standardize our reuse practice in all Thales.

## References

1. Corba Component Model Specification. https://www.omg.org/spec/CCM/4.0/PDF. Accessed 7 July 2020
2. Barros-Justo, J.L., Pinciroli, F., Matalonga, S., Martínez-Araujo, N.: What software reuse benefits have been transferred to the industry? A systematic mapping study. Inf. Softw. Technol. **103**, 1–21 (2018)
3. Bauer, V.M.: Analysing and supporting software reuse in practice. Ph.D. thesis, Technische Universität München (2016)
4. Bernstein, L.: Foreword: importance of software prototyping. J. Syst. Integr. **6**(1–2), 9–14 (1996)
5. Bonnet, S., Voirin, J.L., Exertier, D., Normand, V.: Not (strictly) relying on SYSML for MBSE: language, tooling and development perspectives: the Arcadia/Capella rationale. In: 2016 Annual IEEE Systems Conference (SysCon). IEEE (2016)
6. Ducasse, S., Nierstrasz, O., Schärli, N., Wuyts, R., Black, A.P.: Traits: a mechanism for fine-grained reuse. ACM Trans. Program. Lang. Syst. (TOPLAS) **28**(2), 331–388 (2006)

7. Ducasse, S., et al.: Pharo by Example 5. Square Bracket Associates (2017). http://books.pharo.org
8. Dutriez, C., Verhaeghe, B., Derras, M.: Switching of GUI framework: the case from spec to spec 2. In: Proceedings of the 14th Edition of the International Workshop on Smalltalk Technologies, Cologne, Germany (2019)
9. Ingalls, D., Kaehler, T., Maloney, J., Wallace, S., Kay, A.: Back to the future: the story of squeak, a practical smalltalk written in itself. In: Proceedings of the 12th ACM SIGPLAN Conference on Object-Oriented Programming, Systems, Languages, and Applications, OOPSLA 1997, pp. 318–326. Association for Computing Machinery, New York (1997)
10. Land, R., Sundmark, D., Lüders, F., Krasteva, I., Causevic, A.: Reuse with software components - a survey of industrial state of practice. In: Edwards, S.H., Kulczycki, G. (eds.) ICSR 2009. LNCS, vol. 5791, pp. 150–159. Springer, Heidelberg (2009). https://doi.org/10.1007/978-3-642-04211-9_15
11. Lau, K.K., Wang, Z.: Software component models. IEEE Trans. Softw. Eng. **33**(10), 709–724 (2007)
12. Lidwell, W., Holden, K., Butler, J.: Universal Principles of Design. Rockport Publishers, Beverly (2010)
13. Lynex, A., Layzell, P.J.: Organisational considerations for software reuse. Ann. Softw. Eng. **5**(1), 105–124 (1998)
14. Mohagheghi, P., Conradi, R.: Quality, productivity and economic benefits of software reuse: a review of industrial studies. Empir. Softw. Eng. **12**(5), 471–516 (2007)
15. Rein, P., Taeumel, M., Hirschfeld, R.: Towards exploratory software design environments for the multi-disciplinary team. In: Meinel, C., Leifer, L. (eds.) Design Thinking Research. UI, pp. 229–247. Springer, Cham (2019). https://doi.org/10.1007/978-3-319-97082-0_12
16. Schärli, N., Ducasse, S., Nierstrasz, O., Black, A.P.: Traits: composable units of behaviour. In: Cardelli, L. (ed.) ECOOP 2003. LNCS, vol. 2743, pp. 248–274. Springer, Heidelberg (2003). https://doi.org/10.1007/978-3-540-45070-2_12
17. Szyperski, C., Bosch, J., Weck, W.: Component-oriented programming. In: Moreira, A. (ed.) ECOOP 1999. LNCS, vol. 1743, pp. 184–192. Springer, Heidelberg (1999). https://doi.org/10.1007/3-540-46589-8_10
18. Tesone, P., Ducasse, S., Polito, G., Fabresse, L., Bouraqadi, N.: A new modular implementation for stateful traits. Sci. Comput. Program. **195**, 102470 (2020)
19. Verhaeghe, B., et al.: GUI migration using MDE from GWT to angular 6: an industrial case. In: 2019 IEEE 26th International Conference on Software Analysis, Evolution and Reengineering (SANER), Hangzhou, China (2019). https://hal.inria.fr/hal-02019015
20. Voirin, J.L.: Model-based System and Architecture Engineering with the Arcadia Method. Elsevier, Amsterdam (2017)

# CxDev: A Case Study in Domain Engineering for Customer eXperience Management

Imen Benzarti[1,2](✉) ⓘ, Hafedh Mili[1,2] ⓘ, and Abderrahmane Leshob[1,3] ⓘ

[1] LATECE Lab, Université du Québec à Montréal, Montréal H3C 3P8, Canada
{benzarti.imen,mili.hafedh,leshob.abderrahmane}@uqam.ca
[2] Département d'Informatique, Université du Québec à Montréal,
Montréal H3C 3P8, Canada
[3] ESG-UQAM, Université du Québec à Montréal, Montréal H3C 3P8, Canada
http://www.latece.uqam.ca

**Abstract.** Customer experience management (CXM) denotes a set of practices, processes, and tools, that aim at personalizing a customer's interactions with a company around the customer's needs and desires [18]. Marketing specialists have been imagining context-aware CXM applications that exploit the IoT, AI, and cloud computing to provide rich and personalized customer experiences. However, there is no methodology to elicit/specify the requirements for such applications, nor domain level reusable components that can be leveraged to implement such applications. An e-commerce software vendor asked us to do just that, in a domain with a fragmented scientific literature, and with no portfolio of applications to draw upon. In this paper, we describe our domain engineering *strategy*, present the main elements of the *technical approach*, and discuss the main difficulties we faced in this domain engineering effort.

**Keywords:** Domain engineering · Customer Experience Management · Cognitive modeling · Ontologies · Metamodeling · Metaprogramming

## 1 Introduction

Jane walks into her favorite grocery. As she drops items in her shopping cart, the food labels are displayed on her phone or a head-up display. As she drops a box of crackers, she is warned of the sodium level, given her blood pressure. Walking through the produce section, she gets notices about the latest arrivals of fair trade certified products, being an active member of an environmental advocacy organization. Walking into the meat section, an MMS mentions a special on lamb chops that her significant other enjoys. As she drops a rack into her cart, she receives two thumbs up for a Syrah wine from northern Rhone, and one thumb up for a Merlot. While getting toothpaste, she gets an SMS about the special on size 4 diapers, since she has been buying size 3 diapers for the past six months!

© Springer Nature Switzerland AG 2020
S. Ben Sassi et al. (Eds.): ICSR 2020, LNCS 12541, pp. 100–116, 2020.
https://doi.org/10.1007/978-3-030-64694-3_7

Six years ago, the CEO of an e-commerce software vendor presented us with this scenario and asked "what software frameworks do I need to include with my product so that my customers [retailers] can design [i.e. *specify*] and integrate [develop and integrate] such experiences into their implementations of our solution". Customer Experience Management (CXM) denotes a set of practices, processes, and tools that aim at personalizing a customer's interactions with a company around the customer's needs and desires [18]. This personalization depends on the type of service/product, the type of customers, and how much a company knows about them. Effective personnalization depends on communicating the right information (*what*), in the right format (*how*), at the appropriate time (*when*); otherwise, customer *experience* becomes customer *harassment*.

In software engineering terms, we were tasked to develop a *domain-specific framework* to help retailers *instrument* existing purchasing processes as they are managed by the deployed e-commerce solutions. This *instrumentation* may involve enhancing the information communicated to the customer–the food label display, and the various warnings in the scenario above. It could also *augment* the process, by *adding extra steps* not typically covered by the e-commerce solution– e.g. the lamb chops and diaper suggestions in the scenario above.

To solve this problem, we need to perform four tasks, in sequence. *First*, we need to understand the *purchasing process* (or *customer journey*), modulo *variabilities* that account for the different *types* of products (e.g. a detergent versus a car), regardless of an IT implementation, i.e. some sort of a *Computation Independent Model* of purchasing. *Second*, based on this understanding, we need to identify when it is *possible* and *appropriate* to 'enhance' this process, and *how*, based on business requirements (more 'purchases', healthier purchases, brand loyalty, etc.). *Then (third)*, we can start specifying the *user* and *functional requirements* for such enhancements, and *finally (fourth)*, develop reusable artifacts that enable us to implement such enhancements.

The *technology* for implementing such scenarios is available: 1) the IoT, for context-awareness, 2) machine learning *libraries*, for various analytical capabilities, and 3) cloud/edge computing, for a distributed, virtual computing infrastructure. Further, software engineering work on *context-aware*/IoT-enabled applications does address some of the computational/architectural issues that underlie such applications, including event loops, integration, middleware, cloud/edge load distribution, etc. [1,10,16,17]. This addresses some of the issues in the last two tasks above, but provides little help with the first two tasks. Accordingly, we turned to the marketing literature, the social psychology of *consumer behavior* (e.g. [2,3]), and the *Service-design* literature (e.g. [9,19]), to help fill-in *some* of the gaps. Then, we faced the challenge of translating this understanding into software *requirements*, and, *eventually*, reusable software *artifacts* [13].

Section 2 summarizes the principles underlying our approach. An overview of the domain framework is presented in Sect. 3. Our tool for specifying custom purchase scenarios/customer journeys is presented in Sect. 4. The generation of *domain-specific ontologies* from the specification of purchase scenarios, and a generic CXM ontology, is described in Sect. 5. We describe the process of generating CXM code in a target technology–Java in our case–in Sect. 6. Reflections on this domain engineering effort are presented in Sect. 7. We conclude in Sect. 8.

## 2    A Conceptual Framework for CXM

### 2.1    Overview

Customer Experience Management (CXM) aims to manage the interactions between a consumer and a provider, each executing its own processes, and pursuing its own objectives. Consumers are dynamic systems whose processes (stay alive, pursue happiness, etc.) require a number of resources (e.g. food) or states (e.g. fun or health), triggering consumption processes to replenish the resources ("we are out of milk") or to attain those states ("I need to exercise"). Commercial enterprises are also dynamic systems that build products to sell to consumers.

The 'customer experience' is where the consumer's purchasing process meets the enterprise's selling process. To properly manage this experience, an enterprise needs to *first*, answer the following questions:

- Q1: what are the steps of the customer purchasing process? In particular : 1) what are the *decision points* in this process, and 2) which *factors* influence those decisions? Example *decision points* include the very decision to *initiate the purchasing process* for a particular product; I could use the latest iPhone, a bigger car, and more RAM for my laptop, but I decided to go for the RAM. Other decisions include the product specs, the retailer, etc.
- Q2: which of these steps *requires* or *lends itself* to interactions between the consumer and the enterprise? indeed, personalization can only happen at touch-points between the two processes, the consumer's and the seller's,
- Q3: how to customize such interactions to 'enhance' the overall *experience*?

Here, 'enhance' can mean make faster, make more pleasant, provide more relevant information, or spend more at the cash register. In turn, Q3 leads to three sub-questions. First (Q3.1), what kind of customizations to offer? the scenario showed several examples, including different flavors of *recommendation*, based on purchase history (lamb chops, diapers) and product associations (Syrah wine), and *dissuasion*, based on medical history (crackers). Second (Q3.2), what data is needed to support those customizations? as we just saw, purchase history, product assortment, and medical history are helpful, but can knowledge of consumers' mental states and the factors influencing their decisions be used? Third (Q3.3), how to obtain that data, in an ethical and privacy-preserving way.

To answer these questions, we relied, in part, on a *psychological modeling* of the purchasing process. Consumer behavior has been studied thoroughly by social psychologists trying to understand its mechanics (see e.g. [2–4]). The different theories recognize that purchasing decisions are determined by a combination of objective and rational factors - such as the ability of a product to fulfill a biological need - and subjective or irrational factors such as self-image (e.g., being fashionable), and personal values (e.g. being eco-friendly). Bagozzi [3] proposed a model that integrates all of the influences that have been identified by researchers. The model takes 'consumption' in a broad sense, to account for both the *acquisition of a product/service*, such as buying a computer or subscribing to video streaming services, and *adopting a behavior*, such as dieting or exercising. The model identifies the different steps (see Fig. 4 in Sect. 4.1) and the factors that are known to influence the decisions at those steps [3]. There are different paths through this process, depending on the complexity of the consumption decisions [3,13], as explained in Sect. 4.1.

Bagozzi's model answers Q1 and parts of Q2, but does not tell us when or whether it is appropriate to interact with the consumer (Q2), and how to customize the interaction (Q3). Part of the answer relies on an *operationalization* of Bagozzi's model, as illustrated in Fig. 1. Basically, a consumer has a number of 'ongoing processes' (living, raising kids, pursuing happiness) that generate a number of needs that, in turn, trigger consumption processes. Such processes involve a number of steps (see above), some of which are internal (Step $i$ in Fig. 1), i.e. in the 'consumer's head', while others *require* ("do you have these in size 12?") or lend themselves ("would you like to try it out?") to interactions with the consumer (Steps $i-1$ and $i+1$). Such steps ($i-1$ and $i+1$) may involve decision making that is influenced by *immutable factors* ("RO (Read-Only) influence factor" in Fig. 1), e.g. shoe size, income, or social identity; or *mutable factors* (RW (Read-Write) influence factor), including the desirability of a product (*anticipated positive emotions* [3]).

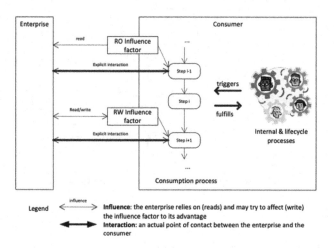

**Fig. 1.** A pattern for operationalizing touchpoints and influence factors for CXM.

Based on this pattern, a product/service provider gains from knowing how far along in the purchasing process the customer is ("are you looking for something in particular?"), and the "values" of the relevant influence factors, to customize its interactions, and when possible, modifying those values. Thus, *the influence factors embody useful data elements of the consumer profile* (question Q3.2); how to obtain them (question Q3.3) is a separate issue (see Sect. 4). Finally, knowing that a step *lends itself* to an interaction does not mean that the enterprise *should* initiate one: *service design research* (e.g. [9,19]) helps to ensure that 'customer experience' does not become 'customer harassment' (Sect. 4).

## 2.2  CXM Ontologies

In this section, we formalize our knowledge about consumers and products in a way that supports the customization of customers' interactions with product/service providers. This knowledge is embodied in *ontologies* in the knowledge representation sense, i.e. as a specification of a set of representational primitives used to represent a domain of knowledge [11]; and in sense of reflecting a *shared conceptualization of a domain*–in this case, consumer behavior.

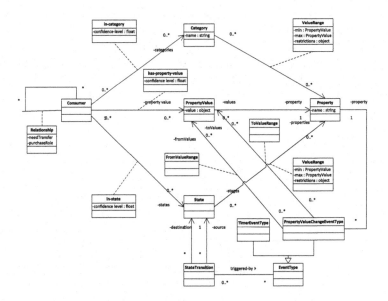

**Fig. 2.** Excerpts from the customer metamodel.

**Consumer Data.** Knowing the consumer is key to a successful CXM. An enterprise may use information about customers to: 1) anticipate their *needs*, before they even engage in a purchasing process, 2) identify those among its products that best address those needs, consistent with customers' known attitudes, biases, emotions, and values, and 3) present those products in a way that appeals to them. Figure 2 shows excerpts from the consumer ontology in UML format. We will comment on the main pieces; full discussion can be found in

[13]. The upper half of Fig. 2 shows that `Consumer`'s (individuals, such as Jane) belong to `Category`'ies (e.g. Yuppies, or Young Urban Professionals). Both have `Property`'ies, such as `income` or `age`, and values for those properties, represented by class `PropertyValue` for individuals (Jane has a single age value), and class `ValueRange` for categories (*yuppies* have an age range from 25 to 40). Both individual's membership to categories, and property values, are qualified with a *confidence level*, reflecting *probability* or *strength* [7]. The lower half of the customer ontology embodies the *life-cycle theory* in marketing [9], where individuals go through different *stages* in life, each having different consumption behavior in terms of needs, attitudes, etc. Life-cycle stages are represented by the class `State` (e.g. married with children), with their own properties and property value ranges. `StateTransition`s are triggered by events (`EventType`), which can be property change events (`PropertyChangeEventType`), as in getting married, or timer events (`TimerEventType`), when a state expires after a given time period–the diapers example in the introductory scenario.

**Product Data.** To take full advantage of our knowledge about the consumer, we need a commensurately rich representation of the products and services sold by the company. Previous work focused on modeling products to configure them and manage their manufacturing life-cycle [8,12]. Product modeling is commonly multilayer, where we distinguish, the category of the product, model of product and the physical item. Space limitations does not allow us to go into the details. Suffice it to say that our product ontology supports: 1) different levels of instantiation–the multi-layer idea, 2) product assortments (lamb with red wine), 3) includes information about *physical attributes* (e.g. dimensions), *functional attributes* (what they are for), 4) *packaging* (presentation, aesthetics, etc.), and 5) *manufacturing process*, to include the kinds of properties that can be matched to consumers' attitudes and *second-order moral values* [3,13].

## 3    A Software Framework for CXM

Section 2 laid the *conceptual* groundwork needed to develop a *software framework for CXM applications*. If anything, it showed the wide conceptual gap between the *concepts* emanating from (a fragmented) CXM theory, and the *operationalization* of those concepts in *domain software artifacts*. Model-Driven Engineering (MDE) provides a useful guide to decompose the functionalities of our *software framework*, shown in Fig. 3.

As mentioned in Sect. 2.1, the *purchasing process* depends heavily on the type of product or service being sold, e.g. a carton of milk versus an appliance, computer or a car. Section 2.2 showed *representational primitives* needed to support CXM functionalities, but we still need to specify relevant *data models* for a specific product type. Both need to be specified by a *marketing analyst*, who typically is neither a *social psychology* researcher, or a modeling guru! Accordingly, the first tool in our framework is one for specifying *purchase scenarios*, to be used by marketing analysts that produces a *domain-level, computation-independent*

*model* (CIM) of the purchase scenario. This tool, described in Sect. 4, relies on:
1) an encoding of Bagozzi's model, and 2) a *library of interactions*, from which
the analyst can pick ones that are relevant to the process at hand. The contents
and format of these *interactions*, which embody the state of the art in *service
design*, will be described in Sect. 4.3.

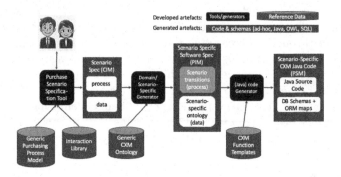

**Fig. 3.** Software framework for CXM.

The next tool in our MDE chain (Domain/Scenario-Specific Generator) takes
the specifications produced by the first tool, and the generic CXM ontology, to
produce a *platform independent model* (PIM) consisting of a scenario-specific
ontology that represents the data, and an abstract description of the process. The
current implementation does *not* generate the process component, but generates
the specific ontology. The generator is described in Sect. 5.

Finally, the Java Code Generator takes the output of the Scenario-Specific
Generator, and a library of CXM function templates, and generates Java code
that implements the data layer of the purchase scenario at hand, and the CXM
customization functions (e.g. recommendation) tailored to that data (see Sect.
6).

## 4    A Tool for Specifying Purchase Scenarios

The tool for specifying purchase scenarios is a question-driven tool for *marketing
analysts*, that elicits the different pieces of information relevant to the *purchase
scenario* in a language and format that they can understand. The gist of the
functionalities for selecting process steps (Sect. 4.1) and specifying the data
model (Sect. 4.2) have been implemented; those for selecting interactions ( Sect.
4.3) have not.

### 4.1    Selecting Process Steps and Influence Factors

Figure 4 shows a simplification of the *purchasing process* (Bagozzi's model [3])
that *drives* the selection of the process steps, using the terminology of marketing

theory. The ovals 'Goal desire', 'Goal Intention', 'Behavioral Desire', 'Implementation Intention', 'Trying', 'Goal-Directed Behavior', 'Goal attainment/Failure' and 'Feedback' represent the different activities of the process. The remaining ovals represent the *influence factors* for each of the activities. The models tells us that desiring the latest iPhone (Goal Desire), e.g., is influenced, among other things, by how easy it is to acquire it (Goal Feasibility), e.g. its affordability; how good we will feel if we get it (Anticipated Positive Emotions); and how likely are we to get it (Outcome Expectancies), e.g. its in-stock availability online. We know from marketing theory that there are different paths through this

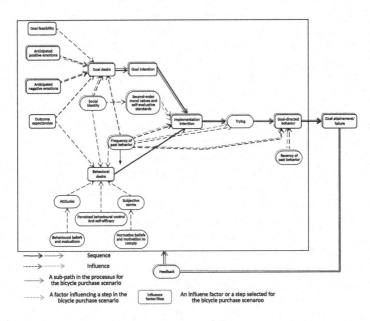

**Fig. 4.** Bagozzi's purchasing/behavior adoption model

process, depending on the complexity of the purchase. Habitual purchases that fulfill biological needs require no arbitration between competing desires (Goal Intention), and no elaborate planning (Implementation Intention): we simply stop at the grocery store, and grab a carton of milk. Contrast that with the process of buying a game console, or a mid-range bicycle, which involves all the steps. Our tool has pre-coded paths through the process in Fig. 4, corresponding to prototypical purchase scenarios; it picks one based on the analyst's answer to a high-level question such as 'is this a habitual [carton of milk] purchase'. For each one of these prototypical processes, we filtered the influence factors leaving only the salient ones. Indeed, it is unlikely that *social identify* plays a role in one's desire to purchase milk. The transitions and influences that are overlaid in red correspond to the *subset* of the full process that applies to the purchase of a mid-range (few hundred $) bicycle [6], which is a combination of a *utilitarian purchase* (transportation) and a *lifestyle purchase* (fitness).

## 4.2   Specifying Data Model

The specification of the data model involves: 1) specifying the *product/service* being offered, i.e. product categories and models, and their properties (see Fig. 5), 2) specifying the customer and customer categories, by selecting among a set of prototypical properties for both, and 3) specifying properties to be added to both *customer* and *product models* to *properly handle the relevant influence factors for the purchase scenario at hand.* We discuss the three aspects in turn.

With regard to products, we use three levels of abstraction: 1) product *categories*, 2) products *models*, and 3) product *items*. For a car, product *categories* include things such as SUVs, Japanese cars, Mazda cars, or Ford SUVs. Product categories can be *nested*. For example, `MazdaSUV` is a subcategory of `MazdaCar` *and* `SUV`. A product *model* (e.g. the *Ford Explorer XLT 2020*) belongs to a category. A product *item* is an *instance* of a *model*, e.g. Jane's Ford Explorer. Each one of these levels has its own properties. Category nesting leads to *restrictions* on *properties*. For example, whereas the `manufacturer` of a `JapaneseCar` is the `PropertyValueRange` {Honda, Mazda, Mitsubishi,...}, the `manufacturer` of a `MazdaCar` is the singleton {Mazda}. Figure 5 shows the data specification GUI.

The specification of customer profiles is slightly different: analysts are provided with a predefined list of attributes that are *typically* used in customer profiles to choose from. Analysts have the option to specify *customer categories* with property *value ranges*, to encode preexisting marketing knowledge about consumer behavior. This was a feature requested by our industrial partner, to allow his customers (retailers) to bootstrap the system with "manual customer categories until they gather enough consumer data to create their own", but derided by marketing academics 'socio-demographics are dead; long live big data'. Finally, the analyst is prompted for the properties that are needed, for both products and consumers, to account for the influence factors. Take the example of *goal feasibility*: we know from marketing theory that goal feasibility influences the desirability of a goal (*Goal Desire*), and its likelihood to be retained/selected (*Goal Intention*) as *the object* of the purchasing process (see Fig. 4). The challenge is to identify those characteristics of the product that are potential obstacles to its acquisition, and to record the corresponding characteristic of customer that can help assess their *capacity to overcome those obstacles*.

Take the example of *price*. If price can be an issue for this type of purchase, it helps to record the customer's *income*. Price is not the only obstacle: *yuppies* may be able to afford a fancy treadmill, but *space* might be an *obstacle* if they live in a condo. Thus, we need to make sure that: 1) the product dimensions are recorded, and 2) the "living space" of the consumer is recorded, somehow.

We have encoded 'proof of concept' questions for the *goal feasibility* influence factor in the current implementation of the tool. But as the above example shows, we must carefully analyze each influence factor to figure out: 1) what it could mean in the context of a particular product type, and 2) how to guide the analyst to add the required properties to both product and customer.

**Fig. 5.** The GUI for specifying product categories.

### 4.3 Selecting Interactions

This is the crux of the *experience design*. Having identified the process steps and the salient influence factors for the purchase scenario at hand, we now figure out whether and how to intervene at each step.

One of the *major challenges* in CXM is figuring out how far along the customer currently is, in a process such the one in Fig. 4. As mentioned in Sect. 2.1, many process steps are in the consumer's head, and until they initiate an interaction, we don't know where they are. Further, retailers now offer multiple *channels* through which consumers can approach them, e.g. online or in a brick-and-mortar store. *Experienced* salespeople are *excellent* at figuring out where a consumer is at, simply from their body language and 'browsing patterns'. And once they figure out where you are, they will present you with the most appropriate options and suggestions, to steer you towards a 'happy state'. The challenge is to *codify* such expertise and embody it in software artifacts that, at run-time, will steer the process in a way that enhances the 'customer experience'.

Accordingly, we need to augment prototypical processes with interactions, for two purposes: 1) figuring out how far along the purchasing process the consumer is, and 2) knowing the current stage, initiate an interaction or respond to one, in a way that transitions the customer to a desirable stage. Both can be expressed as *transitions* in the process of Fig. 4, using the quadruple format (<initial stage/state, trigger, action, end stage/state>, illustrated below:

- **[Initial stage]** [Unknown] **and [Trigger]** [Consumer did an online search on a specific product model] **then [Action]** [display positive product reviews **and** offer to beat best price by 10%] **[End Stage]** [Trying (executing a plan)]
- **[Initial stage]** [Trying] **and [Trigger]** [Customer calls to ask about store hours] **then [Action]** [give store opening hours **and** point to a store near them **and** give them URL of online store] **[End stage]** [Trying]

Findings from *service design* are helping us develop a library of transitions [5]. The transitions depend on the channel used to communicate with the consumer. We are encoding transitions for online channels based on browsing patterns [5]. The library of transitions, and the tool functionality to select them, are not yet complete. We are considering three competing formats for the representation of the process/control component of customer experiences, BPMN, CMMN, and Harel State Charts. Each provides useful metaphors, and is potentially executable, enabling simulation; see Sect. 7.3 for a further discussion.

## 5    Generating Scenario-Specific Software Specifications

Recall from Fig. 3 that the scenario-specific generator takes the specification produced by the scenario specification tool (Sect. 4), and the generic CXM ontology; to produce a platform independent model (PIM), consisting of a scenario-specific ontology and an abstract description of the process. For the time being, the description of the process is empty (see Sect. 4.3), and thus, only the generation of the scenario-specific ontology is implemented, discussed next.

First, note that the generic CXM ontology, excerpted in Fig. 2 (the customer metamodel part), was implemented in OWL using the *Protege* tool (see [6]). Further, the data specification produced by the Scenario Specification Tool (Sect. 4) contains: 1) the product category hierarchy (see Fig. 5), along with the definition of the category properties, 2) product models, along their properties and associated categories, and 3) consumer categories, with their properties, and 4) the consumer profile, with its properties. This information is provided in JSon format, through a REST API of the scenario specification tool.

The scenario-specific generator takes the scenario data specification file, parses it, and generates OWL API code to create, programmatically, the corresponding OWL entities, using the representation primitives of the generic CXM ontology. The generation of the scenario-specific ontology relies on the following rules:

- Each product (customer) category is mapped to an *instance* of the generic CXM ontology *concept* `ProductCategory` (`CustomerCategory`)
- Each product (customer) category property is mapped to an *instance* of the generic CXM ontology concept `ProductProperty` (`CustomerProperty`)
- If a property $P_A$ of a category $A$ is defined by the analyst as a *restriction* of a property $P_B$ of a super category $B$, then $P_A$ is defined as a subconcept of $P_B$, and the restriction is enforced at the range (value type) level.

Figure 6 illustrates the above rules. In this case, the marketing analyst identified the category `Bicycle`, and its subcategory `MountainBicycle`. Both are created as *instances* of `ProductCategory`. Because the analyst stated that `MountainBicycle` 'restricts' the `WheelDiameter` property of `Bicycle`, the generator created a separate property for `MountainBicycle` (`MountainWheelDiameter`) that is a subconcept of `WheelDiameter`.

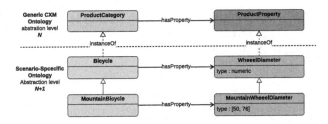

**Fig. 6.** An illustration of the ontology generation rules for the bicycle scenario [6]

## 6 Generating Technology-Specific CXM Code

Recall from Fig. 3 that the Java code generator takes two inputs: 1) an *abstract software specification* of the CX scenario at hand (PIM), produced by the scenario-specific generator (see Sect. 5), and 2) a library of CXM function templates. It produces as *output* executable code in the target platform; in this case Java with a relational database for object persistence. As mentioned earlier, the interaction selection functionality (Sect. 4.3) is yet to be completed, and hence all the downstream functionalities are yet to be implemented. Thus, the scenario-specific software specification (PIM) contains *only* the data model. This model is used for two purposes. First, we use it to generate the Java classes and corresponding databases tables that represent the entities of the purchase scenario (products and consumers). Second, we use it to 'instantiate'/generate the *customization functions* for the purchase scenario at hand. We explain them in turn.

First, using the scenario-specific OWL ontology as an input, we used OWL API 5.1.0 , a reference API for creating and manipulating OWL ontologies (http://owlapi.sourceforge.org), and Hermit Reasoner (1.3.8), to:

- generate database schemas and fill out the tables to store: 1) product information, including the hierarchy of categories, models, and the corresponding property values, and 2) customer categories, states, and individuals.
- generate the corresponding Java classes, with their attributes and accessors, enforcing property-value restrictions expressed in OWL (see Sect. 5).
- generate the Object Relational Mapping between the Java classes and the relational data store.

More details, including an example, are presented in [6]. With regard to the *customization functions*, illustrated with various types of *recommendations* in the introductory scenario, we sought a way of encoding those functions in a way that does not refer *explicitly* to the data model at hand. We will illustrate the problem with an example.

Assume that you want to buy a bicycle to ride in the city, e.g. to commute to work. Thus, 'ride in the city' would be the value of a `bicycleUsage` property of customers. Assume now that we have three bicycle categories, `MountainBicycle`,

HybridBicycle, and RacingBicycle, each with a `function` attribute, representing the potential *usages* of the category. Our application should recommend a *bicycle category* bc, if all the *usages* intended by the customer are supported by the category, i.e. if:

$$(\forall \ bc \in BC) \ \ bicycleUsage(myCustomer) \subseteq function(bc) \ => \atop recommend \ bc \ \text{models to} \ myCustomer \tag{1}$$

This encoding refers *explicitly* to *data elements* of the purchase scenario at hand. Further, the matched attributes (`[Customer.]bicycleUsage` and `[BicycleCategory.]function`) don't even have the same name, though they have *similar semantics* and the same *range*.

To handle this problem, we sought a codification of CXM customization functions that abstracts away *domain specificity* and focuses on the *intensional* and *computational aspects*. This is like *domain genericity* where the *domain variable* is *semantically constrained*. Thus, we developed a *template language* that relies on a Java-like syntax, and that refers to meta-level constraints on the *scenario-specific ontology* to encode customization algorithms in a domain-independent way (see Fig. 7). Concretely, we used the *Velocity* templating engine. So far, we encoded a handful of *faceted concept matching functions*, including simple recommendation functions, as proofs of concept. We are currently working on more complex *processing chains*, of the kind we use in machine learning tasks.

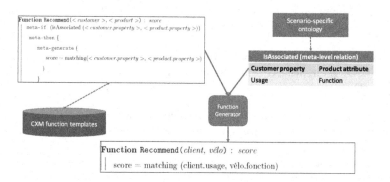

**Fig. 7.** Generating CXM Customization Functions

## 7   Why Was This Hard?

This *domain engineering* effort was *hard*, as we faced many obstacles atypical of domain engineering efforts. This was not a *typical* domain engineering effort in many respects. We discuss the specifics of CXM in this section.

## 7.1   CXM: A to Be-Defined Domain

Domain *analysis* or *engineering* is typically a *maturation* process, where an organization that has been developing applications within a *stable* domain, decides to leverage the *commonalities* between the applications into a methodology and set of software artifacts that facilitate the development and maintenance of future applications. CXM does not fit the bill, as explained below.

First, it is not a *mature domain*, as the fragmented literature shows (see Sect. 2), with *abstractions* coming from different fields (marketing, social psychology, service design). Further, there are no easy mappings from those abstractions to IT. For example, in typical business domains, there is a relatively simple mapping from *domain concepts* to *software concepts*: real-world entities (customer, product, etc.) that the system needs to track are mapped to similarly named entities (objects, tables, etc.). Contrast that with the tortuous path of *influence factors* and how we included them in the consumer profile (see Sect. 2.1, Sect. 2.2, and Sect. 4.2).

A *corollary* of the lack of maturity of the CXM domain, is the absence of existing CXM applications that we could draw upon, for analysis, design, or implementations. First, while the *concept* of CXM is not new, there are no methodical industrial implementations. Most e-commerce tool vendors, like our industrial partner, recognize the potential of CXM functionalities. However, they don't offer *CXM frameworks* beyond, perhaps, standalone machine learning or text mining libraries. Industrial implementations such as Amazon's Go store are more like one-of-a-kind *technology showcases*.

## 7.2   Don't Call Us, We Will Call You

Typical application frameworks rely on what is called the *Hollywood Principle* to: 1) maximize the scope of the shared logic, and 2) minimize the dependencies between the user code and the framework code. Typically, a framework would define a number of *hotspots* (variation points) that correspond to *contracts* (typically, *interfaces*) that *user code has to implement* to benefit from the services offered by the framework. This way, user code does not need to invoke those services explicitly ("don't call us"); however, by "registering with the framework" (instantiating its 'hotspots'), the methods it implemented to "fulfill its contractual obligations" will get called ("we will call you"), thereby benefiting from the services offered by the framework.

This metaphor, which works well with *infrastructure services*, becomes a bit more tenuous with *domain services*, where *contracts* need to be specified in domain-specific terms. This is even more difficult with CXM functionalities, where the problem goes beyond the issue of *domain vocabulary*.

We showed in Sect. 6 how we alleviated this problem by encoding some of the CXM functionality using a *templating language* where *template variables* are defined *intensionally*. However, this does not address the bigger problem with CXM functionalities that involve machine learning. Machine-learning functionalities involve two related, decisions: 1) choosing an *algorithm* appropriate for the data and task at hand, 2) choosing an *encoding* of the input data appropriate for that algorithm. Both decisions involve a combination of technical expertise, domain insights, and trial and error, that are difficult to encode for reuse.

### 7.3  Process Versus Case Management

We were asked to develop a software framework that helps retailers *instrument* the 'purchasing processes' (or customer journeys) enabled by their e-commerce applications, in a way that 'enhances the customer experience'. We used a *process metaphor* to describe the purchasing experience, as is common in both the marketing and the software engineering literature. We saw in Sect. 2.1, 3 and 4.1, that no single process can characterize all purchasing scenarios. In particular, our tool for specifying purchasing scenarios enables marketing analysts to, *first* select a 'sub-pattern' of Bagozzi's generic process (Sect. 4.1), and *second*, add custom interactions to handle the different situations (Sect. 4.3).

We are starting to see the limit of the *process* metaphor, for many reasons. From an *epistemological* point of view, advocates of the *experiential view* of consumption object to the view of purchasing/consumption as a linear process where *decisions* are made based on *rational factors*–subjective *influence factors* notwithstanding. More pragmatically, we see two additional related problems. For all but the most trivial purchasing scenarios (carton of milk), the number of potential interactions is fairly high, especially if we integrate the various *channels* through which a consumer communicates with the retailer. Second, except for the most trivial purchases, no two shopping experiences are likely to be similar, i.e. there is a great variety between *process instances*. In particular, one process instance could start with one objective (*goal desire*), and end-up with a different one; one of the authors was once looking for *one* spare motorcycle helmet, and responding to an ad, ended-up buying the seller's *motorcycle* and *two* helmets!

Process complexity and instance-specificity are symptomatic of situations where a *case management* metaphor is more appropriate. *Case management* is appropriate for low-volume, high-complexity, data-driven, knowledge-intensive processes [14]. That is what most purchasing processes–above a carton of milk– feel like to the average consumer. From a modeling perspective, *case management* adopts a *declarative style* that focuses on specifying *constraints* placed on process execution, as opposed to modeling all of the potential contingencies. We are currently exploring the use of OMG's Case Management Model and Notation [15] to model prototypical purchase scenarios (Sect. 4.1) and CXM interactions (Sect. 4.3).

## 8  Conclusion

The IoT, AI, and cloud computing enable us to develop applications that provide rich and personalized customer experiences around existing e-commerce platforms; *if only* we knew *what* to develop, from a functional point of view, and incidentally, *how* to develop it by leveraging reusable components. That is the *domain engineering* mandate given to us by our industrial partner, the vendor of an e-commerce product suite.

*Domain engineering* is usually done as a logical step in the maturation process of an organization that accrues a deep expertise and a 'large' portfolio of applications within a relatively limited domain. By contrast, we had to contend with some *fundamental questions* about CXM, that a fragmented literature only partially addressed; we also had no existing application portfolio to start with, beyond the 'fantasies' of marketing and IT visionaries. In this paper, we discussed the main challenges, and described our strategy for addressing them. Our work is still in its infancy. It raised many more *domain* questions than it answered, and there is a lot of development work ahead of us, both in terms of tooling and domain content, before we can start thinking about *validation*. However, we hope that our general approach enables us–and others–to research these issues in a methodical manner.

# References

1. Alegre, U., Augusto, J.C., Clark, T.: Engineering context-aware systems and applications: a survey. J. Syst. Software **117**, 53–83 (2016)
2. Azjen, I.: The theory of planned behavior. In: Organisational Behaviour and Human Decision Processes (1991)
3. Bagozzi, R.P., Gurhan-Canliu, Z., Priester, J.R.: The Social Psychology of Consumer Behavior. Open University Press (2007)
4. Bagozzi, R.P., Warshaw, P.R.: Trying to consume. J. Consumer Res. **17**(2), 127–140 (1990)
5. Benzarti, I.: Un Cadre Logiciel de Développement Pour la Gestion de l'Expérience Client. Ph.D. thesis (2020)
6. Benzarti, I., Mili, H.: A development framework for customer experience management applications: principles and case study. In: 2017 IEEE 14th International Conference on e-Business Engineering (ICEBE), pp. 118–125. IEEE (2017)
7. Jiang, F., Berry, H., Schoenauer, M.: Supervised and evolutionary learning of echo state networks. In: Rudolph, G., Jansen, T., Beume, N., Lucas, S., Poloni, C. (eds.) PPSN 2008. LNCS, vol. 5199, pp. 215–224. Springer, Heidelberg (2008). https://doi.org/10.1007/978-3-540-87700-4_22
8. Bock, C., Zha, X., Suh, H.W., Lee, J.H.: Ontological Product Modeling for Collaborative Design, vol. 24, pp. 510–524. Elsevier (2010)
9. Cook, L.S., Bowen, D.E., Chase, R.B., Dasu, S., Stewart, D.M., Tansik, D.A.: Human issues in service design. J. Oper. Manag. **20**(2), 159–174 (2002)
10. Dey, A.K., Abowd, G.D., Salber, D.: A conceptual framework and a toolkit for supporting the rapid prototyping of context-aware applications. Hum. Comput. Interact. **16**, 2–3 (2001)
11. Gruber, T.: Ontologies, web 2.0 and beyond (2007)
12. Lee, J.H., et al.: A semantic product modeling framework and its application to behavior evaluation. IEEE Trans. Autom. Sci. Eng. **9**(1), 110–123 (2011)
13. Mili, H., et al.: Context aware customer experience management: a development framework based on ontologies and computational intelligence. In: Pedrycz, W., Chen, S.-M. (eds.) Sentiment Analysis and Ontology Engineering. SCI, vol. 639, pp. 273–311. Springer, Cham (2016). https://doi.org/10.1007/978-3-319-30319-2_12

14. Motahari-Nezhad, H.R., Swenson, K.D.: Adaptive case management: overview and research challenges. In: 2013 IEEE 15th Conference on Business Informatics, pp. 264–269. IEEE (2013)
15. Object Management Group: Case Management Model and Notation (2013)
16. Perera, C., Zaslavsky, A., Christen, P., Georgakopoulos, D.: Context aware computing for the internet of things: a survey. In: IEEE Communications Surveys and Tutorials (2014)
17. Preuveneers, D., Novais, P.: A survey of software engineering best practices for the development of smart applications in ambient intelligence. J. Ambit. Intell. Smart Env. 4(3), 149–162 (2012)
18. Walker, B.: The emergence of customer experience management solutions. For eBusiness & Channel Strategy Professionals (2011)
19. Zomerdijk, L.G., Voss, C.A.: Service design for experience-centric services. J. Serv. Res. 13(1), 67–82 (2010)

# Reengineering

# Modular Moose: A New Generation of Software Reverse Engineering Platform

Nicolas Anquetil[1]([✉]) [ID], Anne Etien[1] [ID], Mahugnon H. Houekpetodji[1,2],
Benoit Verhaeghe[1,3], Stéphane Ducasse[1] [ID], Clotilde Toullec[1],
Fatiha Djareddir[2], Jerôme Sudich[3], and Moustapha Derras[3]

[1] Université de Lille, CNRS, Inria, Centrale Lille, UMR 9189 – CRIStAL,
Lille, France
nicolas.anquetil@univ-lille.fr
[2] CIM, Lille, France
[3] Berger-Levrault, Montpellier, France

**Abstract.** Advanced reverse engineering tools are required to cope with
the complexity of software systems and the specific requirements of
numerous different tasks (re-architecturing, migration, evolution). Consequently, reverse engineering tools should adapt to a wide range of situations. Yet, because they require a large infrastructure investment, being
able to reuse these tools is key. Moose is a reverse engineering environment answering these requirements. While Moose started as a research
project 20 years ago, it is also used in industrial projects, exposing itself
to all these difficulties. In this paper we present MODMOOSE, the new version of Moose. MODMOOSE revolves around a new meta-model, modular
and extensible; a new toolset of generic tools (query module, visualization engine, ...); and an open architecture supporting the synchronization
and interaction of tools per task. With MODMOOSE, tool developers can
develop specific meta-models by reusing existing elementary concepts,
and dedicated reverse engineering tools that can interact with the existing ones.

## 1 Introduction

As software technologies evolve, old systems experience a growing need to follow
this evolution. From the end-user point of view, they need to offer functionalities
entirely unforeseen when they were first conceived. From the developer point
of view, they need to adapt to the new technologies that would allow one to
implement these functionalities [8].

Given the size of these systems and lack of resources in the industry, such
evolution can only happen with the help of automated tooling [3,14]. Concur-
rently, because such tooling requires a large infrastructure investment, it must
be generic and reusable across technologies and reverse engineering tasks. This
tooling needs to cope with the following problems:

© Springer Nature Switzerland AG 2020
S. Ben Sassi et al. (Eds.): ICSR 2020, LNCS 12541, pp. 119–134, 2020.
https://doi.org/10.1007/978-3-030-64694-3_8

- *Diversity of languages and analyses.* Many programming languages and versions of such languages are used in the industry. Meta-modeling was proposed to cope with that diversity, but it does not solve all problems. Software reverse engineering requires to represent source code with a high degree of details that are specific to each programming language and to the reverse engineering tasks themselves. How to model the different needs for details while remaining generic is an issue meta-models have not tackled yet.
- *Sheer amount of data.* Tools are particularly useful for large systems (millions of lines of code). The size of the analyzed systems stresses the modeling capabilities of the tools and the efficiency of the analyses.
- *Reverse engineering task diversity.* The evolution needs are numerous, from restructuring a system towards a micro component architecture [5], to migrating its graphical user interface [23], evolving its database [7], or cleaning the code [2]. This calls for various tools (query module, visualizations, metrics, navigation, analyses) that must integrate together to answer each need still acting as a coherent tool.
- *Specific tasks require specific tools.* Some tools can be useful in various situations, but specialized tools are also needed[1]. If a tool is too specific to a technology, its advantages are lost when working with others. It is important that they can be easily added and integrated into a reverse engineering environment.

We report here our experience with Moose, a software analysis platform answering to the basic needs of reverse engineering, reusable in different situations, extensible and adaptable to new needs [20]. Moose was initiated as a research project and still fulfills this role. But it is also used in a number of industrial projects [2,7,23].

Our redesign of Moose has the following goals: (1) the ability to develop specific meta-models by reusing existing elementary concepts, (2) the ability to develop dedicated reverse engineering tools by configuring and composing existing tools or developing new ones, (3) the ability to seamlessly integrate new tools in the existing reverse engineering environment. MODMOOSE, the new version of Moose described in this article, revolves around a modular extensible meta-model, a new toolset of generic tools (*e.g.,* query module, visualization engine) and an open architecture supporting the synchronization and interaction of tools.

The contributions of this article are (1) the description of MODMOOSE new generation reverse engineering environment, (2) FAMIXNG supporting the definition of new meta-models based on the composition of elementary concepts implemented using stateful traits, and (3) a bus architecture to support the communication between independent and reusable tools.

In the following sections, we discuss the difficulties of having a generic, multi-language, software meta-model (Sect. 2) and how we solved them with FAMIXNG (Sect. 3). Then, we briefly present the new generic tools and how the new open

---

[1] According to Bruneliere [6], the plurality of reengineering projects requires adaptable/portable reverse engineering tools.

architecture of MODMOOSE supports the collaboration of group of tools and their synchronization (Sect. 4). We conclude in Sect. 5.

## 2   Software Representation and Reverse Engineering Tool Challenges

To analyze code, tools need to represent it. Such a representation should be *generic* (programming languages are all build around similar concepts that should be reusable), support *multi-language*, and *detailed* (a proper analysis must pay attention to little, meaningful, details).

Each one of these challenges may be tackled by meta-models. For example, existing IDEs (Integrated Development Environments) like Eclipse, or software quality tools (*e.g.,* CAST, SonarQube) offer tools based on an internal representation of the source code. But in Eclipse, the model is not the same for version management and source code highlighting. In that way, they can represent with enough details the analyzed systems. The Lightweight Multilingual Software Analysis approach proposed by Lyons *et al.,* uses different parsers (one for each programming language analyzed) to populate their *different* models: "variable assignment locations", or "reverse control flow". The challenge is still how to support the development of multiple dedicated and specific meta-models for different languages in a tractable way.

### 2.1   Problem: Handling the Diversity of Languages

Many publications highlight the need, for modern software analysis tools, to deal with multi-language systems (*e.g.,* [9,12,17–19]). The generality and reusability of the analysis tools depend on their ability to work with all these languages.

Meta-models were supposed to solve this issue. Naively, one could hope that a single "object-oriented meta-model" would be able to represent programs in all OO programming languages and another "procedural meta-model" would represent all procedural programming languages.

Thus, for example, in the Dagstuhl Middle Meta-model [17] "the notions of routine, function and subroutine are all treated the same." But in practice, one soon realizes that "various programming languages have minor semantic differences regarding how they implement these concepts" ([17] again.) To be meaningful and allow precise analyses, the meta-models must represent these little differences and the tools must "understand" their specific semantics. As a consequence, Washizaki *et al.,* [24] report that "even if a meta-model is stated to be language independent, we often found that it actually only supports a very limited number of languages." A good meta-model must represent all details to allow meaningful analyses. Software is not linear, small details may have huge impacts. Reverse engineering is about abstracting from the source code, but also sticking tightly to it because one does not know in advance what "details" are making a difference for different tasks.

Visibility rules are a concrete example of the complexity to represent varying details for apparently universal concepts: Abstracting the API of a class requires understanding the visibility rules of classes, methods, and attributes. They are not exactly the same for Java (public, protected, private, default package, and now export) or C++ (public, protected, private, and friend). And the tools need to be aware of each different semantics to make the proper inferences.

Other problems are raised by the containment relationship (*i.e.,* ownership). Many meta-models assume a hierarchical containment tree: all entities (except the root entity) are owned by exactly one parent entity. However, in C#, class definitions may be scattered over several files (*partial* definitions), and in Objective-C or Smalltalk a package may add methods to a class defined in another package (extension methods). In these contexts, the notion of single owner is less consensual.

Our experience designing and using a programming language meta-model, Famix, for more than 15 years showed that we need dedicated meta-models for each language.

## 2.2    Single Inheritance: Tyranny of the Dominant Decomposition

Moose was based on a single meta-model (Famix [9,10,20]) extensible with plugins. It did allow to model many different programming languages[2] (Ada, C, C++, FORTRAN, 4D[3], Java, JavaScript, Mantis[4], Pharo, PHP, PostgresSQL/PgPlSQL, PowerBuilder[5]), and even other sources of information (*e.g.,* SVN logs). But extending Famix was an awkward process since it relied on a single inheritance tree of concepts.

To address language variety, the choice was to have core entities representing "typical features" of programming languages (*e.g.,* function, methods, package, class) and extend this core for language specific entities (*e.g.,* the macros in C). The Dagstuhl Middle Meta-model [17] made the same choice.

However this was only possible through a careful definition of the meta-model and the hierarchy of modeled entities. In practice, Famix core was tailored towards Java and Smalltalk, its initial focus. Several extensions covered other OOP languages with varying degrees of success. For example, Enum and Class were both Types (see Fig. 1, right). In Java, both accept an implements relationship to Interface (another type). Therefore this relationship is defined at the level of the Type concept. But then, a PrimitiveType (also a Type) inherits this same property which does not make sense in Java, and also an Interface is allowed to implements another Interface, which again is not correct in Java.

Other generic meta-models have the same issue. In the Dagstuhl Middle Metamodel [17] (see Fig. 1, left), all relationships (*e.g.,*IsMethodOf, Includes, Invokes) may occur between ModelElements (*e.g.,*Type, Routine, Field). As a result many entities (*e.g.,*Field) accept relationships (*e.g.,*IsMethodOf) that they don't use.

---

[2] Some languages are only partially supported.

[3] http://en.wikipedia.org/wiki/4th_Dimension_(software).

[4] http://www.lookupmainframesoftware.com/soft_detail/dispsoft/339.

[5] http://en.wikipedia.org/wiki/PowerBuilder.

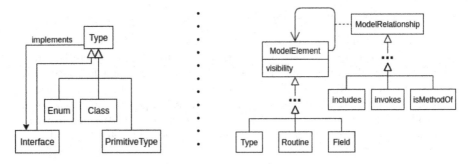

**Fig. 1.** Examples of the Dominant Decomposition problem in the Dagstuhl Middle Meta-model (left) and in Famix (right)

A generic single inheritance meta-model thus turns out to be too permissive with entities owning properties that they don't use. Incidentally, this has consequences on the size of the models since these properties occupy uselessly memory that multiplied by the number of instances (tens or hundreds of thousands) adds up to significant memory loss.

EMF (Eclipse Modeling Framework) attempts to solve the problems raised by single inheritance tree. EMF implementation uses inheritance and interfaces, thus mimicking multiple inheritance. But this still imposes to choose one dominant decomposition for inheritance and the other decompositions have to implement interfaces' API.

### 2.3    ModMoose's Goals

To design a new generation and modular reverse engineering environment we set goals at two different levels: meta-modeling and tooling.

*Meta-modeling goals.* We are looking for generic modeling that leaves open a wealth of analyses (metrics, dead-code, design patterns, anti-patterns, dependency analysis, etc). So we needed a unified representation that:

1. Supports the precise representation of various programming language features (identified in [21]);
2. Is compatible with many analysis tools (the *processing environment* identified in [24]);
3. Is wary of memory consumption (identified in [16]);
4. Is extensible (allow for easy addition of new languages).

*Tooling Goals.* Tools are needed to [3,14]:

- Automate tedious tasks to bring tremendous speed-up with less errors.[6]
- Handle large quantity of data and in our case all the details of multi-millions lines of code. If information size can become an issue even for automated tools, this is several orders of magnitude above what a human can handle.
- Summarize data to allow a human abstracting a big picture understanding.
- Quickly verify hypotheses so that there is little or no cost attached to wrong hypotheses, and several concurrent hypotheses can easily be compared.

# 3    A Composable Meta-model of Programming Languages

FAMIXNG is a redesign of Famix around the idea of composing entities from language properties represented as traits [22]. With FAMIXNG (See Sect. 3.1), one defines a new meta-model out of reusable elements describing elementary concepts (See Sect. 3.2).

## 3.1    FamixNG

To support the reuse of elementary language concept, FAMIXNG relies on *stateful traits* [22].
*What is a trait?* "A trait is a set of methods, divorced from any class hierarchy. Traits can be composed in arbitrary order. The composite entity (class or trait) has complete control over the composition and can resolve conflicts explicitly". In their original form, traits were stateless, *i.e.,* pure groups of methods without any attributes. Stateful traits extend stateless traits by introducing a single attribute access operator to give clients of the trait control over the visibility of attributes [22]. A class or another trait is composed from traits and it retains full control of the composition being able to ignore or rename some methods of the traits it uses.

In FAMIXNG, all properties that were previously defined in classes are now defined as independent traits: For example, the trait TNamedEntity only defines a name property (a string) and may belong to trait TNamespaceEntity. Therefore any entity using this trait will have a name and can be part of a namespace entity. Similarly, entities (presumably typed variables or functions) composed with the trait TTypedEntity have a declaredType pointing to an entity using the trait TType.

Four types of traits can be used to compose a new meta-model:

**Associations** represent usage of entities in the source code. This includes the four former associations of Famix: inheritance, invocation (of a function or a method), access (to a variable), and reference (to a type). In FAMIXNG, we also found a need for three more specialized associations: Dereferenced-Invocation (call of a pointer to a function in C), FileInclude (also in C), and TraitUsage.

---

[6] A source code model computes in seconds a method call graph that takes weeks to recover by hand. We had the case in two different companies.

**Technical** traits do not model programming language entities but are used to implement Moose functionality. Currently, this includes several types of TSourceAnchors, associated to TSourcedEntity to allow recovering their source code (a typical TSourceAnchor contains a filename, and start and end positions in this file.) Other *Technical traits* implement software engineering metric computation, or are used to implement the generic query engine of Moose (see Sect. 4.2). There are 16 *Technical traits* currently in FAMIXNG.

**Core** traits model composable properties that source code entities may possess. This includes TNamedEntity and TTypedEntity (see above), or a number of entities modeling ownership: TWithGlobalVariables (entities that can own TGlobalVariables), TWithFunctions (entities that can own TFunctions),... There are 46 *Core traits* currently in FAMIXNG including 38 traits modeling ownership of various possible kind of entities.

**Terminal** traits model entities that can be found in the source code such as Functions, Classes, Exceptions, ... These entities are often defined as a composition of some of the *Core traits*. For example, TClass is composed of: TInvocationsReceiver (class can be receiver of static messages), TPackageable, TType (classes can be used to type other entities), TWithAttributes, TWithComments, TWithInheritances, TWithMethods. The name *Terminal trait* refers to the fact that they can be used directly to create a programming language concept (a class, a package), whereas *Core traits* are typically composed with other traits to make a meaningful programming language concept. There are 38 such *Terminal traits* currently in FAMIXNG.

Contrary to the old Famix, the *Terminal traits* are rather minimal definitions (intersection of languages) than maximal ones (union of languages). They are intended to have only the properties found in any programming language. For example TClass does not use the TWithModifiers trait (for attaching visibility) since not all languages explicitly define visibility of classes. For any given meta-model, additional properties may be added to these *"Terminal traits"*, for example JavaClass uses the traits TClass and TWithModifiers since Java classes can be declared public, private, ... More specialized languages (*e.g.,* SQL) can always compose new entities from the set of *Core traits* offered by FAMIXNG.

We validated this new approach by defining different meta-models (*e.g.,* GUI meta-model [23], Java, OpenStack cloud infrastructure, Pharo, PowerBuilder, SQL/PLPGSQL).

## 3.2   Creating a New Meta-model with FamixNG

To create a new meta-model, the developer may extend an existing meta-model or start from scratch. This later case can be relevant if the language to model is quite different from what MODMOOSE currently handles, such as a specific domain or SQL. For example, while being different from procedural languages, stored procedures in SQL bear resemblance to functions and can be composed from the same FAMIXNG traits.

Figure 2 shows the definition of a toy meta-model (left) with the meta-model itself (right). There are four entities: the root Entity, and File, Commit and Author.

In grey, the TNamedEntity trait, part of FAMIXNG. The embedded DSL needs first the entity creation, then definition of inheritance relationships, properties of each entity, and finally the relationships between entities. To improve readability, entity descriptions are stored in variables having the same name (*e.g.,* author variable for Author entity description). One can see an example of using a predefined trait, TNamedEntity that adds a "name : String" property to the classes using it. The same syntax, "--|>", is used for class inheritance and traits usage. From this, the builder generates all the corresponding classes and methods.

```
entity := builder newClassNamed: 'Entity'.
file   := builder newClassNamed: 'File'.
commit := builder newClassNamed: 'Commit'.
author := builder newClassNamed: 'Author'.

"inheritance"
file   --|> entity.
file   --|> TNamedEntity.
commit --|> entity.
author --|> entity.
author --|> TNamedEntity.

"properties"
commit property: 'revision' type: #Number.
commit property: 'date' type: #Object.
commit property: 'message' type: #String.

"associations"
file *-* commit.
commit *- author.
```

**Fig. 2.** A simple File/Commit/Author meta-model (left: building script; right: UML view; gray: predefined FAMIXNG trait)

*Meta-model Reuse and Extension.* The extension of existing meta-model is done by specifying which meta-model to extend (similarly to import instruction in Java), then the existing traits can be reused at will. It is also possible to manage multi-language systems by composing several meta-models. We cannot illustrate these two points for lack of space.

## 4    ModMoose: A Reverse Engineering Environment

Program comprehension is still primarily a manual task. It requires knowledge on computer science, the application domain, the system, the organization using it, etc [1]. Yet the sheer size of the current software systems (millions of lines of code, hundred of thousands of entities modeled) precludes any software development team to fully understand these systems. Any significant program comprehension activity imposes the use of specialized tools.

MODMOOSE lets software engineers design specialized reverse engineering tools by (1) using infrastructure tools (see Sect. 4.2); (2) taking advantage of a bus architecture supporting smart interactions between tools (see Sect. 4.3); and, (3) reuse a set of generic and configurable tools (see Sect. 4.4).

## 4.1  ModMoose Architecture

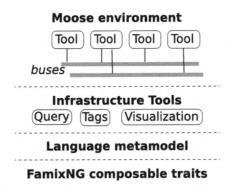

**Fig. 3.** MODMOOSE architecture.

MODMOOSE is architectured on the following principles:

- Tools are part of the MODMOOSE environment which acts as a master and centralizes data;
- Tools communicate through buses, they "read" model entities on their bus(es) and "write" entities back on their bus(es) (see below);
- Tools are focusing on a single task: *e.g.,* the Query Browser works on a set of model entities and produces another set of entities.

  These simple principles ensure that tools can be easily added to MODMOOSE and collaborate between themselves in a flexible manner.

## 4.2  Infrastructure Tools

We identified three important requirement to analyze software systems: (i) query and navigate a model to find entities of interest; (ii) visualise the software to abstract information; and (iii) annotate entities to represent meaning and reach a higher level of abstraction.

**Moose Query** is an API to programmatically navigate FAMIXNG models. For any FAMIXNG meta-model, Moose Query[7] computes the answer to generic queries:

---

[7] https://moosequery.ferlicot.fr/.

– containment: parent or children entities of a given type from a current entity.
– dependencies: following incoming or outgoing associations from or to a given entity. Dependencies are also deduced from parent/children relationships, *e.g.*, dependencies between methods can be uplifted to dependencies between their parent classes or parent packages.
– description: all properties of a given entity.

In a FAMIXNG meta-model, relationships denoting a containment are declared as such in the association part of the meta-model construction (see Fig. 2), *e.g.*, method `*-<>` `class` or `class` `<>-*` `method`. Containment queries may go up and down the containment tree based on the expected entity type: *e.g.*, from a Method one can ask to go up to any entity(ies) of type Class owning it.

Navigating dependencies is based on containment and association relationships. It is possible to navigate through a specific association (*e.g.*, "all invoked methods") or all types of association (*e.g.*, "all dependencies") to other elements. Direction of navigation (incoming, outgoing) must be specified. Dependencies between children of entities can be automatically abstracted at the level of their parents.

*Package Level Communication Example.* A frequent query is to find how packages interact with each other via method calls. This can be done by iterating over all the methods of all the classes of a package, collecting what other methods they invoke. From this one finds the parent classes and parent packages of the invoked methods.

With Moose Query, such a query is simply expressed:
`(aPackage queryOutgoing: FamixInvocation)`
`atScope: FamixPackage` (*i.e.*, find all invocations stemming from `aPackage`, and raise the result at the level of the receiving package).

*Stored Procedures Referencing a Column Example.* In SQL, one may want to know all the stored procedures[8] accessing a given column of a database table. These stored procedures can directly reference columns, in the case of triggers, or contain SQL queries that reference the columns. SQL queries contain clauses that themselves can contain other queries. So, the answer can be computed from a given column of a table, by collecting the references targeting this column, and recursively analyze them to identify the ones that are inside a stored procedure. Due to the possible nesting of SQL queries, this has to be a recursive process.

With Moose Query, this query is simply expressed as follows:
`aColumn queryIncomingDependencies`
`atScope: FamixSQLStoredProcedure` (*i.e.*, find all incoming dependencies to `aColumn` and raise the result at the level of the stored procedures. Incoming dependencies not stemming from a stored procedures are simply dropped here).
*Analysis.* These examples show that MooseQuery API is independent from the meta-model used. Obviously, each query depends on the meta-model of the model

---

[8] functions directly defined inside the database management system.

it is applied (one cannot ask for methods in a SQL model). In the first example (Java), there are different kind of dependencies in the model (invocation, inheritance, access, reference), therefore the kind one is interested in must be specified (`queryOutgoing: FamixInvocation`). In the second example there exist only one kind of dependencies to a column. Consequently, the query can be simpler: `queryIncomingDependencies`.

In the second example, Moose Query implicitly filters out all queries that do not stem from a stored procedure. In the first example, no such filtering occurs since all methods belong to a package in Java.

**Visualisation Engines:** MODMOOSE uses Roassal [4], a generic visualization engine, to script interactive graphs or charts. Roassal is primarily used to display software entities in different forms or colors and their relationships. Possible examples are to display the classes of a package as a UML class diagram, or as a Dependency Structure Matrix[9]. Roassal visualization are interactive.

MODMOOSE also uses the Telescope, more abstract, visualization engine that eases building new visualizations in terms of entities, their relationships, their forms and colors, positioning, etc [15]. Telescope offers abstractions such as predefined visualizations and interaction, and relies on Roassal to do the actual drawing. For example, Telescope offers a predefined "Butterfly" visualization, centered on an entity and showing to the left all its incoming dependencies and to the right all its outgoing dependencies.

**Tags** are labels attached by the user to any entities either interactively or as result of queries [13]. Tags enrich models with extra information. They have many different uses:

- to decorate entities with a virtual property *e.g.,* tagging all methods directly accessing a database.
- to represent entities that are not directly expressed in the programming language constructs: *e.g.,* representing architectural elements or tagging subsets of a god class' members as belonging to different virtual classes [2].
- to mark *to do* and *done* entities in a repetitive process.

An important property of MODMOOSE tags is that they are first class entities. Tags are not only an easy way to search entities, they can also be manipulated as any other model entity: a query may collect all dependencies from or to a tag, the visualization engines may display tags as container entities with actual entities within them, one can compute software engineering metrics (*e.g.,* cohesion/coupling) on tags considered as virtual packages.

## 4.3  Smart Tool Interactions Through Buses

The power of MODMOOSE comes from the generic interaction of specialized tools. In particular, it is key that: (i) different tools display the *same entities*

---

[9] https://en.wikipedia.org/wiki/Design_structure_matrix.

from different points of view, or (ii) different instances of the same tool may be used to compare different entities from the same point of view. MODMOOSE supports such scenarios using an open architecture based on buses and tool behavior controls.

*Communication Buses.* Tools communicate through buses. They read entities produced by other tools on the buses and write entities on the same buses for other tools to consume. Several buses can be created, and groups of tools can be set on different buses. This allows one to explore different parts of the model or different courses of actions: *e.g.,* imagine two buses each one attached to a Query browser and a Dependency Graph browser (described in Sect. 4.4). Each Query browser selects different entities from the model, the Dependency Graph browsers display them, and the two buses ensure interaction within each pair of browsers.

Tools can also be detached from all available buses to keep their current result and presumably allow one to compare it with other results from other instances of the same tools.

Since tools can be attached to more than one bus, a tool can be set as a bridge between all buses: It listens to all buses and forwards activity on them. A natural candidate for this is the Logger (described in Sect. 4.4). By selecting an interesting set of entities in the Logger, one can propagate these entities to all buses, thus synchronizing them.

*Tool Behavior Controls.* On top of the bus architecture, three behavior controls (*frozen, highlighting, following*) fine-tune the tool reaction to bus events:

- *Following* is the default state where a tool reads entities that pass on its bus(es) and writes entities to the same bus(es). In such mode, a tool reacts to read entities.
- *Frozen* is a state where the tool does not listen to the bus(es) for incoming entities and therefore keeps its state and display independent of entities written on the bus(es). The tool is not detached from bus(es) and can still write entities on them. A reverse engineer can interact with a frozen tool and other tools will be informed of this.
- *Highlighting* is a sort of intermediary state, where the current entities on which the tool works remain the same (similar to *Frozen*), but when new entities pass on the bus(es), the tool looks for them in its "frozen" display and highlight them if they are present (they are ignored otherwise). This is useful to highlight a new result in the context of a preceding result that was already displayed in the tool.

## 4.4   Specialized Reusable Tools

On top of the modular meta-model (Sect. 3) and infrastructure tools (Sect. 4.2), MODMOOSE offers some specialized tools that answer different recurring needs in software analysis.

There is a number of reusable tools already implemented, among which:

**Model Browser:** Imports or creates new models of given software systems, selects a model, and browses the model entities. It outputs the selected model. This is the entry point for working with the environment.

**Entity Inspector:** Lists all properties of a selected entity and their values (such as metrics, tags and others). If the input is a group of entities, it lists all their common properties. It allows navigating the model when the value of

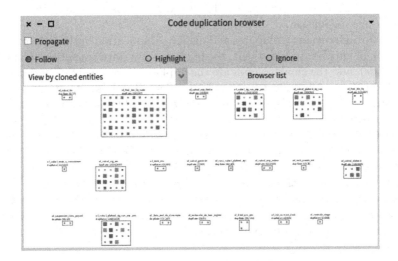

**Fig. 4.** MODMOOSE example of specialized tools: Duplication browser.

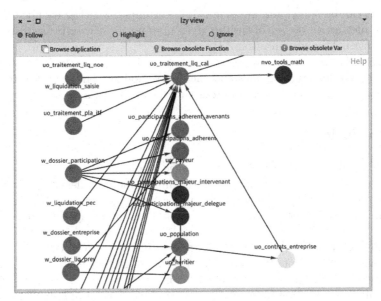

**Fig. 5.** MODMOOSE example of specialized tools: Call graph browser.

a property is another entity (*e.g.,* the methods property of a Class). It outputs any entity selected for navigation.

**Query Browser:** Offers a graphical interface to the Query module (Sect. 4.2). It works on the entities found on the bus(es) and can filter and/or navigate from these entities. It outputs the result of the queries.

**Dependency Graph Browser:** Shows as a graph all direct incoming and outgoing dependencies of a group of entities (see Fig. 5, right). Entities are selectable and are written on the bus for other tools to read them allowing interactive navigation.

**Duplication Browser:** Computes and displays duplication in the source code of a group of entities. In Fig. 4, left, the big boxes are software entities (typically methods), and the small squares are the duplication fragments found in them. Each duplication fragment has a color to identify it in all its occurrences (in the various software entities). Entities are selectable and can be output on the bus(es).

**Source Code:** Displays the source code of an input entity. If there are several entities in input or an entity with no source code (a model for example), does not do anything. Currently produces no output.

**Logger:** Records all entities (individually or in a group) that pass on a bus. It lets the user come back to a previous stage by selecting the entities that were produced at that stage. It can export entities in files (txt, csv). It outputs any selected entity or group of entities.

### 4.5   Creating a New Tool

New tools can be added and are planned, for example, a metric dashboard with standard metrics on the set of entities given in input, or new software maps such a Distribution Map visualisation [11].

Since tools are specialized, they are easy to develop, particularly with the help of the visualization engines and the query module. The open architecture with the buses makes the integration of new tools smooth and easy.

## 5   Conclusion

From literature and our industrial experience, we identified key aspects that a program comprehension environment must fulfill: a meta-model easily extensible and adaptable to represent new programming languages or sources of information; interoperating tools that can be adapted to the comprehension task at hand.

In this paper, we presented the new architecture of MODMOOSE, our reverse engineering environment. It is first based on FAMIXNG a new way to express meta-models by composing new entities from a set of traits, each describing individual properties that are generally encountered in programming languages. We developed *infrastructure* tools to manipulate models and an architecture with specialized end-user tools that interact through information buses.

This is not the end of the road. We will complete our tool suite to respond to other aspects of reverse engineering and re-engineering. Two research directions are drawing our attention: (1) how to more easily develop importers for new programming languages; (2) how to generate new code from the models in any programming language for which we have a meta-model.

# References

1. Anquetil, N., de Oliveira, K.M., de Sousa, K.D., Batista Dias, M.G.: Software maintenance seen as a knowledge management issue. Inf. Softw. Technol. **49**(5), 515–529 (2007)
2. Anquetil, N., Etien, A., Andreo, G., Ducasse, S.: Decomposing God Classes at Siemens (2019)
3. Bellay, B., Gall, H.: An evaluation of reverse engineering tools. J. Softw. Maintenance Res. Pract. (1998)
4. Bergel, A.: Agile Visualization. LULU Press (2016)
5. Bragagnolo, S., Anquetil, N., Ducasse, S., Abderrahmane, S., Derras, M.: Analysing microsoft access projects: building a model in a partially observable domain. In: International Conference on Software and Systems Reuse, ICSR2020, Dec 2020. in submission
6. Bruneliere, H., Cabot, J., Dupé, G., Madiot, F.: Modisco: a model driven reverse engineering framework. Inf. Softw. Technol. **56**(8), 1012–1032 (2014)
7. Delplanque, J., Etien, A., Anquetil, N., Ducasse, S.: Recommendations for evolving relational databases. In: Dustdar, S., Yu, E., Salinesi, C., Rieu, D., Pant, V. (eds.) CAiSE 2020. LNCS, vol. 12127, pp. 498–514. Springer, Cham (2020). https://doi.org/10.1007/978-3-030-49435-3_31
8. Demeyer, S., Ducasse, S., Nierstrasz, O.: Object-Oriented Reengineering Patterns. Morgan Kaufmann (2002)
9. Demeyer, S., Ducasse, S., Tichelaar, S.: Why unified is not universal. In: France, R., Rumpe, B. (eds.) UML 1999. LNCS, vol. 1723, pp. 630–644. Springer, Heidelberg (1999). https://doi.org/10.1007/3-540-46852-8_44
10. Demeyer, S., Tichelaar, S., Ducasse, S.: FAMIX 2.1 – The FAMOOS Information Exchange Model. Technical report, University of Bern (2001)
11. Ducasse, S., Gîrba, T., Kuhn, A.: Distribution map. In: Proceedings of 22nd IEEE International Conference on Software Maintenance, ICSM 2006, pp. 203–212, Los Alamitos CA, IEEE Computer Society (2006)
12. Egyed, A., Medvidovic, N.: A formal approach to heterogeneous software modeling. In: Maibaum, T. (ed.) FASE 2000. LNCS, vol. 1783, pp. 178–192. Springer, Heidelberg (2000). https://doi.org/10.1007/3-540-46428-X_13
13. Govin, B., Anquetil, N., Etien, A., Ducasse, S., Monegier Du Sorbier, A.: Managing an industrial software rearchitecting project with source code labelling. In: Complex Systems Design & Management Conference (CSD&M), Paris, France, December 2017
14. Kienle, H.M., Müller, H.A.: The tools perspective on software reverse engineering: requirements, construction, and evaluation. In: Advanced in Computers, vol. 79, pp. 189–290. Elsevier (2010)
15. Larcheveque, G., Bhatti, U., Anquetil, N., Ducasse, S.: Telescope: a high-level model to build dynamic visualizations. In: International Workshop on Smalltalk Technologies (IWST 2015) (2015)

16. Laval, J., Denier, S., Ducasse, S., Falleri, J.-R.: Supporting simultaneous versions for software evolution assessment. J. Sci. Comput. Program. (SCP) **76**(12), 1177–1193 (2011)
17. Lethbridge, T., Tichelaar, S., Plödereder, E.: The dagstuhl middle metamodel: a schema for reverse engineering. Electron. Notes Theor. Comput. Sci. **94**, 7–18 (2004)
18. Lyons, D.M., Bogar, A.M., Baird, D.: Lightweight multilingual software analysis. Challenges and Opportunities in ICT Research Projects (2018)
19. Mayer, P.: A taxonomy of cross-language linking mechanisms in open source frameworks. Computing **99**(7), 701–724 (2016). https://doi.org/10.1007/s00607-016-0528-3
20. Nierstrasz, O., Ducasse, S., Gîrba, T.: The story of Moose: an agile reengineering environment. In: Wermelinger, M., Gall, H. (eds.) Proceedings of the European Software Engineering Conference, ESEC/FSE 2005, pp. 1–10. ACM Press, New York (2005). Invited paper
21. Shatnawi, A., et al.: Static Code Analysis of Multilanguage Software Systems, June 2019. arXiv: 1906.00815
22. Tesone, P., Ducasse, S., Polito, G., Fabresse, L., Bouraqadi, N.: A new modular implementation for stateful traits. Science of Computer Programming (2020)
23. Verhaeghe, B., et al.: GUI migration using MDE from GWT to Angular 6: an industrial case. In: 2019 IEEE 26th International Conference on Software Analysis, Evolution and Reengineering (SANER) (2019)
24. Washizaki, H., Gueheneuc, Y.-G., Khomh, F.: A taxonomy for program metamodels in program reverse engineering. In: 2016 IEEE International Conference on Software Maintenance and Evolution (ICSME), pp. 44–55, IEEE, Raleigh, NC, USA, October 201

# DeepClone: Modeling Clones to Generate Code Predictions

Muhammad Hammad[1(✉)], Önder Babur[1], Hamid Abdul Basit[2],
and Mark van den Brand[1]

[1] Eindhoven University of Technology, Eindhoven, Netherlands
{m.hammad,o.babur,m.g.j.v.d.brand}@tue.nl
[2] Prince Sultan University, Riyadh, Saudi Arabia
hbasit@psu.edu.sa

**Abstract.** Programmers often reuse code from source code repositories to reduce the development effort. Code clones are candidates for reuse in exploratory or rapid development, as they represent often repeated functionality in software systems. To facilitate code clone reuse, we propose *DeepClone*, a novel approach utilizing a deep learning algorithm for modeling code clones to predict the next set of tokens (possibly a complete clone method body) based on the code written so far. The predicted tokens require minimal customization to fit the context. Deep-Clone applies natural language processing techniques to learn from a large code corpus, and generates code tokens using the model learned. We have quantitatively evaluated our solution to assess (1) our model's quality and its accuracy in token prediction, and (2) its performance and effectiveness in clone method prediction. We also discuss various application scenarios for our approach.

**Keywords:** Language modeling · Deep learning · Code clone · Code prediction

## 1 Introduction

Writing new code is an expensive activity, consuming considerable time and effort. Developers frequently perform adhoc code reuse, searching for code snippets over the web or in some codebase, followed by judicious copying and pasting [7]. Features like code snippet search, code prediction, code auto-completion and code generation can help developers to write code quickly and easily. Lately, language modeling have been effectively employed for these tasks [15,17,27].

A Language Model (LM) estimates the likelihood of sequences of tokens based on a training dataset, by assigning probabilities to tokens (words, subwords, or punctuation marks) or character sequences (sentences or words occurring after a given sequence [15]). Shannon first used language modeling [19] to predict the next element following some given English text. Since then, several language models have been developed to perform different tasks. Various statistical and

© Springer Nature Switzerland AG 2020
S. Ben Sassi et al. (Eds.): ICSR 2020, LNCS 12541, pp. 135–151, 2020.
https://doi.org/10.1007/978-3-030-64694-3_9

Deep Neural Networks (DNN) based techniques for language modeling have been applied to natural languages. These techniques are also applicable to programming languages [2,4,10,24].

DNN techniques are powerful machine learning models that perform well in language modeling for source code, outperforming statistical language modeling techniques [15]. Performance of DNN techniques improves automatically through experience by learning data patterns; their power arising from the ability to perform parallel computations for a large number of training steps. LMs constructed using DNNs are called Neural Language Models (NLM), which have been used for various software development tasks like code completion [15,27] and code clone detection [24] etc.

One common application of language modeling is code prediction [2,4] - a technique for predicting next likely token(s) on the basis of user input (i.e., code written so far), by learning the source code features. These code predictions have a fixed threshold for the length of generated token sequence. In this work, we show how clone methods of arbitrary length, extracted from a large code repository, can enhance regular code generation and prediction applications.

Code clones are repeated patterns in code, usually created with the copy-paste adhoc reuse practice. Around 5 to 50% of the code in software applications can be contained in clones [18]. Clones are generally considered harmful, and several techniques exists for avoiding and eliminating them [8]. However, clones can be useful in certain software development scenarios [14], one of them being exploratory development where the rapid development of a feature is required, and the remedial unification of newly generated clone is not clearly justified. Also, a piece of cloned code is expected to be more stable and poses less risk than new development.

We believe that clone methods, together with the non-cloned code, can be a useful component of a LM, as they represent commonly used functionality, and can be used for code prediction and completion. In this work, we exploit the re-usability aspect of code clones to build a NLM for predicting code tokens up-to the level of method granularity. We believe that our approach can help in improving the quality of code prediction by also predicting complete method bodies of arbitrary length based on clone methods. In this work, we have made the following contributions:

1. We present a novel approach for code prediction by explicitly modeling code clones along with non-cloned code.
2. Our approach can generate code predictions of complete method body of arbitrary length on the basis of user input.
3. We have quantitatively evaluated our approach using the BigCloneBench dataset, in terms of model quality and performance in various tasks including token prediction, and clone method prediction.

## 2   Related Work

To the best of our knowledge, no previous techniques has modeled code clones together with non-cloned code for predicting code tokens up-to the complete method granularity. However, many techniques have explored language modeling for token prediction, code suggestions or code completion. White et al. [25] applied Recurrent Neural Network (RNN) to model Java source code for code prediction. Bold [4] modeled Java language method statements and English language datasets by using Long Short Term Memory (LSTM). He compared the performance of next token prediction task with each other, arguing that method statements highly resemble English language sentences and are comparable to each other. Hellendoorn and Devanbu [10] noticed that source code NLMs underperform due to the unlimited vocabulary size as new identifiers keep coming with higher rates, and limiting vocabulary is not a good solution for NLMs. They proposed a nested scope, dynamically updatable, unlimited vocabulary count-based n-gram model, which outperforms the LSTM model on the task of token prediction. In contrast, Karampatsis et al. [15] solved the issue of unlimited vocabulary size by applying byte-pair encoding (BPE) technique in modeling the code. They compared the performance of n-gram and Gated Recurrent Unit (GRU) language models trained on source code datasets, and demonstrated that NLM trained on GRU can outperform n-gram statistical models on code completion and bug detection tasks if BPE technique is applied. Zhong et al. [27] applied the LSTM model with sparse point network to build a language model for JavaScript code suggestion. Deep TabNine[1] is a recently developed software programming productivity tool, successfully fine-tuned by using GPT-2 on approximately two million GitHub files capturing numerous programming languages, to predict the next chunk of code.

## 3    BigCloneBench for Code Clones

BigCloneBench [20, 21] is the largest clone benchmark dataset, consisting of over 8 million manually validated clone method pairs in IJaDataset 2.0[2]- a large Java repository of 2.3 million source files (365 MLOC) from 25,000 open-source projects. BigCloneBench contains references to clones with both syntactic and semantic similarities. It contains the references of starting and ending lines of method clones existing in the code repository. In forming this benchmark, methods that potentially implement a given common functionality were identified using pattern based heuristics. These methods were manually tagged as true or false positives of the target functionality by judges. All true positives of a functionality were grouped as a clone class, where a clone class of size $n$ contains $\frac{n(n-1)}{2}$ clone pairs. The clone types and similarity of these clone pairs were later identified in a post-processing step. Currently, BigCloneBench contains clones corresponding to 43 distinct functionalities. Further details can be found in the relevant publications [20, 21].

---

[1] https://tabnine.com/blog/deep.
[2] https://sites.google.com/site/asegsecold/projects/seclone.

### 3.1   Dataset Preparation

We are using a reduced version of IJaDataset containing only the source files whose clone method references exist in BigCloneBench [20,21]. The dataset is distributed into a number of smaller subsets, on the basis of 43 distinct functionalities.

   We have performed several pre-processing steps to build our mutually exclusive training, testing, and validation datasets. First, we filtered IJaDataset files, keeping those which have references of true positive clone methods and discarding false positive clone references in BigCloneBench dataset (*Filtering*). Next, we distributed the set of files into training, validation, and testing datasets (*Distribution*). We adopted stratified sampling [22] to ensure that all types of clone methods appear in training, validation, and testing datasets. We distributed the set of files in each functionality folder into portions as per the following ratio: 80% training, 10% validation, and 10% testing. Then, we copied those files from original distribution to three separate folders such as training, validation, and testing. If any of the file already exist in one of those folders, we discarded it to avoid exact duplication [1]. Tables A5[3] and 3 show the statistics of our datasets. Next, we marked the clone methods in the IJaDataset files by placing the meta-token $\langle soc \rangle$ at the start, and $\langle eoc \rangle$ at the end (*Marking*). We normalized our code by removing whitespaces, extra lines, comments (*Normalization*), and tokenized it by adapting Java 8 parser from Javalang[4] Python library. We also replaced integer, float, binary, and hexadecimal constant values with the $\langle num\_val \rangle$ meta-token (*Replacement*). Similarly, string and character values were replaced with $\langle str\_val \rangle$. This reduced our vocabulary size, leading to faster training of the model [15,25]. Finally, we merged all the tokenized data from the training, validation and testing files into three text files, i.e. train.txt, valid.txt, and test.txt (*Merging*). Table A4 demonstrates the pre-processing steps on an example of binary search clone method, while Table 3 gives an overview of our experimental dataset.

## 4    Neural Language Models for Code Clones

A number of techniques were available for developing a LM for BigCloneBench dataset such as n-gram [10], LSTM [12], GRU [5], GPT-2 [17]; as well as parameter settings for training those models. We could not evaluate all the possible combinations (hundreds) and especially very large scale models/training due to the resource limitations. We selected GRU [5] and GPT-2 [17] as they have been reported to outperform other comparable models with recommended configurations. In the following sections we describe the two models.

---

[3] Tables A1, A2, A3, A4 and A5 can be accessible through link https://www.win.tue.nl/~mhammad/deepclone.html.

[4] https://github.com/c2nes/javalang.

## 4.1 Gated Recurrent Units (GRU)

Gated recurrent units (GRUs) are a gating mechanism in RNNs [5], which is similar to LSTM [12] but has a forget gate and fewer parameters as it lacks an output gate. However, it is known to perform better than LSTM on certain tasks. To prepare our dataset (Sect. 3.1), we applied the recently proposed configuration settings for GRU deep learning model by Karampatsis et al. [15], which outperforms n-gram models on code completion and bug detection tasks. They used byte-pair encoding (BPE) technique to solve the unlimited vocabulary problem [2]. This problem makes it infeasible to train LMs on large corpora. BPE is an algorithm originally designed for data compression, in which bytes that are not used in the data replace the most frequently occurring byte pairs or sequences [6]. BPE starts by splitting all the words in characters. The initial vocabulary contains all the characters in the data set and a special end-of word symbol @@, and the corpus is split into characters plus @@. Then, it finds the most common pair of successive items in the corpus (initially characters, then tokens). This pair is merged in a new token which is added to the vocabulary; all occurrences of the pair are replaced with the new token. The process is repeated n times, which is called a merge operation (MO). We applied static settings with a large training set (50 epochs, 64 mini-batch size) and chose 10000 BPE MOs as it performs better than other BPE MOs such as 2000 and 5000. Static settings have been used to train a model on a fixed training corpus, and later evaluated on a separate test dataset. To train the LM, we first learned encoding by using the training set with the help of subword library[5]. Then, we segmented the training, validation, and test sets using the learned encoding, and applied the MOs from BPE to merge the characters into subword units in the vocabulary.

## 4.2 Generative Pretrained Transformer 2 (GPT-2)

OpenAI developed a large-scale unsupervised LM called GPT-2 (Generative Pre-trained Transformer 2) [17] to generate several sound sentences of realistic text by extending any given seed. GPT-2 is a large transformer-based LM with 1.5 billion parameters, trained on a dataset of 8 million web pages. GPT-2 is trained with a simple objective: predict the next word, given all of the previous words within some text. We focus on fine-tuning a GPT-2 transformer [17] pre-trained model for generating code clones, even though it has been trained on English language. We applied fine-tunning of a pre-trained model on IJaDataset - a Java language dataset - as there exists a large amount of overlapping vocabulary with English language. GPT-2 transformer has demonstrated impressive effectiveness of pre-trained LMs on various tasks including high quality text generation, question answering, reading comprehension, summarization, and translation [17].

GPT-2 also has built in BPE tokenizer. We selected a small version of GPT2 (GPT2-117) as our base model, as it does not take too much time and resources to fine-tune, and is enough to evaluate our approach. The GPT2-117 [17] pre-trained model has vocabulary size of 50257, 117M parameters, 12-hidden layers,

---

[5] https://github.com/rsennrich/subword-nmt

768-hidden states, and 12-attention heads. We have fine-tuned our GPT-2 based model on the partition of a GPU-1080Ti cluster (276 CPU cores, 329728 CUDA cores, 5.9 TB memory)[6] for approximately 9 hours by using HuggingFace Transformer Library. In our experiment, we have performed training and evaluation with batch size per GPU of 1 for 5 epochs. We have used a learning rate of 5e-5 and the gradient accumulation steps (number of update steps to accumulate before performing a backward/update pass) as 5. Default values have been used for other hyper-parameters, as mentioned in the language modeling code[7].

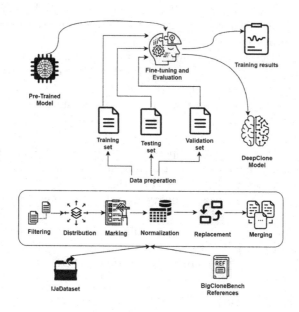

**Fig. 1.** DeepClone training process

## 5     Comparative Evaluation: GRU Vs GPT-2 Based Models

We perform both intrinsic and extrinsic evaluations of GRU and GPT-2 based models to compare their performance. We calculate the perplexity scores (as done in related work [25,26]) to measure the quality of models (i.e. intrinsic evaluation), which is an inverse of cross-entropy (as used in [10,15]). Perplexity is a measurement of how well a given LM predicts sample data. It estimates the average number of code tokens to select from at each point in a sequence [2]. It is

---

[6] https://userinfo.surfsara.nl/.

[7] https://github.com/huggingface/transformers/blob/master/examples/language-modeling.

a natural evaluation metric for LMs, which represent a probability distribution over a subsequence or an entire dataset (Eq. 1):

$$P(L) = exp(-\frac{1}{M} \sum_{i}^{M} \log P(t_i|t_0 : t_{i-1}))  \tag{1}$$

$P(t_i|t_0 : t_{i-1})$ is the conditional probability assigned by the model to the token $t$ at index $i$. By applying *log* of conditional probability, cross-entropy loss is calculated. $M$ refers to the length of tokens. Hence, perplexity is an exponentiation of the average cross entropy loss from each token $[0, M]$. We calculate the perplexity on the validation set (**P1**) and the testing set (**P2**) for GRU and GPT-2 based models, which clearly displays that the GPT-2 based model outperforms the other by a large margin (Table 1).

We further measure the performance of both models on specific tasks such as token prediction (i.e. extrinsic evaluation). Given a number of code sequences as input, we collect the top 10 predictions from GRU and GPT-2 based models, and compute the top-k accuracy (the fraction of times the correct prediction appears in the top k predictions) for k $\in$ [1, 10]. Moreover, we measure the Mean Reciprocal Rank (MRR) scores of both language models (LM), which has been used by many researchers for evaluating code prediction such as [10, 15]. For each prediction done by the LM, we collect a ranked list of 10 predictions. For each of those lists, the reciprocal rank corresponds to the multiplicative inverse of the rank of the first correct answer. MRR in turn is the average of reciprocal ranks for all the input sequences used in the evaluation.

Table 1 shows the top-k accuracies as well as the MRR scores. Clearly, the results suggest that the GPT-2 based model performs more accurately compared to the GRU based model on pre-processed Java source code containing clone methods. The table also indicates that there is almost 77.808% chance to get a correct token in the first option, and 94.999% chance to have a correct output in the top-10 predicted outcomes for GPT-2 based model. To further quantify the accuracy of our models for token prediction task, we report an MRR score of 83%, which indicates an excellent performance in evaluating a ranked list of predictions for GPT-2 based model. As GPT-2 based model gives us highest performance in terms of perplexity on validation set (**P1**) and test set (**P2**), MRR, and top-k accuracy, we continue with that model for the rest of paper, named it as DeepClone model for further evaluation.

**Table 1.** Comparative evaluation results for GPT-2 and GRU models

| Model | Perplexities | | Accuracies | | | | |
|-------|-----------------|-----------|---------|--------|----------|---------|---------|
|       | Validation (P1) | Test (P2) | MRR     | Top 1  | Top 3    | Top 5   | Top 10  |
| GPT-2 | 2.145           | 2.146     | 84.329% | 77.808% | 90.040% | 92.766% | 94.999% |
| GRU   | 13.92           | 13.86     | 73.507% | 66.948% | 79.0715% | 82.02%  | 84.787% |

# 6   Further Evaluation of DeepClone Model

In this section we describe further evaluations of DeepClone on additional aspects of the model.

**Training Evaluation.** At each checkpoint (the 500th logging step) of the training steps, we evaluate DeepClone model performance by calculating the perplexity on the validation set. Figure 2(a) describes the variations in perplexity on the validation set after each checkpoint. We observe that we achieve lowest perplexity **P1** (2.145) at step 24500. Figure 2(c) displays the convergence of the learning rate after each checkpoint. Learning rate helps in determining how quickly a neural network model learns a problem by adjusting the weights of a network with respect to the value of loss function. Another measure called loss function calculates a model error, which identifies how well a model predicts the expected outcome for any data point in the training set. GPT-2 uses cross-entropy loss function, which is to measure the performance of a LM whose output is a probability value between 0 and 1. Figure 2(b) displays a convergence of training losses after each checkpoint, which indicates how well the model behaves after each checkpoint of optimization. The loss value is finally minimized to 0.75 at step 24500, which is a sign of a well optimized deep learning model. Figure 1 describes the training process of the GPT-2 based model, which mentions the steps described in Sect. 3 that are used to perform the fine-tuning of our model. All these numbers imply a successful training and an accurate model. We have published our training results online[8].

(a) Perplexity over the validation dataset

(b) Training average losses

(c) Convergence of the learning rate

**Fig. 2.** Training graphs

**The Effect of Using Clone Markers.** Besides the overall perplexity on the testing dataset (**P2**), we re-calculate the perplexity using the testing dataset but without the clone method markers (i.e. $\langle soc \rangle$ and $\langle eoc \rangle$). The motivation for this

---

[8] https://tensorboard.dev/experiment/tk1XqDi8RMqtrMjmVyQ9Sg.

additional measurement is as follows. Hindle et al. [11] observed that due to the repetitive nature of the code, there exist predictable statistical properties, which n-gram language models can capture and leverage for software engineering tasks. The sign of a good model is that it can capture the patterns in the dataset very well, which is particularly important for the task of clone method prediction. In Table 1, we can see an increase (3.6%) when comparing the original perplexity score of 2.146 (**P2**) and the perplexity on the test dataset without clone markers of 2.182 (**P3** see Table 4), showing that DeepClone performs better when the code has marked clone methods.

**Evaluation per Clone Method.** In order to determine which clone method snippets are more predictable compared to the others, we calculate average perplexity score ($\overline{PPL}$) for each functionality type (see Table A5). We first extract the code snippet for each type of clone method for our testing dataset, and calculate the perplexity score. The scores, as depicted in Table A5, indicate how likely these can be predicted by DeepClone model. We also analyze several factors which can affect the perplexity of clone methods. BigCloneBench contains syntactic similarity scores for each clone method pair on the basis of tokens, calculated by using a line-based metric after normalization. We calculated the mean ($\mu$) and variance ($\sigma^2$) values to determine the overall syntactic similarity of all the clone methods per each type of functionality, as listed in Table A5.

We observe that the perplexity scores vary according to the syntactic similarity between clone methods, as well as the number of clone method snippets in the training set. From the results, we can see that the "Test palindrome" type of clone method (number 44), which is used to test if a string is a palindrome, has the lowest perplexity score. It's thus well predicted by DeepClone. We attribute this to the high mean syntactic similarity ($0.903 \pm 0.040$) among those types of clone methods, and the relatively small number of snippets (133) used in training. Too few number of snippets in the training may lead to (a) high perplexities and low predictability e.g. for "GCD" (number 26) to find the greatest common denominator and (b) no evaluation performed for "Decompress zip archive" clone method (number 5). Note that factors beside syntactical similarity and number of clone methods in the training set can also affect the perplexity score. In BigCloneBench, there are many false positive clone methods and other non-clone code snippets, which may be syntactically similar to true positive clone methods. Other factors such as clone types and hyper-parameters for GPT-2 are left to be explored in future work.

**Non-Clone Methods Vs Clone Methods.** Allamanis [1] noticed that a language model achieves low perplexity scores for code duplication, and high perplexity score for less duplicated code. In order to observe that difference, we calculated the perplexity scores for all the clone method snippets and non-clone method snippets in the testing dataset. We extracted clone method snippets by tracing the tokens, which come inclusively between $\langle$soc $\rangle$ and $\langle$eoc $\rangle$ tokens. All other snippets were considered to be a part of non-cloned code. We then calculate the perplexity for each snippet. Finally, we take an average of the perplexities for both type of code snippets. Table 4, **P4** represents the average perplexity score for the clone method snippets, and **P5** represents the average perplexity of the non-cloned method snippets. We performed one-tailed Wilcoxon rank sum test to statistically compare **P4** with **P5**, which indicates that P4 is indeed less than P5 ($p< 0.001$). This shows that DeepClone correctly predicts clone method snippets much better than non-cloned snippets in general.

**Performance on Other Datasets.** To evaluate the performance of DeepClone on another Java dataset, we use Allamanis et al.'s corpus [2] that contains over 14 thousand popular Java projects from Github. For base-lining, we focus only on 38 test projects that have been used in previous studies [10,15]. We follow the same steps for dataset preparation as mentioned in Sect. 3.1, i.e., normalization, replacement, and merging. The dataset does not contain clone markers as no corresponding clones reference benchmark is available. As the main purpose of clone markers is to help in predicting clone methods, so it will not severely affect the results of predicting next tokens, as also noticed in Sect. 6. On this dataset, we achieve a perplexity of 2.996 (**P6**) equivalent to 1.097 as cross-entropy. We further calculate other accuracy measures like MRR (81.523%), top-1 (74.416%), top-3 (87.613%), top-5 (90.704%), and top-10 (93.152%). These results (see Table 2) outperform the static settings of previous studies [10,15]. This indicates that DeepClone model is perfectly fine-tuned with GPT-2 over Java corpus in general, and it contains an excessive amount of overlapping vocabulary with Allamanis et al.'s [2] selected corpus.

**Table 2.** Performance of Allamanis et al.'s [2] dataset on different models

| Model | Settings | Cross-Entropy | MRR |
|---|---|---|---|
| LSTM/300 [10] | Static | 3.22 | 66.1% |
| LSTM/650 [10] | Static | 3.03 | 67.9% |
| BPE NLM (512) [15] | BPE 10000, Static, Small train | 4.77 | 63.75% |
| DeepClone | Sect. 4.2 | 1.097 | 81.523% |

# 7   Clone Method Prediction

In this section, we demonstrate how clone methods can be predicted from Deep-Clone model on the basis of user context. Furthermore, we measure its various aspects like rapid development and quality.

## 7.1  Experimental Design

For predicting a clone method based on the user context, there exist several text generation methods such as beam search [23] and nucleus sampling [13]. All these methods have a specific decoding strategy to shape the probability distribution of LM with higher probabilities assigned to higher quality texts. We selected nucleus sampling as it is claimed to be best the strategy for generating large amount of high quality text, comparable to human written text [13]. By using a fine-tuned model and nucleus sampling, we can expect a coherent set of code tokens for clone method prediction. Holtzman et al. [13] have also achieved coherent text generation results with similar settings.

We performed a small scale (100 context queries) experiment to predict next token subsequences by choosing different subsequence sizes of 10, 20, 30, 50, and 100 tokens. Among these, subsequences with size 20 gave us the best results in terms of top-k accuracy and MRR. We extracted subsequences of 20 tokens from the testing dataset, and moved the sliding window one step ahead to obtain further subsequences. From these we randomly selected 735 subsequences containing a total of 14,700 tokens, in which $\langle soc \rangle$ token is a part of each subsequence, indicating a start of clone method. We passed these one by one to DeepClone model, and kept on predicting new tokens with nucleus sampling (threshold value 0.95) until the meta-token $\langle eoc \rangle$ (i.e. end of clone) appeared. We used the text generation script[9] of HuggingFace Transformer Library in this case. Note that certain parameters, e.g. the number of subsequences and size of tokens per subsequence are chosen to perform a preliminary evaluation, to be fine-tuned and optimized in a follow-up study. The focus of this paper is to demonstrate the feasibility of our methodology for predicting clone methods. We have mentioned examples from our results in Tables (A1, A2, A3). To make the outputs readable in the tables, we have formatted the code by using the online tool[10] along with little manual editing, which we plan to automate in future.

## 7.2  Evaluation

**Rapid Development.** In this experiment, we successfully generated 92,926 tokens associated with clone methods. Given the 735 cases, this amounts to an average of ~126 tokens per case. As a comparison, other approaches [13,23] traditionally employ a threshold-based strategy of generating a certain number of code tokens up to a maximum threshold value of t. Note that t is typically a low value, e.g. 1 for simple token prediction, and 5–20 for the popular Deep TabNine auto-completer. Nevertheless, we can see that DeepClone, with the clone marking strategy, is able to outperform threshold-based strategies even with an extremely generous configuration of t = 50 or even 100. Furthermore, threshold-based strategies may not generate a set of code tokens for a complete method in a single pass, as the length of complete method varies. Marking the clone method

---

[9] https://github.com/huggingface/transformers/blob/master/examples/text-generation/run_generation.py.

[10] https://www.tutorialspoint.com/online_java_formatter.htm.

regions in the dataset helps DeepClone to generate complete methods in a single pass. We conclude DeepClone model not only helps developers to code rapidly, but also provides a coherent set of code tokens for a complete method.

**Quality.** We measured the quality of DeepClone output by using ROUGE (Recall-Oriented Understudy for Gisting Evaluation) [16]. It is designed to compare an automatically generated summary or translation against a set of reference summaries (typically human-generated). In our context, it helps us to automatically determine the quality of original DeepClone output by comparing it with the ground truth. ROUGE doesn't try to assess how fluent the clone method is. It only tries to assess the adequacy by simply counting how many n-grams in the DeepClone output match the ones in the ground truth. As ROUGE is based only on token overlap, it can determine if the same general concepts are discussed between an automatic and a reference summary, but it cannot determine if the result is coherent or the clone method is semantically correct. High-order n-gram ROUGE measures try to judge fluency to some degree.

We calculated precision (P), recall (R), and F-measure (F) of ROUGE-1 ROUGE-2, and ROUGE-L between DeepClone output and ground truth. ROUGE-1 refers to the overlap of unigrams between some reference output and the output to be evaluated. ROUGE-2, in turn, checks for bigrams instead of unigrams. The reason one would use ROUGE-1 over or in conjunction with ROUGE-2 (or other finer granularity ROUGE measures), is to also indicate fluency as part of the evaluation. The intuition is that the prediction is more fluent if it more closely follows the word orderings of the reference snippet. Finally, ROUGE-L measures longest matching sequence of tokens between machine generated text/code and human produced one by using longest common subsequence (LCS). LCS has a distinguishing advantage in evaluation: it captures in-sequence (i.e. sentence level flow and word order) matches rather than strict consecutive matches. DeepClone predicted clone method can be extremely long, capturing all tokens in the retrieved clone methods, but many of these tokens may be useless, making it unnecessarily verbose. This is where precision comes into play. It measures what portion of the DeepClone output is in fact relevant and desirable to be kept with respect to the reference output.

$$\text{Precision} = \frac{\text{\# of overlapping tokens}}{\text{total tokens in the predicted output}} \qquad (2)$$

Recall in the context of ROUGE measures what portion of the reference output was successfully captured by the DeepClone output.

$$\text{Recall} = \frac{\text{\# of overlapping tokens}}{\text{total \# tokens in reference snippet}} \qquad (3)$$

We also report the F-measure which provides a single score that balances both the concerns of precision and recall.

$$\text{F-Measure} = 2 * \frac{\text{Precision * Recall}}{\text{Precision + Recall}} \tag{4}$$

We have measured different ROUGE scores, i.e. ROUGE-1, ROUGE-2, and ROUGE-L, to evaluate the similarity (and the quality to a certain extent) of the DeepClone output to ground truth. In this step, we extract only the tokens between $\langle soc \rangle$ and $\langle eoc \rangle$ (inclusive) from the DeepClone output and ground truth (see Tables A1, A2, and A3). We observe quite reasonable scores for ROUGE-1 and ROUGE-L against ROUGE-2 (Table 5). This depicts that the DeepClone output contains reasonably well overlap of uni-grams and longest sequence matches of tokens with the ground truth compared to bi-grams.

In our qualitative investigation, we experienced two different scenarios based on the input context. The first one is when the context contains the method name. It is straightforward for the neural language technique to generate the predicted clone method following the given method name and current context. Table A1 gives an example of this scenario, where "transpose" method name is mentioned in the context and our approach predicts the clone method, whose functionality type matches the ground truth. The second scenario is based on the context that does not contain a method name. This can have two different output sub-scenarios. The first one is when the functionality type of the ground truth do not match. As we see in Table A3, the context does not have the full signature of the clone method. This makes the generated output by DeepClone using nucleus sampling deviate from the functionality type of the ground truth. Ground truth belongs to "copy file" functionality, while DeepClone output belongs to "delete directory", which eventually leads to low and largely deviating ROUGE scores between the DeepClone output and the ground truth (see Table  5 and the example in Table A3. These clone methods may or may not fulfil the desired goal of the user. So, it might be useful to guide the users to include the clone method name in the context for better results. The other output sub-scenario is when we manage to successfully generate DeepClone output whose functionality type matches with the ground truth. In Table A2, "copy file" method name is not mentioned in the context, but the functionality type of the DeepClone output matches with the ground truth. We notice that the total number of "copy file" clone methods used in DeepClone training are 2,454, which allows nucleus sampling to generate DeepClone output closer to ground truth in example A2. Overall, we believe our approach yields good results and can assist the developers by correctly predicting clone methods in different scenarios.

## 8   Discussion

Our approach leads to promising results. The performance metrics in the training (learning rate approaching 0, minimized loss) and validation (perplexity of 2.145) phases all indicate a fine-tuned model. The series of calculated perplexity scores allow us to conclude that DeepClone model can predict regularities successfully

**Table 3.** Final Distribution of Big-CloneBench Dataset

|            | Files  | Clone Methods | Tokens     |
|------------|--------|---------------|------------|
| Training   | 9,606  | 11,991        | 16,933,894 |
| Validation | 1,208  | 1,499         | 2,130,360  |
| Testing    | 1,234  | 1,502         | 2,235,982  |
| Total      | 12,048 | 14,992        | 21,300,236 |

**Table 4.** Perplexities

| P3    | P4    | P5    | P6    |
|-------|-------|-------|-------|
| 2.182 | 2.410 | 2.767 | 2.996 |

**Table 5.** Empirical evaluation results between DeepClone output and ground truth

| ROUGE-1   |                   |
|-----------|-------------------|
| Precision | 0.667 ± 0.192     |
| Recall    | 0.559 ± 0.226     |
| F-measure | 0.56 ± 0.185      |
| ROUGE-2   |                   |
| Precision | 0.479 ± 0.217     |
| Recall    | 0.398 ± 0.218     |
| F-measure | 0.4 ± 0.202       |
| ROUGE-L   |                   |
| Precision | 0.652 ± 0.165     |
| Recall    | 0.586 ± 0.183     |
| F-measure | 0.599 ± 0.153     |

in terms of clone markers, including the code in general and the individual clone snippets in particular. The extrinsic evaluation reveals that we achieve high accuracy, notably 95% in the top 10 suggestions, as well as larger number of tokens than a threshold-based strategy even with a generous threshold of 100. With a high quality and accurate model as the foundation, we next discuss the potential use cases to exploit our model, as well as the limitations to our work.

**Use Cases for DeepClone.** DeepClone model can be utilized to assist developers in various scenarios. Some of these have already been mentioned above: predicting the next token (as typically done by many LMs) or the complete clone method body. The latter, while seemingly straightforward, can be enhanced with a more elaborate ranking and retrieval mechanism rather than simply generating the most likely sequence of tokens one after another. For that purpose, the additional information in BigCloneBench, including the exact clone method clusters (methods representing the same functionality), clone types, and so on can be exploited. Another use case might involve clone refactoring (and avoidance), by recommending extract method refactoring instead of predicting a complete clone method snippet. In combination with some additional code transformations, the clone methods can be converted to reusable assets (e.g. in the form of libraries). The model can also be used to perform code search for common functionalities.

**Limitations and Threats to Validity.** Our approach is the first step for code prediction that raises the granularity level to complete methods. However, we cannot expect exactly the same clone method being predicted or completed as the one used in training by DeepClone model. In prediction tasks, generating well-formed outputs is challenging, which is well-known in natural language generation [9]. The desired output might be a variation of another, previously observed sample [9], due to the probabilistic nature of the LM; the space of possible clone methods that could be generated grows exponentially with the length of the clone methods. An extension of the current work would involve displaying the most similar cloned methods (as is) from the dataset to the user.

Some limitations originate from the selected dataset. BigCloneBench only contains clone references of methods for the 43 common functionalities, i.e. not all the clones are marked in the dataset. Although it is enough to validate our methodology, modeling all the clones might result in more interesting findings. Although BigCloneBench is a well-known dataset, it does not necessarily represent Java language source code entirely (a threat to external validity).

In our study, we relied on the HuggingFace transformer implementation of GPT-2 to train and evaluate DeepClone model. While GPT-2 is a reliable architecture used in many NLP experiments [17], HuggingFace transformer implementation is still an emerging project. However, our results and trends are aligned with those obtained in the field of NLP. Hence, we are positive that the results are reliable. As for the clone method prediction, we have only used nucleus sampling. Other techniques such as beam search can also be explored.

## 9   Conclusion and Future Work

In this work, we proposed DeepClone, a deep learning based cloned code language model. We have performed intrinsic and extrinsic evaluations to determine its performance in predicting clone methods. The extensive evaluation suggests that our approach significantly improves code prediction by exploiting deep learning and code clones. In future work, we plan to implement the potential use cases of this model (Sect. 8). The proposed LM can be improved by hyper-parameter optimizations, as well as by better training (e.g. on a larger dataset or larger pre-trained GPT-2 models). We also plan to investigate how to tackle different types and granularity levels of code clones such as simple clones, structural clones, file clones, and clones of other artifact types such as models [3,8].

**Acknowledgment.** Dr. Sohaib Khan (CEO at http://hazen.ai/Hazen.ai) provided valuable feedback on the experimentation. https://userinfo.surfsara.nl/SURFsara provided credits for experiments. The project is partly funded by Prince Sultan University Faculty Research Fund.

# References

1. Allamanis, M.: The adverse effects of code duplication in machine learning models of code. In: Proceedings of the 2019 ACM SIGPLAN International Symposium on New Ideas, New Paradigms, and Reflections on Programming and Software, pp. 143–153 (2019)
2. Allamanis, M., Sutton, C.: Mining source code repositories at massive scale using language modeling. In: Proceedings of the 10th Working Conference on Mining Software Repositories, pp. 207–216. IEEE Press (2013)
3. Babur, Ö., Cleophas, L., van den Brand, M.: Metamodel clone detection with SAMOS. J. Comput. Lang. **51**, 57–74 (2019)
4. Boldt, B.: Using LSTMs to model the java programming language. In: Lintas, A., Rovetta, S., Verschure, P.F.M.J., Villa, A.E.P. (eds.) ICANN 2017. LNCS, vol. 10614, pp. 268–275. Springer, Cham (2017). https://doi.org/10.1007/978-3-319-68612-7_31
5. Cho, K., et al.: Learning phrase representations using RNN encoder-decoder for statistical machine translation. arXiv preprint arXiv:1406.1078 (2014)
6. Gage, P.: A new algorithm for data compression. C Users J. **12**(2), 23–38 (1994)
7. Gharehyazie, M., Ray, B., Filkov, V.: Some from here, some from there: cross-project code reuse in github. In: 2017 IEEE/ACM 14th International Conference on Mining Software Repositories (MSR), pp. 291–301. IEEE (2017)
8. Hammad, M., Basit, H.A., Jarzabek, S., Koschke, R.: A systematic mapping study of clone visualization. Comput. Sci. Rev. **37**, 100266 (2020)
9. Hashimoto, T.B., Guu, K., Oren, Y., Liang, P.S.: A retrieve-and-edit framework for predicting structured outputs. In: Advances in Neural Information Processing Systems, pp. 10052–10062 (2018)
10. Hellendoorn, V.J., Devanbu, P.: Are deep neural networks the best choice for modeling source code? In: Proceedings of the 2017 11th Joint Meeting on Foundations of Software Engineering, pp. 763–773. ACM (2017)
11. Hindle, A., Barr, E.T., Gabel, M., Su, Z., Devanbu, P.: On the naturalness of software. Commun. ACM **59**(5), 122–131 (2016)
12. Hochreiter, S., Schmidhuber, J.: Long short-term memory. Neural Comput. **9**(8), 1735–1780 (1997)
13. Holtzman, A., Buys, J., Forbes, M., Choi, Y.: The curious case of neural text degeneration. arXiv preprint arXiv:1904.09751 (2019)
14. Kapser, C.J., Godfrey, M.W.: "cloning considered harmful" considered harmful: patterns of cloning in software. Empirical Softw. Eng. **13**(6), 645 (2008)
15. Karampatsis, R.M., Babii, H., Robbes, R., Sutton, C., Janes, A.: Big code!= big vocabulary: Open-vocabulary models for source code (2020)
16. Lin, C.Y.: Rouge: a package for automatic evaluation of summaries. In: Text Summarization Branches Out, pp. 74–81 (2004)
17. Radford, A., Wu, J., Child, R., Luan, D., Amodei, D., Sutskever, I.: Language models are unsupervised multitask learners. OpenAI Blog **1**(8), 9 (2019)
18. Roy, C.K., Cordy, J.R.: A survey on software clone detection research. Queen's School of Comput. TR **541**(115), 64–68 (2007)
19. Shannon, C.E.: Prediction and entropy of printed english. Bell Syst. Techn. J. **30**(1), 50–64 (1951)
20. Svajlenko, J., Islam, J.F., Keivanloo, I., Roy, C.K., Mia, M.M.: Towards a big data curated benchmark of inter-project code clones. In: 2014 IEEE International Conference on Software Maintenance and Evolution, pp. 476–480. IEEE (2014)

21. Svajlenko, J., Roy, C.K.: Bigcloneeval: a clone detection tool evaluation framework with bigclonebench. In: 2016 IEEE International Conference on Software Maintenance and Evolution (ICSME), pp. 596–600. IEEE (2016)

22. Trost, J.E.: Statistically nonrepresentative stratified sampling: a sampling technique for qualitative studies. Qualit. Sociol. **9**(1), 54–57 (1986)

23. Vijayakumar, A.K., et al.: Diverse beam search for improved description of complex scenes. In: Thirty-Second AAAI Conference on Artificial Intelligence (2018)

24. White, M., Tufano, M., Vendome, C., Poshyvanyk, D.: Deep learning code fragments for code clone detection. In: Proceedings of the 31st IEEE/ACM International Conference on Automated Software Engineering, pp. 87–98. ACM (2016)

25. White, M., Vendome, C., Linares-Vásquez, M., Poshyvanyk, D.: Toward deep learning software repositories. In: Proceedings of the 12th Working Conference on Mining Software Repositories, pp. 334–345. IEEE Press (2015)

26. Zaremba, W., Sutskever, I., Vinyals, O.: Recurrent neural network regularization. arXiv preprint arXiv:1409.2329 (2014)

27. Zhong, C., Yang, M., Sun, J.: Javascript code suggestion based on deep learning. In: Proceedings of the 2019 3rd International Conference on Innovation in Artificial Intelligence, pp. 145–149 (2019)

# Analysing Microsoft Access Projects: Building a Model in a Partially Observable Domain

Santiago Bragagnolo[1,2]($\boxtimes$) (ID), Nicolas Anquetil[1] (ID), Stephane Ducasse[1] (ID),
Seriai Abderrahmane[2], and Mustapha Derras[2]

[1] Université de Lille, CNRS, Inria, Centrale Lille,
UMR 9189 – CRIStAL, Lille, France
{santiago.bragagnolo,nicolas.anquetil,stephane.ducasse}@inria.fr
[2] Berger-Levrault, Paris, France
{santiago.bragagnolo,seriai.abderrahmane,
mustapha.derras}@berger-levrault.com
http://www.inria.fr

**Abstract.** Due to the technology evolution, every IT Company migrates their software systems at least once. Reengineering tools build system models which are used for running software analysis. These models are traditionally built from source code analysis and information accessible by data extractors (that we call such information *observable*). In this article we present the case of Microsoft Access projects and how this kind of project is partially observable due to proprietary storing formats. We propose a novel approach for building models that allows us to overcome this problem by reverse engineering the development environment runtime through the usage of Microsoft COM interface. We validate our approach and implementation by fully replicating 10 projects, 8 of them industrial, based only on our model information. We measure the replication performance by measuring the errors during the process and completeness of the product. We measure the replication error, by tracking replication operations. We used the scope and completeness measure to enact this error. Completeness is measured by the instrumentation of a simple and scoped diff based on a third source of information. We present extensive results and interpretations. We discuss the threats to validity, the possibility of other approaches and the technological restrictions of our solution.

**Keywords:** Model-driven engineering · Migration · Software analysis · Software reuse · Reverse engineering · Re engineering

## 1 Introduction

With the fast evolution of programming languages and frameworks, companies must evolve their systems. This evolution may imply the full migration of their

© Springer Nature Switzerland AG 2020
S. Ben Sassi et al. (Eds.): ICSR 2020, LNCS 12541, pp. 152–169, 2020.
https://doi.org/10.1007/978-3-030-64694-3_10

applications to new technological environments. Our work takes place in collaboration with Berger-Levrault, a major IT company selling information systems developed in Microsoft Access among others. Microsoft Access is ageing and not able to respond to the architectural needs of modern times. This migration is critical, since Berger-Levrault has more than 90 Microsoft Access applications.

Migration has been a research topic for a long time. The scientific community has proposed many different ways of tackling down this problem [3, 6, 8–11, 16, 22]. Nevertheless, migration is hard, tightly related with its circumstances and therefore, still challenging and not completely solved [20].

Most of the programming language compilers use plain text files as input for the programs they should compile or for configuration, such as XML, YML, properties, etc. Therefore, reengineering tools [12] often use the same approach for producing their internal models [6, 8, 11, 13, 16, 21, 22]. Work has already been done to mix static and dynamic analysis[1] [7, 15, 18, 19]. However, not all the languages are based on text files. Some of them, such as Microsoft Access (Access for short), Oracle Forms, Flash, Flex and many other Rapid Application Development (RAD), use some kind of binary format. In our particular case, we study the applications developed in Access. Access uses a proprietary binary format for storing the programs. Due to this policy and the lack of exporting capabilities, an Access application lacks full text representation.

Knowing that our migration involves the splitting of code in between front-end and back-end, the reengineering of the UI from desktop application to web application and the backend into good quality micro-services.

We propose the next three research questions to lead the research:

**#RQ1:** Can we obtain an application representation by querying the IDE runtime?

**#RQ2:** Are we able to re-engineer the meta-data sources into a model useful for migration?

**#RQ3:** Is the obtained model suitable for migration?

Using these questions as general guidelines and getting inspiration from previous work on a different domain [1, 2], we propose a model fully built on binary sources by applying reverse engineering on the run-time of the Access development environment, and re-engineering to transform the available data into an unified model.

Section 2 details the background of our research and in particular we describe Access as a *partially observable* domain and stress its *opacity*. We overview available technologies for accessing binary information. We propose an approach and implementation (Sect. 4) based on reverse and re-engineering taking into account the underlying challenges. We validate our approach and implementation by fully replicating 10 projects, 8 of them industrial, based only on our model information. We measure the replication performance by measuring the errors during the process and completeness of the product. We measure the replication error, by

---

[1] For space reasons, we do not consider tools performing analyses of system runtime. Such approaches instrument applications and produce various traces [4].

tracking replication operations. We used the scope and completeness measure to enacte this error. Completeness is measured by the instrumentation of a simple and scoped diff based on a third source of information (Sect. 5).

# 2    Microsoft Access: A Partially Observable System

Access is a relational database management system (RDBMS) that besides offering the relational Microsoft Jet Database Engine, also offers a graphical user interface and software-development tools. We briefly present and stress the key problems to extract information about Access applications.

## 2.1    Access

Visual Basic for Applications (VBA) is provided as a programming language. VBA is an object-based [23] extension of Visual Basic. Access is a fourth-generation language (4GL), comparable with Oracle forms or Visual Fox-pro. With the same mission of easing the GUI creation.

Access proposes a hybrid paradigm that aims to tackle down GUI, data storing and processings in a fully controlled and centralized environment. A program developed in Access solves problems by the orchestration of its first-class citizens: forms, modules, class, tables, queries, reports and macros.

To ease the work of GUI development, Access provides a point and click GUI Builder. As many other GUI builders in the market, such as Android Studio, Eclipse or Microsoft Visual Studio, Access also has to face the problem of distinguishing the generated content from the hand-crafted content. Android Studio uses the R class[2] for scoping generated code, Visual Studio.Net uses partial classes[3], and JavaFX uses xml files and annotations.

In the case of Access, Forms and Reports are split into two parts: (1) the VBA code, produced and modified only by the developer, (2) the component internal structure, produced and managed by the IDE, accessible to the developer only through point and click.

As many other 4GL languages, and Microsoft products, Access uses a proprietary binary format. This format organisation is undocumented, implying that attempting to extract data directly from the file would require a huge reverse engineering effort. Furthermore, Access uses entity specific formats for each first-class-citizen type, and in some cases, such as forms and reports, it has two formats, to respond to the internal division, required for managing code generation, explained above. This variety of formats leads to a more complex problem, threatening the generalization of a solution.

---

[2] https://developer.android.com/reference/android/R.

[3] https://docs.microsoft.com/en-us/dotnet/csharp/programming-guide/classes-and-structs/partial-classes-and-methods.

## 2.2    Limited Exporting

Access provides a visual interface to export some entities by point and click. This process is time consuming and prone to error. It is not tractable for full applications and in addition not all the elements can be exported. Leading to what we call a *partially observable* domain, since, by the usage of given tooling we cannot obtain artefact to analyze.

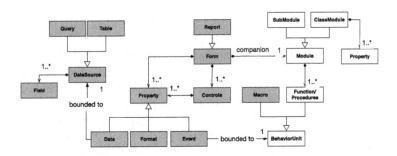

**Fig. 1.** Access simplified model

Figure 1 shows a simplified model of Access main elements. In grey we show the elements that **cannot** be exported from the GUI, in white those that can. Most of the structural entities are not available for export such as the table definitions, the query SQL definition, reports and forms structures not even the macros. The main GUI exporting features are related to the visual basic part of the project, including modules, class-modules, and the report or form companion-modules. The latter happens to be useless since their structure is not migrated. All analysis proposed over this partial content should be fully based on heuristics.

## 2.3    Programmatic Exporting

Access provides an undocumented function for programmatically exporting a text representation for all the first-class citizens. Using this function requires the implementation of specific software. This function is leveraged by third-party vendors that propose enhanced exporting features for control source version purposes. Solutions such as Oasis[4], Ivercy[5], MSAccess SVN[6], and others. We compare and extend on this subject in Sect. 7

---

[4] https://dev2dev.de/index.php?lang=en.

[5] https://ivercy.com/.

[6] https://archive.codeplex.com/?p=accesssvn.

## 2.4    Requirements and Constraints

Our work happens in the context of an industrial research on migration from Access to different kinds of technologies. We aim to migrate full applications from one monolith origin to a front-end and a micro service-based back-end (disregarding the database migration and restructuring since is out of scope).

The main features expected for the migration process are (1) selectiveness (the developer must be able to choose what he wants to migrate). (2) iterative (being able to propose short loops of migrations easy to verify and cheap to reject). (3) interactiveness (to be able to establish a dialog with the developer to better achieve the selective migration).

Such a migration process must coexist with an original project that is under maintenance and development. These requirements imply the following constraints: (1) The CPU and memory usage must be scoped to selective migrations (the migration solution must be able to run cheaply in the working environment of the developers without performance penalties). (2) The model must be able to supply as much data as possible. (3) The model must be able to supply up-to-date data (all modifications should be reflected immediately in the model).

Following the direction of [8,16] that work over the model of Oracle Forms, we recognize the importance of having a model based on the first-class-citizens of the language. Following the abstract idea behind [14], we propose a representation close to the language, that responds to Fig. 1.

## 3    COM Technological Overview

In this Section we provide a technological overview that will be used to enumerate the challenges of a solution based on the usage of Access COM API.

### 3.1    Microsoft COM and Access

Through COM, Access exposes a large and powerful API, that allows high interoperability in between different applications.

Access documentation[7] is heterogeneous. It provides good quality content for the popular usages, but vague, superfluous or even nonexistent for less popular usages. We insist on a technological overview that will help us answer our #RQ1, and shed light on the challenges.

### 3.2    Data Access

For interacting with Access through COM we must interact with an object model, composed by the followings.

*Remote Handle.* For interacting with remote Access entities COM provides remote memory addresses. We call these addresses handles.

---

[7] https://docs.microsoft.com/en-us/office/vba/api/overview/access.

*Application.* First instance to access through COM. This application object is bound to a running instance of Access. It exposes an explorable API, and it allows access to the project components, directly or indirectly.

*DoCmd.* (Do Command) is an object that reifies most of the available operations to apply on the application. It must be used for opening a project, databases and others. Most of the objects below have this object as a dependency.

*References.* This collection contains *Reference objects* describing a project's static dependencies.

*CurrentProject.* Depends on *DoCmd*. It holds basic metadata for each element in the project, by pointing to the collections *AllForms, AllReports, AllMacros, AllModules* that contains objects describing each form, report, macro and module correspondingly.

*CurrentData.* Depends on *DoCmd*. It holds metadata for each element related with data structures. In this object the available collections are *AllTables, AllQueries* that contains objects describing each table and query correspondingly.

*DbEngine.* Depends on *DoCmd*. It is the main access point to the data model. It provides access to *workspaces*.

*Workspace.* Depends on *DbEngine*. Represent database schemes, and provides access to the scheme elements by pointing to the collections *QueryDefs* and *TableDefs*.

*TableDef and QueryDef.* Depends on *Workspace*. Each of these objects contains a description. For the TableDefs name and *fields*. For the QueryDefs name and SQL.

*Forms, Reports and Modules.* Depends on *DoCmd*. Finally, we have three main collections where we can find the Form, Report and Module objects with their inner composition. This internal definition includes composed controls (textbox, labels, etc.), properties (layout, naming, companion-module, etc.) and VBA source code.

## 3.3  COM Model Re-engineer Challenges

To re-engineer COM data into an unified model has challenges:

*The Reading of a Property of the COM Entity, may Give Back Another COM Entity.* In some cases, we are going to read native type or self-contained information. But in some other cases the value of an attribute may be another handle. For these cases, we have to map the read value with a model entity type.

*One Model Entity may Correspond to more than one COM Entity.* The COM model provides two different objects for representing each of the first-class citizens. By example, *AllForms* contains form's metadata, *Forms* contains a form internal representation.

*One COM Entity Type may be Mapped to Different Model Entity Types.* Most of the objects in the COM model have properties represented with the same type, but to be able to structure the analysis (visiting, for example), we need them belonging to different classes. This implies that some of the entities with the same type may have to be mapped to different types in our model.

*Loadable Objects.* The first-class citizen objects must be dynamically loaded to reach their internal information. For loading, they require access to many COM entry points. This implies that some objects require specific extra steps for acquiring the desired data.

*Summary.* The overview shows that COM delivers a large access to the binary model of an Access application. This remote binary representation (from now on **COM model**) is also a very low level model that responds to the need for interaction between applications. We also understand that an approach in this direction must respond at least to the traditional challenges of reverse and re-engineering processes.

## 4    Mixing Static and Internal Access Information

To answer *Are we able to re-engineer the meta-data sources into a model useful for migration?*, (#RQ2), we propose the approach of online model from the point of view of a migration, followed by an implementation of the proposed approach and an explanation of how our approach and implementation address each constraint and challenge stated above.

### 4.1    Approach

As a general approach we propose to define our model as an online projection of the COM model. By **online** we mean that all the data is obtained by the COM bridge, therefore, any change done in the code impacts immediately our model. For achieving this we propose to let our model use COM as a back-end. Our model must conform to the meta model proposed in Fig. 1. By delegating to COM we aim to get all the possible data to be gathered from the analyzed software on demand. We expect this strategy to give immediate feedback and to allow quick and agile modifications over the used information, without requiring to do further extractions reducing the need of planning the data (constraint stated in Sect. 2), and allows us to implement quick migration experiments.

### 4.2    Architecture Implementation

As general architecture we propose to create a model that uses the COM model as a back-end as shown in the Fig. 2. We propose lazy access to the COM model back-end, what will guarantee that we access and load only what is needed. This feature aims to limit the memory usage (constraint stated in Sect. 2) by construction. The lazy approach will also allow us to map each binary-model-entity

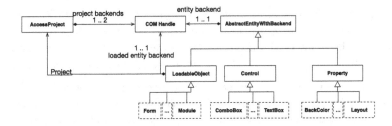

**Fig. 2.** Architecture

to a model-entity one at a time. We also propose to cache the results, for reducing the COM calls and therefore CPU time and inter-process communication.

Regarding the mapping between the COM model entity-type and our model, we propose to use two kinds of mapping: by type and by attribute value. First-class citizen entities are represented by two COM models, and that is why all of them subclass from a *LoadableObject* class, which maps two COM models instead of one.

For mapping the binary-model-entities to model-entity types, we propose to use factories. The mapping factory by type maps one binary-entity-type to one model-entity-type. The mapping factory by attribute value maps one binary-entity to one specific model-entity-type according to one specific binary-entity value.

### 4.3  Microsoft Access Model Implementation

Our model extends from the architecture implementation, and inherits the mapping to COM remote entities. This model is meant to be visited by a visitor pattern, in order to perform analysis. In order to define the structural composition to be visited, it relies on the usage of stateful traits. At the level of stateful traits we define, by example, the widget - control composition.

### 4.4  Meeting the Challenges and Constraints

*The Reading of a Property of the COM Entity, may Give Back Another COM Entity.* Each model type must know which readings will give back a COM model entity. In these reads we use a factory that maps the COM model type with a model type. After creating a new instance, it sets up the given COM model entity as a back-end.

*One Model Entity may Correspond to more than one COM Entity.* There are two kind of objects with more than one back-end, the first-class citizens, subclass of LoadableObject, and AccessProject, that is a convenient class for managing the generality of COM usage. Since there are only two specific cases they are treated individually.

*One COM Entity Type may be Mapped to Different Model Entity Types.* While loading properties we use a factory pattern that defines the class to instantiate according to the name of the property. Since the only COM model entity with this kind of mapping is the property, we did not generalize this kind of mapping.

*Loadable Objects.* For loadable objects, we defined a specific branch in the hierarchy, that before accessing to remote properties related to the loaded object back-end, it ensures that the back-end has been loaded and bounded. For ensuring this, the Loadable Object subclass does a typed double dispatch with the AccessProject, which delegates to DoCmd.

*Contain Computational Resources Usage.* If we want to access all possible data, we risk having a model that is too big to be managed. For approaching a solution to this problem, we propose to specialize the access on demand in our implementation by using **lazy loading** and **cache**. Lazy loading scopes the memory usage to the effectively needed data. Cache scopes the inter-process communication and CPU time for remote access to one time per object.

*Accessing all Accessible Data.* Our proposal is conceived to get data on demand. This is why the very nature and particularity of this model is to be connected to the Access development runtime. If the data is reachable by COM, therefore it should be accessible.

*Accessing Up-to-date Data* The online nature of our approach is the main key for ensuring up-to-date data, since the data obtained is meant to be obtained from the developer's Microsoft Access running instance.

## 5    Validation

Our validation is aligned with #RQ3: *Is the obtained model suitable for migration?* Since our model is meant to be used for migration, we propose to fully migrate some projects to the same technology. That is to say to replicate or clone. For doing so, we perform a replication of 10 different access projects. For this performance we use our model and the COM extensions to produce the replicated project programmatically.

### 5.1    Methodology

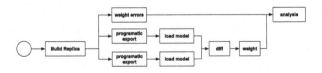

**Fig. 3.** Validation methodology overview

*Chosen Projects.* For this validation we used 10 different projects (described in Table 1). 8 of them are base libraries used by Berger-Levrault in all the Access projects. One is an open source example found in GitHub[8]. The last one is the Microsoft Northwind Traders (Northwind for short)[9] example project. This project is used for learning Access and it uses most of the standard techniques and available graphical features of the language.

**Table 1.** Projects descriptions

| Project | Remote table | Table | Remote query | Query | Module | Classes | Report | Forms |
|---|---|---|---|---|---|---|---|---|
| Northwind | 0 | 20 | 0 | 27 | 6 | 2 | 15 | 34 |
| CUTLCOMP | 0 | 1 | 0 | 0 | 3 | 0 | 0 | 0 |
| CUTL | 7 | 3 | 0 | 1 | 26 | 62 | 0 | 8 |
| CRIR | 5 | 4 | 0 | 16 | 6 | 0 | 2 | 3 |
| CPDI | 0 | 1 | 0 | 0 | 2 | 0 | 0 | 0 |
| CHABIL | 11 | 2 | 0 | 27 | 8 | 1 | 1 | 10 |
| CDDE | 0 | 1 | 0 | 0 | 2 | 0 | 0 | 0 |
| CAUNIT | 0 | 1 | 0 | 0 | 4 | 15 | 0 | 1 |
| ACCUEIL | 25 | 7 | 0 | 13 | 6 | 67 | 5 | 33 |
| Access Examples | 0 | 10 | 2 | 14 | 11 | 1 | 8 | 13 |

*Error Tracking & Weighting.* All errors happening during the replication process are tracked down for further analysis and correlation with the original/replica comparison. The error tracking composition responds to the same composition as the proposed model. In a nutshell, we count the operations required to replicate the project. We obtain a proportion of errors by contrasting this counting according to the outcome: successful or failure. More details including the formula are given in the annex Sect. A.

*Programmatic Export for Obtaining File Definitions.* For obtaining the file definition of each component we leverage the COM function named SaveAsText (this function is explained in Sect. 7). The output of this function differs by each type of entity as follow: For Modules and class-modules it offers VBA (.bas) files. For Queries it offers an SQL output. For tables it uses XML format. For Forms and Reports, offers an output that hybridizes the structure definition and the VBA code of the companion-module.

*File Diff & Weighting.* We instrument a diff in between pairs of files of each original/replica exported project. The result of this diff is a differential graph expressing all the required operations for transforming the original project to the replica project. In a nutshell, we count the comparisons and contrast according to the outcome: added/removed element, modified value, exact replication. More details including the formula are given in the annex Sect. B.

---

[8] https://github.com/Access-projects/Access-examples.

[9] https://docs.microsoft.com/en-us/powerapps/maker/canvas-apps/northwind-install.

## 5.2   Results

Table 2 offers an overview of the process of replication of each of our projects. Most of the main elements are replicated. The tables and queries not replicated happen to be remote tables that we cannot access, since we lack access to the remote server.

**Table 2.** Export overview

|            | Reference | Table | Query | Module | Report | Forms | Total |
|------------|-----------|-------|-------|--------|--------|-------|-------|
| #Elements   | 70        | 98    | 100   | 222    | 31     | 102   | 623   |
| #Replicated | 69        | 50    | 98    | 222    | 31     | 102   | 572   |
| #Failures   | 1         | 48    | 2     | 0      | 0      | 0     | 51    |

Below compare the different aggregation of completeness with the aggregation of error tracking per project per type of element. We do not include modules nor macros because the result is **complete** in all the projects. Since both completeness and error series respond mostly to a hyperbolic distribution, we propose to measure the rate of success and error by using the median.

**Table 3.** Query comparison

Queries

| Projects | Completeness | | | | Failures | | | |
|----------|-----|-----|--------|------|-----|-----|--------|------|
|          | Max | Min | Median | SDev | Max | Min | Median | SDev |
| Northwind | 100 | 100 | 100 | 0 | 15 | 0 | 0 | 3.05 |
| CUTLCOMP | – | – | – | – | – | – | – | – |
| CUTL | 100 | 100 | 100 | 0 | 0 | 0 | 0 | 0 |
| CRIR | 100 | 88.46 | 100 | 2.88 | 0 | 0 | 0 | 0 |
| CPDI | – | – | – | – | – | – | – | – |
| CHABIL | 100 | 93.49 | 100 | 1.25 | 0 | 0 | 0 | 0 |
| CDDE | – | – | – | – | – | – | – | – |
| CAUNIT | – | – | – | – | – | – | – | – |
| ACCUEIL | 100 | 95.76 | 100 | 1.17 | 0 | 0 | 0 | 0 |
| Access Examples | 100 | 0 | 100 | 25.81 | 100 | 0 | 0 | 34.15 |

**Table 4.** Table comparison

Tables

| Projects | Completeness | | | | Failures | | | |
|----------|-----|-----|--------|-------|-----|-----|--------|-------|
|          | Max | Min | Median | SDev | Max | Min | Median | SDev |
| Northwind | 100 | 0 | 100 | 23.72 | 22 | 0 | 0 | 5.14 |
| CUTLCOMP | 100 | 0 | 100 | 27.62 | 0 | 0 | 0 | 0 |
| CUTL | 100 | 0 | 98 | 5041 | 10 | 0 | 0 | 46.43 |
| CRIR | 100 | 0 | 99 | 46.04 | 100 | 0 | 0 | 44.42 |
| CPDI | 100 | 0 | 100 | 27.62 | 0 | 0 | 0 | 0 |
| CHABIL | 100 | 0 | 0 | 50.65 | 100 | 0 | 0 | 50.38 |
| CDDE | – | – | – | – | – | – | – | – |
| CAUNIT | 100 | 98 | 100 | 0.75 | 0 | 0 | 0 | 0 |
| ACCUEIL | 100 | 0 | 0 | 49.6 | 100 | 0 | 100 | 50.63 |
| Access Examples | 100 | 0 | 99.5 | 32.34 | 90 | 0 | 0 | 17.65 |

Table 3 show some very good results. We fully replicate most of the queries. Table 4 has also very good results, since most of the failures happen on tables that are remote. **CUTL, CRIR, CHABIL, ACCUEIL** and **Access Examples**, all of them high standard deviations, and all of them have remote tables. There are some cases where there are no errors during the process, but we don't meet full completeness, such as the cases **CUTLCOMP, CAUNIT** and **CPDI**. These cases happen because system tables are not replicated, and the replication targets a newer Access version.

**Table 5.** Form comparison

| Forms | | | | | | | | |
|---|---|---|---|---|---|---|---|---|
| Projects | Completeness | | | | Failures | | | |
| | Max | Min | Median | SDev | Max | Min | Median | SDev |
| Northwind | 86.24 | 61.55 | 69 | 4.72 | 8.68 | 5.32 | 9 | 0.73 |
| CUTLCOMP | – | – | – | – | – | – | – | – |
| CUTL | 86.73 | 63.46 | 82 | 8.45 | 7.62 | 1.66 | 5 | 1.79 |
| CRIR | 74.73 | 73.06 | 74 | 0.96 | 8.31 | 8.18 | 9 | 0.064 |
| CPDI | – | – | – | – | – | – | – | – |
| CHABIL | 78.3 | 65.89 | 70.5 | 4.14 | 8.95 | 5.44 | 6 | 1.134 |
| CDDE | 100 | 98 | 100 | 0.83 | 0 | 0 | 0 | 0 |
| CAUNIT | 79.96 | 79.96 | 79.96 | 0 | 5.27 | 5.27 | 5.27 | 5.27 |
| ACCUEIL | 92.71 | 70.01 | 78 | 6.22 | 15.71 | 2.49 | 6 | 2.7 |
| Access Examples | 88.52 | 61.91 | 76 | 8.35 | 34.05 | 6.6 | 9 | 7.25 |

**Table 6.** Report Comparison

| Reports | | | | | | | | |
|---|---|---|---|---|---|---|---|---|
| Projects | Completeness | | | | Failures | | | |
| | Max | Min | Median | SDev | Max | Min | Median | SDev |
| Northwind | 71.55 | 65.97 | 70 | 1.5 | 16.57 | 11.33 | 16 | 1.3 |
| CUTLCOMP | – | – | – | – | – | – | – | – |
| CUTL | – | – | – | – | – | – | – | – |
| CRIR | 73.13 | 71 | 73 | 1.5 | 20.64 | 15.64 | 18.5 | 3.54 |
| CPDI | – | – | – | – | – | – | – | – |
| CHABIL | 71.21 | 71.21 | 71.21 | 0 | 13.87 | 13.87 | 13.87 | 0 |
| CDDE | – | – | – | – | – | – | – | – |
| CAUNIT | – | – | – | – | – | – | – | – |
| ACCUEIL | 74.57 | 73.34 | 74 | 0.53 | 14.16 | 13.87 | 14 | 0.13 |
| Access Examples | 90.14 | 66.1 | 72.5 | 7.48 | 18.15 | 13.87 | 16 | 1.51 |

In the particular case of reports and forms (Table 5, Table 6) we see less interesting outcomes from the point of view of completeness, but we can observe an inversely proportional relation with the errors. There is also a restriction of implementation, many values that are stored in byte array structures, even if we can read them, we cannot write them. This makes impossible the replication of printing configuration, custom controls based on ActiveX or OCX technologies and image contents. These properties do not figure in between the errors, because they are avoided by construction of the process. Finally, Fig. 4 provides an idea of the confidence interval of the measures. Both sides show a correlated existence of isolated measures. In the case of the *Tables* the completeness confidence is too large. We can relate it with the scattered error measures. Forms and Reports completeness show shorter intervals, that we can correlate with the error intervals and the distance between the isolated cases. Finally, modules and queries have a really good interval. The centre is placed almost in 0 in the failures plot, even having some isolated cases themselves.

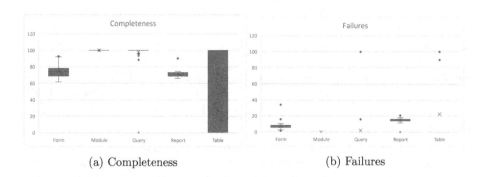

(a) Completeness                    (b) Failures

**Fig. 4.** Confidence

## 5.3   Human Insight and Opinion

We check each of the replicas and compare manually with the original, and also with the extracted data. Most of the meaningful parts of the applications were properly replicated, even when some of the most appealing graphical features are not maintained because of the impossibility of writing this kind of data. Nevertheless, we spent time specially on the execution of many functionalities of the project Northwind and found out that most of the behaviors are maintained, since all the macros and source code has been correctly replicated and bound to the proper structures. After migrating all the example data available from the original to the replica, we can observe that the login works as expected in all the tests we manually checked. Figure 5(a) and Fig. 5(b) give material evidence of the outcome, by exposing the most complex form in the replicated system. All this insight is highly positive. Our most positive but opinionated insight is that we achieve to develop the validation faster than we expected, thanks to the model that we are presenting. We got constant assessment from it getting fast feedback and understanding of the replication process target.

(a) Original Home screen          (b) Replicated Home screen

Fig. 5. Original replica comparison

## 6   Threats to Validity

*Empirical Study.* Our validation is based on the replication of ten projects. This gives about 534 first-class-citizen components, thousands of controls and table fields. There may exist many kinds of projects that are not represented by those that we have.

*Multiple Versions.* We have seen how the non-replication of system tables available in other versions of access came out as a difference in between the original and replicate code because of the policy of non-exporting system tables. This does not happen to be a false positive. And we did not find any false positive or false negative, but we cannot completely ensure yet with this validation this cannot happen in other projects.

*Undocumented Features Leveraging.* For allowing the file comparison done for our validation, we had to leverage some undocumented functions (widely explained in Sect. 7). This function could change or not be accessible anymore, threatening the reliability of the process.

# 7   Discussion

*Source Version Control-Oriented Solution.* As we pointed out in Sect. 2, there are third party solutions for source control that could be helpful for solving this problem. This software produces different text formats able to reproduce the exact same project. The available tools developed for source control are based on the usage of **SaveAsText** undocumented function provided by Access DoCmd command. This function exports each entity to a text format, producing XML for the tables, VBA for the source code and an Access specific DSL for defining forms and reports. Their stability is tested already for many years by the market, meaning that could be a good starting point for software analysis.

*Undocumented Features.* Even taking into account the fact that these tools have been in the market for a long time, we do not really know how they have changed during their lifetime. As we pointed just above, these solutions are based on the usage of the undocumented functions SaveAsText and LoadFromText. This presents two risks: (1) Microsoft may change their behavior, or even make them unavailable in the future, (2) the format of the exported text has no documentation either, which means that different versions could have singularities.

*Context and Performance.* Besides that, our approach of software migration is based on augmenting the developer. For this reason, we see it more useful to be able to see exactly what the developer is actively working on, to have more context and insight. Finally, we see that delegate the management of the information to the same access and using the IDE as a database has a high potential for reducing memory consumption and model complexity, allowing us to develop tools that can run on a working environment, without requiring extra infrastructure.

*What our Validation does not Validate.* The exported files have the minimal amount of information required to build again the whole application. This is a lot. But it does not include default values. While in a file, a complex component may define about ten different properties, when accessed through COM, we have access to more than 100 properties per control. This means that the text representation reveals to be incomplete, *partially observable*. From the point of view of software analysis and migration, to have systematic access to default values without having to manually specify them is a great asset.

# 8   Related Works

OMG in [13] and [21], in the context of Architecture driven modernization, proposes successive transformations over the extracted Abstract Syntax Tree model (ASTM) [14], which is obtained by parsing source code. [6] Claims an efficient implementation of model-driven Engineering (MDE) with models obtained by parsing source code and obtaining an ASTM. [16] proposes to reverse engineer GUI Layouts from Oracle Forms. They export the Form structure as XML and use EMF[10] tools for generating models. [11] for the particular case of analyz-

---

[10] http://www.eclipse.org/modeling/emf/.

ing flex UI, it proposes the usage of Adobe Wallaby[11] for transforming Flash's SWF binary proprietary format files into HTML, and then parsing. [8] proposes to parse all the files representing an Oracle Forms for obtaining a model the article does not specify the kind of file they used for analyzing But according to [16] and to the existence of Oracle exporting tools[12] from Form to XML we suspect that they follow the same path. [22] proposes the usage of Famix [5]. Famix extraction for Java applications is achieved by using VervaineJ[13]. This library transforms the source code to a Family of Languages representation. One of the main differences with an AST is that it is a Graph with scoping and it binds all the static relationships. To reach this deeper knowledge, it analyses the application by parsing its files in the context of the eclipse java compiler. To the best of our knowledge, at least within the MDE based approaches: (1) there is no other model extraction technique but by parsing: either the source code of the source application or the exportation from a binary format to a text format (for example XML/HTML). (2) The approaches are based on batch processing instead of online access. Some of these model extracting tools VervaineJ, Proleap[14], SMACC[15], ANTLR[16], and many others. [19] overviews several dynamic (based on run-time analysis) reverse engineering techniques and their challenges in the context of the software migration and evolution. [18] Proposes a hybrid analysis approach for reverse-engineering web applications, obtaining a model by crawling the widgets from the run-time, and augment the results by parsing the event handlers code and recognize what are the possible navigation options. [17] Points out the complexity of accurate GUI analysis by code interpretation. Extracts a technology-agnostic UI model by crawling the application run-time using AOP, for enabling portability to android.

## 9    Conclusion and Future Work

*Contribution.* In this article we explained the problem of opacity in Access. We enunciate three research questions for our work. We offered a technological overview for using COM as a bridge for accessing data, aiming to answer #RQ1. We offered the novel approach and implementation of model to shape a COM model into an application model, answering #RQ2. We conducted an exhaustive and detailed validation process guided by and answering #RQ3. We offered a compendium of the threats to validity that we found during our experiments. We compared our solution with related work and proposed a discussion on why to choose the usage of COM over exported files. We position our work with the state of the art on the part of software migration and how software is analyzed towards this goal.

---

[11] https://en.wikipedia.org/wiki/Adobe_Wallaby.

[12] https://blogs.oracle.com/apex/forms-to-apex-converting-fmbs-to-xml.

[13] https://github.com/NicolasAnquetil/VerveineJ.

[14] https://github.com/uwol/proleap-vb6-parser.

[15] https://refactory.com/smacc/.

[16] https://www.antlr.org/.

*Future.* From this point we have several paths opening. Adapt parsing techniques over the modules, class-modules and companion-modules, for being able to build a full AST on demand, and being able to control its creation on demand, without losing reference information. Find the minimal migration from Access to Angular/TypeScript based in our online metamodel.

## A    Annex 1: Error Tracking and Weighting

*Error Tracking.* COM is not intensively used to create projects programmatically. Many standard procedures, after running, make Access unstable and easy to fail in any next attempt of modification. Failures that may imply from non created widgets to missing properties. During the whole process we track down all the errors happened during this process, for being able to plot alongside with the results on the comparisons. This error is tracked down at the level of replication operation and typified. (1) ChildCreatedSuccessfully (2) FailureToCreateChild (3) FailureToWriteProperty (4) PropertyWrittenSuccesfully. The tree of error tracking composition responds to the same composition as the proposed model.

*Error Weighting.* We measure the failure of a replication process, by the weighting and summarization of the tree of operations.

Let $o$ be the result of an operation of replication. Let $c_o$ be the children creation operation under the scope of the operation $o$. Let $p_o$ be the properties creation operation under the scope of the operation $o$.

$$F(o) = \begin{cases} 1 & o \in \{Failure\} \\ 0 & o \in \{Success\} \wedge |c_o| = 0 \wedge |p_o| = 0 \\ (0.9\frac{\sum_{i=1}^{|c_o|} F(c_o i)}{|c_o|} + 0.1\frac{\sum_{i=1}^{|p_o|} F(p_o i)}{|p_o|})0.5 & o \in \{Success\} \wedge |c_o| > 0 \\ \frac{\sum_{i=1}^{|p_o|} F(p_o i)}{|p_o|} & o \in \{Success\} \wedge |c_o| = 0 \end{cases} \quad (1)$$

This recursive function calculates the proportion of error in terms of errors in terms of composed errors. For our work those elements that are composed of elements (by example, the controls inside a form) are specially represented by their children. This is why one formula branch uses coefficients: 10% based on the component properties, and 90% on the children completeness.

## B    Annex 2: File X File Diff & Weighting

*File Diff.* For being able to diff each pair of files we used different techniques Modules, Macros, and Queries are loaded as nodes with name and plain text content. Tables are loaded as XML trees including name, indexes and fields with their name and type. Forms, Reports are loaded with a simple parser that produces a tree of report/form with their controls and properties.

Each of these entities are loaded from original and replica. For each pair we calculate the differential tree expressing all the needed operations for transforming the original graph into the replica graph. We define the following operations: (1) Add (2) Remove (3) Same (4) ModifyChild (5) ModifyProperty.

*Diff Weighting.* We measure the completeness of each of the elements on the differential graph. Let $u$ be the result of comparing an element from the original project with its equivalent of the replica.

$$Completeness(u) = (1 - M(u)) * 100) \tag{2}$$

Magnitude $M(u)$ is the weighting of the difference in between two elements. Let $u_o$ and $u_r$ being respectively original and replica side of $u$. Let $c_u$ be the set of children that belong to the $u$. Let $p_u$ be the set of properties that belong to the $u$.

$$M(u) = \begin{cases} 1 & u \in \{Add, Remove\} \\ 0 & u \in \{Same\} \\ (0.9\frac{\sum_{i=1}^{|c_u|} M(c_u i)}{|c_u|} + 0.1\frac{\sum_{i=1}^{|p|} M(p_u i)}{|p_u|})0.5 & u \in \{ChildModif\} \wedge |c_u| > 0 \\ \frac{\sum_{i=1}^{|p_u|} M(p_u i)}{|p_u|} & u \in \{ChildModif\} \wedge |c_u| = 0 \\ u_r - u_o & u \in \{PropertyModif\} \wedge u_r, u_o \in \{Native\ type\} \end{cases} \tag{3}$$

This recursive function calculates the magnitude of the difference in terms of the composed differences. The coefficients used in this formula respond to the same explanation as those used on the error weighting formula explained above.

# References

1. Bragagnolo, S., Marra, M., Polito, G., Boix, E.G.: Towards scalable blockchain analysis. In: 2019 IEEE/ACM 2nd International Workshop on Emerging Trends in Software Engineering for Blockchain (WETSEB), pp. 1–7 (2019)
2. Bragagnolo, S., Rocha, H., Denker, M., Ducasse, S.: SmartInspect: solidity smart contract inspector. In: 2018 International Workshop on Blockchain Oriented Software Engineering (IWBOSE), pp. 9–18 (March 2018). Electronic ISBN: 978-1-5386-5986-1
3. Brant, J., Roberts, D., Plendl, B., Prince, J.: Extreme maintenance: transforming Delphi into C#. In: 2010 IEEE International Conference on Software Maintenance (ICSM), pp. 1–8 (2010)
4. De Pauw, W., Jensen, E., Mitchell, N., Sevitsky, G., Vlissides, J., Yang, J.: Visualizing the execution of Java programs. In: Diehl, S. (ed.) Software Visualization. LNCS, vol. 2269, pp. 151–162. Springer, Heidelberg (2002). https://doi.org/10.1007/3-540-45875-1_12
5. Ducasse, S., Anquetil, N., Bhatti, U., Cavalcante Hora, A., Laval, J., Girba, T.: MSE and FAMIX 3.0: an interexchange format and source code model family. Tech. rep., RMod - INRIA Lille-Nord Europe (2011)
6. Fleurey, F., Breton, E., Baudry, B., Nicolas, A., Jézéquel, J.-M.: Model-driven engineering for software migration in a large industrial context. In: Engels, G., Opdyke, B., Schmidt, D.C., Weil, F. (eds.) MODELS 2007. LNCS, vol. 4735, pp. 482–497. Springer, Heidelberg (2007). https://doi.org/10.1007/978-3-540-75209-7_33
7. Francesca, A.F., Fabrizio, P., Claudia, R., Stefano, R.: Behavioural design pattern detection through dynamic analysis. In: Proceedings of 4th PCODA at the 15th Working Conference on Reverse Engineering (WCRE 2008), pp. 11–16 (2008)

8. Garcés, K., et al.: White-box modernization of legacy applications: the Oracle forms case study. Comput. Stand. Interfaces **57**, 110–122 (2017)
9. Govin, B., Anquetil, N., Etien, A., Ducasse, S., Monegier Du Sorbier, A.: Managing an industrial software rearchitecting project with source code labelling. In: Complex Systems Design & Management conference (CSD&M), Paris, France (December 2017)
10. Govin, B., Anquetil, N., Etien, A., Monegier Du Sorbier, A., Ducasse, S.: How can we help software rearchitecting efforts? Study of an industrial case. In: Proceedings of the International Conference on Software Maintenance and Evolution, (Industrial Track), Raleigh, USA (October 2016)
11. Hayakawa, T., Hasegawa, S., Yoshika, S., Hikita, T.: Maintaining web applications by translating among different RIA technologies. GSTF J. Comput. **2**, 250–256 (2012)
12. Kienle, H.M., Müller, H.A.: The tools perspective on software reverse engineering: requirements, construction, and evaluation. In: Advanced in Computers, vol. 79, pp. 189–290. Elsevier (2010)
13. Newcomb, P.: Architecture-driven modernization (ADM). In: 12th Working Conference on Reverse Engineering (WCRE 2005), p. 237 (2005)
14. Object Management Group: Abstract syntax tree metamodel (ASTM) version 1.0. Tech. rep., Object Management Group (2011)
15. Richner, T., Ducasse, S.: Recovering high-level views of object-oriented applications from static and dynamic information. In: Yang, H., White, L. (eds.) Proceedings of 15th IEEE International Conference on Software Maintenance (ICSM 1999), pp. 13–22. IEEE Computer Society Press, Los Alamitos (September 1999)
16. Sánchez Ramán, O., Sánchez Cuadrado, J., García Molina, J.: Model-driven reverse engineering of legacy graphical user interfaces. In: Proceedings of the IEEE/ACM International Conference on Automated Software Engineering, ASE 2010, pp. 147–150. ACM (2010)
17. Shah, E., Tilevich, E.: Reverse-engineering user interfaces to facilitate porting to and across mobile devices and platforms. In: Proceedings of the Compilation of the Co-located Workshops on DSM 2011, TMC 2011, AGERE! 2011, AOOPES 2011, NEAT 2011, & VMIL 2011, pp. 255–260. ACM (2011)
18. Silva, C.E., Campos, J.C.: Combining static and dynamic analysis for the reverse engineering of web applications. In: Proceedings of the 5th ACM SIGCHI Symposium on Engineering Interactive Computing Systems, p. 107. ACM Press (2013)
19. Stroulia, E., Systä, T.: Dynamic analysis for reverse engineering and program understanding. SIGAPP Appl. Comput. Rev. **10**(1), 8–17 (2002)
20. Terekhov, A.A., Verhoef, C.: The realities of language conversions. IEEE Softw. **17**(6), 111–124 (2000)
21. Ulrich, W.M., Newcomb, P.: Information Systems Transformation: Architecture-Driven Modernization Case Studies. Morgan Kaufmann, Burlington (2010)
22. Verhaeghe, B., et al.: GUI migration using MDE from GWT to Angular 6: an industrial case. In: 2019 IEEE 26th International Conference on Software Analysis, Evolution and Reengineering (SANER), Hangzhou, China (2019)
23. Wegner, P.: Dimensions of object-based language design. In: Proceedings OOPSLA 1987, ACM SIGPLAN Notices, vol. 22, pp. 168–182 (December 1987)

# Recommendation

# Automated Reuse Recommendation of Product Line Assets Based on Natural Language Requirements

Muhammad Abbas[1,2]([✉]) [ID], Mehrdad Saadatmand[1] [ID], Eduard Enoiu[2] [ID], Daniel Sundamark[2], and Claes Lindskog[3]

[1] RISE Research Institutes of Sweden, Västerås, Sweden
{muhammad.abbas,mehrdad.saadatmand}@ri.se
[2] Mälardalen University, Västerås, Sweden
{muhammad.abbas,eduard.paul.enoiu,daniel.sundmark}@mdh.se
[3] Bombardier Transportation AB, Västerås, Sweden
claes.lindskog@rail.bombardier.com

**Abstract.** Software product lines (SPLs) are based on reuse rationale to aid quick and quality delivery of complex products at scale. Deriving a new product from a product line requires reuse analysis to avoid redundancy and support a high degree of assets reuse. In this paper, we propose and evaluate automated support for recommending SPL assets that can be reused to realize new customer requirements. Using the existing customer requirements as input, the approach applies natural language processing and clustering to generate reuse recommendations for unseen customer requirements in new projects. The approach is evaluated both quantitatively and qualitatively in the railway industry. Results show that our approach can recommend reuse with 74% accuracy and 57.4% exact match. The evaluation further indicates that the recommendations are relevant to engineers and can support the product derivation and feasibility analysis phase of the projects. The results encourage further study on automated reuse analysis on other levels of abstractions.

**Keywords:** Software product line · Reuse recommender · Natural language processing · Word embedding

## 1 Introduction

With the increasing customization needs from customers, quality, and quick delivery of software products are of paramount importance. Meeting this demand requires an effective software engineering process. Software Product Lines (SPL/PL) [21] are created to help achieve quick delivery of quality products by systematically reusing features across variants. These PL features satisfy a

This work is funded by the ITEA3 XIVT [25], and Knowledge Foundation's ARRAY Projects.

S. Ben Sassi et al. (Eds.): ICSR 2020, LNCS 12541, pp. 173–189, 2020.
https://doi.org/10.1007/978-3-030-64694-3_11

set of standard requirements in a particular domain and are realized by reusable assets. Variations in the assets are introduced to cope with varying customization requirements of the same product.

A common industrial practice to the adoption of SPL is through the incremental development of overloaded assets, which are reused in a clone-and-own manner (e.g., in the railway industry [1]). While clone-and-own reuse is generally not recommended in SPL engineering, it does have some benefits, e.g., the reuse is very high speed with little domain engineering, needs less coordination, and has less adoption cost. In such cases, in the derived products, some assets are reused as-is, while for some, a copy of the asset is modified to address the particular customer requirements. This way of working results in many functional variants of the assets. Companies following clone-and-own based reuse practices faces problems among others, when implementing a new requirements, it might be required to know a) if a similar requirement has already been implemented by a PL asset or its functional variant, and b) if that is not the case, which asset or its functional variant is the closest one that can be modified to realize the new requirement. To achieve the aforementioned objectives, a reuse analysis is performed.

A reuse analysis process may have the following activities (as per [12,13], summarized in [19]). Note here that we modified the activities to match our industrial partner's practices in the context of a PL: (1) identify high-level system functions that can realize the new customer requirements, (2) search existing projects to shortlist existing owned assets (that implements the system functions), (3) analyze and select from the shortlisted PL assets, and (4) adapt the selected assets to new customer requirements. The current (requirements-level) process for reuse analysis lacks automated support, is time-consuming, and is heavily based on the experience of engineers. Our approach aims to support the first three steps.

We support the reuse analysis and recommendation of PL assets early at the requirements level. The approach proposed in this paper is motivated by an industrial use case from the railway domain, where the same PL engineering practices (clone-and-own based reuse via overloaded assets) are followed. In our partner's company, requirements are written at various levels of abstraction (i.e., customer level, system level, subsystem level, SPL Assets description). Compliance with safety standards requires our partner to maintain the links between customer requirements and PL asset descriptions realizing them. Unfortunately, most of the existing reuse approaches (e.g., [2,6,15]) do not make use of this information (existing cases) to recommend reuse of PL assets and their functional variants. In addition, many existing approaches are limited to recovering traces between one requirement abstraction level sharing term-based or semantic similarity. In our case, the customer requirements share less semantic similarity with the asset descriptions.

In this paper, we propose an approach for requirement-level case-based reuse analysis and recommendation of (existing) PL assets. The approach is developed and evaluated in close collaboration with Bombardier Transportation, Sweden.

Our approach uses NLP techniques to clean the input customer requirements, train a word embedding model on the existing requirements, and cluster them. The trained model and clusters can then be used to generate recommendations (five at most, in our case) for PL assets (Simulink models in our case) reuse for new customer requirements.

*Contributions.* To this end, we make the following contributions: i) a proposed approach for the recommendation of PL asset reuse, ii) an evaluation of different word embedding algorithms on an industrial use case, and iii) a focus group evaluation to report engineer's view on the results.

Results obtained from this evaluation on two projects (derived products of the Power Propulsion Control (PPC) system's PL) show that our approach can recommend reuse of PL assets given unseen customer requirements with 74% accuracy[1] and 57.4% of exact match percentage[2]. The results obtained using thematic analysis on the focus group transcript show that our approach's recommendations are highly relevant and useful for practitioners.

*Structure.* The remainder of the paper is structured as follows. Section 2 presents our proposed approach for reuse analysis and recommendation. Section 3 evaluates the proposed approach and state-of-the-art word embedding algorithms in the context of reuse, Sect. 3.1 discusses the results obtained from the evaluation and the focus group, Sect. 3.2 discusses threats to validity. Section 4 presents the related work, Finally, Sect 5 concludes the paper.

## 2   Approach

Our approach supports the reuse analysis of PL assets at the requirements-level. The approach has three distinct phases (shown in Fig. 1), namely **Pre-Process**, **Training** and **Asset Reuse Recommender**. The first step of the approach (**Pre-Process**) is responsible for cleaning the requirements text for the later steps. Cleaning requirements include the removal of stop words, Part-Of-Speech (POS) tagging, and lemmatization. **Training** takes in existing cleaned customer requirements with their links to assets, realizing them. Clean requirements are used to train a feature extraction model (word embedding) and produce meaningful vectors for the existing customer requirements. The derived vectors are clustered using unsupervised clustering. The **Asset Reuse Recommender** phase takes in unseen cleaned customer requirements and recommends PL assets that can be reused to realize them. This is achieved by inferring meaningful feature vectors for the new requirements, predicting cluster for vectors of new requirements in the existing clusters, retrieving closest neighbors' reuse links to the PL assets or their functional variants, and finally ranking the reused PL assets. To demonstrate our approach, we use a running example (LOG4J2) from the SEOSS

---

[1] A reuse recommendation is accurate if the recommended list contains the ground truth.

[2] A reuse recommendation is an exact match if the recommended list contains the ground truth on top.

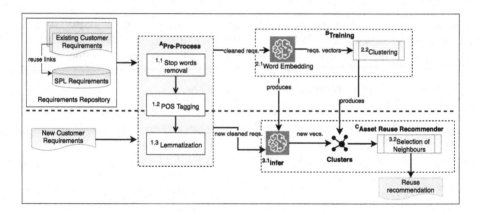

**Fig. 1.** An overview of the approach for reuse analysis and recommendation

**Table 1.** The Running example of LOG4J2 and its corresponding issue text

| ID | Issue Text | Target |
|---|---|---|
| 1292 | 1274 added the encode(LogEvent, ByteBufferDestination) method to Layout. Appenders implementing the ByteBufferDestination interface can call Layout.encode. This enables Layout implementations to process LogEvents without creating temporary objects. This ticket is to track the work for letting RandomAccessFileAppender (and its Rolling variant) implement the ByteBufferDestination interface and call Layout.encode instead of Layout.toByteArray | 1274 |
| 1291 | 1274 added the encode(LogEvent, ByteBufferDestination) method to Layout. The default... | 1274 |
| 1305 | Logging in a binary format instead of in text can give large performance improvements... | 1397 |
| 1424 | In non-garbage-free mode, the logged Message objects are immutable and can be simply... | 1397 |
| 1517 | Add ThreadContext.setContext(Map< $String, String$ >). Note that we... | 1516 |
| 1519 | Add API ThreadContext.putAll(Map< $String, String$ >). My immediate goal is to be able... | 1516 |
| 1349 | The current ThreadContext map and stack implementations allocate temporary objects.... | 1516 |

33 data-set [22]. The running example is a subset of issues to issues data-set shown in Table 1. The Issue Text column can be mapped (to our data-set) as customer requirements, and the Target column can be mapped as PL assets. Note that the running example is just for demonstration purposes and contains implementation details unlike requirements. In this section, we discuss each step of our approach in more detail.

**Table 2.** Pre-processed text of issue 1292

| |
|---|
| **Text:** 1274 add encode(logevent bytebufferdestination method layout appender implement bytebufferdestination interface layout.encode enable layout implementation process logevent create temporary object ticket track work let randomaccessfileappender roll variant implement bytebufferdestination interface layout.encode instead layout.tobytearray |
| **Vector:** $<0.66987733, -0.12908074, 0.01017888, 0.01252554>$ |

***A. Pre-Process.*** The pre-processing step of our approach is responsible for cleaning the text of requirements. The approach makes no assumption on the structure of the requirements. However, we do assume that the input requirements are written in English. The input to this step is processed following the steps below:

*1.1 Stop Words Removal.* Removal of language-specific stop words is important since most of the NLP models expect clean input. We use the spaCy[3] library for tokenizing the requirements and removing the English stop words from the text of the requirements. We also remove some of the domain-specific stop-words (e.g., system).

*1.2 POS Tagging.* Utilizing the full features of our pre-process pipeline, we also tag each of the tokens with their POS tags to guide lemmatization.

*1.3 Lemmatization.* We use the pre-trained English model from spaCy for the lemmatization of the requirements text. This step is necessary in order to avoid different interpretations of the same word in other forms. First row of Table 2 shows the text of issue 1292 after pre-processing.

***B. Training.*** The training step expects clean requirements, and their reuse links to the PL assets realizing them.

Each of the cleaned requirement is a training sample for the word embedding model. After training the word embedding model, the step produces vectors for the training set and a model that can be used to infer vectors for unseen requirements. The vectors obtained from the training set are given as an input to the unsupervised clustering algorithm. The unsupervised clustering algorithm (K-Means) is fitted to the input vectors, and the

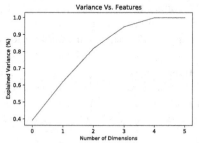

**Fig. 2.** Selected dimensions Vs. explained variance

vectors are iteratively clustered to $n$ number of clusters (calculated using the elbow method). The clustering step produces clusters and a model for later use. The running example (other than issue 1517) is used for the training phase.

---

[3] spaCy: Industrial-Strength NLP, https://spacy.io/.

**Table 3.** Clusters for the running example

| Cluster | Members |
| --- | --- |
| 1 | 1349 (linked to 1516), 1424 (linked to 1397), 1519 (linked to 1516) |
| 2 | 1291 (linked to 1274), 1292 (linked to 1274), 1305 (linked to 1397) |

*2.1 Word Embedding.* is a set of feature extraction and learning approaches used to extract numeric vectors from raw text. This is done by mapping the words and phrases of the requirements into vectors of real numbers. This allows the application of complex mathematical operations (such as Euclidean distance calculation) on the vectors representing the requirements. The effectiveness of the resultant pipeline is heavily dependent on the choice of the word embedding method. Thus we also presented an evaluation of different pipelines on an industrial data-set. Three different word embedding methods (and their variants) are supported by our approach and can be selected by the end-users. We presented each word embedding method supported by our approach below:

*Term Document Matrix-Based Word Embedding.* Our approach's default word embedding is based on the term co-occurrence matrix called Term Frequency Inverse Document Frequency (TFIDF). TFIDF vectors mostly contain redundant features, contributing to the high dimensionality of the vectors. We apply a dimensionality reduction technique called Principal Component Analysis (PCA) to remove the redundant and co-related features from the vectors. The resultant vectors are considered as a final output for clustering. The vectors generated for the running example are of 1051 dimensions. After applying PCA (as shown in Fig. 2), 1047 features can be dropped since those features do not contribute to the explained variance. Resultant vector for the issue 1292 is shown in Table 2.

*Neural Network-Based Word Embedding.* Our approach also supports vectors from the state-of-the-art Doc2Vec algorithm [14]. The Doc2Vec is designed for learning paragraph vectors and can be later used for inferring vectors for unseen paragraphs. Another neural network-based word embedding algorithm supported by our approach is the FastText [3]. FastText is another neural network-based approach for learning word vectors, utilizing character-level information. This makes FastText an ideal choice for domain-specific NLP tasks (such as word embedding for requirements). Note that vectors obtained from neural network-based word embedding usually do not require dimensionality reduction.

*2.2 Clustering* existing (vectors of) customer requirements aid the case-based recommendation process for the PL asset's reuse. This is done by predicting clusters for new customer requirements in the existing clusters, and the nearest neighbors' top reused PL assets are recommended for reuse. We use the K-Mean algorithm to cluster the vectors of existing customer requirements iteratively. While clustering the existing requirements, we also keep track of the links to the reused PL assets. This step produces clusters containing the vectors of exist-

**Table 4.** Generated Reuse recommendations

(b) For one industrial requirement
**Input: CUS-REQ-450**

(a) For the running example
**Input: 1517**

| Reuse | Sim. Score | Based on |
|-------|-----------|----------|
| *1516* | 0.84 | 1519 |
| 1397 | 0.06 | 1424 |

| Reuse | Sim. Score | Based on |
|-------|-----------|----------|
| *PL-1249* | 0.988 | CUS-REQ-449 |
| PL-1252 | 0.939 | CUS-REQ-451 |
| PL-906 | 0.901 | CUS-REQ-426 |
| PL-1069 | 0.879 | CUS-REQ-409 |
| PL-1333 | 0.622 | CUS-REQ-377 |

ing requirements. The produced clusters are stored for later use. The running example is clustered into two clusters, shown in Table 3.

***C. Asset Reuse Recommender.*** In this final step, the new customer requirements are cleaned following the same pre-process pipeline. The cleaned customer requirements are given as an input to the word embedding model obtained from the training phase. The model infers (computes) a vector for each customer requirements using the learned policy. The computed vectors for all new requirements are given as an input to the K-Means model to predict clusters for the new requirements' vectors in the existing clusters. For each new requirement, the existing closest customer requirement from the predicted cluster is selected, and their reused PL assets are retrieved. The retrieved PL assets (five at most) are then ranked based on the similarity between their source vectors (existing requirements) and the new vector (new requirement). Note that the approach recommends multiple PL assets because one requirement can be satisfied by one or many PL assets. For the running example, issue 1517 (predicted cluster, in this case, is 1) is given as an input to the Asset Reuse Recommender, and the output is shown in Table 4a. The Reuse column shows the recommended PL assets based on similarity (Sim. Score) with the existing customer requirements shown in Based on column. The actual (ground truth) reused PL asset is shown in italic in Table 4a. Table 4b shows a real run of the approach on an industrial case.

## 3    Evaluation

This section presents the evaluation of our approach on a data-set from the railway industry in detail. From a high-level view, we started the evaluation by considering the following four research questions.

*RQ1. Which word embedding algorithm produces the most accurate results in the context of PL asset reuse recommendation?* We investigate the accuracy of different word embedding algorithms for PL asset reuse recommendation on a real industrial data set.

**Table 5.** Summary of the pre-processing

| Reqs. | Before | | After | |
|---|---|---|---|---|
| – | Words | AVG. Words | Words | AVG. Words |
| 188 | 4527 | 24.079 | 2421 | 12.877 |

*RQ2. Are pre-trained word embedding models suitable in the context of PL asset reuse recommendation?* Since neural network-based word embedding models require large amounts of data for training (which might not be available), we investigate if pre-trained models can be used for reuse recommendations.

*RQ3. What is the execution time of different pipelines for reuse recommendations?* We aim at identifying the most efficient pipeline in terms of the time it takes to produce recommendations.

*RQ4. What are the potential benefits, drawbacks, and improvements in our approach in an industrial setting?* This research question captures the engineers' qualitative view on the results of the approach.

*Implementation.* All the pipelines (shown and discussed in sub-sect. 3) are implemented in Python 3. The pipelines are configured to process spreadsheets containing requirements and their reuse links exported from the requirements management tool. For neural network-based word embedding algorithms, we used the Gensim implementation [23], and for TFIDF word embedding and clustering, we used sci-kit learn implementation [20].

*Data Collection and Preparation.* We used two recently deployed industrial projects (derived products of the PPC product line at the company). The SPL is actively developed in the safety-critical domain by a large-scale company focusing on the development and manufacturing of railway vehicles. A manual reuse analysis was already performed on the customer requirements of these two projects, and therefore the data set contains the ground-truth.

We selected a relevant subset of requirements out of the requirements available in the two documents. We removed the non-requirements (explanation text and headings) inside both documents. The rest of the requirements were further filtered out by excluding 78 requirements having reuse links to a PL asset that is not reused by any other requirement in the data-set. A final set of 188 requirements was reached. The application of the above criteria was necessary to ensure that the training phase uses suitable data. The PL reuse frequency in the date-set is spanning between 2 and 12. The text of the 188 selected requirements was passed through our pre-process pipeline (outlined already in Fig. 1). Table 5 reports the total number of words and an average number of words per requirement both before and after pre-processing.

Besides, we conducted a two hours face-to-face focus group session. A focus group instrument was developed containing three topical questions based on RQ4. We recruited a convenience sample of individuals affiliated with our indus-

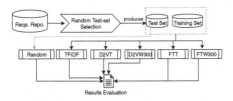
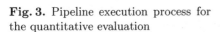
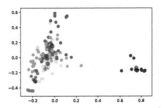

**Fig. 3.** Pipeline execution process for the quantitative evaluation

**Fig. 4.** Clustered requirements (training set) using K-Means

trial partner's organization. The participants in the focus group were five employees, all with more than ten years of experience. The participants work closely with requirements, bids, and product line engineering during their work hours. Note here that three of the participants were involved in the product derivation and requirements engineering activities in the selected projects. The interview was transcribed and then analyzed using Braun and Clarke's guidelines for thematic analysis [5]. Themes are high-level abstractions of the transcribed data. In our case, these themes were predefined and extracted from RQ4 (i.e., benefits, drawbacks, and improvements). We did a data-driven analysis for the actual thematic analysis without trying to make it fit into an existing theoretical framework. The transcription was coded independently by two authors to encourage diversity of codes, sub-themes, and themes.

*Evaluation Metrics for the Pipelines.* We used the standard metric accuracy (A) and exact match percentage (E) for the evaluation of our pipelines. We randomly selected 25% of our data for validation. A recommendation is correct if the recommendations generated by the pipeline contains the ground truth. In our case, accuracy is calculated as the ratio between the total number of correct recommendations and total instances in the test set. In addition, we use a stricter evaluation metric (i.e., exact match percentage). This is calculated using the ratio between the number of exactly correct recommendations (where the ground truth is ranked on the top of the list of recommendations) and the total number of instances in the test set.

*Procedure.* To answer our first three research questions, we executed our approach with different word embedding algorithms and included both term document matrix-based and neural network-based word embedding algorithms. We also include a random recommender as a pipeline. Two neural network-based pre-trained models (trained on Wikipedia documents) are also included in our evaluation to answer RQ2. Each pipeline (other than random) is given the same randomly selected 75% of the 188 requirements as the training set and the rest of the 25% of the data is used to validate the pipeline. Figure 3 shows the execution process of the resultant pipelines. Due to randomness involved in the algorithms, each pipeline is executed 15 times.

**Table 6.** Summary of pipelines validation

| Stats. | Random | | TFIDF | | D2VT | | D2VW300 | | FTT | | FTW300 | |
|---|---|---|---|---|---|---|---|---|---|---|---|---|
| %→ | A | E | A | E | A | E | A | E | A | E | A | E |
| AVG | 11.73 | 2.24 | **74** | **57.4** | 10.71 | 2.24 | 65.2 | 41.45 | 56.53 | 43.30 | 59.38 | 44.35 |
| SSD | 5.01 | 2.93 | 3.87 | 4.26 | 4.59 | 1.67 | 3.72 | 3.42 | 4.80 | 4.75 | 6.25 | 5.25 |
| VARS | 25.17 | 8.60 | 14.99 | 18.21 | 21.10 | 2.81 | 13.86 | 11.71 | 23.07 | 22.57 | 39.12 | 27.57 |

**Table 7.** Average time taken for pipelines (RQ3)

| Stats. | PP | Ran. | TFIDF | | D2VT | | D2VW300 | | FTT | | FTW300 | | C | RG |
|---|---|---|---|---|---|---|---|---|---|---|---|---|---|---|
| – | – | – | T | I | T | I | L(s) | I | T | I | L(s) | I | – | – |
| AVG. | 12.94 | 0.08 | 5.55 | 0.62 | 18.5 | 0.04 | 4.04 | 3.55 | 67.04 | 0.70 | 261.9 | 1.46 | 1.55 | 17.6 |
| SSD | 0.44 | ≈0 | 0.33 | 0.06 | 5.36 | ≈0 | 0.49 | 0.98 | 2.63 | 0.02 | 2.60 | 0.33 | 1.09 | 1.12 |
| VARS | ≈0 | ≈0 | 0.11 | ≈0 | 28.75 | ≈0 | 0.24 | 0.97 | 6.92 | ≈0 | 6.76 | 0.10 | 1.20 | 1.25 |
| TT | – | – | **38.26 ms** | | 50.63 ms | | 4.07 s | | 99.8 ms | | 261.9 s | | – | – |

All the pipelines were executed on an Apple MacBook Pro, 2018 with Intel Quad-Core i7 Processor (2.7 GHz) and 16 GB of primary memory. We further discuss the execution setup for each pipeline in the remainder of this section.

The *Random* pipeline was configured to randomly generate (for each requirement in the test set) five unique reuse recommendations from the list of 50 PL assets.

The *TFIDF* pipeline was configured to the maximum (0.5) and minimum (6) term frequencies. We considered the n-gram ranging from 1 to 8. The TFIDF pipeline is configured to build the matrix on the training set. The produced vectors (of 2750 dimensions) from the training-set are reduced with PCA configured to automatically select the top features (i.e., 95% or more of the explained variance of the data is captured by the selected dimensions). The reduced vectors of 86 dimensions from the PCA are stored and clustered using K-Means preserving the reuse links to PL assets. We used the Elbow method to compute the number of clusters using the vectors obtained from the PCA. Five clusters are used in all pipelines. Figure 4 shows the K-Means clusters of the data-set (with cluster's centers in light black color), showing only two dimensions of the training vectors obtained from one run. For each requirement in the test-set, the vectors from the TFIDF are generated and are reduced by PCA. The reduced vectors are plotted in the existing clusters produced by K-Means (during training), and at-most five recommendations for reuse are generated by looking into the reuse links of closest neighbors.

For *Doc2VecTraining (D2VT) and Doc2VecWiki300 (D2VW300)*, a model is trained with a vector size of 300. The model is configured to consider a minimum term frequency of two. A pre-trained Doc2Vec model from the Gensim data[4] is also considered for this evaluation. The model has a vocabulary size of 35556952,

---

[4] https://github.com/RaRe-Technologies/gensim-data.

and a vector size of 300. The cleaned customer requirements are vectorized using both of these configurations.

For *FastTextTraining (FTT) and FastTextWiki300 (FTW300)*, a model is trained with a vector size of 100. This model is configured to consider a minimum term frequency of one. We also considered a pre-trained model with a vector of size 300. The pre-trained model is trained on one million words from Wikipedia on the sub-words level. The obtained requirements vectors are clustered, and recommendations for reuse are generated.

## 3.1   Results and Discussion

To answer the stated research questions, we executed each pipeline 15 times using the same training and test set (selected randomly in each run). We also performed a focus group session with engineers. This section presents the answers to all of our research questions with essential bits in *Italic*.

*RQ1*: *Accuracy Results.* Table 6 shows the average accuracy and exact match results (from 15 runs) for each pipeline (shown in Fig. 3). The best accuracy and exact match ratio percentage are shown in bold text in Table 6. To summarize each run of each pipeline, we presented some of the descriptive statistics in the `Stats.` column. A sample standard deviation (SSD), and sample variance (VARS) is presented to give insights on the runs. *Automated reuse analysis using term document matrix-based pipeline (TFIDF) outperformed all other approaches in terms of accuracy (74%) and exact match percentage (57.4%).*

The second best word embedding algorithm (in terms of accuracy) in our context is the pre-trained Doc2Vec model (D2VW300). However, the exact match percentage score for the FastText pre-trained model is higher than the D2VW300 pipeline. It is also important to note that the Random pipeline outperformed the D2VT pipeline. This is because the neural network-based approaches require a huge data-set for learning. In cases where the data-set is small, *self trained models for word embedding should be avoided.* However, the FastText's self-trained (FTT) pipeline performed significantly better than the D2VT pipeline. This is because the FTT model utilizes sub-word information for learning, and this makes it more accurate than other self-trained pipelines.

*RQ2*: *Pre-Trained Models' Results.* Table 6 includes results from two pre-trained models (D2VW300 & FTW300). Our results suggest that the use of pre-trained models might be good in cases where the data-set is small. The second best pipeline for reuse recommendation is the pre-trained Doc2Vec pipeline (D2VW300). *Pre-trained models in automated reuse analysis produced more accurate results than self-trained models.* This is because of less data provided to the self-trained models. In many cases, transfer learning might be an ideal choice and is one of our future focuses.

*RQ3*: *Execution Time Results.* Table 7 shows the time taken by each pipeline. `Stats.` column shows average time (AVG.), Sample standard deviation of time (SSD), and sample variance of time (VARS). Pre-processing time (PP), each pipeline execution time, clustering time (C), and recommendation generation time (RG) are also shown in the table. All the values (except model loading) are the time taken values per requirement and are in milliseconds (ms). The time for model loading (L) is the time taken (in seconds) to load the pre-trained model. The time for the Random (Ran.) pipeline is the average time taken (ms) per recommendation. The total time (TT row) represents the total average time per requirement for the pipeline execution $(PP + Pipeline + C + RG)$. *TFIDF is the most efficient pipeline (in terms of execution time per requirement) for PL asset reuse analysis.*

Note that the Random pipeline takes even less time than the TFIDF pipeline, but produces inaccurate results. Our results also suggest that the FastText based pipelines might take significantly more time than other pipelines. However, this does not limit the application of FastText based pipelines in practice (since the model is loaded once per run).

***RQ4***: *Focus Group Results.* To answer this research question, we performed a thematic analysis of the data obtained from the focus group. In the first 15 min, our approach with the TFIDF pipeline was presented and executed on the dataset. After the pipeline generated the recommendations for the test-set), the participants reviewed six cases (i.e., one exact match, one with ground truth ranked down in the list, and four incorrect cases). After the participants reviewed the recommendations and their similarity scores, the participants were asked to discuss how accurate these recommendations are and what are the potential benefits, drawbacks, and improvements in the use of our approach. The rest of this section presents the findings related to three themes (also in Table 8).

**Table 8.** Identified sub-themes for the main themes.

| Theme | Sub-Theme |
| --- | --- |
| 1. Benefits | 1.1 Aid in the automation of PL reuse analysis |
| | 1.2 Relevant and useful recommendations |
| | 1.3 Quicker reuse analysis |
| 2. Drawbacks | 2.1 Lack of proper documentation |
| | 2.2 Effective selection of the training set |
| | 2.3 Tool integration in development processes |
| 3. Improvements | 3.1 Threshold tuning for similarity values |
| | 3.2 Careful consideration of cases for training |

*Theme 1.* Participants found that our approach is beneficial for automating the process of reuse analysis. Currently, this analysis is manual, and the use of a tool that recommends reuse can be very useful for quicker analysis. Several participants stated the pipeline could provide relevant and useful recommendations early on in the development process and can avoid redundancy of assets.

*Theme 2.* Several challenges has been identified during the focus group. According to the participants, the lack of proper documentation for how this approach works and the underlying algorithms used for recommendations can hinder the adoption of such a tool. Another challenge mentioned by the participants was the effective selection of the training set of requirements. When asked how the practitioners would integrate the reuse analysis method into their process setting, we got varying answers depending on the team setting. However, all practitioners saw the full potential of automated reuse analysis if integrated into their existing tool-chains.

*Theme 3.* After reviewing the six cases, the participants discussed the accuracy results. For two cases, the recommendations were considered correct, relevant, and useful. In four other cases, the recommendations given by our approach were considered wrong. Note here that for these cases, the similarity values were consistently low. Participants suggested that the pipeline should not recommend reuse in cases where the recommendations are based on a similarity value below a certain threshold. For one of these cases, our approach accurately recommended the PL asset, but participants stated that it was the wish of the customer to include a relevant alternative PL asset. In addition, participants recommended that the pipeline should not include such cases for training.

## 3.2   Validity Threats

In this section, we present the validity threats following guidelines proposed by Runeson and Höst [24].

The requirements-level similarity might not be the best predictor of actual software reuse. To mitigate the internal validity threat, we verified that requirements-level similarity could be used to recommend PL asset reuse. This initial verification was performed by the use of topic modeling, where we verified that requirements sharing common topics are indeed realized by common PL assets. We also reviewed the current process of reuse analysis at our industrial partner's company and found that requirements-level similarity plays a significant role in reuse analysis.

Our results are based on data from one company using a data-set of 188 requirements created by industrial engineers. To mitigate potential external validity threats, we based our evaluation on requirements from two different projects, originated from different sources. Even if the number of requirements can be considered quite small, we argue that having access to real industrial requirements created by engineers working in the safety-critical domain can be representative. More studies are needed to generalize these results to other systems and domains. In addition, our work is based on the assumption that traceability links are maintained between assets and requirements. This assumption limits the applicability of our approach.

Finally, we address the threats to the reliability of our results by providing enough details on the setup of each pipeline. Our results are also based on 15 runs of each pipeline to address the randomness involved in the process.

## 4   Related Work

The related work in this area can be classified into three different lines of research. This section summarizes each class of related work.

*Feature Extraction.* Over the years, a huge amount of research has been focused on feature model extraction and feature recommendation for SPL [16]. Most of these approaches look for commonalities and variability to suggest features and extract feature diagrams. Public documents are being used for mining common domain terminologies and their variability(e.g., [9]). These approaches focus on aggregating natural language requirements to extract a high-level system feature model. Latent semantic analysis (LSA) is used to calculate the similarity between requirements pairs [27]. This approach clusters the requirements based on similarity and extracts feature trees. The Semantic and Ontological Variability Analysis (SOVA) [11] uses semantic role labeling to calculate behavioral similarity and generate feature model. In addition, bottom-up technologies for reuse (BUT4Reuse [17]) are used for reverse engineering variability from various artifacts.

*Requirements Reuse.* Another class of approaches [10] are focused on deriving and structuring a generic set of requirements that can be reused for PL and configured for derived products. For example, Zen-ReqConfig [15] uses models to aid in the structuring of requirements, reuse, and configuration at the requirements level. Arias et al. [2] proposed a framework for managing requirements that uses a defined taxonomy to aid the reuse of requirements in an SPL. Pacheco *et al.* proposed an approach for functional requirements reuse focused on small companies with no PL architecture [19]. In addition, Moon *et al.* [18] proposed a systematic method for deriving generic domain requirements as core reusable assets by analyzing the existing legacy requirements.

*Traceability.* Another set of approaches are focused on traceability link recovery [4]. These approaches recommend possible traceability links between different artifacts (e.g., requirements, source code). Yu *et al.* proposed an approach to recover traceability links between features and domain requirements [28]. The approach extracts and merge application feature models and establish their traceability links. Wang *et al.* proposed a co-reference-aware approach to traceability link recovery and also proposed an algorithm for automated tracing of dependability requirements [26]. IR-based approaches for traceability link recovery are well-known solutions to trace recovery (e.g., [7]. These approaches mostly uses term-document matrix-based similarity for tracing requirements.

The approaches classified in Feature Extraction & Requirements Reuse categories are focused on extracting feature models and domain requirements. On the other hand, the approaches included in the Traceability category are closely related to our approach since these are focusing on establishing the links between requirements and other artifacts. Compared to our work, the traceability approaches are not directly recommending the reuse of PL assets in a PL context but can be tailored for reuse recommendation. In addition, existing approaches also do not make use of existing cases for reuse reasoning. To the best of our knowledge, we are the first to support the reuse analysis of PL assets in a context of a clone-and-own reuse process.

## 5 Conclusion

In this paper, we proposed an automated approach for requirements-level reuse analysis of product line assets. The approach uses existing customer requirements to recommend possible PL assets that can be reused to implement new requirements. We evaluated our approach in the railway industry. The results show that the proposed approach was able to recommend reuse of PL assets with 74% average accuracy and 57.4% exact match ratio. We also presented an evaluation of five different pipelines with varying word embedding algorithms, which demonstrated that the document matrix-based word embedding algorithm performed significantly better than other pipelines. We also found that the self-training of the neural network-based word embedding algorithm should be avoided if the data-set is small. In such cases, transfer learning should be performed with existing pre-trained models. Our results also show that the Doc2Vec pre-trained model performed better than the FastText's pre-trained model. In terms of the practicality of the pipelines, we found that the maximum end-to-end execution time of the approach is around 262 s. The validation of the results in our focus group session with five engineers also confirmed the applicability of such pipelines in practice. In particular, results shows that the approach automates the reuse analysis with highly relevant reuse recommendations.

Our future work includes an empirical evaluation of requirements-level reuse recommenders. We aim to investigate the teams performing reuse analysis with and without a reuse recommender. Investigating Bidirectional Encoder Representations from Transformers (BERT [8]) model for requirement-level reuse is also one of our future focus.

## References

1. Abbas, M., Jongeling, R., Lindskog, C., Enoiu, E.P., Saadatmand, M., Sundmark, D.: Product line adoption in industry: an experience report from the railway domain. In: 24th ACM International Systems and Software Product Line Conference. ACM (2020)
2. Arias, M., Buccella, A., Cechich, A.: A framework for managing requirements of software product lines. Electron. Not. Theor. Comput. Sci. **339**, 5–20 (2018)
3. Bojanowski, P., Grave, E., Joulin, A., Mikolov, T.: Enriching word vectors with subword information. Trans. Assoc. Comput. Linguist. **5**, 135–146 (2017)
4. Borg, M., Runeson, P., Ardö, A.: Recovering from a decade: a systematic mapping of information retrieval approaches to software traceability. Empir. Softw. Eng. **19**(6), 1565–1616 (2013). https://doi.org/10.1007/s10664-013-9255-y
5. Braun, V., Clarke, V.: Using thematic analysis in psychology. Qual. Res. Psychol. **3**(2), 77–101 (2006)

6. Dag, J.N.O., Gervasi, V., Brinkkemper, S., Regnell, B.: A linguistic-engineering approach to large-scale requirements management. IEEE Softw. **22**(1), 32–39 (2005)
7. De Lucia, A., Oliveto, R., Tortora, G.: Adams re-trace: traceability link recovery via latent semantic indexing. In: International Conference on Software Engineering, ICSE 2008, New York, NY, USA, pp. 839–842. ACM (2008)
8. Devlin, J., Chang, M.W., Lee, K., Toutanova, K.: Bert: pre-training of deep bidirectional transformers for language understanding. arXiv preprint arXiv:1810.04805 (2018)
9. Ferrari, A., Spagnolo, G.O., Orletta, F.D.: Mining commonalities and variabilities from natural language documents. In: International Software Product Line Conference, Tokyo, Japan, pp. 116–120. ACM (2013)
10. Irshad, M., Petersen, K., Poulding, S.: A systematic literature review of software requirements reuse approaches. Inf. Softw. Technol. **93**(2017), 223–245 (2018)
11. Itzik, N., Reinhartz-Berger, I., Wand, Y.: Variability analysis of requirements: considering behavioral differences and reflecting Stakeholders' perspectives. IEEE Trans. Software Eng. **42**, 687–706 (2016)
12. Krueger, C.W.: Software reuse. ACM Comput. Surv. **24**(2), 131–183 (1992)
13. Lam, W., McDermid, T., Vickers, A.: Ten steps towards systematic requirements reuse. In: International Symposium on Requirements Engineering, pp. 6–15 (1997)
14. Le, Q.V., Mikolov, T.: Distributed representations of sentences and documents. CoRR abs/1405.4053 (2014). http://arxiv.org/abs/1405.4053
15. Li, Y., Yue, T., Ali, S., Zhang, L.: Enabling automated requirements reuse and configuration. Softw. Syst. Model. **18**(3), 2177–2211 (2017). https://doi.org/10.1007/s10270-017-0641-6
16. Li, Y., Schulze, S., Saake, G.: Reverse engineering variability from natural language documents: a systematic literature review. In: Proceedings of Software Product Line Conference, Sevilla, Spain, vol. 1, pp. 133–142 (2017)
17. Martinez, J., Ziadi, T., Bissyandé, T.F., Klein, J., Traon, Y.L.: Bottom-up adoption of software product lines: a generic and extensible approach. In: International Conference on Software Product Line, SPLC 2015, Nashville, TN, USA, July 20–24, 2015, pp. 101–110 (2015)
18. Moon, M., Yeom, K., Chae, H.S.: An approach to developing domain requirements as a core asset based on commonality and variability analysis in a product line. IEEE Trans. Software Eng. **31**(7), 551–569 (2005)
19. Pacheco, C., Garcia, I., Calvo-Manzano, J.A., Arcilla, M.: Reusing functional software requirements in small-sized software enterprises: a model oriented to the catalog of requirements. Requirements Eng. **22**(2), 275–287 (2016). https://doi.org/10.1007/s00766-015-0243-1
20. Pedregosa, F., et al.: Scikit-learn: machine learning in Python. J. Mach. Learn. Res. **12**, 2825–2830 (2011)
21. Pohl, K., Böckle, G., van Der Linden, F.J.: Software Product Line Engineering: Foundations, Principles and Techniques. Springer, Heidelberg (2005). https://doi.org/10.1007/3-540-28901-1
22. Rath, M., Mäder, P.: The SEOSS 33 dataset - Requirements, bug reports, code history, and trace links for entire projects. Data in Brief **25** (2019)
23. Řehůřek, R., Sojka, P.: Software framework for topic modelling with large corpora. In: Proceedings of the LREC 2010 Workshop on New Challenges for NLP Frameworks, pp. 45–50. ELRA, May 2010
24. Runeson, P., Höst, M.: Guidelines for conducting and reporting case study research in software engineering. Empir. Softw. Eng. **14**(2), 131–164 (2009)

25. Schlingloff, H., Kruse, P.M., Saadatmand, M.: Excellence in variant testing. In: Proceedings of the 14th International Working Conference on Variability Modelling of Software-Intensive Systems, VAMOS 2020. ACM (2020)
26. Wang, W., Niu, N., Liu, H., Niu, Z.: Enhancing automated requirements traceability by resolving polysemy. In: International Requirements Engineering Conference, RE 2018, pp. 40–51. IEEE (2018)
27. Weston, N., Chitchyan, R., Rashid, A.: A framework for constructing semantically composable feature models from natural language requirements. In: International Software Product Line Conference, pp. 211–220 (2009)
28. Yu, D., Geng, P., Wu, W.: Constructing traceability between features and requirements for software product line engineering. In: Proceedings - Asia-Pacific Software Engineering Conference, APSEC, vol. 2, pp. 27–34. IEEE (2012)

# Learning to Recommend Trigger-Action Rules for End-User Development
## A Knowledge Graph Based Approach

Qinyue Wu, Beijun Shen[✉], and Yuting Chen[✉]

School of Electronic Information and Electrical Engineering, Shanghai Jiao Tong University, Shanghai, China
{wuqinyue,bjshen,chenyt}@sjtu.edu.cn

**Abstract.** Trigger-action programming (TAP) is a popular programming paradigm in the IoT world. It allows non-professional end users to program by themselves, in a form of a set of *trigger-action rules*, for automating IoT devices and online services meeting their needs. Since the number of smart devices/services keeps increasing and the combinations between triggers and actions become numerous, it is challenging for novice users to present their demands through TAP. On the other hand, a number of TAP rules do exist in TAP communities; it is promising to collect these rules and recommend appropriate ones to end users during their development. This paper conducts a preliminary empirical study, revealing three problems in recommending TAP rules, *i.e.*, the *cold-start* problem, the *repeat-consumption* problem, and the *conflict* problem. To solve these problems, we propose rtar, a semantic-aware approach to recommending trigger-action rules: (1) it designs a trigger-action knowledge graph (TaKG) for modeling the relationships among IoT devices/ services, triggers, and actions; and (2) it learns to recommend trigger-action rules by extracting features from TaKG and training a ranking model. We evaluate rtar against *RecRules* (a state-of-the-art approach) on real user data collected from IFTTT, one of the largest TAP communities. The results clearly show the strengths of rtar. In particular, rtar outperforms *RecRules* by 26% in $R@5$ and 21% in $NDCG@5$, indicating that rtar is of higher precision than *RecRules* in rule recommendations.

**Keywords:** End user development · Trigger-action programming · Rule recommendation · Knowledge graph

## 1 Introduction

End user development allows end users without programming experiences to develop their software artifacts [1,18]. One popular paradigm is trigger-action programming (TAP). TAP facilitates end users to program by themselves for automating IoT devices [12] and/or online services (*e.g.*, social medias [25], and scientific computations [5]). Due to its simplicity and popularity, TAP has

© Springer Nature Switzerland AG 2020
S. Ben Sassi et al. (Eds.): ICSR 2020, LNCS 12541, pp. 190–207, 2020.
https://doi.org/10.1007/978-3-030-64694-3_12

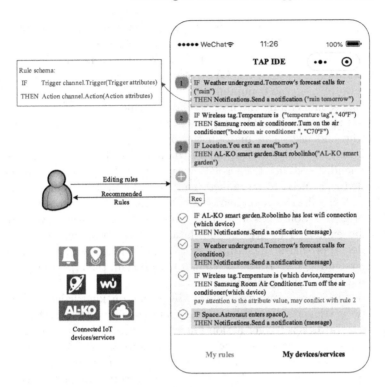

**Fig. 1.** An example of a TAP rule recommendation.

been promoted by many communities and organizations, such as IFTTT [14], Microsoft Power Automate [20], Zapier [29], and Mozilla WebThings [21].

A TAP program usually consists of one or more *trigger-action rules*, each having the form of

$$\text{rule: [If } \underline{\text{trigger}} \text{ Then } \underline{\textit{action}}]$$

Each rule specifies a *triggering event* and an *action* that should be carried out. For instance, a user may write a rule, saying that <u>she/he needs to be notified</u> (the action) when <u>the weather forecast says it will rain tomorrow</u> (the trigger).

One notable phenomenon is that the number of smart devices and online services keeps growing. Each device (or service) has its triggers and actions, and the potential rules (*i.e.*, the combinations between triggers and actions) are thus numerous. Rules also need to be systematically organized in one TAP program, targeting at multiple goals. It becomes challenging for non-professional users to design rules presenting complex, yet commonly desired, activities.

On the other hand, many TAP rules are available in TAP communities, such as IFTTT and Zapier. It is promising to collect these rules and recommend appropriate ones to end users during their development: a user only needs to search for a TAP rule meeting her/his demands followed by making minor revisions. Meanwhile, few TAP communities support personalized rule recommendations. Let IFTTT be an example. It only provides users with hottest rules; it also allows users to search for TAP rules, while a user must present her/his demand accurately, as the community only performs textual-textual similarity comparisons, recommending the user the hottest rule.

A state-of-the-art is *RecRules* [8], which recommends one or more TAP rules such that the end users can pick up the most appropriate ones during their software development. However, it is non-trivial to develop such a trigger-action rule recommender system—trigger-action rules need to be fuzzy searched, the recommended rules need to be ranked, and the rules picked up need to be customized *w.r.t.* the devices and their states. Furthermore, we use a web crawler to collect trigger-action rules in IFTTT and create a dataset **TAPData**. As what will be explained in Sect. 2, the dataset reveals that existing TAP rule recommender approaches (including *RecRules*) are faced with three problems when recommending TAP rules: the cold-start problem, the repeat-consumption problem, and the conflict problem.

To solve these problems, we build a trigger-action knowledge graph TaKG and propose a trigger-action rule recommendation approach rtar for end-user development. TaKG is a trigger-action knowledge graph modeling trigger-action rules, IoT devices/ services, users, and their relationships. rtar is a semantic and context-aware approach to recommending trigger-action rules. As Fig. 1 shows, rtar aids an end user in editing TAP rules: it learns to recommend trigger-action rules through extracting features from TaKG and training a ranking model.

This paper makes the following contributions:

1. **A preliminary empirical study.** We collect a dataset from IFTTT, and perform a preliminary empirical study. The study reveals that a rule recommender system may be faced with three problems: the cold-start problem, the repeat-consumption problem, and the conflict problem.
2. **Knowledge graph.** We design a knowledge graph TaKG. TaKG models both of the ontological concepts and the instances in the TAP domain. It is a hybrid model, consisting of functionality hierarchies and rule collaborative graphs. TaKG guides rtar to reveal the latent (and usually the semantic) relationships among rules and users, recommending semantically relevant rules to end users.
3. **Approach.** We design rtar to recommend trigger-action rules. rtar is a learning-to-recommend technique; it extracts three types of well-designed features from TaKG and trains a ranking model for rule recommendations: 1) the collaborative features for collaborative-filtering-based recommendations, 2) the content matching feature for content-based recommendations, 3) the behavior features for solving the repeat consumption problem.
4. **Evaluation.** We evaluate rtar against state-of-the-art trigger-action rule recommendation approaches on TAPData. The results show that rtar is effective in recommending trigger-action rules for end user development. More specifically, it solves the three above-mentioned problems; it also outperforms

**Table 1.** A rule example in TAPData.

| Type | Field | Value |
|------|-------|-------|
| Trigger | Channel | Smanos connect |
| | Event | System armed |
| | Description | This Trigger fires when your smanos system is armed to away mode with no one in the house |
| Action | Channel | Tado air conditioning |
| | Event | Turn AC off |
| | Description | This Action will turn your AC off |
| Auxiliary data | Author | tony09 |
| | Created Time | 2020-03-22 08:29:23 -0700 |
| | Description | If smanos is set to away mode, then turn tado AC off |

*RecRules* by 26% in $R@5$ and 21% in $NDCG@5$, indicating that rtar is of higher precision than *RecRules* in rule recommendations.

The rest of the paper is organized as follows. Section 2 presents a preliminary empirical study, in which we reveal three problems in recommending TAP rules. Section 3 presents the trigger-action knowledge graph and describes the technical details of the rtar approach. Section 4 evaluates rtar on the TAPData dataset. Section 5 presents related work. Section 6 concludes.

## 2    A Preliminary Empirical Study

We use a web crawler to collect trigger-action rules in IFTTT and create a dataset **TAPData**. TAPData contains 72,107 rules created by 39,480 authors. Each rule, as Table 1 shows, specifies the trigger (Channel, Event, and Description) and the action (Channel, Event, and Description). Auxiliary data items are also collected, including the author who has created a rule, the creation time, and a description of the rule.

An analysis of the dataset also reveals that rule recommendation approaches are faced with three practical problems:

1. *The cold-start problem.* As Fig. 2(a) shows, each author creates 1–837 rules (2 on average); 84% of authors are cold users, having created only one or two rules. It clearly indicates a rule recommender system can face a cold-start problem—Let many end users be cold users having few records in a rule corpus. Learning to recommend TAP rules to these cold users is a challenging task.
2. *The repeat-consumption problem.* As Fig. 2(b) shows, 12% of the authors have created and/or used repeated rules (with minor revisions), and up to 28% of the rules in the dataset are similar. It implies a rule in end user development

can be a mixture of a repeated rule and some novelties. A TAP recommender system needs to tackle the repeat-consumption problem.

3. *The conflict problem.* Some TAP rules in a rule corpus can be conflict with each other. Users may also write inconsistent rules. We randomly selected the TAP rules written by 100 users from TAPData. It can be observed that the rules of 15% of users are of conflicts. It will save many development efforts if end users can obtain rules that do not conflict with their demands.

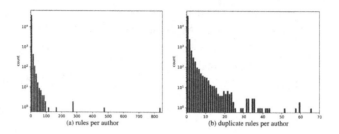

**Fig. 2.** Analysis of TAPData.

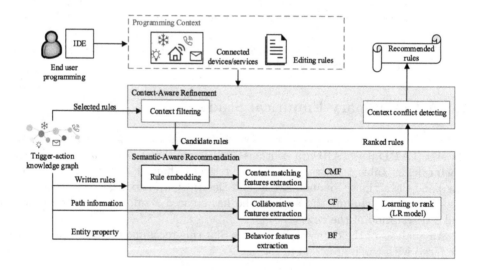

**Fig. 3.** Overview of rtar.

## 3  Approach

rtar learns to recommend trigger-action rules to end users. As Fig. 3 shows, it designs a TAP knowledge graph (Sect. 3.1), and performs a semantic and context-aware approach to recommending trigger-action rules (Sect. 3.2 and 3.3).

### 3.1    Trigger-Action Knowledge Graph

We follow an ontology approach to design TaKG, a domain-specific knowledge graph for the TAP paradigm. As Fig. 4 shows, TaKG has *an ontology layer* and *an instance layer*. The ontology layer contains a hybrid model with two sub-models:

1. *Rule collaboration graph*. This sub-model defines users, rules, devices/services and their collaborative relations.
2. *Functionality hierarchy*. This sub-model defines two functionality hierarchies for triggers and actions. The functions of the triggers and the actions are organized at the high, the medium, and the low levels.

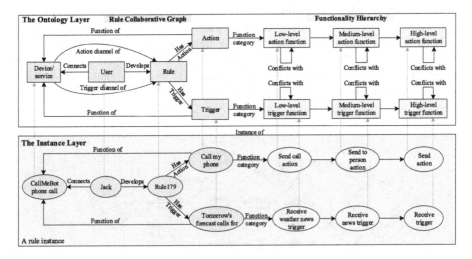

**Fig. 4.** Overview of the TaKG knowledge graph. The ovals, the rectangles, and the edges represent instances, classes, and relations, respectively.

Each instance in the instance layer corresponds to a trigger-action rule. An instance is also composed of a rule collaboration graph and a functionality hierarchy, which can be mapped into the model on the ontology layer.

**Construction of TaKG.** We perform a schema analysis of TAPData, and construct the ontology layer of the rule collaboration graph. The functionality hierarchies are extracted from EUPont [7], an ontological representation of end-user development in the IoT. Since conflicts can exist among actions (*e.g.*, an action that is to increase the temperature and another to decrease the temperature) [3], we further add the "conflicts with" relations among functionalities. These relations are used to filter out the rule candidates conflicting with the editing rules.

Given a set of trigger-action rules and descriptions of connected IoT devices/ services, we build the instance layer through extracting information from the rules. The two sub-models are then connected through categorizing trigger-action rules by their functions. Relations are checked by the TAP experts to guarantee their correctness.

**Semantic Reasoning.** With the functionality hierarchies of TaKG, the similarities among rules are calculated in terms of their shared functionalities. That is, the rule similarities can be semantically reasoned by analyzing the categories and super-categories of the triggers and the actions involved in [8]. The conflict relations can be used for semantic reasoning as well.

Figure 5 shows an example of the user-rule collaborations in TaKG. Syntactically, the users and the rules are less relevant—The actions "Electric switch on" (Rule2) and "Start heating" (Rule3) look independent; Rule3 may be related with Rule4 since they have the same action channel.

TaKG allows engineers to mine paths among trigger-action rules and capture their latent relations. First, Rule2 and Rule3 are related with each other because (1) both of their actions have the "Enable heating" action functionality; (2) there exists a path (Rule2, $hasAction$, $action1$, $functionCategory$, $function1$, $functionCategory^{-1}$, $action2$, $hasAction^{-1}$, Rule3), denoting that the two rules share some functionalities. Second, Rule3 conflicts with Rule4, because a path between them contains a conflict relation.

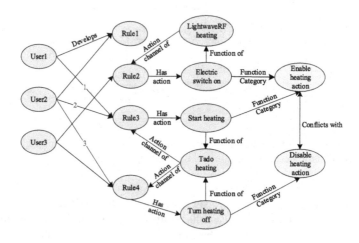

**Fig. 5.** An example of user-rule collaborations in TaKG.

### 3.2   Semantic-Aware Recommendation

To compute the top-N recommendations, rtar performs a feature engineering on TaKG and trains a ranking model; it learns a scoring function, sorting the rule candidates according to their relevances.

rtar employs a *pointwise* technique with a logistic regression model [16]. First, each of the features extracted is normalized

$$\hat{x} = \frac{x - x_{min}}{x_{max} - x_{min}}$$

where $x_{max}$ and $x_{min}$ denote the max and the min values of the features, respectively. Next, the features are concatenated as the input to the ranking model and the rules are recommended by their output scores.

For each rule candidate $r \in R_u^c$ and the set of rules $R_u^w$ written by the user $u$, we extract several features from TaKG for constructing the model. Table 2 summarizes the features used by rtar, including one content matching related feature, five collaborative related ones, and three behavior related ones.

**Content Matching-Related Feature (CMF).** This feature is designed for content-based recommendation. It measures whether a rule matches the user preference.

**Table 2.** Summary of features.

| Type | Description |
|---|---|
| Content Matching Related | ① CMF (*Content Matching Feature*): the matchings of the rule candidates and the user preference. They are calculated by the DKN model and enhanced by the knowledge graph embedding |
| Collaborative Related | ② UCF (*User Collaborative Feature*): the possibility of the user choosing a rule. It calculates how many similar users prefer this rule |
| | ③ ACCF (*Action Channel Collaborative Feature*): the similarity of action channels between the user's previous rules and the rule candidates |
| | ④ ACF (*Action Collaborative Feature*): the similarity of actions between the user's previous rules and the rule candidates |
| | ⑤ TCCF (*Trigger Channel Collaborative Feature*): the similarity of trigger channels between the user's previous rules and the rule candidates |
| | ⑥ TCF (*Trigger Collaborative Feature*): the similarity of triggers between the user's previous rules and the rule candidates |
| Behavior Related | ⑦ RPF (*Rule Popularity Feature*): the total number of usages of the rule by all of the users |
| | ⑧ URF (*User Repeat-consumption Feature*): the number of duplicates of the rule for a user |
| | ⑨ RRF (*Rule Repeat-consumption Feature*): the number of duplicates of the rule for all of the users |

rtar employs the Kim CNN [17] to encode a rule candidate by combining the entity embedding of the rule and the function category embeddings of the rule entities in TaKG. Embeddings of all rules written by the user are concatenated as the user preference. Let $e(u)$ be the user $u$'s embedding. Let $e(r_j)$ be the embedding of a candidate rule $r_j \in R_u^c$. The probability of $u$ choosing $r_j$ is predicted by a neural network $G$. DKN [26], a knowledge-aware neural network then computes the matching degree of the user and the candidate rule using

$$\text{CMF}_{u,r_j} = G(e(u), e(r_j))$$

**Collaborative-Related Features (CF).** The collaborative features are extracted for both of the user- and the item-based collaborative filtering recommendations. We extract five collaborative features for modeling user preferences.

(1) *UCF* computes the number of paths between the given user and the candidate rule. An intuition is that users are similar to each other if they have written similar rules. UCF is defined as:

$$\text{UCF}_{u,r_j} = \#P_{u,r_j},$$

where $\#P_{u,r_j}$ is the number of paths between $u$ and $r_j$. Each path has the form of $P_{u,r_j} = (u, develops, r_x, develops^{-1}, u_y, develops, r_j)$, where $u_y \neq u$ and $r_x \neq r_j$.

The more paths between the rule and the user, the more likely the user is interested in the rule.

(2) *ACF* computes the shortest path between two rules in terms of their action channels. The shorter the length, the more similar the two rules. Here we have

$$\text{ACF}_{u,r_j} = \sum_{r_i \in R_u^w \cap r_i \neq r_j} computeSim_{r_j, r_i},$$

where the similarity between two rules is computed

$$computeSim_{r_j, r_i} = \frac{1}{|P_{r_j, r_i}|},$$

where $P_{r_j, r_i} = (r_j, hasAction, action1, functionCategory, function1, ..., func-tionN, functionCategory^{-1}, ..., functionm, hasAction^{-1}, actionn, hasAction^{-1}, r_i)$, and $|P_{r_j, r_i}|$ returns the length of a path between $r_i$ and $r_j$ ($r_j \neq r_i$).

*ACCF, TCCF* and *TCF* can be similarly computed.

**Behavior-Related Features (BF).** Behavior features model the users' repeating behaviors. We extract three behavior features from users' history interactions.

(1) *RPF.* It sums up the usage of a popular rule by all of the users.

$$\text{RPF}_r = \sum_{u \in U} \alpha_{u,r},$$

where $\alpha_{u,r}$ denotes the number of path $(u, develops, r)$. This feature is designed because a popular rule can be frequently chosen by end users [6].

(2) *URF*. Given a rule $r$, it computes the duplicates of the rule for a user $u$. Since users may have different repeating habits, it is necessary to model a user and her/his individual behaviors.

$$\mathrm{URF}_{u,r} = \alpha_{u,r} - 1$$

(3) *RRF*. It computes the total duplicates of a given rule *w.r.t.* all of the users. Intuitively, a rule is likely to be repeated if it has been repeated frequently.

$$\mathrm{RRF}_r = \sum_{u \in U} \mathrm{URF}_{u,r}$$

### 3.3  Context-Aware Refinement

rtar is also a context-aware recommendation approach. It refines candidate/recommended trigger-action rules according to a user's programming context, where the context includes the rules under development and the connected IoT devices/services.

Before the learning to recommend stage, rtar performs a context filtering. It guarantees all recommended rules are executed by one of the connected IoT devices/services. When a user is editing rules in IDE, rtar captures the programming context, including the editing rules and the IoT devices/services; it then retrieves the rules related with the connected IoT devices/services, by querying TaKG, as the candidates.

After the learning to recommend stage, rtar also performs a conflict detection. Inconsistent actions and rules are detected and reported during this phase. Note that a rule having `conflicts with` relations with the existing rules can still be recommended. It relies on the end user to make a decision on either rejecting this rule or accepting it with revisions.

## 4  Evaluation

We have evaluated rtar on the TAPData dataset. The evaluation is designed to answer two research questions:

- **RQ1.** Is rtar precise in recommending trigger-action rules?
- **RQ2.** Has rtar solved the cold-start problem, the repeat-consumption problem, and the conflict problem when recommending the TAP rules?

### 4.1  Setup

**Methods Under Comparisons.** We compare rtar with the following state-of-the-art techniques. These techniques are implemented atop a publicly available software library for recommender systems [13]:

1. *Pop*. It sorts rules on the basis of their popularities, and recommends the top-n rules.

2. *User-KNN* [15]. *User-KNN* is a user-based collaborative filtering method. It recommends items to a user on the basis of other users' opinions to these items.
3. *Item-KNN* [15]. It is an item-based collaborative filtering method. A rating is estimated by ratings made by the same user on similar items.
4. *RecRules* [8]. It is a trigger-action rule recommender system equipped with a learning-to-rank technique.

Note that the above methods cannot deal with the three problems. For example, the original *RecRules* repeatedly recommends rules to 97% of the users. Thus, we make some modifications—repeated rules with low confidences are removed from the results; we also let *RecRules* be equipped with TaKG and path information be extracted for rule recommendations.

**Dataset.** We use the rules in TAPData for training and testing. We select users who have 2+ rules in TAPData. The dataset is split into a training set with 70% rules as positive samples, a testing set with 20% rules, and a validating set with 10% rules for tuning the hyperparameters. We also add negative samples, as [22] suggests.

**Metrics.** $R@k$ (Recall) and $NDCG@k$ (Normalized Discounted Cumulative Gain) are selected to measure the precision of the recommendation approaches. Here, $R@k$ calculates the percentage of recommended rules in all rules a user really write, and $NDCG@k$ measures the normalized discounted cumulative gain of the result list.

These metrics are defined as follows:

$$R@k = \frac{1}{|U|} \sum_{u \in U} \left| \frac{Hits_u}{Test_u} \right|,$$

where $Hits_u$ denotes the rules really used by the user $u$, $Test_u$ the test set of the user $u$, and $U$ the set of $u$.

$$NDCG@k = \frac{DCG@k}{IDCG@k}$$

and

$$DCG@k = \sum_{i=1}^{k} \frac{2^{rel_i} - 1}{log_2(i + 1)},$$

where $DCG$ (Discounted Cumulative Gain) is a measure of ranking quality by calculating gain of the result list, with the gain of each result discounted at lower ranks, $rel_i$ is the relevance score (0/1), and $IDCG$ (Ideal Discounted cumulative Gain) is the maximum possible $DCG$, letting all relevant documents be sorted by their relevances.

To evaluate whether the repeat-consumption problem can be solved, we use another two metrics: $SR$ and $SNR$. $SR$ represents the ability of recommending a repeated rule successfully. The higher the $SR$ value, the stronger the recommendation approach in recommending repeated rules.

$$SR_u = \begin{cases} 1 & Test_u \cap Hits_u \cap Train_u \neq \varnothing \\ 0 & otherwise \end{cases}$$

$$U_{reru} = u \in U, Test_u \cap Train_u \neq \varnothing$$

$$SR = \frac{1}{|U_{reru}|} \sum_{u \in U_{reru}} SR_u$$

$SNR$ represents whether a user receives at least one repeated rule that the user has never written. The lower the $SNR$ value, the better the approach.

$$SNR_u = \begin{cases} 1 & Test_u \cap Train_u = \varnothing, Hits_u \cap Train_u \neq \varnothing \\ 0 & otherwise \end{cases}$$

$$U_{nore} = u \in U \cap u \notin U_{reru}$$

$$SR = \frac{1}{|U_{nore}|} \sum_{u \in U_{nore}} SNR_u$$

### 4.2    RQ1: Precision

We evaluate the five approaches in recommending the top-5 rules. One reason for this is that many users only focus on the top-5 rules, especially when they develop their programs in a small TAP IDE on smart devices. Table 3 shows the evaluation results. The results indicate that:

- Among all the methods, *Pop* achieves the worst results. A popularity-based predictor is not customized, without realizing the differences among users. Consequently, *Pop* is not precise enough compared with the other approaches.
- The two collaborative filtering methods (*User-KNN* and *Item-KNN*) are of low precisions. One reason is that the dataset is a mixture of hot and cold data, while the traditional collaborative filtering methods do not deal with cold-start scenarios.
- *RecRules* achieves a higher precision than *Pop* and the collaborative filtering methods. It indicates that the side information provided by the knowledge graph enhances trigger-action rule recommendations. However, *RecRules* only leverages path-based features for generating a learning-to-recommend model, but fails to solve the repeat-consumption problem.

Comparatively, rtar achieves the highest precision. rtar leverages the path information and the embeddings of the knowledge graph, and designs specific features for learning-to-recommending trigger-action rules. It achieves the $R@5$ value (0.24) and the $NDCG@5$ value (0.41), implying rtar can effectively recommend the rules a user needs and sort the rules such that highly relevant rules can be placed on highly ranked positions. In particular, rtar outperforms *RecRules* by 26% in $R@5$ and 21% in $NDCG@5$, indicating that rtar is more precise than *RecRules* in recommending trigger-action rules.

**Table 3.** A comparison of the precisions.

| Metrics | Pop | User-KNN | Item-KNN | RecRules | rtar |
|---------|-----|----------|----------|----------|------|
| R@5 | 0.11 | 0.15 | 0.14 | 0.19 | **0.24** |
| NDCG@5 | 0.13 | 0.21 | 0.18 | 0.34 | **0.41** |

**Table 4.** A comparison of the precisions in cold start scenarios.

| Metrics | Pop | User-KNN | Item-KNN | RecRules | rtar |
|---------|-----|----------|----------|----------|------|
| R@5 | 0.13 | 0.08 | 0.10 | 0.17 | **0.20** |
| NDCG@5 | 0.15 | 0.11 | 0.12 | 0.23 | **0.27** |

### 4.3 RQ2: Problem Solving

We make some further comparisons among the five approaches and check whether they are able to solve the three problems.

**The Cold-Start Problem.** We evaluate the five approaches on cold users. The results are shown in Table 4. In cold-start scenarios, *Pop* is of higher precision than the traditional collaborative filtering methods—for cold users without interaction records, recommending popular rules is simplest, but still effective.

For hot users, *Pop* is not precise enough. The precisions achieved by *RecRules* and rtar indicate that leveraging the knowledge graph helps alleviate the cold-start problem. In addition, rtar leverages the path information and the embeddings of the knowledge graph, providing hot/cold users with a semantic-aware recommendation solution.

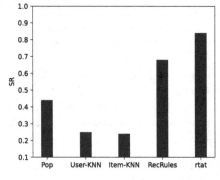 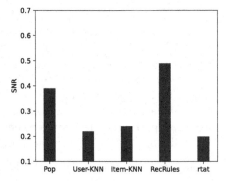

**Fig. 6.** Repeated rules users want.  **Fig. 7.** Repeated rules users do not want.

**The Repeat-Consumption Problem.** Figure 6 shows how recommender systems meet the users' needs in receiving repeated rules. Figure 7 reveals a user may or may not need repeated rules. Figures 6 and 7 show that (1) *User-KNN* and *Item-KNN* are not designed for solving the repeat-consumption problem, and thus they fail to capture the rule repetitiveness during rule recommendations. (2) *RecRules* can, with slight modifications, recommend repeated rules. However, it is difficult to balance the novelty and the repetitiveness in rule recommendations. (3) rtar takes several factors into consideration, such as a rule's popularity, its repetitiveness, and the user's preference for repeating this rule. It achieves a balance between $SR$ and $SNR$.

**The Conflict Problem.** We randomly pick up a user, extract his information from the training set and the test set, and then compare the recommended rules. As Table 5 shows, both of *RecRules* and rtar are able to recommend the rules the user needs (Rules in blue). However, rtar highlights some rules if they conflicts with the editing rules, while the other techniques (including *RecRules*) cannot reveal conflicts.

In addition, *RecRules* recommends rules having similar functions, since many rules define triggers `at specific time` and actions `sending notifications`. Comparatively, rtar recommends rules with different functions, exploring rules with rich triggers and actions. It helps find out and recommends the most appropriate rules for end-user development.

## 5   Related Work

This section discusses related work on (1) knowledge graph for recommendation and (2) generation of trigger-action rules.

**Knowledge Graph for Recommendation.** Knowledge has been found to be useful in many tasks, such as recommendations and question answerings, which speeds up the popularity of knowledge graphs (KGs). While quite a few KGs have been published, such as DBpedia, OpenCyc, Wikidata, and YAGO, only some researches exist on developing TAP KGs. One well-known TAP KG is EUPont (End-User Programming Ontology) [7], an ontological representation of TAP in the IoT, proposed by Corno *et al.* EUPont captures the key concepts and their relations in TAP, including rules, actions, triggers, users, locations, services/devices. Inspired by EUPont, we design TaKG for modeling the TAP rules, actions, triggers, *etc.*. Comparatively, EUPont is small-scale, composed of only ontological concepts; TaKG is designed with rich entities and relations, facilitating a recommender system to search for semantically relevant rules.

Incorporating KGs into recommender systems has attracted many attentions in recent years [4]. There are two mainstreams of utilizing KGs in recommendations: path- and embedding-based methods. Path-based methods compute similarities of users or items by comparing their paths in the KG. Sun *et al.* reveal a fact that two users or items are similar if they are linked by many paths in the graph [24]. They propose *PathSim* to measure the similarities of users or

**Table 5.** A comparison of the rules recommended by *RecRules* and rtar.

| User's written rules in the training data | |
|---|---|
| 1 | IF Weather underground. Sunrise, THEN Wemo light switch. Turn off |
| 2 | IF Date&time. every day at, THEN Notifications. send a notification |
| 3 | IF Weather underground. tomorrow's forecast calls for, THEN Notifications. Send a notification |
| 4 | IF Location. You enter an area, THEN Android device. Turn on wifi |
| 5 | IF Date&time. every day at, THEN Notifications. send a notification |
| **User's written rules in the testing data** | |
| 1 | IF Weather underground. tomorrow's forecast calls for, THEN Notifications. Send a notification |
| 2 | IF Location. You exit an area, THEN Android device. Turn off wifi |
| **Recommended rules for user** | |
| RecRules | IF Weather underground. tomorrow's forecast calls for, THEN Notifications. Send a notification |
| | IF Date&time. every day at, THEN Notifications. send a notification |
| | IF Weather underground. Sunrise, THEN Notifications. Send a notification |
| | IF Date&time. every day at, THEN Wemo light switch. Turn on |
| | IF Weather underground. Sunrise, THEN Android device. Update device wallpaper |
| rtar | IF Weather underground. tomorrow's forecast calls for, THEN Notifications. Send a notification |
| | IF Date&time. every day at, THEN Wemo light switch. Turn on. (Pay attention to the attribute value. This rule may conflict with rule1) |
| | IF Weather underground. Sunrise, THEN Android device. Update device wallpaper |
| | IF Android device. Connects to a specific wifi, THEN Notifications. Send a notification |
| | IF Location. You exit an area, THEN Android device. Turn off wifi. (Rule4 triggers a sustained action, and will not roll back automatically) |

items. *Hete-MF* [27] calculates item-item similarity in a path using a weighted non-negative matrix factorization method. Yu *et al.* [28] propose *HeteRec-p*, assuming that meta-paths should vary from user to user.

Embedding-based methods merge the properties and relations of entities in the KG together to improve the effectiveness of recommendations. Wang *et al.* [26] propose an embedding-based DKN model to recommend news. The key component of DKN is a multi-channel and word-entity-aligned knowledge-aware CNN (convolutional neural network) that fuses semantic- and knowledge-level representations of news. Dadoun *et al.* [9] propose a neural network based approach with knowledge graph embeddings to predicting for travelers the next trip destination. However, neither of the two approaches fully utilizes KGs. Comparatively, rtar leverages path information and KG embeddings to recommend trigger-action rules, and as well solve the cold-start and the conflict problems.

**Generation of Trigger-Action Rules.** The first research to recommend trigger-action rules for end users is proposed by Domínguez *et al.* [10]. Although Domínguez's technique does not outperform traditional algorithms, the results still inspire researches on rule recommendations since end users lacks of professional skills. To best of our knowledge, there are only two recommender systems for trigger-action rules: one proposed by Domínguez *et al.* [10] and *RecRules* proposed by Corno *et al.* [8]. rtar is inspired by *RecRules*, while it is different from *RecRules* in two respects. First, *RecRules* only leverages similarities of entities in different paths. Comparatively, rtar employs a unified method which combines path- and embedding-based techniques. The embedding technique helps preserve the inherent property of the knowledge graph and enrich the item representations. Second, *RecRules* fails to address some practical problems, while rtar detects rule conflicts and captures the repeat-consumption behaviors of end users.

Another notable effort for supporting end user development is TAP program synthesis. Quirk *et al.* [23] first proposes an idea of synthesizing trigger-action rules from natural language. Two recent approaches use sequence-to-sequence model [11] and an ensemble of a neural network and a logistic regression model [2] to synthesize rules, respectively. Liu *et al.* [19] propose an end-to-end neural architecture. While channels and functions are treated as distinct multi-class labels, the model jointly predicts all of the recipe components using the shared latent attention mechanism. It is believed that our knowledge graph TaKG also facilitates rule synthesis, which will be remained as one of our future work.

# 6   Conclusion

rtar is a semantic and context-aware method for end users to reuse and customize trigger-action rules. It constructs a knowledge graph TaKG for assisting rule recommendations, leverages different types of features for training a learning-to-recommend model, and actively detects and eliminates potential conflicts among rules. The evaluation results show that rtar outperforms some state-of-the-art techniques.

**Acknowledgment.** This research was sponsored by National Key R&D Program of China (Project No. 2018YFB1003903) and National Nature Science Foundation of China (Grant No. 61472242, 61572312).

# References

1. Barricelli, B.R., Cassano, F., Fogli, D., Piccinno, A.: End-user development, end-user programming and end-user software engineering: A systematic mapping study. J. Syst. Softw. **149**, 101–137 (2019)
2. Beltagy, I., Quirk, C.: Improved semantic parsers for if-then statements. In: ACL 2016 (2016)
3. Brackenbury, W., et al.: How users interpret bugs in trigger-action programming. In: CHI 2019, p. 552 (2019)
4. Çano, E., Morisio, M.: Hybrid recommender systems: a systematic literature review. CoRR abs/1901.03888 (2019)
5. Chard, R., et al.: High-throughput neuroanatomy and trigger-action programming: a case study in research automation. In: Proceedings of the 1st International Workshop on Autonomous Infrastructure for Science, AI-Science@HPDC 2018 (2018)
6. Chen, J., Wang, C., Wang, J., Yu, P.S.: Recommendation for repeat consumption from user implicit feedback. In: ICDE 2017, pp. 19–20 (2017)
7. Corno, F., Russis, L.D., Roffarello, A.M.: A high-level semantic approach to end-user development in the internet of things. Int. J. Hum. Comput. Stud. **125**, 41–54 (2019)
8. Corno, F., Russis, L.D., Roffarello, A.M.: Recrules: recommending IF-THEN rules for end-user development. ACM TIST **10**(5), 58:1–58:27 (2019)
9. Dadoun, A., Troncy, R., Ratier, O., Petitti, R.: Location embeddings for next trip recommendation. In: WWW 2019, pp. 896–903 (2019)
10. Domínguez, N., Ko, I.-Y.: Mashup recommendation for trigger action programming. In: Mikkonen, T., Klamma, R., Hernández, J. (eds.) ICWE 2018. LNCS, vol. 10845, pp. 177–184. Springer, Cham (2018). https://doi.org/10.1007/978-3-319-91662-0_13
11. Dong, L., Lapata, M.: Language to logical form with neural attention. In: ACL 2016 (2016)
12. Ghiani, G., Manca, M., Paternò, F., Santoro, C.: Personalization of context-dependent applications through trigger-action rules. ACM Trans. Comput. Hum. Interact. **24**(2), 14:1–14:33 (2017)
13. Guo, G., Zhang, J., Sun, Z., Yorke-Smith, N.: Librec: a Java library for recommender systems. In: UMAP 2015 (2015)
14. IFTTT: Ifttt: Every thing works better together. Online document ifttt.com/
15. Jalili, M., Ahmadian, S., Izadi, M., Moradi, P., Salehi, M.: Evaluating collaborative filtering recommender algorithms: a survey. IEEE Access **6**, 74003–74024 (2018)
16. Hosmer Jr., D.H., Lemeshow, S.: Applied logistic regression. Technometrics **34**(3), 358–359 (2013)
17. Kim, Y.: Convolutional neural networks for sentence classification. In: EMNLP 2014, pp. 1746–1751 (2014)
18. Lieberman, H., Paternò, F., Klann, M., Wulf, V.: End-user development: an emerging paradigm. In: Lieberman, H., Paternò, F., Wulf, V. (eds.) End User Development, pp. 1–8. Springer, Dordrecht (2006). https://doi.org/10.1007/1-4020-5386-X_1

19. Liu, C., Chen, X., Shin, E.C.R., Chen, M., Song, D.X.: Latent attention for if-then program synthesis. In: Advances in Neural Information Processing Systems 29: Annual Conference on Neural Information Processing Systems 2016, pp. 4574–4582 (2016)
20. Microsoft: Power automate documentation. Online document docs.microsoft.com/en-us/power-automate/
21. Mozilla: Mozilla IoT webthings: An open platform for monitoring and controlling devices over the web. https://iot.mozilla.org/
22. Pan, R., et al.: One-class collaborative filtering. In: ICDM 2008, pp. 502–511 (2008)
23. Quirk, C., Mooney, R.J., Galley, M.: Language to code: learning semantic parsers for if-this-then-that recipes. In: ACL 2015, pp. 878–888 (2015)
24. Sun, Y., Han, J., Yan, X., Yu, P.S., Wu, T.: Pathsim: meta path-based top-k similarity search in heterogeneous information networks. Proc. VLDB Endow. **4**(11), 992–1003 (2011)
25. Surbatovich, M., Aljuraidan, J., Bauer, L., Das, A., Jia, L.: Some recipes can do more than spoil your appetite: analyzing the security and privacy risks of IFTTT recipes. In: WWW 2017, pp. 1501–1510 (2017)
26. Wang, H., Zhang, F., Xie, X., Guo, M.: DKN: deep knowledge-aware network for news recommendation. In: WWW 2018, pp. 1835–1844 (2018)
27. Yu, X., Ren, X., Gu, Q., Sun, Y., Han, J.: Collaborative filtering with entity similarity regularization in heterogeneous information networks. IJCAI HINA **27** (2013)
28. Yu, X., et al.: Personalized entity recommendation: a heterogeneous information network approach. WSDM **2014**, 283–292 (2014)
29. Zapier: Connect your apps and automate workflows. Online document zapier.com/

# AndroLib: Third-Party Software Library Recommendation for Android Applications

Moataz Chouchen[1], Ali Ouni[1(✉)], and Mohamed Wiem Mkaouer[2]

[1] Ecole de Technologie Superieure, University of Quebec, Montreal, QC, Canada
moataz.chouchen.1@ens.etsmtl.ca, ali.ouni@etsmtl.ca
[2] Rochester Institute of Technology, Rochester, NY, USA
mwmvse@rit.edu

**Abstract.** Android mobile applications (apps) rely heavily on third-party libraries as a means to save time, reduce implementation costs, and increase software quality while offering rich, robust, and up-to-date features to end users. The selection of third-party libraries is an essential element in any software development project, and particularly, in Android apps given the fast-changing and evolving mobile app ecosystem. Indeed, deciding which libraries to choose is a challenging problem, especially with the exponentially increasing number of available libraries in the Android ecosystem. In this paper, we introduce, AndroLib, a novel approach to recommend third-party libraries for Android apps. In particular, we formulate the problem as a multi-objective combinatorial problem and use the non-dominated sorting genetic algorithm (NSGA-II) as a search method to find and recommend relevant libraries. We aim at guiding the search process towards the best trade-off three objectives to be optimized (*i*) maximize libraries historical co-usage, (*ii*) maximize libraries functional diversity, and (*iii*) maximize libraries reuse from highly rated apps. We conduct an empirical experiment to evaluate our approach on a benchmark of real-world Android apps libraries. Results show the effectiveness of AndroLib compared with three recent state-of-the-art library recommendation approaches.

**Keywords:** Third-party Software Library · Android apps · Software reuse · Search based software engineering

## 1 Introduction

Android has been the dominating operating system developed by Google for mobile apps [24], experiencing a tremendous expansion of its user base over the past few years. It currently has approximately 86% of the smart phones market around the world with over 2.5 billion monthly active users[1]. Several

---

[1] https://venturebeat.com/2019/05/07/android-passes-2-5-billion-monthly-active-devices.

© Springer Nature Switzerland AG 2020
S. Ben Sassi et al. (Eds.): ICSR 2020, LNCS 12541, pp. 208–225, 2020.
https://doi.org/10.1007/978-3-030-64694-3_13

factors contribute to the vibrancy of Android including its flexibilities for vendor customizations, facility of third-party libraries integration along with the richness of the functionalities it provides in its platform that ease the development and evolution of apps that cover ever-broadening domains of applications [32].

The use of third-party libraries become a common and essential practice for mobile apps developers to speed up the development process and reduce its costs [11, 27]. One particular feature of Android apps resides on their small code base and their extensive reuse of third-party libraries, such as advertisement libraries, graphics, social network libraries, mobile analytic tools, etc. These libraries usually constitute a considerable part of code in Android apps. Indeed, a recent study shows that sub-packages from external libraries account for 60% of code in Android software [31], and over 90% of Android apps use 5 libraries or more [11]. Hence, Android developers take the benefit from freely reusing functionality provided by well-tested and mature third-party libraries through their Application Programming Interfaces (APIs) [13, 14, 23, 26]. Third-party software libraries provide developers with customized functionality, relieving them from the burden of "reinventing the wheel" [14].

However, finding the appropriate libraries is a challenging task in Android apps development given the volatile mobile apps market as well as the fast-evolving user needs. The number of available libraries is growing exponentially in various repositories such as Android Arsenal[2]. While such growth and heterogeneity provide developers more options, it also complicates their selection process. Hence, developers need to spend a lot of effort to search for relevant libraries [17, 25]. Despite the need for better support to developers in this task, very little work has been conducted to provide techniques that facilitate the search for suitable libraries for mobile apps. Most of existing library recommendation techniques, *e.g.*, CrossRec [17], LibRec [28], LibFinder [23], and LibCUP [26] are designed to support Open Source Software (OSS) developers to recommend individual libraries, while ignoring the specific characteristics of Android apps development. Indeed, Android library recommendation is rather a complex decision making problem where several considerations should be balanced. These complex multi-objective decision problems with competing and conflicting constraints are well suited to multi-objective search techniques [9, 10, 19–22].

In this paper, we introduce, AndroLib, a novel approach that formulates the Android libraries recommendation problem as a multi-objective search-based optimization problem to find and recommend a set of libraries that are most relevant to the implementation of a given Android app. In particular, our approach learns from successful Android apps available in Google Play Store, the largest Android apps repository. Given an Android app that utilizes a set of libraries, AndroLib aims at recommending relevant libraries to the developer that are most appropriate to his app implementation requirements. The recommendation process aims at finding a trade-off among three main objectives to be optimized (1) maximize libraries co-usage, *i.e.*, the recommended libraries have been commonly used together in other apps, (2) maximize functional diversity, *i.e.*, the

---

[2] https://android-arsenal.com.

recommended set of libraries implement distinct functionality to prevent redundant/similar libraries recommendations, and (3) maximize the reuse of library from highly rated apps by adopting a weighting mechanism. We adopt the non-dominated sorting genetic algorithm (NSGA-II) [6] to find the best trade-off between the three objectives. The complexity of the addressed library recommendation problem is combinatorial since our formulation consists of finding a set of libraries that match with the current libraries of a given app while being commonly used in other successful apps.

AndroLib aims at supporting mobile app developers who have already utilized some libraries in their app, and search for recommendations of additional libraries that could be useful (if any). It exploits a multi-objective search mechanism to recommend further combinations libraries, instead of individual one, that may be useful based on training data from other successful apps in the market. To the best of our knowledge, this is the first attempt to employ search-based techniques to recommend third-party libraries for mobile app development.

We conduct an empirical evaluation on a dataset curated from GitHub. The statistical analysis of our results indicates that AndroLib outperforms state-of-the-art approaches including LibRec [28], CrossRec [17], and LibCUP [26] based on various performance metrics. The statistical analysis of the obtained results indicate that our approach achieves better accuracy than existing approaches, while identifying relevant libraries in the first ranks of the recommendation list.

The rest of the paper is organized as follows. Section 2 presents the related works. Section 3 describes our approach, AndroLib, for Android library recommendation. Section 4 reports on the design of our empirical study while presenting and discussing the obtained results. Sect. 5 describes the threads to validity. Finally, we conclude and present our future work in Sect. 6.

## 2    Related Work

In this section, we summarize related work on recommendation systems for software libraries and frameworks.

*API and Method Recommendation.* Most of the existing recommendation approaches have focused on the method/API level. Heinemann et al. [12] introduced an approach for recommending library methods using data mining for learning term-method associations based on identifiers similarity, similarly to our approach. Rascal [15] uses collaborative filtering to suggest API methods based on a set of already employed methods within a class. Similarly, Javawock [30] utilizes the same technique to recommend API classes instead of methods. Nguyen et al. [18] introduced FOCUS, a recommender system that mines API calls and usage patterns by leveraging collaborative filtering technique and mutual relationships among projects using a tensor. Chang et al. [5] proposed a greedy sub-graph search algorithm to find APIs with high textual similarity while leveraging space-efficient compressed shortest path indexing scheme to recover the exact shortest path. Later, Thung et al. [29] have proposed a technique for recommending API methods based on textual description of feature requests and method history usage. While most of these API and method level approaches suppose that developer has already found his library and she/he needs support on how to use it, our approach aims at finding and recommending whole library.

*Library and Framework Recommendation.* Thung et al. [28] proposed an approach called *LibRec* that combines association rule mining and collaborative filtering on historic software artifacts to determine commonly used together libraries. Later, Saied et al. [26] proposed LibCUP, a recommender system that suggests libraries based on the extent to which they are used together. The proposed approach uses a clustering technique based on the DBSCAN algorithm to mine and recommend library co-usage patterns. Ouni et al. [23] introduced a recommender system called LibFinder to recommend useful Maven libraries using a search-based approach by leverage libraries usage and source code semantic similarity. The proposed works on-the-fly to identify missed reuse opportunities. Recently, He et al. [11] proposed, LibSeek, a collaborative filtering-based approach to predict useful libraries for developers. It uses an adaptive weighting mechanism to neutralize the bias caused by the popularity of specific libraries by leveraging information about similar third-party libraries and systems. Nguyen et al. [17] proposed CrossRec, a recommender system that uses collaborative filtering to recommend libraries to OSS developers by relying on the set of dependencies, which are currently included in the project being developed.

While most of the existing approaches have shown relatively acceptable performance in recommending libraries/frameworks in traditional software systems, they are not directly applied in the context of mobile apps. The main limitation of these existing approaches resides in the fact that libraries are recommended individually, while ignoring the innate relationships among Android libraries that need to be recommended collectively, *i.e.*, combined recommendations, such as social network libraries and image loading libraries which are typically used together. Moreover, due to the nature of Android apps, a small fraction of popular libraries dominates the market while most other libraries are *ill-served*. We argue that basing the recommendation on libraries usage records, may hurt other relevant libraries. As a consequence, newly published or unpopular libraries have little or no chance to appear in the recommendation results. Ultimately, such challenges call for new recommendation approaches to find groups of libraries and better balance the '*wisdom of the crowd*' as reflected by libraries usage.

# 3 Approach

In this section, we describe in detail our approach, AndroLib, for Android library recommendations. We first provide an overview of our approach, then describe how we adapted NSGA-II to the Android libraries recommendation problem.

## 3.1 Approach Overview

Figure 1 shows the general framework underlying the AndroLib approach. In a typical usage scenario of AndroLib, we assume that an Android developer is implementing a new app, or evolving an existing app, in which she/he has already adopted some libraries and looking for other relevant libraries to her/his current implementation. AndroLib takes as input (1) a query from an Android app developer who is seeking for new libraries recommendations based on the currently used libraries in her/his app, and (2) third-party libraries usage record from a set of apps available on Google Play Store. As output, AndroLib returns a collection of recommended libraries that are relevant to the current app.

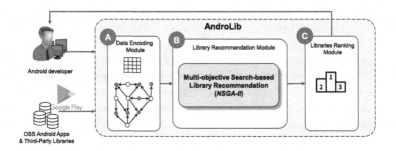

**Fig. 1.** An overview of the AndroLib approach.

The recommendation process is based on combinatorial multi-objective search to find a set of libraries that are commonly used together in existing apps. Given the nature of Android libraries ecosystem where multiple libraries are reused together to deliver a given functionality, such libraries should be recommended collectively instead of individually, to fulfill various and rich functionalities while avoiding potential library incompatibility problems. For example, most of the apps that use the `Facebook`[3] library, to communicate with the popular Facebook social network, also use another image loading and management library such as the `Glide`[4] library. Both libraries are commonly used together in Android apps to perform social media based tasks. This indicates that such combination of both libraries is needed for adding social functionalities to apps as many popular apps have benefited from them. At the same time, other apps that use the `Facebook` library are using other alternative image management libraries to `Glide`, such as the `Picasso`[5] or `Fresco`[6] libraries. Thus, to build a successful app, it is rewarding to learn from other successful apps, *i.e.*, those implementing similar features and having high rating in the Google Play Store from users. This helps to avoid incompatibility problems while increasing the chance user satisfaction. Other criteria need to be considered to get relevant recommendations such as functionality matching and diversity.

---

[3] https://github.com/facebook/facebook-android-sdk.
[4] https://github.com/bumptech/glide.
[5] https://github.com/square/picasso.
[6] https://github.com/facebook/fresco.

As depicted in Fig. 1, our approach consists of three main modules to support the recommendation process (*i*) data encoding module, and (*ii*) library recommendation module, and (*iii*) libraries ranking module.

**Module Ⓐ: Data Encoding Module.** This module collects data from OSS repositories, and uses a specific graph-based encoding to facilitate their exploration in the recommendation module. Our encoding is largely inspired from recommendation systems for online services [8,17] which are based on three main elements, namely users, items, and ratings. Usually, the mutual relationships among these elements are represented all together by means of a user-item ratings matrix. Such ratings matrix consists of a table where each row represents a user, each column represents a specific item, and each entry represents the rating given by the user to the particular item [8]. For library recommendation, instead of users and items, we consider apps and third-party libraries, *i.e.*, an app may adopt various libraries to implement its functionalities. We derive an analogous user-item ratings matrix to represent the app-library inclusion relationships. In this matrix, each row represents an Android app and each column represents a library. A cell in the matrix is set to 1 if the library in the column is included in the app indicated in the row, and 0 otherwise. An example of our data matrix encoding is illustrated in Fig. 2a.

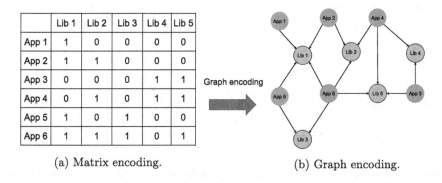

|        | Lib 1 | Lib 2 | Lib 3 | Lib 4 | Lib 5 |
|--------|-------|-------|-------|-------|-------|
| App 1  | 1     | 0     | 0     | 0     | 0     |
| App 2  | 1     | 1     | 0     | 0     | 0     |
| App 3  | 0     | 0     | 0     | 1     | 1     |
| App 4  | 0     | 1     | 0     | 1     | 1     |
| App 5  | 1     | 0     | 1     | 0     | 0     |
| App 6  | 1     | 1     | 1     | 0     | 1     |

Graph encoding

(a) Matrix encoding.                          (b) Graph encoding.

**Fig. 2.** An example of the data encoding model adopted by AndroLib.

To facilitate the exploration of such search space within the recommendation module of AndroLib, we use a representation model that addresses the semantic relationships among different components including the apps, libraries, and their mutual interactions as an ecosystem, as adopted by Nguyen et al. [17]. We adopt a graph-based model to represent different relationships in the Android apps ecosystem, and allow calculating various similarity and usage measures to derive libraries recommendation list. It is acknowledged that the graph model is a convenient approach in the context of mining OSS repositories, since it allows for flexible data integration and various computation techniques. This representation allows transforming the initially encoded apps-libraries matrix shown in Fig. 2a into a directed graph as illustrated in Fig. 2b.

To calculate the similarities between the graph nodes, *i.e.*, libraries, we rely on techniques successfully employed in various information retrieval studies [7,16,17]. Among other relationships, two graph nodes are considered to be similar if they point to the same node with the same edge. For instance, we observe from the graph in Fig. 2b, that Lib4 and Lib5 have a high usage similarity score (we refer to as "*co-usage*", in the remainder of the paper) as they both have dependencies with the nodes App3, and App4. This co-uasge is also based on the premise that similar apps implement common pieces of functionality by using a shared set of libraries as pointed out by McMillan et al. [16].

Formally, to compute the co-usage between two libraries, $Lib_i$ and $Lib_j$, in our graph-based model, let us consider that $Lib_i$ has a set of neighbor nodes $(App_1, App_2, .., App_n)$. The features of $Lib_i$ are represented by a vector $\vec{\omega} = (\omega_1, \omega_2, \ldots, \omega_n)$, with $\omega_i$ being the weight of node $App_i$. It is computed as the term-frequency inverse document frequency (TF-IDF) score as follows:

$$\omega_i = Dep(App_i) \times \log \left( \frac{|P|}{Dependency(App_i)} \right) \tag{1}$$

where $Dep(App_i)$ returns the number of dependencies of $Lib_i$ in $App_i$, *i.e.*, either 0 or 1. $|P|$ is the total number of considered apps in the graph; $Dependency(App_i)$ is the count of libraries that are connected to $App_i$. Hence, the co-usage score between $Lib_i$ and $Lib_j$ having their corresponding feature vectors $\vec{\omega} = (\omega_1, \omega_2, \ldots, \omega_n)$ and $\vec{\vartheta} = (\vartheta_1, \vartheta_2, \ldots, \vartheta_m)$, respectively, is calculated as follows:

$$co\text{-}usage(Lib_i, Lib_j) = \frac{\sum_{t=1}^{n}(\omega_t \times \vartheta_t)}{\sqrt{\sum_{t=1}^{n}(\omega_t)^2} \times \sqrt{\sum_{t=1}^{n}(\vartheta_t)^2}} \tag{2}$$

where $n$ is the cardinality of the set of apps that use both $Lib_i$ and $Lib_j$ [7]. Intuitively, $Lib_i$ and $Lib_j$ are characterized by using vectors in an n-dimensional space, and $co\text{-}usage(Lib_i, Lib_j)$ measures the cosine of the angle between the two vectors.

**Module Ⓑ: Library Recommendation Module.** To explore the extracted data about libraries and apps relationships, efficient search techniques are needed. Our approach aims at supporting Android developers by recommending relevant library combinations that match with their currently adopted libraries. AndroLib recommends library sets based on three main aspects (1) the '*wisdom of the crowd*', *i.e.*, libraries that are commonly co-used together in other similar and successful apps, (2) the user rating of the apps that use the recommended libraries, and (3) the diversity in the recommended libraries to avoid redundant recommendation lists.

The number of potential solutions (*i.e.*, library combinations) could be very large or even infinite [10] as the number of available libraries and apps and in the Android market are experiencing a tremendous expansion over the past few years. Indeed, the task of searching for commonly used libraries, is fastidious, complex and time-consuming. Thus, dedicated intelligent algorithms, namely meta-heuristics, are known to solve such search problems with a high degree of objectives and constraints satisfaction [10, 19]. In particular, our approach adopts the non-dominated sorting genetic algorithm (NSGA-II) [6] to recommend a relevant sets of services by finding the optimal trade-off among the considered objectives. NSGA-II finds multiple optimal, *i.e.*, non-dominated, solutions instead of single one, based on the *Pareto optimality principle* [6]. It shows a variety of optimal solutions in the search space, which allow the developer to explore a solution space that provides optimal trade-offs between the optimized objectives. Thus, the developer makes his selection according to his preferences.

**Module ©: Library Ranking Module.** AndroLib comprises an automatic ranking module for all recommended libraries in the different optimal solutions returned by the search algorithm. All the recommended libraries that appear in all the optimal solutions, *i.e.*, library sets, returned in the *Pareto front* by NSGA-II, are then sorted based on their occurrence count in all the returned solutions. The more the number of optimal solutions in which a library appears, the more the library is relevant for the concerned app. For instance, suppose the search algorithm returns 10 optimal solutions, *i.e.*, a combination of libraries, where the library `Picasso` appears in 7 solutions, and the service `Glide` appears in 5 solutions. Then, `Picasso` will be ranked first with a score of 0.7, while the *Glide* rank will be 0.5.

## 3.2 NSGA-II Overview

We adopt the widely used multi-objective search algorithm, NSGA-II [6] that has proven good performance in solving many software engineering problems [10, 19]. NSGA-II starts by randomly creating an initial population $P_0$ of individuals encoded using a specific representation. Then, a child population $Q_0$ is generated from the population of parents $P_0$ using genetic operators, *i.e.*, crossover and mutation. Both populations are merged into an initial population $R_0$ of size $N$. Then, the whole population that contains $N$ individuals (solutions) is sorted using the dominance principle [6] into several fronts based on their dominance levels. When NSGA-II has to cut off a front $F_i$ and select a subset of individual solutions with the same dominance level, it relies on the crowding distance [6] to make the selection. This parameter is used to promote diversity within the population. Then, a new population $Q_{t+1}$ is created using selection, crossover and mutation. This process will be repeated until reaching the last iteration according to a stop criteria.

## 3.3 NSGA-II Adaptation

Various element need to be formulated in any attempt to use a multi-objective search algorithm for a given problem, including ($i$) the solution representation, ($ii$) fitness function, and ($iii$) change operators.

**Solution Representation.** A candidate solution is typically represented in the form of a number of decision variables that need to be optimized through an evolutionary search process. We encoded a feasible solution for our problem as chromosomes of length $n$ using a vector representation, where each gene, *i.e.*, vector dimension, represents a candidate library. The chromosome's length, $n$, is variable and corresponds to the number of libraries to be recommended. Figure 3 represents a simplified example of a chromosome that contains five recommended libraries.

| MPAndroidChart | Picasso | Facebook | CAMView | Dagger |
|---|---|---|---|---|

**Fig. 3.** A simplified example of solution representation.

**Fitness Function.** An appropriate fitness function should be defined to evaluate how good is a candidate solution. Let $L$ a candidate solution, *i.e.*, chromosome, that consists of a set of libraries $L = \{l_1, ..., l_n\}$ to be recommended for a given Android App $A$ that currently uses a set of libraries $L_A = \{l_{A_1}, ..., l_{A_m}\}$. To evaluate the fitness of each solution, we use three objective functions to be optimized.

1. **Maximize Recommended Library Co-Usage (RLC):** This objective function aims at discovering third-party libraries that are commonly used together based on the co-usage score, while reducing incompatibility risks. The RLC score is calculated as follows:

$$RLC(L) = \sum_{i=1}^{n} \sum_{j=1}^{m} \text{co-usage}(ls_j, l_i) \times \frac{1}{m} \times \frac{1}{n} \quad (3)$$

   where the function $lco\text{-}usage(ls_j, l_i)$ is given by Eq. 2.

2. **Maximize Library Functional Diversity (LFD):** This objective function aims at maximizing the diversity among the recommended libraries in terms of their functionality as captured by the library categories, *e.g.*, image loader, animation, graphics, advertisement, camera, etc. Diversified list of recommended libraries is of pivotal importance as developers are unlikely to look at redundant list of recommendations. Inspired from biodiversity, we use the *Shannon diversity index* (H), a mathematical measure of species diversity in a given community, based on the species richness (the number of species present) and species abundance (the number of individuals per species). Let $C = \{c_1, ..., c_N\}$ the list of categories in both libraries in the recommendation list $L$ and libraries currently used $L_A$ in the app $A$, LFD is calculated as follows:

$$LFD(L) = - \sum_{\forall c_i \in C} P(c_i) \ln P(c_i) \quad (4)$$

   where $P(c_i)$ returns the proportion $(n/N)$ of libraries $(n)$ having one particular category $c_i$ recommended divided by the total number of library categories $(N)$, and $ln$ is the natural logarithm.

3. ***Maximize Reuse from Successful Apps (RSA)***: This objective function aims at increasing the chance of recommending commonly used libraries in apps having high user rating, while decreasing the chance to recommend those from low rated apps. RSA is used as an adaptive weighting mechanism that reduces the bias caused by the popularity of libraries. We argue that basing the recommendation only on the library usage record, *i.e.*, popularity, may hurt other newly released libraries. It has been shown that a small fraction of popular libraries dominates the recommendation results [11]. RSA is a dominance index as it gives more weight to libraries commonly used in highly rated apps. In this case, new emerging libraries or libraries having low usage record but adopted in highly rated and successful apps will have a higher chance to be recommended. RSA of a candidate solution $L$ is calculated as follows:

$$RSA = \frac{1}{\mid L \mid} \sum_{\forall l_i \in L} AppsRating(l_i) \tag{5}$$

where $AppsRating(l_i)$ returns of the average rating of all apps adopting $l_i$ in the training dataset, based on the current apps rating in Google Play Store.

**Change Operators.** Change operators such as crossover and mutation allow to change the solution's phenotype. These changes are intended to evolve candidate solutions to a near-optimal state.

The *crossover* operator creates offspring solutions, *i.e.*, a re-combination of solutions, from the current generation to create a new offsprings. In our NSGA-II adaptation, we use a single, random cut-point crossover operator. The operation starts by randomly choosing then splitting two solutions from the current generation. Thereafter, two offspring solutions are generated by combining, for the first offspring, the left part of its first parent solution with the right part of the second parent solution, and vice versa for the second offspring.

The *mutation* operator aims at introducing slight changes into selected solutions to drive the search process into different solutions within the search space that cannot be reached via pure recombinations in order to avoid converging the population towards few or specific elite solutions. We employ a mutation operator that selects at random one or more libraries from their solution vectors and substitutes them by other random libraries.

## 4    Empirical Evaluation

In this section, we describe our experimental study design to evaluate the performance of AndroLib, and compare it with three state-of-the-art approaches, namely LibRec [28], CrossRec [17], and LibCUP [26]. Then, we report and discuss the obtained results.

### 4.1   Research Questions

Our study aims at addressing the following research questions:

- **RQ1. (State-of-the-art comparison)** How does AndroLib compare with the state-of-the-art approaches in terms of recommendation accuracy?
- **RQ2. (Ranking performance)**  How does AndroLib perform in terms of ranking of recommended libraries?

### 4.2   Dataset

To evaluate the effectiveness of our approach, we carried out our experiments on an existing dataset[7] that consists of a total of 2,752 open-source Android apps [27]. The dataset was collected from the F-Droid and AndroidTimeMachine repositories while considering a set of selection criteria to make sure that the apps (*i*) make use of third-party libraries, and (*ii*) have dependencies that are still available, (*iii*) available in Google Play Store. All the selected apps provide their source code in a public repository on GitHub and use Gradle as build system. Library dependencies were collected by parsing the `Gradle` build files to retrieve the declarations of third-party libraries dependency for each app. The libraries were reported with the general pattern:

```
<configuration> <group> : <name> : <version>
```

All the libraries are publicly available on different repositories, *e.g.*, Maven, JCenter, Bintray. It is worth noting that we focus in our experiments on unique libraries based on their unique `<group>` ID and `<name>`, and did not consider the granularity of library `<version>`. For each app, we also extract the metadata from the Google Play Store to identify the current app user rating.

**Table 1.** Experimental dataset statistics.

| Statistics | Value |
|---|---|
| # of Android apps | 2,752 |
| # of third-party libraries | 979 |
| # of library categories | 76 |
| Average number of libraries per app | 4.62 |

### 4.3   Evaluation Method and Metrics

To evaluate the performance of the four approaches, *i.e.*, AndroLib, LibRec [28], CrossRec [17], and LibCUP [26], we applied ten-fold cross validation, where we split the dataset into 10 equal folds (each contains 275 apps), considering 9 parts

---

[7] https://doi.org/10.6084/m9.figshare.9366341.

for training and the remaining part for testing. Thereafter, for each testing app, a half of its libraries are randomly taken out and saved as ground truth data. We adopt this evaluation method as it has been widely used in baseline methods and prior works [17,23,26,29]. Due to the stochastic nature of the NSGA-II algorithm, we run it for each problem instance, $i.e.$, app, 30 times, then take the median value [2].

To respond **RQ1**, we use common performance metrics, including the success rate@k, precision@k and recall@k. These metrics are commonly used for evaluating recommendation systems for software reuse [17,23,26,28,29]. Library ranking is based on the frequency count of a library in the recommendation list as described in Sect. 3.3. Let $D$ denotes the experimental dataset (c.f. Sect. 4.2). For a given iteration, we test the considered approach on the part $P_x \in D$, while training from the 9 other parts $P_T$ where $P_T = D \setminus \{P_x\}$. For each app $A_i \in P_x$ having a set of libraries $L$, let $L_d \subset L$ the subset of dropped libraries ($i.e.$, ground truth) where $\mid L_d \mid = \lfloor \frac{|L|}{2} \rfloor$. We consider the following metrics:

**Success Rate:** The recommendation $SuccessRate@k$ for $P_x$ is calculated as follows.

$$\text{SuccessRate@}k(P_x) = \frac{\sum\limits_{\forall A_i \in P_x} match(REC_{A_i}, L_d)}{\mid P_x \mid} \times 100\% \qquad (6)$$

where the function $match(REC_{A_i}, L_d)$ returns 1 if at least one of recommended libraries $REC_{A_i}$ is part of the ground truth $L_d$, and 0 otherwise.

**Accuracy:** We also use widely-adopted accuracy metrics [3], $i.e.$, $precision@k$ and $recall@k$, to better evaluate the accuracy of each approach. $Precision@k$ is the ratio of the top-k recommended libraries that belong to the ground-truth dataset $L_d$, while $recall@k$ is the ratio of the ground truth libraries appearing in the top-k recommended libraries [3,7,17,18]. Both $precision@k$ and $recall@k$ are defined as follows:

$$Precision@k(A_i) = \frac{\mid REC_{A_i} \cap L_d) \mid}{k} \times 100\% \qquad (7)$$

$$Recall@k(A_i) = \frac{\mid REC_{A_i} \cap L_d) \mid}{\mid L_d \mid} \times 100\% \qquad (8)$$

The overall precision@k and recall@k for $P_x$ correspond to the average $Precision@k(A_i)$, and $Recall@k(A_i)$, respectively, $\forall A_i \in P_x$.

**Ranking Quality:** To answer **RQ2**, we use two common metrics to evaluate the ranking of the returned list of recommended libraries, the Mean Reciprocal Rank (MRR) and the Normalized Discounted Cumulative Gain ($NDCG@k$) [1,3]. Both $MRR$ and $NDCG@k$ are defined in Eqs. 9 and 10, respectively. The higher $MRR$ and $NGCD@k$, the better is the recommendation accuracy.

Given a list of recommended libraries $L$, the reciprocal rank corresponds to the multiplicative inverse of the rank of the first true positive (*i.e.*, belongs to the ground truth) library recommended in a ranked list. Then, MRR corresponds to the average of the reciprocal ranks of a set of library recommendations for a given app. Let $REC_{A_i}$ the list of recommended library for app $A_i$, then MRR is calculated as follows:

$$MMR = \frac{\sum\limits_{\forall l \in REC_{A_i}} rank(l)}{|REC_{A_i}|} \tag{9}$$

where $rank(l)$ refers to the rank of the first correct library in the recommendation list.

Unlike *MRR*, the metric *NDCG@k* emphasizes on the precision of the first few $(1st, 2nd, 3rd, \ldots)$ recommendations. Formally, *NDCG@k* is calculated as follows:

$$NDCG@k = \frac{1}{S_k} \times \sum_{j=1}^{k} \frac{2^{r(j)} - 1}{log_2(1 + j)} \in [0, 1] \tag{10}$$

where $r(j)$ is associated with $j^{th}$ recommended library, as being its relevant score, and whose value is binary (0 or 1). $S_k$ is the best (maximum) score that any element can cumulatively reach.

### 4.4   Inferential Statistical Test Methods

To assess the differences in the performance of each of the approaches under comparison, AndroLib, CrossRec, LibRec and LibCUP, we rely on suitable statistical methods. In particular, we use the Wilcoxon ranked sum test, where each fold of the cross-validation is considered as a data point. We fix the confidence level, $\alpha = 0.05$. Moreover, to analyze the magnitude of the difference, we use the Cliff's delta ($d$) effect size measure, which is interpreted as negligible (N) if $|d| < 0.147$, small (S) if $0.147 \leq |d| < 0.33$, medium (M) if $0.33 \leq |d| < 0.474)$ and large (L) $|d| \geq 0.474$. We also use the Bonferroni method [4] to adjust *p-values* since multiple tests are being performed.

### 4.5   Results

**Results for RQ1.** Table 2 reports the average *SucessRate@k*, *Precision@k* and *Recall@k* results achieved by AndroLib, CrossRec, LibRec and LibCUP for $k = \{1, 3, 5, 10, 15\}$, as well as the statistical test results. The success rate score achieved by AndroLib are always superior than those of CrossRec, LibRec and LibCUP. The maximum success rate@15 of AndroLib is 0.91, whereas the competing approaches achieved maximum success rates scores being 0.82, 0.69, and

0.63 for CrossRec, LibCUP and LibRec, respectively, for $k = 15$. We also observe from the statistical analysis that AndroLib significantly outperforms the competing approaches with medium/large effect sizes, except for $k = 1$. Indeed, for this experiment, $k = 1$, we observe that while AndroLib achieves superior success rate than CrossRec, the effect size is negligible and results are not statistically significant. Overall, the obtained results suggest that our approach is more efficient for longer lists of recommendations due to the employed diversity component to be optimized during the recommendation process.

**Table 2.** The achieved *SucessRate@k*, *Precision@k* and *Recall@k* results.

| Metric | k | AndroLib | CrossRec | LibRec | LibCUP | AndroLib vs CrossRec | | AndroLib vs LibRec | | AndroLib vs LibCUP | |
|---|---|---|---|---|---|---|---|---|---|---|---|
| | | | | | | p-value | Effect size | p-value | Effect size | p-value | Effect size |
| SuccessRate@k | 1 | **0.52** | 0.51 | 0.40 | 0.40 | 0.07 | 0.12 (N) | <0.05 | 0.87 (L) | <0.05 | 1.00 (L) |
| | 3 | **0.67** | 0.55 | 0.48 | 0.51 | <0.05 | 0.41 (M) | <0.05 | 0.83 (L) | <0.05 | 0.90 (L) |
| | 5 | **0.81** | 0.72 | 0.51 | 0.58 | <0.05 | 0.35 (L) | <0.05 | 0.90 (L) | <0.05 | 0.98 (L) |
| | 10 | **0.87** | 0.76 | 0.59 | 0.64 | <0.05 | 0.52 (L) | <0.05 | 0.95 (L) | <0.05 | 1.00 (L) |
| | 15 | **0.91** | 0.82 | 0.63 | 0.69 | <0.05 | 0.49 (L) | <0.05 | 0.82 (L) | <0.05 | 0.83 (L) |
| Precision@k | 1 | **0.78** | 0.75 | 0.67 | 0.68 | <0.05 | 0.28 (S) | <0.05 | 0.92 (L) | <0.05 | 0.76 (L) |
| | 3 | **0.70** | 0.64 | 0.62 | 0.60 | <0.05 | 0.41 (M) | <0.05 | 1.00 (L) | <0.05 | 0.84 (L) |
| | 5 | **0.64** | 0.55 | 0.50 | 0.52 | <0.05 | 0.73 (L) | <0.05 | 0.83 (L) | <0.05 | 1.00 (L) |
| | 10 | **0.58** | 0.48 | 0.46 | 0.45 | <0.05 | 0.70 (L) | <0.05 | 0.98 (L) | <0.05 | 0.84 (L) |
| | 15 | **0.49** | 0.42 | 0.43 | 0.42 | <0.05 | 0.35 (M) | <0.05 | 0.64 (L) | <0.05 | 0.69 (L) |
| Recall@k | 1 | **0.53** | 0.48 | 0.44 | 0.45 | <0.05 | 0.49 (L) | <0.05 | 0.88 (L) | <0.05 | 0.81 (L) |
| | 3 | **0.59** | 0.51 | 0.42 | 0.41 | <0.05 | 0.58 (L) | <0.05 | 0.90 (L) | <0.05 | 0.87 (L) |
| | 5 | **0.64** | 0.56 | 0.35 | 0.36 | <0.05 | 0.57 (L) | <0.05 | 0.78 (L) | <0.05 | 0.75 (L) |
| | 10 | **0.75** | 0.65 | 0.32 | 0.33 | <0.05 | 0.52 (L) | <0.05 | 0.92 (L) | <0.05 | 0.94 (L) |
| | 15 | **0.81** | 0.71 | 0.30 | 0.29 | <0.05 | 0.55 (L) | <0.05 | 0.82 (L) | <0.05 | 0.90 (L) |

We also investigate the precision@k and recall@k results to get a more qualitative sense of the accuracy results, as the success rate@k does not reflect the whole picture of the recommendation accuracy. The results from Table 2 indicate that AndroLib achieves a maximum precision score of 0.78 for $k = 1$ which is superior to the three competing methods CrossRec, and LibCUP, LibRec, having maximum scores of 0.75, 0.68 and 0.67, respectively. Moreover, we observe from the results that there is a marginal difference in performance in terms of the recall score in favor of AndroLib which also achieves the highest superiority with a recall of 0.81 for $k = 15$. To better understand the performance of AndroLib as compared to the competing approaches, we investigated the internal design of each approach. First, our approach recommends a collection of libraries that are commonly used together instead of individual libraries, which helps finding patterns of libraries to implement features. Second, AndroLib utilizes meta-heuristic search to explore various combinations of libraries while giving more importance on the diversity of libraries as well as libraries used by highly rated apps, even though the recommended library is newborn and not yet popular in the current library ecosystem. Hence, AndroLib adopts a completely different metaheuristic approach to find optimal solutions that balance various problem specific objectives, while the competing approaches are mainly based on deterministic approaches using simple collaborative filtering, association rule mining, or clustering techniques. Furthermore, CrossRec is based on graph representation and assigns a weight to each library node to disproportionate the level of importance of a node to its popularity, which ressembles to our formulation. While this mechanism is important in the Android apps ecosystem, still the diversity of the recommended libraries an important aspect to be considered when recommending libraries, as developers are unlikely to go through long lists of similar or redundant items.

**Results for RQ2.** Figure 4a reports the Mean Reciprocal Rank (MRR) reflecting the overall ranking performance. As shown in the figure, AndroLib achieves a MRR score of 0.72 while CrossRec, LibCUP, and LibRec achieved 0.66, 0.59, 0.58, respectively, for all the studied apps. These results indicate that our approach provides a higher chance of recommending appropriate library in first ranks.

In terms of *NDCG@k*, results from Fig. 4b show that AndroLib achieves superior performance in providing accurate library recommendations in the first few ranks of 0.63 for the top-10 recommended libraries, *i.e.*, $k = 10$. Whereas, LibCUP and LibRec achieve the lowest performance of 0.53 and 0.52, respectively, for $k = 10$. This could be due to the fact that libraries are recommended individually, than considering the link between them. Moreover, each of the CrossRec, LibCUP, and LibRec methods also consider a set of k-nearest neighbor similar projects for finding libraries, while neglecting the success of such projects in terms of user rating by considering all projects in the same way. Moreover, a key feature of AndroLib is providing suitable diversity mechanisms to avoid the redundancy issue and recommend libraries from distinct, yet complementary category groups.

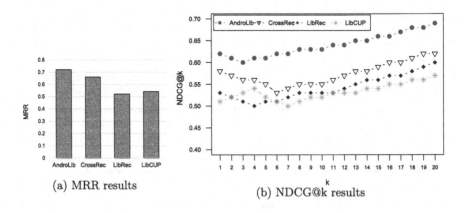

(a) MRR results

(b) NDCG@k results

**Fig. 4.** The achieved ranking scores, *NDCG@k* and *MRR* by each approach.

# 5  Threats to Validity

*Threats to construct validity* could be related to the performance measures. We basically used standard performance metrics such as success rate, precision, recall that are widely used in recommender systems for software engineering [3,17,18,23,26,28]. We also plan to conduct a user study with Android developers to better evaluate the usefulness of our approach from developer's perspective. Another potential threat could be related to the selection of search algorithm. Although we use NSGA-II which is known to have high performance in solving several software engineering problems [10], there are other techniques. To mitigate this threat, we plan to compare the performance of our approach with other search algorithms.

*Threats to internal validity* relate to errors in our experiments. We have double checked our experiments and the datasets collected following the literature guidelines, still there could be errors that we did not notice. Other threats could be related to the stochastic nature of search algorithms employed [2]. To mitigate this, we conducted non-parametric statistical testing. We used the Wilcoxon Signed Rank test over 30 independent runs with a 95% ($\alpha < 0.05$) confidence level along with Cliff's delta effect size for measuring the difference magnitude. We are, thus, confident that the observed statistical relationships are significant. Other threats to internal validity refers to experimenter bias. Most of our experimental process is automated and randomized. Thus we believe there is little experimenter bias.

*Threats to internal validity* could relate to the generalizability of our results. The To ensure the generalizability of our findings across various types of libraries, we have used a large dataset of 2,752 Android apps that are hosted in Google Play Store, and 979 libraries that belong to multiple domains. We have also performed cross-validation to mimic real-world scenarios. However, to further challenge our recommender system, we plan on testing it on a wider variety of mobile apps from both Android and iOS environments to better generalize our findings.

# 6  Conclusion and Future Work

In this paper, we introduced AndroLib to support the adoption and reuse of third-party libraries in Android development by tackling their recommendation as a multi-objective optimization problem. Our designed tool, namely AndroLib, provides developers with a set of libraries that are most adequate to fit their needs, based on their common usage in other apps, based on the extent to which their functionality is diverse, and based on their rating, as a mean to only consider well-engineered apps. Our experiments have shown the value of AndroLib, in successfully recommending libraries, when tested using a dataset of 979 third-party libraries, with of score of 0.91 of success rate, 0.78 of precision, and 0.81 of recall. Results indicate also that our approach provides a higher chance of recommending the appropriate libraries in the first ranks of the recommendation list. As part of our future work, we plan to test AndroLib with a larger set of libraries from both Android and iOS environments. We plan on also challenging the choice of NSGA-II by testing with other competitive evolutionary algorithms that are known for handling a higher number of objectives, when increasing our objective space. Moreover, we plan to conduct a user study with developers to better evaluate the usefulness of our approach from developer's perspective.

# References

1. Almarimi, N., Ouni, A., Bouktif, S., Mkaouer, M.W., Kula, R.G., Saied, M.A.: Web service api recommendation for automated mashup creation using multi-objective evolutionary search. Appl. Soft Comput. **85**, 105830 (2019)
2. Arcuri, A., Briand, L.: A practical guide for using statistical tests to assess randomized algorithms in software engineering. In: International Conference on Software Engineering (ICSE), pp. 1–10 (2011)
3. Avazpour, I., Pitakrat, T., Grunske, L., Grundy, J.: Dimensions and metrics for evaluating recommendation systems. In: Recommendation Systems in Software Engineering, pp. 245–273 (2014)
4. Bland, J.M., Altman, D.G.: Multiple significance tests: the bonferroni method. BMJ **310**(6973), 170 (1995)
5. Chan, W.K., Cheng, H., Lo, D.: Searching connected API subgraph via text phrases. In: ACM SIGSOFT International Symposium on the Foundations of Software Engineering (FSE), p. 10 (2012)
6. Deb, K., Pratap, A., Agarwal, S., Meyarivan, T.: A fast and elitist multiobjective genetic algorithm: NSGA-II. IEEE Trans. Evolutionary Comput. **6**(2), 182–197 (2002)
7. Di Noia, T., Mirizzi, R., Ostuni, V.C., Romito, D., Zanker, M.: Linked open data to support content-based recommender systems. In: International Conference on Semantic Systems, pp. 1–8 (2012)
8. Di Noia, T., Ostuni, V.C.: Recommender systems and linked open data. In: Reasoning Web International Summer School, pp. 88–113 (2015)
9. Harman, M., Jones, B.F.: Search-based software engineering. Inf. Softw. Technol. **43**(14), 833–839 (2001)
10. Harman, M., Mansouri, S.A., Zhang, Y.: Search-based software engineering: trends, techniques and applications. ACM Comput. Surv. **45**(1), 11 (2012)
11. He, Q., Li, B., Chen, F., Grundy, J., Xia, X., Yang, Y.: Diversified third-party library prediction for mobile app development. IEEE Transactions on Software Engineering (2020)
12. Heinemann, L., Bauer, V., Herrmannsdoerfer, M., Hummel, B.: Identifier-based context-dependent api method recommendation. In: European Conference on Software Maintenance and Reengineering (CSMR), pp. 31–40 (2012)
13. Kula, R.G., German, D.M., Ouni, A., Ishio, T., Inoue, K.: Do developers update their library dependencies? Empirical Softw. Eng. **23**(1), 384–417 (2017). https://doi.org/10.1007/s10664-017-9521-5
14. Larios-Vargas, E., Aniche, M., Treude, C., Bruntink, M., Gousios, G.: Selecting third-party libraries: The practitioners' perspective. In: European Software Engineering Conference and Symposium on the Foundations of Software Engineering (2020)

15. Mccarey, F., Cinnéide, M.Ó., Kushmerick, N.: Rascal: a recommender agent for agile reuse. Artif. Intell. Rev. **24**(3–4), 253–276 (2005)
16. McMillan, C., Grechanik, M., Poshyvanyk, D.: Detecting similar software applications. In: International Conference on Software Engineering, pp. 364–374 (2012)
17. Nguyen, P.T., Di Rocco, J., Di Ruscio, D., Di Penta, M.: Crossrec: supporting software developers by recommending third-party libraries. J. Syst. Softw. **161**, 110460 (2020)
18. Nguyen, P.T., Di Rocco, J., Di Ruscio, D., Ochoa, L., Degueule, T., Di Penta, M.: Focus: a recommender system for mining api function calls and usage patterns. In: International Conference on Software Engineering (ICSE), pp. 1050–1060 (2019)
19. Ouni, A.: Search based software engineering: challenges, opportunities and recent applications. In: Proceedings of the Genetic and Evolutionary Computation Conference, pp. 1114–1146 (2020)
20. Ouni, A., Kessentini, M., Inoue, K., Cinnéide, M.O.: Search-based web service antipatterns detection. IEEE Trans. Serv. Comput. **10**(4), 603–617 (2017)
21. Ouni, A., Kessentini, M., Sahraoui, H., Boukadoum, M.: Maintainability defects detection and correction: a multi-objective approach. Automated Softw. Eng. **20**(1), 47–79 (2013)
22. Ouni, A., Kessentini, M., Sahraoui, H., Inoue, K., Deb, K.: Multi-criteria code refactoring using search-based software engineering: an industrial case study. ACM Trans. Softw. Eng. Methodol. **25**(3), 1–53 (2016)
23. Ouni, A., Kula, R.G., Kessentini, M., Ishio, T., German, D.M., Inoue, K.: Search-based software library recommendation using multi-objective optimization. Inf. Softw. Technol. **83**, 55–75 (2017)
24. Research, I.D.C.I.: Android dominating mobile market. https://www.idc.com/promo/smartphone-market-share/os (2020)
25. Robillard, M., Walker, R., Zimmermann, T.: Recommendation systems for software engineering. IEEE Software **27**(4), 80–86 (2010)
26. Saied, M.A., Ouni, A., Sahraoui, H., Kula, R.G., Inoue, K., Lo, D.: Improving reusability of software libraries through usage pattern mining. J. Syst. Softw. **145**, 164–179 (2018)
27. Salza, P., Palomba, F., Di Nucci, D., De Lucia, A., Ferrucci, F.: Third-party libraries in mobile apps: when, how, and why developers update them. Empirical Softw. Eng. **25**(3), 2341–2377 (2020)
28. Thung, F., Lo, D., Lawall, J.: Automated library recommendation. In: 20th Working Conference on Reverse Engineering (WCRE), pp. 182–191, October 2013
29. Thung, F., Wang, S., Lo, D., Lawall, J.: Automatic recommendation of api methods from feature requests. In: IEEE/ACM International Conference on Automated Software Engineering, pp. 290–300, November 2013
30. Tsunoda, M., Kakimoto, T., Ohsugi, N., Monden, A., Matsumoto, K.: Javawock: a java class recommender system based on collaborative filtering. In: International Conference on Software Engineering and Knowledge Engineering, pp. 491–497 (2005)
31. Wang, H., Guo, Y., Ma, Z., Chen, X.: Wukong: A scalable and accurate two-phase approach to android app clone detection. In: International Symposium on Software Testing and Analysis, pp. 71–82 (2015)
32. Zhang, Z., Cai, H.: A look into developer intentions for app compatibility in android. In: International Conference on Mobile Software Engineering and Systems. pp. 40–44 (2019)

# Empirical Analysis

# Investigating the Impact of Functional Size Measurement on Predicting Software Enhancement Effort Using Correlation-Based Feature Selection Algorithm and SVR Method

Zaineb Sakhrawi[1]([⊠]) , Asma Sellami[2] , and Nadia Bouassida[2]

[1] Faculty of Economics and Management of Sfax, University of Sfax, Sfax, Tunisia
zeinab.sakhraoui@fsegs.rnu.tn
[2] Higher Institute of Computer Science and Multimedia, University of Sfax, Sfax, Tunisia
{asma.sellami,nadia.bouassida}@isims.usf.tn

**Abstract.** The software Functional Size Measurement (FSM) is one of the major factors affecting the effort estimation. Several FSM methods have been proposed since they are useful when development/ enhancement effort must be estimated. However, the greatest challenge for the project managers and other stakeholders is how to identify the effectiveness of an FSM method and select an accurate enhancement effort prediction model. There is only one 2nd generation FSM method- the Common Software Measurement International Consortium (COSMIC) method and four first-generation FSM, including the International Function Point Users Group (IFPUG) method. The main goal of this paper is to investigate the effectiveness of the first and the second FSM generations, respectively, IFPUG and COSMIC methods for sizing functional changes, and their use for predicting software enhancement maintenance effort. In this paper, the Correlation-based-Feature Selection (CFS) algorithm is combined with the Support Vector Regression (SVR) model. The dataset used for training and testing the prediction model is obtained from the International Software Benchmarking Standards Group (ISBSG) Release 12. To make comparisons between the impact of enhancement functional size generated from COSMIC and IFPUG methods on the enhancement effort prediction, two types of experiments were conducted, one with the use of the IFPUG and the other with the use of the COSMIC. Results show that the use of COSMIC functional change size measurement as input for predicting enhancement effort provides significantly better results than IFPUG in terms of MAE (Mean Absolute Error) = 0.0382 and Root Mean Square Error (RMSE) = 0.1082.

**Keywords:** Software functional size measurement · Software enhancement effort prediction · COSMIC · IFPUG · Correlation-based Feature Selection (CFS) · Support Vector Regression (SVR)

© Springer Nature Switzerland AG 2020
S. Ben Sassi et al. (Eds.): ICSR 2020, LNCS 12541, pp. 229–244, 2020.
https://doi.org/10.1007/978-3-030-64694-3_14

# 1   Introduction

Software Maintenance is the field of Software Engineering which have been ignored over the last period of time. It has not received the same degree of attention that the other phases have [34]. Nevertheless, it is the most crucial field in the software life [1]. In fact, one of the most challenging problems in managing software project is how to obtain an accurate estimate when requirements are likely to change. The ISO/IEC-14764 defines Enhancement Maintenance (EM) as a modification to an existing software product to satisfy a new requirement. Note also that, there are two types of software enhancements, adaptive and perfective. Adaptive maintenance provides enhancements necessary to accommodate changes in the environment in which a software product must operate. These changes are those that must be made to keep pace with the changing environment [27]. On the other hand, perfective maintenance provides enhancements for improvement of program documentation, and improvement of software performance, maintainability, or other software attributes [27]. As indicated by the results of the Standish Group analyses, the success rate for such projects has never gone beyond 35% [17]. This is due to the lack of a standardized verification process.

Despite the large number of proposals interested in finding accurate estimates, there is no clear evidence in determining which model is the best for estimating enhancement effort (*i.e.*, the considerations for selecting one model from others). It is therefore paramount that the inputs to estimation models be identified and evaluated. Inaccurate estimates lead to customer dissatisfaction, and project failure. In contrast, accurate estimates reduce uncertainty and support software project management in a more effective manner. An estimator has to deal with both linear and non-linear relationships of the dependent variable and independent variables.

In this context, software size is widely recognized as a predominant cost driver for the effort and cost needed for software projects. Researchers consider that the size variables are closely related to the required effort [18]. Knowing the COSMIC functional size of the software to be developed/re-developed is valuable. In fact, software size can be used for improving organizational performance, estimating the effort/cost of new development, estimating the enhancement effort, and controlling software development, etc. [15,16]. In the literature, there are a number of studies on the use of software functional size generated from IFPUG and COSMIC methods for estimating software effort [13,30]. However, very few of them investigate their effectiveness and impact on predicting enhancement effort [21,22,40]. Thus, in this work we assess the effectiveness of the most popular FSM methods (IFPUG and COSMIC) for measuring functional changes and, therefore, to be used as independent variables for predicting software enhancement effort. The prediction is carried out differently by applying CFS algorithm and SVR method separately and by using data from the ISBSG dataset. The following hypothesis is made:

"The use of a precise measurement of the COSMIC functional change provides significantly better results than IFPUG for predicting enhancement effort".

The first step is to understand whether the selected FSM methods might be used in the context of enhancement effort prediction using the CFS algorithm. Then, an effort prediction model is built using Support Vector Regression model. The results (the estimates) are compared against some standard baselines that are widely used in the literature (*e.g.,* the Mean of Absolute Residuals (MAR) to check their accuracy. To the best of our knowledge, this is the first study investigating the impact of using FSM methods (IFPUG and COSMIC) on predicting accurately software enhancement maintenance effort.

The rest of the paper is structured as follows: Sect. 2 provides the reader with background knowledge on IFPUG, COSMIC, CFS algorithm and SVR method, and on the related work. The design of our empirical study is described in Sect. 3, while its results and discussion are provided in Sect. 4. Conclusion and future work conclude the paper.

## 2    Background

This section describes the most widely used FSM methods (IFPUG ISO 20926 and COSMIC ISO 19761), the CFS algorithm, the SVR method and discusses the works related to this research.

### 2.1    IFPUG FPA Method

The IFPUG was formed to foster and promote the evolution of the Function Points method [28]. Since then, the method has been named IFPUG Function Point Analysis (or simply IFPUG, for short) and has been standardized as ISO/IEC 20926:2009. The IFPUG sizing method is used to measure the functionality impacted by software development, enhancement and maintenance independently of technology used for implementation. IFPUG sizes an application starting from its Functional User Requirements (or by other software artifacts that can be abstracted in terms of FURs). In particular, to identify the set of "features" provided by the software, each FUR is functionally decomposed into Base Functional Components (BFC), and each BFC is categorized into one of five Data or Transactional BFC Types [28]. For more details about the application of the IFPUG method, readers may refer to the counting manual [25].

### 2.2    COSMIC FSM Method

The COSMIC method was proposed in 1999 to correct some of the structural deficiencies of the first-generation FSM methods and overcame a number of their limitations [10]. The COSMIC method was designed to be independent of any implementation decisions embedded in the operational artifacts of the software to be measured. Each data movement is measured as 1 CFP. The COSMIC measurement process [16] includes three phases: Measurement strategy phase, mapping phase and Measurement phase.

The size of a functional process is the sum of all its data movements. There are four types of data movements: Entry, exit, Write, and Read [16]. An Entry moves a single data-group from a user to the functional process. An exit moves a single datagroup from a functional process to the user. A Write moves a single data-group inside the functional process to a persistent storage. And, a Read moves a single data-group from persistent storage to the functional process. The Functional Size of a Functional Process (noted by FS(FP)) (*i.e.*, UC) is given by Eq. 1 [16].

$$FS(FPi) = \sum FS(Entries) + \sum FS(eXits) + \sum FS(Reads) + \sum FS(Writes) \quad (1)$$

COSMIC measures the functional size of a change to software as well as the functional size of software that is added, changed or deleted.

## 2.3   Correlation-Based Feature Selection (CFS) Algorithm

In the literature, a number of feature selection algorithms have been proposed to solve the high-dimensional data problem. However, many published studies [23] confirmed the effectiveness of Features Selection algorithms, as a data preprocessing strategy, and Machine Learning (ML) techniques for software enhancement effort estimation. In this study, we will use Correlation-based Feature Selection (CFS). CFS was proposed by Hall [19]. CFS used correlation to evaluate feature subsets that are derived from Pearson correlation coefficient [19]. This method is a multivariate feature Filter. That means that it assesses different feature subsets and chooses the best one. The CFS evaluates subsets of features according to heuristic evaluation function.

## 2.4   Support Vector Regression (SVR) Method

A review of various ML techniques used in estimating enhancement effort revealed that the accuracy of estimates can be achieved [3,31]. No one method is necessarily better than the other. Strengths and weaknesses are often complementary to each other. The SVR method was first introduced by Vapnik at 1995 [8]. To generalize the Support Vector algorithm to regression estimation, an analogue of the margin is constructed in the space of the target values using Vapnik's insensitive loss function [8]. Variables in the SVR method structure belong to continuous space.

## 2.5   Related Work

FSM methods are nowadays widely applied in software industry for sizing software systems and then using the obtained functional size as independent variable in estimation models [9]. Software effort estimation can be considered as a super domain of many software activities including the prediction of software development effort, testing effort, maintenance effort, etc. [36]. Most of the effort prediction models for software enhancement used the software size as the main input parameter. In this context, from literature review, we analysed:

**The Impact of Software Functional Size Generated from the IFPUG FPA Method on the Software Effort Estimation:** IFPUG is very popular in the software industry [35], IFPUG software size is commonly used as independent variables for estimating the software development/enhancement effort. In fact, the amount of data collected using the IFPUG method in the ISBSG dataset were greatly large when compared to the COSMIC method. However, many FSM specialists found that IFPUG is less effective when measuring software size, even when it is applied in its traditional MIS domain for which it was designed [29]. IFPUG measure only the functional size of the software before and after the change, and the change size is provided as an indirect measurement [20].

**The Impact of Software Functional Size Generated from the COSMIC FSM Method on the Software Effort Prediction:** Several empirical studies confirm that CFP is an effective FSM for web applications, real-time and embedded software [22]. Compared to other FSM methods, COSMIC is designed to objectively measure the functional size of a change to software as well the size of software that is added, changed or deleted [39]. Results from industry demonstrate that the COSMIC sizing has been successfully used for productivity monitoring and estimating [29].

**The Impact of Using Correlation-based Feature Selection (CFS) Techniques on the Performance of Effort Prediction Models:** Researchers [14,42] reported that CFS algorithm outperforms the other feature selection techniques. They showed that the impact of feature selection techniques varies across the studied dataset. Experimental results in [14,42] indicate that the CFS algorithm was reported as the best-performing feature selection techniques. Thus, in this study, we will use Correlation-based Feature Selection (CFS) algorithm. In addition, CFS algorithm evaluates all the possible combinations. It can update the subset of the selected features during the evaluation process instead of the greedy forward selection and greedy backward elimination. These later do not update the subset of features during the evaluation process [23]. Another challenge when using CFS is related to the starting points for feature subsets generation [23], also to handle the missing values in a feature. CFS algorithm replaces the missing values by taking the average value for continuous features and the most common value for discrete features [6]. Our study was based on Hall's hypothesis "A good feature subset is one that contains features highly correlated with the class, yet uncorrelated with each other" [19]. In this study, we will use Correlation-based Feature Selection (CFS) algorithm.

**The Impact of SVR Method on the Performance of Effort Prediction Models:** Most of the common software effort prediction-based methods are Regression [7] and Analogy [38]. In regression-based estimation, the model must be specified in advance in which one dependent variable is plotted against several independent variables [41]. In our case, we selected SVR as a regression model, since it outperforms the other popular cost estimation procedures in terms of accuracy [32].

## 3   Research Methodology

Figure 1 presents our research methodology. Setting up two regression-based models, one using the IFPUG and the other using the COSMIC and making comparison between their prediction accuracies to identify whether the COS-MIC method provides useful information (*i.e.,* a more accurate functional change size than IFPUG) for predicting software enhancement effort, using a training dataset to use subsequently to predict the total enhancements effort for the development of software projects in man-hours.

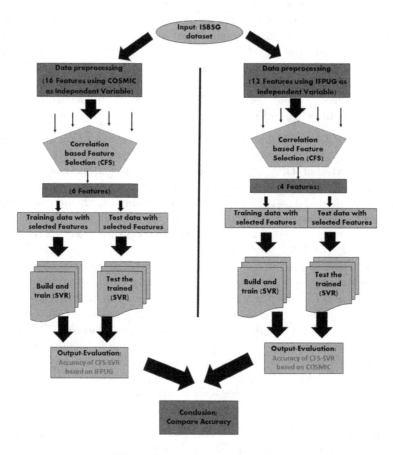

**Fig. 1.** Research method design

## 3.1   Data Preprocessing

The dataset used for training and testing the prediction model is obtained from the ISBSG Release 12 [26]. The ISBSG dataset is widely used for software project estimation [24]. It maintains a repository of data about completed software projects, including new, enhanced and re-developed software projects. ISBSG dataset offers a wealth of information about completed software projects, regarding practices, tools, and methodologies, accompanied by process and product data, to be used in benchmarking, monitoring, quality control, and performance management purposes during the software development process [18]. The ISBSG dataset is the largest available for research in effort estimation, and it has now been used in a large number of studies [7,12,33]. It has been extensively reviewed for its applicability to build effort estimation models, including effects of outliers and missing values [2]. We selected the data regarding "enhancement" as the "development type" where "count approaches" were IFPUG and COSMIC methods. In addition, we consider only data with soundness and high level of integrity (*i.e.*, records having "Data Quality Rating" of "A" or "B"). Table 1 lists the data fields, the corresponding values selected in this study, and the number of projects. After the preprocessing phase, we have selected a total of 17 attributes/features for COSMIC data and a total of 13 attributes/features for IFPUG data.

**Table 1.** First selection of data concerning software enhancement projects from the ISBSG dataset

| ISBSG data field | Selected Values for COSMIC _dataset | Selected Values for IFPUG _dataset | Discarded Values | Projects for COSMIC _dataset | Projects for IFPUG _dataset |
|---|---|---|---|---|---|
| Data quality rating | A, B | A,B | C,D | 4000 | 4000 |
| Count Approach | COSMIC | IFPUG | NESMA, FISMA, etc. | 449 | 3104 |
| development Type | Enhancement | Enhancement | New development and Redevelopment | 302 | 1084 |

## 3.2   Using the Correlation-Based Feature Selection Algorithm

After the project selection with high quality of data (after the preprocessing phase), we propose to use CFS algorithm for selecting the features that are relevant for the software enhancement effort prediction. That is after applying CFS algorithm, we determine which features globally and consistently appear in the optimal set of features. In this step, the filtering is done using the Pearson's Correlation Coefficient algorithm which is the most commonly used algorithms [5]. Pearson's correlation coefficient is a single number that measures both the strength and direction of the linear relationship between two continuous variables. Values can range from $-1$ to $+1$, where 0 is no correlation, 1 is total positive correlation, and −1 is total negative correlation [11]. In our case, we will plot the Pearson correlation heat map. Each feature is ranked based on the attained correlation score p (See Eq. 2) [11]:

$$p = \frac{cov(Xi, Y)}{\sqrt{var(Xi)var(Y)}} \tag{2}$$

where var(Xi) and cov(Xi,Y) represent the variance of feature Xi and the covariance between a feature Xi and the target class Y, respectively.

**Computation of Score P for the Selected Features from COSMIC_dataset Using Pearson's Correlation Coefficient.** After the preprocessing phase we selected a total of 17 attributes where 16 are independent variables and one is the dependent variable (NormalizedWorkEffort). The use of Pearson's correlation coefficient provides a list of features that are sorted based on their degree of correlation to the module class (*i.e.,* NormalizedWorkEffort). In our case, only features having correlation larger than 0.4 (taking into account absolute value) are selected with the output variable. The use of CFS algorithm selects 37.5% (6 out of 16 features) (see Fig. 2).

**Table 2.** Selected Feature correlation when using COSMIC_dataset

| Selected Features | Value - Round(Correlation target) |
|---|---|
| CHANGEWorkEffort | 0.4 |
| UnrecordedWorkEffort | 0.5 |
| FunctionalSize | 0.5 |
| EffortTest | 0.4 |
| SummaryWorkEffort | 0.8 |
| NormalizedWorkEffortLevel1 | 1 |

It has been observed that COSMIC sizing is an efficient method for measuring the functional size of an enhancement that is identified within the enhancement project. Table 2 shows the selected features with their corresponding correlation coefficients value (having score larger than 0.4), computed using COSMIC_dataset, between functional change size (FunctionalSize) and enhancement effort (NormalizedWorkEffort). From the results, the correlation coefficient value has a value of 0.5, indicate an acceptable correlation of functional change size with enhancement effort comparing with other features (such as CHANGEWorkEffort and UnrecordedWorkEffort). Therefore, functional change size is chosen as the primary independent variable.

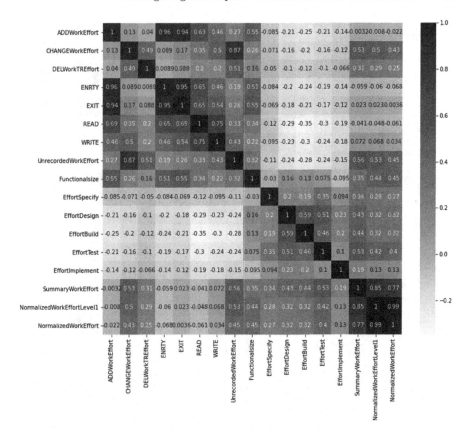

**Fig. 2.** Pearson's correlation heat map for COSMIC_dataset

**Computation of Score P for the Selected Features from IFPUG_dataset Using Pearson's Correlation Coefficient.** After the preprocessing phase, we have selected a total of 13 attributes where 12 are independent variables and one is the dependent variable (NormalizedWorkEffort). Only features having correlation larger than 0.4 (taking into account absolute value) are selected with the output variable. For the IFPUG_dataset, the use of CFS algorithm selects 33.3% (4 out of 12 of the features) (see Fig. 3). When using data from the ISBSG dataset, the correlation coefficient between Functional change size and enhancement effort has a value of 0.1 (see Fig. 3). This value indicates a very weak correlation of functional change size with enhancement effort when compared to other features (such as EffortBuilt and EffortTest). Results show that choosing a functional change size generated from the IFPUG sizing as primary independent variable may not provide an accurate enhancement effort prediction. On the other hand, a careful inspection of the feature list produced by the Pearson's correlation algorithm (see Table 3) indicates that the EffortTest, EffortBuilt, SummaryWorkEffort and NormalizedWorkEffortLevel1 were the most meaningful features that helped in predicting effort.

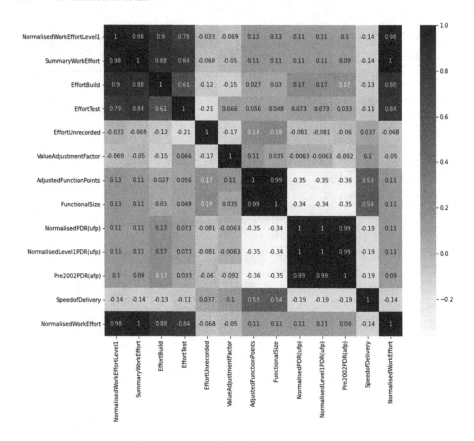

**Fig. 3.** Pearson's correlation heat map for IFPUG_dataset

## 3.3   Constructing Prediction Model

This section conducted a series of experiments to investigate the use of the SVR method. For experiments, the classic approach is to do a simple 70%–30% split. ISBSG dataset is split into training and validation/test sets. The size of the split is specified via the "test_size" argument. In our model 30% of the dataset is allocated to the test set and 70% are allocated to the training set. The training set is used to train the model, and the validation/test set is used to validate it on data it has never seen before. Thereafter, to carry out the experiments, the CFS algorithm and the validation test prediction of SVR method were performed using the Google Colaboratory[1] python programming. Google Colaboratory is widely known as Google Colab. It provides GPU for research to the people who do not have enough resources or cannot afford one. Table 4 lists the predefined range of parameters values of the SVR method.

---

[1] https://colab.research.google.com.

**Table 3.** Selected Feature correlation when using IFPUG_dataset

| Selected Features | Value -Round(Correlation target) |
|---|---|
| EffortBuilt | 0.8 |
| EffortTest | 0.9 |
| SummaryWorkEffort | 1 |
| NormalizedWorkEffortLevel1 | 1 |

**Table 4.** Parameters values for Grid Search

| ML Technique | Parameters |
|---|---|
| SVR | Kernel=Linear; Complexity=1, 2; epsilon=0.2; Deviation=0.001, 0.0001 |

## 3.4  Empirical Results

This section evaluates the prediction performance of SVR used in this study? where two types of experiments are conducted with the use of CFS algorithm. To evaluate the accuracy of the prediction models, we used a widely set of evaluation metrics [24] such as root mean square error (RMSE) and mean absolute error (MAE). We proposed to measure accuracy, using the Standardized Accuracy (SA) metric based on MAE as described by [37].

**Performance Assessment When Using COSMIC Sizing.** SVR is trained and tested using features selected by the CFS algorithm. Using CFS algorithms with the SVR method can lead to more accurate enhancement effort prediction when the Functional Change Size is used as the independent variable (See Table 5). Error metrics (such as MAE and RMSE) reveal quite values using SVR method (MAE = 0.0382; RMSE = 0.1082).

**Table 5.** Prediction analysis using MAE, RMSE and SA for COSMIC_dataset

| Method/ Parameters | MAE | RMSE | SA(%) |
|---|---|---|---|
| SVR | 0.0382 | 0.1082 | 98% |

**Performance Assessment When Using IFPUG Sizing.** SVR is trained and tested using features selected by the CFS algorithm. The selected features (*i.e.*, features selecting by CFS and the IFPUG feature) with SVR method can lead to accurate enhancement effort prediction (see Table 6). Error metrics (such as MAE and RMSE) reveal quite values (MAE = 0.0734; RMSE = 0.1950).

**Table 6.** Prediction analysis using MAE, RMSE and SA for IFPUG_dataset

| Method/ Parameters | MAE | RMSE | SA(%) |
|---|---|---|---|
| SVR | 0.0734 | 0.1950 | 98% |

# 4  Discussion and Comparison

Using the ISBSG dataset, the prediction accuracy increases when the COSMIC method is selected as "count approaches" for "enhancement projects" in comparison with the ISBSG method (see Table 5 and 6). We can accept the following hypothesis as formulated in the Introduction:

"The use of a precise measurement of the COSMIC functional change provides significantly better results than IFPUG for predicting enhancement effort."

The main reason behind selecting Functional size as independent variable in our study, is that software functional size is correlated to software project effort and sensitivity to changes in functional size has a greater impact on the project effort [4]. In order to identify the effective determinants for enhancement effort estimation, the importance of each feature (using COSMIC and IFPUG) is computed using CFS algorithm.

In this study, SVR method is used to provide the effort prediction of a new enhancement (*i.e.*, a new functional change) when software is being developed. The COSMIC FSM method is evaluated to be the most effective when compared to the IFPUG FPA method. It is evident from the results with the minimum MAE of 0.0382 and accurate predictions has a value of 98%. Furthermore, the CFS algorithm results show the importance of Functional Change Size feature using the COSMIC FSM method. As expected, the CFS algorithm in our case has contributed significantly not only in reducing the number of features required to achieve the performance of prediction but also to improve such performance. Summarizing, the benefits of this study suggest that software organizations interested in managing software enhancement effort should choose the right sizing method based on their objectives and capabilities. Hence, A good measurement program is an investment in success by facilitating early detection of enhancement issues.

# 5  Threats to Validy

Threats to validity of our study are pertinent to internal validity, external validity, and finally construct validity.

## 5.1  Internal Validity

The Internal validity is related to the types of features used for assessing the performance of prediction models. We restricted the study to numerical attributes.

A justification of numerical attributes is that they lead to the selection of different types of features in a uniform manner, and therefore providing a common basis for computing feature correlation, but there still remains the case of categorical attributes.

### 5.2  External Validity

The External validity is related to the degree of the generalization of the results. The main threat may come from the CFS algorithm. Although the experiments were performed using CFS algorithm, it is still compulsory to test other FS algorithms with different ML techniques.

### 5.3  Construct Validity

The Construct validity is related to the degree of reliability of the size measurement method used as input for prediction models. In fact, the enhancement effort prediction models in our study used the enhancement size (generated from IFPUG and COSMIC sizing) as independent variables. Although the estimation model using the COSMIC sizing as input has the MAE of 0.0382, the correlation coefficients computed between the COSMIC Functional change size and the enhancement effort still a moderate value. This is due to the fact that Functional Size is identified at the functional process level identifying only the data movements.

## 6  Conclusion

In this study, we investigated the problem of accurately estimate effort for software enhancement projects using two FSM methods including the 1st generation (*e.g.*, IFPUG) and the 2nd generation (*i.e.*, COSMIC). A SVR method based on CFS algorithm was implemented and empirically tested. The constructed model was tested using ISBSG dataset of historical software projects including enhancement functional size using either IFPUG or COSMIC sizing. The findings of our empirical study were as follows:

- The correlation score between IFPUG enhancement size and enhancement effort has a value of 0.1 which denotes a very weak correlation. Therefore, choosing the IFPUG as the primary independent variable cannot give an accurate enhancement effort prediction. However, the estimated effort that results from SVR method provides a good accuracy.
- The correlation score between COSMIC enhancement size and enhancement effort has a value of 0.5 which denotes a good correlation as compared to IFPUG. Therefore, choosing the COSMIC sizing as the primary independent variable provides an accurate enhancement effort prediction. In addition, the estimated effort that results from SVR method provides a good accuracy. Consequently, COSMIC can be considered an effective measurement method for sizing enhancement and thereafter predicting its corresponding effort.

– Using CFS algorithm and SVR method, the experimental results suggested that the COSMIC sizing is significantly better than IFPUG when used as primary in dependant variable for predicting enhancement effort having The results show small MAE has a value of 0.0382 and with quite good performance has a value of 98%.

For future work, several extensions can be made. Only one real world dataset (ISBSG) is used for experiments in our study, because it is the only one that uses COSMIC functional size measurement for enhancement projects. This work will be extended by exploring the accuracy of enhancement effort using boosting machine learning techniques such Gradient Boosting regression and others features selection algorithms.

# References

1. Ali, S.S., Zafar, M.S., Saeed, M.T.: Effort estimation problems in software maintenance-a survey. In: 2020 3rd International Conference on Computing, Mathematics and Engineering Technologies (iCoMET), pp. 1–9. IEEE (2020)
2. Bala, A., Abran, A.: Use of the multiple imputation strategy to deal with missing data in the ISBSG repository. J. Inf. Technol. Softw. Eng. **6**, 171 (2016)
3. Basgalupp, M.P., Barros, R.C., Ruiz, D.D.: Predicting software maintenance effort through evolutionary-based decision trees. In: Proceedings of the 27th Annual ACM Symposium on Applied Computing, pp. 1209–1214 (2012)
4. Bhardwaj, M., Ajay, R.: Estimation of testing and rework efforts for software development projects. Asian J. Comput. Sci. Inf. Technol. **5**(5), 33–37 (2015)
5. Biesiada, J., Duch, W.: Feature selection for high-dimensional data'a pearson redundancy based filter. In: Computer recognition systems, vol. 2, pp. 242–249. Springer, Heidelberg (2007). https://doi.org/10.1007/978-3-540-75175-5_30
6. Blessie, E.C., Karthikeyan, E.: Sigmis: a feature selection algorithm using correlation based method. J. Algorithms Comput. Technol. **6**(3), 385–394 (2012)
7. Cerón-Figueroa, S., López-Martín, C., Yáñez-Márquez, C.: Stochastic gradient boosting for predicting the maintenance effort of software-intensive systems. IET Software **14**(2), 82–87 (2019)
8. Cortes, C., Vapnik, V.: Support-vector networks. Mach. Learn. **20**(3), 273–297 (1995)
9. Di Martino, S., Ferrucci, F., Gravino, C., Sarro, F.: Web effort estimation: function point analysis vs. cosmic. Inf. Software Technol. **72**, 90–109 (2016)
10. Di Martino, S., Ferrucci, F., Gravino, C., Sarro, F.: Assessing the effectiveness of approximate functional sizing approaches for effort estimation. Inf. Softw. Technol. 106308 (2020)
11. Fan, J., Lv, J.: Sure independence screening for ultrahigh dimensional feature space. J. Royal Stat. Soc. Ser. B (Statistical Methodology) **70**(5), 849–911 (2008)
12. García-Floriano, A., López-Martín, C., Yáñez-Márquez, C., Abran, A.: Support vector regression for predicting software enhancement effort. Inf. Softw. Technol. **97**, 99–109 (2018)
13. Gencel, C.: How to use COSMIC functional size in effort estimation models? In: Dumke, R.R., Braungarten, R., Büren, G., Abran, A., Cuadrado-Gallego, J.J. (eds.) IWSM/Mensura/MetriKon -2008. LNCS, vol. 5338, pp. 196–207. Springer, Heidelberg (2008). https://doi.org/10.1007/978-3-540-89403-2_17

14. Ghotra, B., McIntosh, S., Hassan, A.E.: A large-scale study of the impact of feature selection techniques on defect classification models. In: 2017 IEEE/ACM 14th International Conference on Mining Software Repositories (MSR), pp. 146–157. IEEE (2017)
15. Group, I.I.F.P.U.: Cosmic and IFPUG glossary of terms. A Functional Size Measurement Method (2011)
16. Group, I.I.F.P.U.: Cosmic and IFPUG glossary of terms. Common Software Measurement International Consortium (2015)
17. Group, S., et al.: Chaos summary 2009. Online report. Accessed 20 June 2009
18. González-Ladrón-de Guevara, F., Fernández-Diego, M., Lokan, C.: The usage of ISBSG data fields in software effort estimation: a systematic mapping study. J. Syst. Softw. **113**, 188–215 (2016)
19. Hall, M.A.: Correlation-based feature selection for machine learning (1999)
20. Haoues, M., Sellami, A., Ben-Abdallah, H.: Towards functional change decision support based on cosmic FSM method. Inf. Softw. Technol. **110**, 78–91 (2019)
21. Hira, A., Boehm, B.: Function point analysis for software maintenance. In: Proceedings of the 10th ACM/IEEE International Symposium on Empirical Software Engineering and Measurement, pp. 1–6 (2016)
22. Hira, A., Boehm, B.: Cosmic function points evaluation for software maintenance. In: Proceedings of the 11th Innovations in Software Engineering Conference, pp. 1–11 (2018)
23. Hosni, M., Idri, A., Abran, A.: Investigating heterogeneous ensembles with filter feature selection for software effort estimation. In: Proceedings of the 27th International Workshop on Software Measurement and 12th International Conference on Software Process and Product Measurement, pp. 207–220 (2017)
24. Idri, A., Azzahra Amazal, F., Abran, A.: Analogy-based software development effort estimation: a systematic mapping and review. Inf. Softw. Technol. **58**, 206–230 (2015)
25. IFPUG: International function point users group (IFPUG) function point counting practices manual (2000)
26. ISBSG: Repository data release 12'field descriptions, e.field descriptions -data release 12.document provided as a part of data set, International Software Benchmarking and Standards Group (2013)
27. ISO/IEC: International standard-iso/iec 14764 ieee std 14764–2006 software engineering; software life cycle processes & ; maintenance (2006)
28. ISO/IEC: ISO/IEC 20926: Software and systems engineering - software measurement - IFPUG functional size measurement method. In: International Organization for Standardization, Geneva, Switzerland (2009)
29. Jayakumar, K.: why you must change to cosmic for sizing and estimation (2011)
30. Kaur, A., Kaur, K.: A cosmic function points based test effort estimation model for mobile applications. J. King Saud Univ. Comput. Inf. Sci. (2019)
31. Kaur, A., Kaur, K., Malhotra, R.: Soft computing approaches for prediction of software maintenance effort. Int. J. Comput. Appl. **1**(16), 69–75 (2010)
32. Kumari, S., Pushkar, S.: Comparison and analysis of different software cost estimation methods. Int. J. Adv. Comput. Sci. Appl. **4**(1), 41 (2013)
33. López-Martín, C.: Predictive accuracy comparison between neural networks and statistical regression for development effort of software projects. Appl. Soft Comput. **27**, 434–449 (2015)
34. Bourque, R.F.: Guide to the software engineering body of knowledge. In: SWEBOK V3.0. IEEE Computer Society (2014)

35. Quesada-López, C., Jenkins, M.: An evaluation of functional size measurement methods, pp. 151–165 (2015)
36. Sangwan, O.P., et al.: Software effort estimation using machine learning techniques. In: 2017 7th International Conference on Cloud Computing, Data Science & Engineering-Confluence, pp. 92–98. IEEE (2017)
37. Shepperd, M., MacDonell, S.: Evaluating prediction systems in software project estimation. Inf. Softw. Technol. **54**(8), 820–827 (2012)
38. Shepperd, M., Schofield, C.: Estimating software project effort using analogies. In: Series on Software Engineering and Knowledge Engineering, **16**, 64 (2005)
39. Symons, C.: A comparison of the key differences between the IFPUG and cosmic functional size measurement methods. In: Common Software Measurement International Consortium (2011)
40. Tran-Cao, D., Levesque, G.: Maintenance effort and cost estimation using software functional sizes. In: International Workshop on Software Measurement, Montreal, Canada (2003)
41. Walkerden, F., Jeffery, R.: An empirical study of analogy-based software effort estimation. Empirical Softw. Eng. **4**(2), 135–158 (1999)
42. Xu, Z., Liu, J., Yang, Z., An, G., Jia, X.: The impact of feature selection on defect prediction performance: an empirical comparison. In: 2016 IEEE 27th International Symposium on Software Reliability Engineering (ISSRE), pp. 309–320. IEEE (2016)

# How Does Library Migration Impact Software Quality and Comprehension? An Empirical Study

Hussein Alrubaye[1]([✉])[ID], Deema Alshoaibi[1][ID], Eman Alomar[1][ID],
Mohamed Wiem Mkaouer[1][ID], and Ali Ouni[2][ID]

[1] Rochester Institute of Technology, Rochester, NY, USA
{hat6622,da3352,eaa6167,mwmvse}@rit.edu
[2] Ecole de Technologie Superieure, University of Quebec, Quebec City, QC, Canada
ali.ouni@etsmtl.ca

**Abstract.** The process of migration between different third-party software libraries, while being an typical library reuse practice, is complex, time consuming and error-prone. Typically, during a library migration process, developers opt to replace methods from a retired library with other methods from a new library without altering the software behavior. However, the extent to which the process of migrating to new libraries will be rewarded with improved software quality is still unknown. In this paper, our goal is to study the impact of library API migration on software quality. We conducted a large-scale empirical study on 9 popular API migrations, collected from a corpus of 57,447 open-source Java projects. We computed the values of commonly-used software quality metrics before and after a migration occurs. The statistical analysis of the obtained results provides evidence that library migrations are likely to improve different software quality attributes including significantly *reduced coupling, increased cohesion, and improved code readability*. Furthermore, we released an online portal that helps software developers to understand the impact of a library migration on software quality and recommend migration examples that adopt best design and implementation practices to improve software quality. Finally, we provide the software engineering community with a large scale dataset to foster research in software library migration.

**Keywords:** API migration · Software quality · Code comprehension

## 1 Introduction

Software maintenance activities consume up to 70% of the total life-cycle cost of a typical software product [11]. To cope with the expense software evolution, software reuse, through third-party libraries and APIs, has become the backbone of modern software development. However, just like any traditional code, libraries and APIs undergo maintenance and evolution. In order to keep

© Springer Nature Switzerland AG 2020
S. Ben Sassi et al. (Eds.): ICSR 2020, LNCS 12541, pp. 245–260, 2020.
https://doi.org/10.1007/978-3-030-64694-3_15

most up to date libraries, developers need to periodically perform *third-party library migration* [5,8,25,26]. In practice, library migration can be seen as the process of replacing a library with a different one, while preserving the same program behavior. The library migration process tends to be a manual, error-prone, and time-consuming process [5,9,15,27]. Hence, developers have to explore and understand the new library's API, its associated documentation, and its usage scenarios in order to find the right API method(s) to replace in the current implementation belonging to the retired library's API. As a consequence, developers often spend considerable time to verify that the newly adopted features do not introduce any regression. Indeed, previous studies have shown that developers typically spend up to 42 days to migrate between libraries [8]. In the same context, another study shows how the task of library migration is typically given to developers with relatively higher years of coding experience, to reduce the possibility of introducing any regression [6].

Unlike library upgrades, library migrations typically require more fine-grained code changes and refactorings, *e.g.*, changing types of variables and parameters, renaming attributes and methods, etc., since developers need to accommodate the syntactic and semantic mismatch between the added and removed methods [25]. These refactoring changes may account for the overhead needed to fulfill the migration and adjust the existing software design to the newly introduced methods. Typically, API migrations introduce a set of methods and objects with different lexical and naming conventions, which have to be integrated into the existing codebase terminology. That is, developers may refactor their code along with the migration to contextualize the new library methods. These unintended refactoring operations have an impact on software design metrics (*e.g.*, cohesion, coupling, etc.) [4,13] besides the changes in terminology and renaming activities that affect code readability as well [12,20,21].

Various studies have focused on analyzing the impact of API evolution on software quality in terms of change and bug-proneness [17], software usability and rating [16]. Other studies focused on estimating the impact of API documentation on the library adoption and usability which has been investigated in the literature [14]. Moreover, recent studies attempted to identify traces of manually performed library migrations. They provide the community with a set of real-world migrations between popular Java libraries, in various open source projects [8,26,27].

Existing studies reveal the importance of taking into account the software design characteristics when performing the migration to reduce maintenance costs. However, there is little knowledge on the impact of API migration, and its related refactoring changes, on the quality of software's design as well as code comprehension and readability. Indeed, as software systems evolve rapidly, there is a need for appropriate tools, reliable, and efficient techniques to support developers in replacing their deprecated library APIs with up-to-date ones, and maintaining/improving the quality of their software design.

To address the above-mentioned issues, we conducted a large-scale empirical study to assess the impact of library migration on both software design quality and code comprehension. We considered an existing dataset of 9 popular migrations between Java libraries, mined from 57,447 open-source Java projects [8]. Afterward, we shortlisted all commits containing traces of method swaps, as part of migrations under the study. We refined our dataset by untangling each commit to identify the specific code elements involved in the migration using program analysis. Then, for the selected code elements, we calculated the values of their corresponding design and readability metrics, before and after the migration. Finally, we statistically compared the variation of these values, to analyze whether the migration had a significant, positive, or negative impact on design quality and readability. We finally associated a ranking score, to each migration trace, according to the extent to which it was able to improve the design and readability of the existing code. We survey 10 senior developers to assess the usefulness of the ranking score in providing relevant migration code examples.

Our study is driven by the following research questions:

### RQ1. (Design Improvement) What is the Impact of Library Migration on the Quality of Software Design?

To answer this research question, we assess the impact of library migration on software design quality in terms of complexity, coupling and cohesion, widely popular structural metrics [23], and previously used metrics in similar empirical studies [4,18]. For each analyzed source file in the dataset (that we detail later in the next subsection), we measured the value of its coupling and cohesion before and after the migration. As we aggregated all values before and after the migration, we observed the variation in the aggregated values to investigate whether the migration had a positive or negative impact on design quality.

### RQ2. (Code Readability) Does Migration Improve the Code Readability?

Similarly to RQ1, we consider popular state-of-the-art readability tools and metrics [12,22]. For each metric, we measure its pair values in the dataset files, before and after the migration, and then we analyze the values for statistical significance.

### RQ3. (Quality Recommendation) Can We Leverage Design and Readability Metrics to Recommend Better Code Examples for Migration?

Since there are multiple code fragments, belonging to various projects and containing the same mappings, we design a recommendation-based ranking method that aggregates various quality metrics. Our method ranks the collected code fragments based on the extent to which they preserve the design coherence and improve the code comprehension. We then perform a qualitative study with 10 senior developers to evaluate the usefulness of our recommendation-based ranking method.

The paper's key findings show a positive variation of structural and readability metrics, i.e., developers do pay attention to design and readability when performing the migration process. Moreover, results show that code fragments with higher ranking score were also voted by the majority of developers, as good examples of migrations. This study makes the following contributions:

1. We release an online portal[1] that showcases real-world migration fragments, with their corresponding positive or negative impact on coupling, cohesion, and readability.
2. We propose a ranking score, that we label *Migration Quality Score* (MQS), which ensures better API reuse by recommending migration examples that ensure better software quality and comprehension.
3. We survey with senior software engineers at an outstanding company to evaluate MQS's ability to recommend high-quality migration examples for 9 popular migrations. Findings show that MQS effectively recommends high-quality migration examples that facilitates API reusability.

## 2    Background and Terminology

### 2.1    Library Migration

When a software development team made the decision of replacing the current libraries used by the software, they have to specify the **migration rules**. A migration rule is denoted by a pair of a *source* (retired) library and a *target* (replacing) library, *i.e.*, *source* → *target*. For example, *easymock* → *mockito* represent a migration rule where the library easymock is migrated to the new library mockito. Migration rules are not enough to start the migration process. Developers should define the mappings between methods. **Method mapping** is the process of replacing at least one method from the source library by one or multiple methods belonging to the target library.

```
public void addKeyValues(String key, Map value) {
    checkIfKeyDescriptionExist(key);
-   keyValues.put(key, value);
+   keyValues.addProperty(key, new Gson().toJson(value));
}
```

**Fig. 1.** Sample of migration between *json* and *gson*.

### 2.2    Migration Example

We showcase, in Fig. 1, a real-world example of a method-level migration as part of replacing the *json* library with the *gson* library[2]. The method *put(key, value)* has been replaced with two methods, namely *addProperty(key, value)*, and *Gson().toJson(value)*. To have valid input for *addProperty* method, the *Map* object needs to be converted into a *json* object, so another converting method was added. We call this type of change as *Migration fragment* where a block of code changes has methods from removed/added libraries.

---

[1] http://migrationlab.net/index.php?cf=icsr2020.
[2] http://migrationlab.net/redirect.php?cf=icpc2019&p=1.

## 2.3  Software Quality Attributes

Object oriented (OO) software quality attributes reflects the quality change of a refactoring operation. The wide used attributes for software structure design and size are coupling, cohesion and complexity. Coupling measures the level of relationship between modules [24]. While designing the software, low coupling is desirable (*i.e.,* less dependency between modules). Coupling Between Objects (CBO) is a metric for measuring coupling between code objects. The higher the CBO, the higher the class coupling. Cohesion measures the level of relationship within module [18]. While designing the software, high cohesion is desirable (*i.e.,* strong interaction between code elements in a module) since this target helps in fostering code maintainability. Cohesion of Methods (LCOM) metric is used to assess the cohesion of classes. Normalized LCOM metric has been widely recognized in the literature [4,19] as being the alternative to the original LCOM, as the latter addresses its main limitations (misperception of getters and setters, etc.). The lower the LCOM, the higher the class cohesion. Complexity of software indicates effort and time required to maintain the software. Complex software costs more during maintenance and refactoring. Five complexity and volume metrics are used to compute this quality attribute, namely, the Cyclomatic Complexity (CycC), the Line of Code (LOC), the Line with Comments (CLOC), the Ratio of Comment Lines to Code Lines, and the Number of Blank Lines. Normally, higher values of these metrics indicate a higher value of class complexity [13].

Code readability $(CR)$ impacts further code changes conducted by different team members than the original developer or even for the same developer but after a while. Source code readability is one of the important aspects of software engineering. Line length and number of comments are the basic readability metrics obtained from code static analysis. Buse and Weimer [12] derived a relationship between code metrics and human readability notation. Scalabrino et al. [22] extracted code textual features from source code lexicon analysis. The validity and usability of those readability metrics were tested by humans and show high correlation between human conception of code readability and metrics values.

## 3  Empirical Study Setup

### 3.1  Data Collection

Figure 2 provides an overview of our study workflow. To measure the impact of library migration on software quality attributes, we need to analysis the source code before and after library migration has happened. To do so, we used MigrationMiner [7], a command-line based tool used to detect library migration at the method level. Given 57,447 GitHub Java projects, provided by Allamanis et al. [1] as input to MigrationMiner [7], The tool detects 8,938 *migration commits* where a developer migrates the project's source code from using library A to

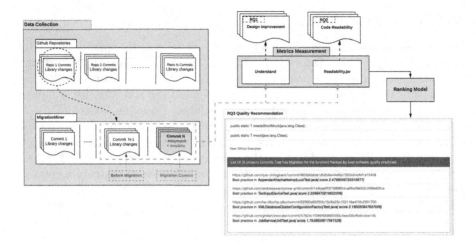

**Fig. 2.** Experimental design overview.

library B (ex *easymock* → *mockito*). To analyze the impact of library migration on code quality, we run  Understand, *readability.jar* [12,22] on migration commit( Commit N) and a commit before migration( Commit N-1).

Each *migration commit* contains at least one or multiple mappings, *i.e.*, fragments of code containing one or multiple removed methods, being replaced with one or multiple added methods, along with other code changes that may or may not be related to the migration. Since any code change, not related to migration represents a noise for this study, we only consider files containing migration fragments in each *migration commit*. We notice that some migrations are *instant i.e.*, all method replacements are located in the same commit, but in multiple source files, and some migrations are *delayed, i.e.*, method replacements are scattered across multiple commits.

The data collection process has analyzed commits belonging to a diverse set of 57,447 projects. We have identified 36,023 classes, each contains at least one mapping. We also enumerated 9,380 unique mappings, already showcased in the dataset's website[3]. Also, we provide our collected data for replication and extension online (Table 1) .

### 3.2   Metrics Measurement

To collect the design metrics, we use, Scitools Understand, a static analysis framework that captures a variety of structural metrics, across languages such as C++ and Java. Based on the computed metrics values, we can calculate the effect of migration-related changes on the system design. In particular, we analyze the following size and structure metrics: Coupling Between Objects (CBO), normalized Lack of Cohesion (LCOM), and Cyclomatic complexity(CycC).

---

[3] http://migrationlab.net/index.php?cf=icsr2020.

**Table 1.** Dataset overview.

| Property | # of instances |
|---|---|
| # unique migrations | 9 |
| # projects | 57,447 |
| # commits have Migration | 393 |
| # Classes involved in migration | 36,023 |

Since each source file may contain multiple migration fragments, and since we only care about these specific files, we calculate metrics only for these fragments and then we average them to construct one value per file. In other terms, each data point in our analysis is a file with an average metric value.

Code readability during the migration process was measured by two state-of-the-art metrics proposed by Buse and Weimer [12], and Scalabrino et al. [22]. On the one hand, Buse and Weimer's Readability metric (BWR) combines the source code size characteristics to approximate its readability. On the other hand, Scalabrino et al.'s Readability metric (SR) does not only look at the structural characteristics of code, and adds another lexical dimension, in which it considers more linguistic properties such as comments consistency with the source code and its coherence etc. Both metrics generate a score that, the higher it is, the better is the readability of the code. Similarly to structural metrics, each data point in our analysis represents an average readability score per source file.

After applying these tools on all predefined *mappings commits*, before and after the migration, we generate a dataset that contains, for each commit, its associated code fragments, structural and readability metrics pairs of values. We then use this dataset as a base of examples that we rank according to how much they improve quality and comprehension. We detail our proposed ranking model in the following Sect. 3.3.

### 3.3   Ranking Model

The migration dataset [8] contains, for each migration rule, *e.g.*, *easymock* to *mockito*, several commits, extracted from various projects, containing similar mappings. Therefore, for the same mapping, there are various real-world examples of how a deprecated method has been replaced with one or multiple replacing methods. Although these examples exhibit similar sets of removed/added methods, they differ in their overhead in the software design, since the migration process is subjective [8,9,26,27], and developers may perform different types of code changes to perform the same type of migration. Moreover, as maintaining a good quality of the source code, in terms of design and readability, is critical for code longevity.

Our aim is to favor the recommendation of source code migration examples that correctly execute the migration while also maintaining, or improving the current client code quality. To do so, we simply leverage the existing software quality attributes metrics, previously explored in the Metrics Measurement Sect. 3.2, and combine them into an overall *Mapping Quality Score* (MQS). For each given library migration in the dataset, we loop through all its method-level mappings, for each mapping, we locate all its instances in the source code (*inst*). Then, for each instance, we calculate its MQS, and finally, we rank them on a descendent order, to favor examples with the highest quality improvement. Formally, we calculate the MQS as follows:

$$MQS(inst) = \sum_{i \in m} \varphi_i(inst) \tag{1}$$

where MQS represents the weighted sum of the software quality attributes ($\varphi_i$). The term $m$ is a set, $m = \{CBO, LCOM, CycC, CLOC, LOC, CR\}$. The term *inst* denotes code instances to be ranked for a given mapping.

Since the combined metrics do not belong to the same scale, we normalize them using *min-max normalizer* that linearly rescales every metric value to the [0,1] interval. Rescaling in the [0,1] interval is done by shifting the values of each feature $x$ so that the minimal value is 0, and then dividing by the new maximal value (which is the difference between the original maximal $max(x)$ and minimal $min(x)$ values).

Moreover, since some metrics are to be minimized, we transform all of them to be maximized using the duality principle. For example, since the lower are the values of coupling, the better they are, we maximize the complement of the normalized value of coupling, *i.e.*, $\varphi_{CBO} = (1\text{-}z(\text{CBO(src)}))$, where $z$ returns the min-max normalized value.

As an illustrative example, we observe in Fig. 2 that for a given mapping between `createStrictMock`, belonging to the removed library *easymock*, and `mock`, belonging to *mockito*, 4 instances are being shown and recommended as migration examples. Note that each example contains a link to the actual location of the code on GitHub. The examples have been ranked according to their MQS. For instance, the first example has the highest MQS of 2.475, while the second example has an MQS of 2.239.

Note that the normalization was restricted to the MQS calculation, we still use the actual *raw* values of the metrics for the results, which are detailed in the following sections. Also note that we weights for the actual MQS score are by default equal to 1 i.e., for this study, we consider all metrics to be equally important, and thus, this can be improved, if any metric has been found to be more influential than others in this context of API migration.

# 4   Results

## 4.1   RQ1. (Design Improvement) What is the impact of library migration on the quality of software design?

Figure 3 outlines the box plots of the values, for each of the structural metrics, calculated before and after the migration. To better understand the statistical significance of the observed results, we setup our statistical analysis as follows: for each metric, we cluster its values according to whether it was measured before or after the migration. We apply this to each code fragment. As a result, we create two groups of equal size, each containing measurements of the same metric before and after the migration. Then, we use the Wilcoxon signed rank test, since these groups are dependent (measurement on the same code fragments), to evaluate the significance of the difference between the values, in terms of their mean.

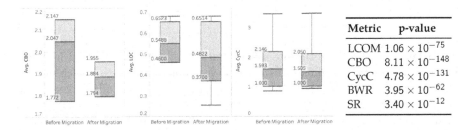

| Metric | p-value |
|--------|---------|
| LCOM | $1.06 \times 10^{-75}$ |
| CBO | $8.11 \times 10^{-148}$ |
| CycC | $4.78 \times 10^{-131}$ |
| BWR | $3.95 \times 10^{-62}$ |
| SR | $3.40 \times 10^{-12}$ |

**Fig. 3.** Box plots of CBO, LCOM, and average CycC values, extracted from migrated code fragments, before and after the migration (lower values are better). Statistical significance of samples difference, before and after API migration, for each of the considered metrics.

Our Null hypothesis indicates no variation in the metric values of pre- and post-migrated code elements. In contrast, the alternative hypothesis advocates for a variation in the metric values. In this research question, a decrease in the mean values is considered desirable (*i.e.*, an improvement in design quality). Additionally, the variation between values of both sets is considered significant if its corresponding p-value is less than 0.05 (a confidence level of 95%). We deploy the same statistical analysis for RQ2 as well, but with a difference in the interpretation, since for readability metrics, an increase in mean value is considered desirable.

As can be seen in Fig. 3, for the coupling between objects metric (CBO), we clearly notice a general trend of values being significantly decreased, just after the migration. The mean CBO value has decreased from 2.047 to 1.884 ($p - value < 0.05$), and the upper quartile has become significantly lower while decreasing from 2.147 to 1.955. Interestingly, we also observe from the figure a similar trend for the Lack of Cohesion of Methods metric (LCOM), since its mean value has gone from 0.548 to 0.482 ($p - value < 0.05$). We also notice a drop in the lower quartile, going from 0.460 to 0.370.

As for the average Cyclomatic complexity, there is a slight decrease in the upper quartile, varying from 2.146 to 2.050, but the mean value has decreased from 1.593 to 1.505 ($p - value < 0.05$).

```
...der/src/test/java/org/jboss/aerogear/unifiedpush/test/archive/UnifiedPushArchiveImpl.java

@@ -93,8 +93,7 @@ public UnifiedPushArchive withApi() {

        @Override
        public UnifiedPushArchive withUtils() {
-           return addPackage(org.jboss.aerogear.unifiedpush.utils.AeroGearLogger.class.getPackage())
-                   .addClasses(ConfigurationUtils.class);
+           return addClasses(ConfigurationUtils.class);
        }
```

**Fig. 4.** Illustrative example of a code migration from *log4j* to *slf4j*, with a positive impact on coupling.

To better understand the observed results, we manually analyze few random instances. Fig. 4 illustrates a code fragment example of such migrations, extracted from Github[4]. In this fragment, the methods `addPackage` with `addClasses`, belonging to the library *log4j*, is being replaced with the method `addClasses`, from *slf4j*. We can observe the difference in the used parameters between the replaced and replacing methods. More precisely, `addPackage` with `addClasses` have a CBO of 4, while `addClasses` only have a CBO of 3, which did improve the overall CBO of all methods by adopting this newly deployed method.

Another interesting example in Fig. 5[5] shows how the newly introduced object `DefaultHttpClient` does not rely on any parameter, unlike the retired object `HttpCLient` whose constructor is initialized with `connectionManager`. Therefore, the new object is more cohesive and it reduces class lack of cohesion.

> **Summary for RQ1.** Our empirical analysis has shown that APIs migration exhibit a positive impact on the software's design quality, in terms of complexity, coupling and cohesion.

---

[4] https://github.com/aerogear/aerogear-unifiedpush-server/commit/
4861157566723bc3179b69d0755e5bf5460d9729.

[5] https://github.com/anthonydahanne/ReGalAndroid/commit/
6410cc8a12246745b19a102da5dd2c92d326b9f9.

```
-       private final HttpClient client;
+       private final DefaultHttpClient client;

        /**
         * defines if the user uses a proxy
@@ -112,8 +113,8 @@ public SessionManager(String login, String motDePasse, String url) {
            this.login = login;
            this.motDePasse = motDePasse;
            this.url = url + "/ws.php";
-           MultiThreadedHttpConnectionManager connectionManager = new MultiThreadedHttpConnectionManager();
-           client = new HttpClient(connectionManager);
+  //       MultiThreadedHttpConnectionManager connectionManager = new MultiThreadedHttpConnectionManager();
+           client = new DefaultHttpClient();
```

**Fig. 5.** Illustrative example of a code migration from *async-http-client* to *httpclient*, with a positive impact on cohesion.

## 4.2 RQ2. (Code Readability) Does migration improve the code readability?

Figure 6a outlines the boxplots of the values, for each of the readability metrics, calculated before and after each API migration.

For the BWR [12] metric, we observe an improvement in its values. In particular, the mean BWR [12] value has increased from 0.474 to 0.482 ($p-value <$ 0.05). Similarly, the lower and the upper quartiles have slightly increased respectively from 0.316 to 0.329, and 0.579 to 0.587. As for the second readability metric, namely SR [22], the improvement is more significant since its mean value exhibits an increase from 0.568 to 0.603 ($p-value < 0.05$). The increase is also seen in the lower quartile, going from 0.461 to 0.484, whereas the upper quartile exhibits a slight decrease from 0.709 to 0.706.

If we take deeper look into the code example[6], illustrated in Fig. 6b, we notice that the developer just moved from using the method put, from *json* to the method addProperty, from *gson*. Note that the developer did not perform any additional activities; however the BWR [12] improved from 0.0013 to 0.0023 since the method name *addProperty* has better readability score than *put*, as shown in the console output of BWR [12] in Fig. 6b.

> **Summary for RQ2.** API migrations do improve code readability, as both BWR [12] and SR [22] readability metrics experience a significant increase when comparing code fragments before and after the migration.

---

[6] https://github.com/groupon/Selenium-Grid-Extras/commit/
4d9bada8aeab5b09e7a27926fc9ecab8bb5a1b51.

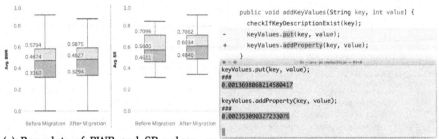

(a) Box plots of BWR and SR values, extracted from migrated code fragments, before and after the migration (higher values are better).

(b) Illustrative example of a code migration from *json* to *gson*, with a positive impact on readability.

**Fig. 6.** Impact of API migration on code readability metrics.

### 4.3 RQ3. (Quality Recommendation) Can we leverage design and readability metrics to recommend better code examples of migration?

To evaluate our ranking model based on the structural and readability metrics, we conducted a qualitative analysis with 10 senior developers from an outstanding software development company. All the participants volunteered to participate in the experiment and were familiar with Java programming, Maven ecosystem, and API usage. The experience of these participants with Java development is 10+ years. Prior to the experiment, the participants were provided with a 30-min. tutorial on the tool usage and the experiment process. Each participant were provided with 10 code fragments to perform 10 migration tasks between libraries including *easymock* to *mokito*, and *json* to *gson*. Then, for each of the migration tasks, the developer runs our migration code examples tool that returns a list of examples but exposed to the developers at a random order (at least for our experimental study to avoid biased selection from a ranked list). Then, the developer reviews all the returned examples and picks the top-3 examples that fit her/his preferences and the quality of the examples.

Figure 7 reports the survey results, where the x-axis represents the index of example($k$) in the ranked list, and the y-axis represents the number of times an example@$k$ has been chosen by a developer as their top choice, divided by all choices. In other terms, the y-axis percentage of developers' choice of an example whose rank is $k$. For instance, the value @$k = 1$ is the percentage of how many times the example number one in the ranked list was chosen at the best example.

According to Fig. 7, we could see that 59% of developers agreed that the first recommended example is the best example. If we allow the top-2 ranked examples ($k <= 2$), our recommendation already captures 80% of developers' choices, which also improves further to become 94% for top-3 ranked examples ($k <= 3$).

We can conclude that our ranking model efficiently recommends what developers consider to be their decision if they are requested to perform the migration.

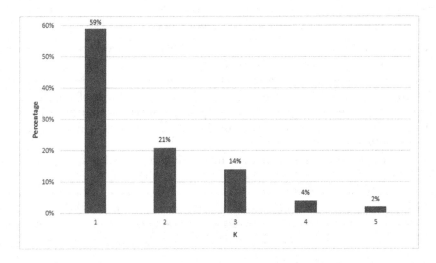

**Fig. 7.** Percentages of the match between developers choices and the $k^{th}$ example.

---

**Summary for RQ3.** The qualitative analysis of our ranking model shows its efficiency to considerably prune the search space for developers when they are searching for good migration examples. Our ranking score was able to match 59% of the developer's chosen examples when recommending top-1 example.

---

## 5  Threats to Validity

**Internal Validity.** Our empirical analysis is mainly threatened by the accuracy of the migration dataset. Since our assumption that all studied commits carried at least one migration, any intruding files would be considered as noise to our analysis. We did not perform any rigorous verification concerning the correctness of the dataset, but we did perform various manual checks when gathering the files for statistical analysis and for qualitatively analyze our findings, and we did not notice any single case where the file we were investigating did not contain at least one migration trace.

The second main threat to the validity of our work is the choice of the metrics used in this study. We have chosen coupling, cohesion, complexity, and readability, as being representative to design quality and popular metrics, being used in similar empirical studies [2–4].

The non diverse set of developers, along with the randomness in assigning them the examples, has a direct impact on the results. The choice of experienced and volunteers was to reduce the effect of non interest to the problem resolution. Developers were genuinely interested to support the work, and they were aware of it being potentially published for the community.

**Construct Validity.** Threats to construct validity describe concerns about the relationship between theory and observation and, generally, this type of threat is mainly constituted by any errors related to measurements. More precisely, any error in the used tools directly impacts the correctness of our findings. For calculating metrics, we have used popular frameworks and libraries such as Understand. Based on our own humble experience, we did not notice any anomaly while using them.

Moreover, in this study, we did not differentiate between instant and delayed migrations, by combining their results. This may not have allowed to fully understand the difference between both, especially that the instant migration is performed faster than the delayed migration, which may hypothesize that developers may have focused on the correctness of their migrated code, rather than optimizing the design of their system. This remains one of our main future experiments.

**External Validity.** Threats to external validity are connected to the generalization of the obtained results. Our empirical study was limited to only open source Java projects. However, we constrained by the tools we use to collect the metrics, and besides Understand, others can only process Java source code. Thus, only the first research question can be extended across languages, if there is such a dataset because the one we have used is also limited to Java libraries.

## 6    Conclusion and Future Work

In this paper, we conducted a large scale empirical study to investigate the impact of software migration between third-party libraries on code quality and comprehension. Our qualitative and empirical analysis indicate that library migrations have a positive impact on software's design, in terms of coupling and cohesion. We also experiment their effect on two state-of-the-art code readability metrics, and we observe an improvement in both metrics. We observed multiple factors that explain the improvement, including the typical better naming conventions and more cohesive API methods. Finally, we leverage structural and readability metrics to define a ranking score for migration examples. To evaluate the effectiveness of our ranking, we surveyed developers to see whether our top recommended examples would match what developers consider to be the best choice. Results show that our top-1 recommended example achieves an agreement of 59%.

These factors drive our future work. We plan to include the execution of selected test cases, to avoid the introduction of regression [10]. recommendation further leveraging API contextual information to recommend better APIs for usage, with respect to a given code fragment. We also plan on extending the structural metrics used to characterize software design quality, such as including the weighted method per class, response for a class, class stability, and depth of inheritance tree.

**Acknowledgements.** This material is based on work supported by the National Science Foundation under Grant No. 1757680.

# References

1. Allamanis, M., Sutton, C.: Mining source code repositories at massive scale using language modeling. In: Proceedings of the 10th Working Conference on Mining Software Repositories, pp. 207–216. IEEE Press (2013)
2. AlOmar, E., Mkaouer, M.W., Ouni, A.: Can refactoring be self-affirmed? an exploratory study on how developers document their refactoring activities in commit messages. In: 2019 IEEE/ACM 3rd International Workshop on Refactoring (IWoR), pp. 51–58. IEEE (2019)
3. AlOmar, E.A., Mkaouer, M.W., Ouni, A.: Toward the automatic classification of self-affirmed refactoring. J. Syst. Softw. **171**, 110821 (2020)
4. AlOmar, E.A., Mkaouer, M.W., Ouni, A., Kessentini, M.: On the impact of refactoring on the relationship between quality attributes and design metrics. In: 2019 ACM/IEEE International Symposium on Empirical Software Engineering and Measurement (ESEM), pp. 1–11. IEEE (2019)
5. Alrubaye, H., Mkaouer, M.W.: Automating the detection of third-party java library migration at the function level. In: Proceedings of the 28th Annual International Conference on Computer Science and Software Engineering, pp. 60–71. IBM Corp. (2018)
6. Alrubaye, H., Mkaouer, M.W., Khokhlov, I., Reznik, L., Ouni, A., Mcgoff, J.: Learning to recommend third-party library migration opportunities at the API level. Appl. Soft Comput. **90**, 106140 (2020)
7. Alrubaye, H., Mkaouer, M.W., Ouni, A.: Migrationminer: an automated detection tool of third-party java library migration at the method level. In: The International Conference on Software Maintenance and Evolution (ICSME). IEEE Press (2019)
8. Alrubaye, H., Mkaouer, M.W., Ouni, A.: On the use of information retrieval to automate the detection of third-party java library migration at the method level. In: Proceedings of the 27th International Conference on Program Comprehension, pp. 347–357. IEEE Press (2019)
9. Alrubaye, H., Wiem, M.: Variability in library evolution. In: Software Engineering for Variability Intensive Systems: Foundations and Applications, p. 295 (2019)
10. Alshoaibi, D., Hannigan, K., Gupta, H., Mkaouer, M.W.: PRICE: detection of performance regression introducing code changes using static and dynamic metrics. In: Nejati, S., Gay, G. (eds.) SSBSE 2019. LNCS, vol. 11664, pp. 75–88. Springer, Cham (2019). https://doi.org/10.1007/978-3-030-27455-9_6
11. Boehm, B., Basili, V.R.: Software defect reduction top 10 list. Found. Empirical Softw. Eng.: Legacy of Victor R. Basili **426**(37), 426–431 (2005)
12. Buse, R.P., Weimer, W.R.: Learning a metric for code readability. IEEE Trans. Softw. Eng. **36**(4), 546–558 (2010)
13. Chidamber, S.R., Kemerer, C.F.: A metrics suite for object oriented design. IEEE Trans. Softw. Eng. **20**(6), 476–493 (1994)

14. Endrikat, S., Hanenberg, S., Robbes, R., Stefik, A.: How do API documentation and static typing affect api usability? In: Proceedings of the 36th International Conference on Software Engineering, pp. 632–642. ACM (2014)
15. Kula, R.G., German, D.M., Ouni, A., Ishio, T., Inoue, K.: Do developers update their library dependencies? Empirical Softw. Eng. **23**(1), 384–417 (2017). https://doi.org/10.1007/s10664-017-9521-5
16. Linares-Vásquez, M., Bavota, G., Bernal-Cárdenas, C., Di Penta, M., Oliveto, R., Poshyvanyk, D.: Api change and fault proneness: a threat to the success of android apps. In: Proceedings of the 2013 9th Joint Meeting on Foundations of Software Engineering, pp. 477–487. ACM (2013)
17. McDonnell, T., Ray, B., Kim, M.: An empirical study of API stability and adoption in the android ecosystem. In: 2013 IEEE International Conference on Software Maintenance, pp. 70–79. IEEE (2013)
18. Mkaouer, M.W., Kessentini, M., Bechikh, S., Deb, K., Ó Cinnéide, M.: High dimensional search-based software engineering: finding tradeoffs among 15 objectives for automating software refactoring using NSGA-III. In: Proceedings of the 2014 Annual Conference on Genetic and Evolutionary Computation, pp. 1263–1270 (2014)
19. Mkaouer, M.W., Kessentini, M., Bechikh, S., Ó'Cinnéide, M., Deb, K.: Software refactoring under uncertainty: a robust multi-objective approach. In: Proceedings of the Companion Publication of the 2014 Annual Conference on Genetic and Evolutionary Computation, pp. 187–188 (2014)
20. Peruma, A., Mkaouer, M.W., Decker, M.J., Newman, C.D.: Contextualizing rename decisions using refactorings, commit messages, and data types. J. Syst. Softw. **169**, 110704 (2020)
21. Peruma, A., Mkaouer, M.W., Decker, M.J., Newman, C.D.: Contextualizing rename decisions using refactorings and commit messages. In: 2019 19th International Working Conference on Source Code Analysis and Manipulation (SCAM), pp. 74–85. IEEE (2019)
22. Scalabrino, S., Linares-Vásquez, M., Poshyvanyk, D., Oliveto, R.: Improving code readability models with textual features. In: 2016 IEEE 24th International Conference on Program Comprehension (ICPC), pp. 1–10. IEEE (2016)
23. Shatnawi, A., Seriai, A.D., Sahraoui, H., Alshara, Z.: Reverse engineering reusable software components from object-oriented APIs. J. Syst. Softw. **131**, 442–460 (2017)
24. Stevens, W.P., Myers, G.J., Constantine, L.L.: Structured design. IBM Syst. J. **13**(2), 115–139 (1974)
25. Teyton, C., Falleri, J.R., Blanc, X.: Mining library migration graphs. In: 2012 19th Working Conference on Reverse Engineering (WCRE), pp. 289–298. IEEE (2012)
26. Teyton, C., Falleri, J.R., Blanc, X.: Automatic discovery of function mappings between similar libraries. In: In 2013 20th Working Conference on Reverse Engineering (WCRE), pp. 192–201. IEEE (2013)
27. Teyton, C., Falleri, J.R., Palyart, M., Blanc, X.: A study of library migrations in java. J. Softw. Evol. Process **26**(11), 1030–1052 (2014)

# How Do Developers Refactor Code to Improve Code Reusability?

Eman Abdullah AlOmar[1(✉)], Philip T. Rodriguez[1], Jordan Bowman[1],
Tianjia Wang[1], Benjamin Adepoju[1], Kevin Lopez[2], Christian Newman[1],
Ali Ouni[3], and Mohamed Wiem Mkaouer[1]

[1] Rochester Institute of Technology, Rochester, NY, USA
{eaa6167,ptr5201,jeb4905,tw7205,ba1724,cdnvse,mwmvse}@rit.edu
[2] California State University, Turlock, CA, USA
klopez43@csustan.edu
[3] ETS Montreal, University of Quebec, Montreal, QC, Canada
ali.ouni@etsmtl.ca

**Abstract.** Refactoring is the *de-facto* practice to optimize software health. While there has been several studies proposing refactoring strategies to optimize software design through applying design patterns and removing design defects, little is known about how developers actually refactor their code to improve its reuse. Therefore, we extract, from 1,828 open source projects, a set of refactorings which were intended to improve the software reusability. We analyze the impact of reusability refactorings on state-of-the-art reusability metrics, and we compare the distribution of reusability refactoring types, with the distribution of the remaining mainstream refactorings. Overall, we found that the distribution of refactoring types, applied in the context of reusability, is different from the distribution of refactoring types in mainstream development. In the refactorings performed to improve reusability, source files are subject to more design level types of refactorings. Reusability refactorings significantly impact, high-level code elements, such as packages, classes, and methods, while typical refactorings, impact all code elements, including identifiers, and parameters.

**Keywords:** Refactoring · Reusability · Software metrics · Quality

## 1 Introduction

Refactoring is defined as the process of changing software system in such way that changes improve software quality and do not alter the software behaviour [7,13]. Refactoring is one of the commonly-used techniques to improve software quality [7,18]. There are different refactoring operations that could be used to improve software quality such as a change in parameter types, move attributes/methods, rename variables/parameters/attributes/methods/classes, extract methods, extract classes, etc. [7].

© Springer Nature Switzerland AG 2020
S. Ben Sassi et al. (Eds.): ICSR 2020, LNCS 12541, pp. 261–276, 2020.
https://doi.org/10.1007/978-3-030-64694-3_16

Refactoring plays an important role in software engineering, as its purpose is to improve software quality. Without refactoring, software quality would continue to deteriorate and make development more difficult. Researchers conducted many studies on refactoring in different areas, such as finding the approach to effectively refactor code and determining the impact of refactoring on software quality. One particular aspect of refactoring is increasing the reusability of software components, which provides developers a more efficient way to utilize existing code to create new functionality. Creating reusable software components facilitates development and maintenance since less work is needed to accomplish additional functionality.

While it is usually true that refactoring improves software quality, it is not known how reusability refactoring impacts metrics. Moser et al. [10] has found that the appropriate refactoring can make the necessary design level changes to improve the software reusability, however, there is no practical evidence on how developers refactor code to improve reusability in practice.

The purpose of this paper is to investigate how developers use refactoring when they state they are improving code reusability. Therefore, we have mined commits from 1,828 well-engineered project, were we have identified 1,957 reusability commits. We refer to a commit as a *reusability commit* where its developer explicitly mentions, in the commit message, that a refactoring is performed to improve reusability. Then we extract all refactorings executed in these reusability commits, and we label them as *reusability refactorings*. To better understand how developers perceive reusability and apply it in real-world scenarios, we examine how these refactorings manifest in the code by examining their impact on code quality. Furthermore, to check if there are some refactoring patterns that are specific to reusability, we report the distribution of reusability refactorings compared to other refactorings and the distribution of the different types of refactored code elements in reusability refactorings. To perform this analysis, we formulate the following research questions:

**RQ1.** *Do developers refactor code differently for the purpose of improving reusability?*

To answer this research question, we execute Refactoring Miner [19] to extract the type of refactorings that are chosen by developers to improve reusability. We also investigate if there are any refactoring patterns that are specific to reusability, by comparing the distribution of reusability-related refactorings, with the distribution of refactorings for other mainstream development tasks. Then, we identify any significant differences between the distribution values in the two populations.

**RQ2.** *What is the impact of reusability refactorings on structural metrics?*

To answer this research question, we consider the state-of-the-art reusability structural metrics, extracted from previous studies [4,10]. We calculate these metrics on files before and after they were refactored for improving reusability. Then we analyze the impact of refactorings on the variation of these metrics, to see if they were capturing the improvement.

The results of our study indicate that when developers make reusability changes, they seem to significantly impact metrics related to methods and attributes, but not parameters or interfaces. Additionally, developers perform reusability changes much less than regular refactoring changes. Aid from our empirical analysis, we provide the software reuse community with a replication package, containing the dataset we crawled, the files containing all the metric values, for the purpose of replication and extension[1].

The remainder of this paper is organized as follows: Sect. 2 includes some existing studies related to our work. Section 3 presents the design of our empirical study, Sect. 4 shows the results of our experiments, Sect. 5 describes the threats the validity to our study and any mitigation we took to minimize those threats, and Sect. 6 summarizes the contributions and results of our study.

## 2 Related Work

Research in refactoring software has covered a variety of aspects, including tools and methods to facilitate refactoring and accurately assess the impact of refactoring on software quality. Pantiuchina et al. [14] talked about determining if there was a difference in how developers perceive refactorings will be helpful, and how the metrics say the refactorings were. That study determined that even if a developer reports that there was a refactoring done it might not be reflected in the metrics. This study focuses on comparing specific refactorings relating to certain metrics, specifically "cohesion", "coupling", "readability", and "complexity", to metrics that measure those attributes, while we focused on using metrics to determine if there was a quantifiable difference, and if so, what that difference was, during self-proclaimed reusability refactorings. Even then, something to take away from this study is that measuring refactoring code changes focusing on quality of life, rather than strictly functional, can have many moving parts not measured by metrics. Metrics do not tell the whole story, and while it is good to see what metrics are affected when developers improve reusability, it could also be helpful to include information and narratives from actual developers alongside the pure metrics.

Fakhoury et al. [6] have shown that the existing readability models are not able to capture the readability improvement with minor changes in the code, and some metrics which can effectively measure the readability improvement are currently not used by readability models. The authors also studied the distribution of different types of changes in readability improvements, which is similar to our research question, which examines the distribution of the different types of refactored code elements in reusability refactorings.

Prior works [1, 2, 15] have explored how developers document their refactoring activities in commit messages; this activity is called Self-Admitted Refactoring or Self-Affirmed Refactoring (SAR). In particular, SAR indicates developers' explicit documentation of refactoring operations intentionally introduced during a code change.

---

[1] https://smilevo.github.io/self-affirmed-refactoring/.

AlOmar et al. [3] showed that there is a misperception between the state-of-the-art structural metrics widely used as indicators for refactoring and what developers consider to be an improvement in their source code. The research aims to identify (among software quality models) the metrics that align with the vision of developers on the quality attribute they explicitly state they want to improve. Their approach entailed mining 322,479 commits from 3,795 open source projects, from which they identified about 1,245 commits based on commit messages that explicitly informed the refactoring towards improving quality attributes. Thereafter, they processed the identified commits by measuring structural metrics before and after the changes. The variations in values were then compared to distinguish metrics that are significantly impacted by the refactoring, towards better reflecting the intention of developers to improve the corresponding quality attribute. Our study also utilized software quality metrics to evaluate the impact of refactoring on reusability.

Research particularly in reusability refactoring by Moser et al. [10] showed that refactoring increases the quality and reusability of classes in an industrial, agile environment. Similar to our paper, their study examines the impact of refactoring on quality metrics related to reusability on the method and class levels, such as Weighted Method per Class (WMC) and Coupling Between Object (CBO), respectively. The results of their experiment revealed that refactoring significantly improved the metrics Response for Class (RFC) and Coupling Between Object classes (CBO) related to reusability. However, the limitations of their study involved a small project consisting of 30 Java classes and 1,770 Lines of Code (LOC) developed by two pairs of programmers over the course of 8 weeks. In addition, the authors considered how general refactoring operations impact metrics related to reusability, rather than specifically reusability refactorings. In our study, we examined 1,828 projects and 154,820 commits that modified Java

**Table 1.** Summary of related studies.

| Study | Year | Focus | Dataset size | Quality attribute | Software metric |
|---|---|---|---|---|---|
| Moser et al. [10] | 2006 | Reusability measurement over time | 30 Java classes | Reusability | LCOM/RFC/CC CBO/WMC/LOC DIT/NOC |
| Pantiuchina et al. [14] | 2018 | Developer's perception & quality | 1,282 commits. | Cohesion/Coupling Complexity/Readability | LOCM/C3/CBO RFC/WMC/B&W Sread |
| Fakhoury et al. [6] | 2019 | Developer's perception & quality | 548 commits | Readability | B& W/Sread/Dorn |
| AlOmar et al. [3] | 2019 | Developer's perception & quality | 1,245 commits | Coupling/Cohesion Complexity/Inheritance Polymorphism/Encapsulation Abstraction/Size | LCOM/CBO/FANIN FANOUT/RFC /CC WMC/Evg/NPATH MaxNest/DIT/NOC IFANIN/LOC/CLOC STMTC/CDL/NIV NIM |
| This work | 2020 | Developer's perception & quality | 1,967 commits | Reusability | LCOM/CBO/RFC CC/WMC/LOC DIT/NOC |

files. We also considered how reusability changes affect software quality metrics and how what kinds of refactoring operations were performed during reusability changes. Table 1 shows the summary of each study related to our work.

# 3    Experimental Design

Depicted in Fig. 1 is an overview of our experiment methodology. We detail each activity of our methodology in the subsequent subsections. The dataset utilized in this study is available for extension and replication purpose [2].

## 3.1    Selection of Quality Attributes and Structural Metrics

We started by conducting a literature review on existing and well-known software quality metrics [5,8,9]. Next, we extracted metrics that are used to assess several object-oriented design aspects in general, and software reusability in particular. For example, the RFC (Response for Class) metric is typically used to measure visibility of a given class in the project, the more a class is responsive, the more it can be accessed and its functionality can be reused by other objects in the system.

The process left us with 8 object-oriented metrics as shown in Table 2. The list of metrics is (1) well-known and defined in the literature, and (2) can assess on different code-level elements, i.e., method, class, package, and (3) can be calculated by the tool we considered. All metrics values are automatically computed using the tool UNDERSTAND[3], a software quality assurance framework.

**Table 2.** Reusability and its corresponding structural metrics used in this study.

| Quality attribute | Study | Software metric |
|---|---|---|
| Cohesion | [4, 10] | Lack of Cohesion of Methods (LCOM) |
| Complexity | [10] | Response for Class (RFC) |
| | [10] | Cyclomatic Complexity (CC) |
| Coupling | [4, 10] | Coupling Between Objects (CBO) |
| Design size | [4, 10] | Weighted Method per Class (WMC) |
| | [4, 10] | Line of Code (LOC) |
| Inheritance | [4, 10] | Depth of Inheritance Tree (DIT) |
| | [4, 10] | Number of Children (NOC) |

---

[2] https://smilevo.github.io/self-affirmed-refactoring/.
[3] https://scitools.com/.

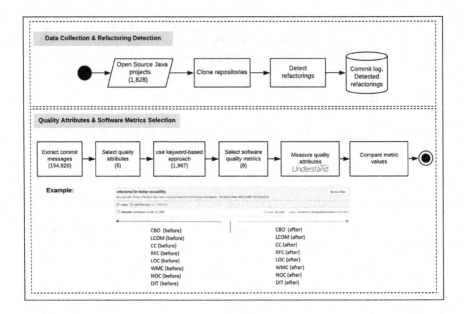

**Fig. 1.** Empirical study design overview.

## 3.2 Refactoring Detection

The projects in our study consist of 1,828 open-source Java projects, which were curated projects hosted on GitHub. These projects were selected from a dataset made available by Munaiah et al. [11], while verifying that these are Java-based projects since this is the only language the Refactoring Miner [19] supports. These projects utilize software engineering practices such as documentation and testing.

We utilize Refactoring Miner [19] for mining refactorings from each project in our dataset. Refactoring Miner is designed to analyze code changes (i.e., commits) in Git repositories to detect applied refactorings. Our choice of the mining tool is driven by its accuracy (precision of 98% and a recall of 87%) and is suitable for a study that requires a high degree of automation since it can be used through its external API.

In this phase, we collect a total of 862,888 refactoring operations from 154,820 commits. An overview of the studied benchmark is provided in Table 3.

**Table 3.** Studied dataset statistics.

| Item | Count |
| --- | --- |
| Studied projects | 1,828 |
| Commits with refactorings | 154,820 |
| Commits with *reus*\*/*reusability* Keywords | 1,967 |
| Reusability refactoring operations | 3,065 |

### 3.3   Reusability Commits Extraction

After extracting all refactoring commit messages detected by Refactoring Miner, our next step consists of analyzing each of the commit messages as we want to only keep commits where refactoring is documented, i.e., self-affirmed refactoring (SAR) [1]. As for the commit message selection, we initially use a keyword-based approach to find those commits that contain the keywords *reus\**[4] and *reusability*. We have chosen these two keywords because of their popularity in the development community as being used by developers to describe software reusability [17]. We then kept commits whose messages contained the two keywords. We performed a manual analysis of all the commits, and we ended up removing any duplicates and false positives. This process resulted in selecting 1,967 commits, containing 3,065 refactorings, as our dataset for this study. Each dataset instance is a commit, along with its corresponding refactorings.

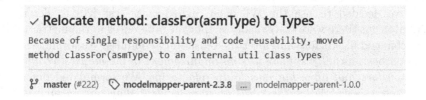

**Fig. 2.** A sample instance of our dataset.

As an illustrative example, Fig. 2 details a commit whose message states the relocation of the method *classFor(asmType)* to an internal class utility class for the purpose of applying the single responsibility principle and code reusability[5]. After running Refactoring Miner, we detected the existence of a *Move method* refactoring from the class *ExplicitMappingVisitor* to the class *Types*. The detected refactoring matches the description of the commit message, and gives more insights about the old placement of the method, which was absent in the textual description. As we explain in the following subsection, we need to locate all the code elements involved in the refactoring (source class, target class, etc.) for the purpose of evaluating the quality of the relocation in terms of impact of structural metrics, such as coupling and cohesion.

### 3.4   Metrics Calculation

To generate the metric values for reusability commits, we ran code evaluation tools, specifically using UNDERSTAND[6]. The metrics we used to evaluate the code quality are summarized in Table 2.

---

[4] Regular expression was used to capture all expansions of reus such as reuses, reusing, reuse, etc.

[5] Link to the commit: https://github.com/modelmapper/modelmapper/commit/6796071fc6ad98150b6faf654c8200164f977aa4.

[6] https://scitools.com/features/.

We then used SQL queries to find reusability commits in the dataset and their associated project links to clone using Git and exported the results from our dataset to a combined Comma-Separated Value (CSV) file. Using a shell script, we cloned the projects, checked out the versions for each commit, and ran the Git diff command to see which files changed in each commit. If files were deleted in a commit, we included the metric values for those files before the commit but not after it. If files were added in a commit, we included the metric values for those files after the commit but not before it. If files were renamed or moved in a commit, then we included the metric values for those files both before and after the commit. Our shell script then ran the UNDERSTAND tool to generate metrics for the changed files for the versions before and after each reusability commit, resulting in two files containing metric values for each commit: (1) one file for the files changed before the commit and (2) another file for the files changed after the commit.

Since each metric value before and after the commit are dependent to each other, we decided to use the Wilcoxon Signed-rank Test [20] to determine whether or not there were statistically significant differences in the metric values for all changed files before and after the reusability commits. We formulated our null hypothesis as follows: *there was no improvement in the metrics we analyzed between before and after the reusability refactoring*. We formulated our alternate hypothesis as follows: *there was an improvement shown as an increase*. To achieve that, we created Python scripts to order and sort all the values from the above results from UNDERSTAND to ensure that the rows in both before and after files are corresponding to each other. Next, we combined the data in the CSV files before and after the commits together into another two CSV files each have a total of 185,244 metric values: one CSV file for all code elements in changed files before the reusability commits, and another CSV file for all code elements in changes files after the commits.

The Wilcoxon Signed-rank Test allowed us to determine if any metrics were statistically significantly changed when developers performed self-proclaimed reusability refactorings.

## 4     Results

This section reports and discusses our experimental results and aims to answer our research questions.

### 4.1     RQ1. Do Developers Refactor Code Differently for the Purpose of Improving Reusability?

This research question aims to compare refactoring activity in reusability commits with the refactoring activity that can be found in mainstream development tasks (feature updates, bug fix, etc.). Since we have a dataset of all refactorings performed in the 1,828 projects that we study, we separate refactorings that belong to the reusability commits (refactorings performed for the purpose of improving reusability), which we refer to as *reusability refactorings*. We refer to the remaining refactorings as *non-reusability refactorings*. Then, for each group, we calculate the percentage of each refactoring type, among the total refactorings of that group.

Figure 3 visualizes, by percentage of the total refactoring operations in each of the respective sets, the distributions of refactoring operations. We observe that the distribution of *reusability refactorings* varies from the *non-reusability refactorings*. In fact, the top frequent types in reusability refactorings are, *Move Method*, *Extract Method*, and *Pull-Up Method*, whose percentages are respectively, 17.29%, 14.85%, and 11.21%. For non-reusability refactorings, the top frequent type were *Rename Attribute*, *Rename Method*, and *Rename Variable*, as their percentages are respectively, 18.96%, 11.92%, and 11.86%. While the *move* related types were highly solicited in reusability refactorings, the *rename* activity was dominant for non-reusability refactorings, which was expected since previous studies who analyzed mainstream refactoring has found that renames are the most popular refactorings [3,15,16,19]. However, reusability refactorings seem to be different. To analyze the extent to which reusability and non-reusability refactorings vary, we compare the distribution of refactoring refactorings identified for each group using the Wilcoxon signed-rank test, a pairwise statistical test verifying whether two sets have a similar distribution [20]. If the p-value is smaller than 0.05, the distribution difference between the two sets is considered statistically significant. The choice of Wilcoxon comes from its non-parametric nature with no assumption of a normal data distribution. Upon running the statistical test, the null hypothesis was rejected and the difference between group distributions was found to be statistically significant.

Another interesting observation that we draw is the popularity of method-level refactoring, being in TOP 3 most frequent reusability refactorings. Figure 4 shows the distribution of code elements impacted by refactorings, and we notice that more than 50% of refactorings were performed at the method level.

To better understand the observed results, we sampled a subset of reusability refactorings, and we have extracted two main patterns:

**Functionality Extraction.** When developers are interested in a needed functionality, which is found inside a long method, containing various functionalities, they extract the code elements, belonging to the needed functionality, into a newly created separate method, and they update the original method with the appropriate method calls. This decomposition process is known as *Extract Method*. The newly extracted method has its own visibility, which is independent from the original method, and so developers can increase its visibility of the purpose of reuse, and so other objects and methods can now access it.

**Functionality Movement.** To increase the reusability of a given method, we have noticed that developers typically move methods from less visible classes, into more visible classes, in the system. Various methods were moved into utility classes, which are eventually offering their services to the other classes in the system, this explains why *Move Method* was the most popular type in reusability refactorings, according to Fig. 3. Our qualitative analysis has also shown scenar-

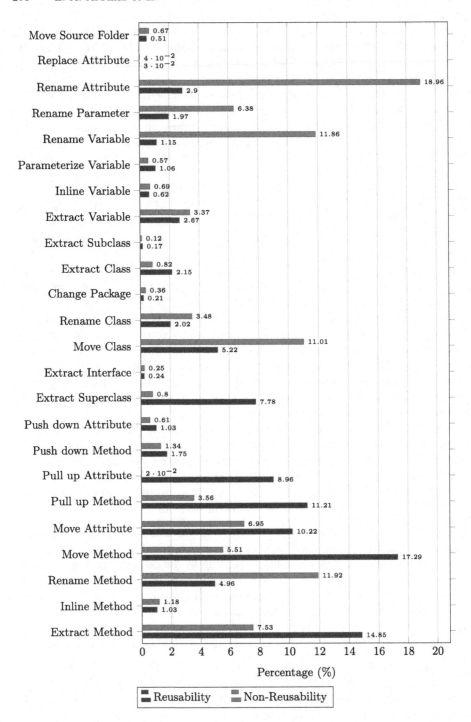

**Fig. 3.** Percentages of *reusability refactoring* and *non-reusability refactorings*, clustered by type.

ios of moving method up, from a child class, into a super class, for the purpose of sharing its behavior across all subclasses through inheritance. This refactoring is known as *Pull-Up Method*, which was found to be the third popular type in reusability refactorings, while being not popular in non-reusability refactorings.

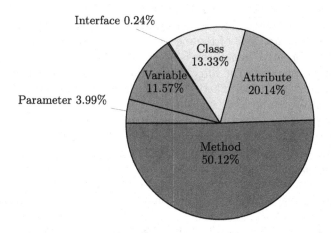

**Fig. 4.** Distribution of code elements in reusability refactoring commits.

**Summary.** We have shown that the distribution of refactoring types, applied in the context of reusability, is different from the distribution of refactoring types in mainstream development. In the refactorings performed to improve reusability, files are subject to more design level types of refactorings (e.g., *Move Method, Extract Method*) in general, and inheritance-related refactorings (e.g., *Pull-up Method, Pull-up Attribute*) in particular, while in other refactorings, files tend to undergo more renames (e.g., *Rename Method, Rename Variable*) and data type changes (e.g., *Change Variable Type*) to identifiers. Reusability refactorings heavily impact, high-level code elements, such as packages, classes, and methods, while typical refactorings, impact all code elements, including identifiers, and parameters.

## 4.2   RQ2. What Is the Impact of Reusability Refactorings on Structural Metrics?

To answer this research question, we investigate the impact of reusability refactorings on the state-of-the-art metrics, which have been used by previous studies, to recommend reusability changes. As a reminder, we aim to look at the variation of each metric value after the execution of the refactoring, therefore, we checkout the project files, right before the reusability commit, and we calculate metrics values, and after the reusability commit, and we recalculate the metrics values. Note that we only consider files that were involved in the commit, as there files are considered part of developer's intention of improving reusability. The results of metrics boxplots are outlined in Fig. 5. To further investigate the significance of difference between the boxplots, we also use the Wilcoxon Signed-rank Test. Statistical settings included using a 0.05 alpha value for the significance level. We hypothesize that reusability refactorings will optimize metrics by reducing them (the lower is the value of the metric, the better is the software structural quality). Our alternative hypothesis is accepted if the *before refactoring* boxplot is significantly larger than the *after refactoring* boxplot. The Wilcoxon Signed-rank Test results indicating whether or not there were statistically significant improvements before and after reusability commits is shown in Table 4.

According to Fig. 5, reusability refactorings had no impact on the Number of Children (NOC) Depth of Inheritance Tree (DIT), and Response for Class (RFC). These results can be explained by the fact that the majority of reusability refactoring are not targeting classes. In fact, if we refer to Fig. 4, only 13.3% of reusability refactoring targeted classes, and exctrating subclasses, which would have impacted these metrics, represent only 0.13%, and so, its impact is negligible.

On the other hand, we measure an increase in the weighted methods per class, and the variation is found to be statistically significant ($p < 0.05$). According to Fig. 3, the *Extract Method* refactoring has been found to be very popular in reusability refactoring, and so, developers tend to create new methods while extracting the reusable code from the longer methods. This implies the sudden increase of methods count, per class. While developers are expected to keep the number of methods lower in classes, the impact of reusable functionality from longer classes, creates free methods that can be pulled up to either superclasses, and be shared with all children, or relocated to operate on variables that may not belong to its original class. This explains decrease of the Coupling Between Objects (CBO) and the slight decrease in the Lack of Cohesion of Methods (LCOM), which means that methods have become more cohesive. However, its corresponding statistical test show no significant different, but its value was close to 0.05. Similarly, we notice slight improvement in the Lines of Code (LOC), with no statistical significance but close p-value (i.e., 0.066). The extraction of methods helps in reducing cloning functionalities in multiple locations in the code. Also, pulling methods up the hierarchy, will allow subclasses to inherit it, and so, lines of code will decrease, unless when the method gets overridden. Moreover, the Cyclomatic Complexity (CC) has decreased after reusability code changes with no statistical significance. A proper extraction of sub-methods tends to break down long methods, and slightly decrease their complexity.

As a meta-review, the majority of state-of-the-art metrics did not capture any improvement, or captured non-significant improvement, when developers refactor their code for the purpose of reusability. This is an interesting finding for our future research directions, as we want to further increase our dataset, in terms of projects, and programming languages, in order to experiment whether

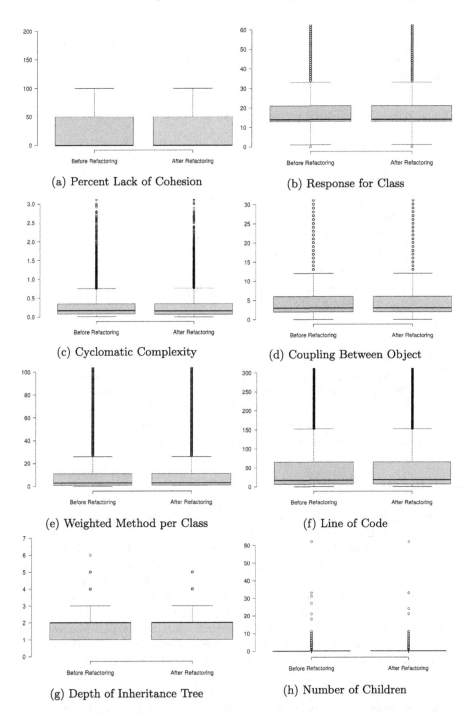

(a) Percent Lack of Cohesion

(b) Response for Class

(c) Cyclomatic Complexity

(d) Coupling Between Object

(e) Weighted Method per Class

(f) Line of Code

(g) Depth of Inheritance Tree

(h) Number of Children

**Fig. 5.** Boxplots for metric values before and after reusability commits for different sets of code elements.

there is a shortage of metrics that properly measure what developers consider to be at design level change to improve reusability. Such investigations will bridge the gap between how existing research on software reuse evaluates code changes, and how developers concretely achieve it.

**Table 4.** Wilcoxon Signed-Rank Test results for all code elements between before-after versions of reusability commits.

| Metric | p-value | Impact | Reject $H_0$? |
|---|---|---|---|
| Percent Lack of Cohesion (LCOM) | 0.0707 | +ve | False |
| Response for Class (RFC) | 0.2925 | No | False |
| Cyclomatic Complexity (CC) | 0.3298 | +ve | False |
| Coupling Between Objects (CBO) | 0.2739 | +ve | False |
| Weighted Method per Class (WMC) | 0.0372 | -ve | True |
| Line of Code (LOC) | 0.06621 | +ve | False |
| Depth of Inheritance Tree (DIT) | 0.7446 | No | False |
| Number of Children (NOC) | 0.5292 | No | False |

**Summary.** When developers refactor their code for the purpose of reusability, we found that the number of methods significantly increased, but the majority of the state-of-the-art metrics did not capture any improvement, or captured non significant improvement.

## 5    Threats to Validity

The first threat is that the analysis was restricted to only open source, Java-based, Git-based repositories. However, we were still able to analyze 1,828 projects that are highly varied in size, contributors, number of commits and refactorings. Additionally, in this paper, we analyzed only the 28 refactoring operations detected by Refactoring Miner, which can be viewed as a validity threat because the tool did not consider all refactoring types mentioned by Fowler et al. [7]. However, in a previous study, Murphy-Hill et al. [12] reported that these types are amongst the most common refactoring types. Moreover, we did not perform a manual validation of refactoring types detected by Refactoring Miner to assess its accuracy, so our study is mainly threatened by the accuracy of the detection tool. Yet, Tsantalis et al. [19] reported that Refactoring Miner has a precision of 98% and a recall of 87% which significantly outperforms the previous state-of-the-art tools, which gives us confidence in using the tool.

Another threat to validity is that, as we mentioned above, while we determined whether a commit has a reusability change, we only look for terms like *reus* in the commit message, although not all reusability commit messages may contain those words.

Another critical threat, is the fact that not all refactorings are root-canal. Developers may be interleaving refactorings with other types of changes, and so, this may become a noise in our measurements. To mitigate this issue, we considered commits that both contain an explicit statement about reusability, and contain at least one refactoring operation, in order to correlate between the refactoring and its documentation. Also, the existence of several unrelated files, in the commit, as part of other changes, can also become a noise for our metrics measurements. To mitigate this threat, we measure the metrics for code elements that are being refactored, and not all the changed files in the reusability commit.

## 6   Conclusion

In this paper, we performed a study on analyzing reusability refactorings based on information in Java projects from our dataset. We found that in reusability refactorings, the changes developers performed would significantly affect metrics pertaining to methods, but not significantly affect metrics regarding comments or cohesion of classes. We also found that less than 0.4% commits are reusability refactorings in 154,820 commits. Another fact we found is that method is modified more frequently in reusability refactoring changes. Our results have shown some existing facts in reusability refactorings, and those findings could help developers to make better decisions while performing reusability refactorings in the future.

Some recommendations that we have for future work involve comparing different subsections of data, and determining what refactorings are related to reusability. Specifically, we think that it would be interesting to compare the results that we got to instances where each individual refactoring detected was analyzed to explore if it was done for reusability or not, to see if us grouping all refactorings in a commit for reusability and non-reusability is similar. We also think that analyzing the code before and after the reusability commits for different metrics that are more usability based, such as adaptability, understandability, or portability, could be an interesting future work, though an issue might arise to finding specific ways to measure those metrics. Moreover, we plan to find a better way to figure out if a commit was a reusability refactoring or not. Since this work relies on the commit message, there could be commits incorrectly labeled, or commits that are reusability but not labeled as such that we are missing.

**Acknowledgements.** This material is based on work supported by the National Science Foundation under Grant No. 1757680.

## References

1. AlOmar, E., Mkaouer, M.W., Ouni, A.: Can refactoring be self-affirmed? An exploratory study on how developers document their refactoring activities in commit messages. In: 2019 IEEE/ACM 3rd International Workshop on Refactoring (IWoR), pp. 51–58. IEEE (2019)

2. AlOmar, E.A., Mkaouer, M.W., Ouni, A.: Toward the automatic classification of self-affirmed refactoring. J. Syst. Softw. **171**, 110821 (2020)

3. AlOmar, E.A., Mkaouer, M.W., Ouni, A., Kessentini, M.: On the impact of refactoring on the relationship between quality attributes and design metrics. In: 2019 ACM/IEEE International Symposium on Empirical Software Engineering and Measurement (ESEM), pp. 1–11. IEEE (2019)

4. Alshayeb, M.: Empirical investigation of refactoring effect on software quality. Inf. Softw. Technol. **51**(9), 1319–1326 (2009)

5. Chidamber, S.R., Kemerer, C.F.: A metrics suite for object oriented design. IEEE Trans. Softw. Eng. **20**(6), 476–493 (1994)

6. Fakhoury, S., Roy, D., Hassan, A., Arnaoudova, V.: Improving source code readability: theory and practice. In: 2019 IEEE/ACM 27th International Conference on Program Comprehension (ICPC), pp. 2–12. IEEE (2019)

7. Fowler, M.: Refactoring: Improving the Design of Existing Code. Addison-Wesley Professional, Boston (2018)

8. Lorenz, M., Kidd, J.: Object-Oriented Software Metrics, vol. 131. Prentice Hall, Englewood Cliffs (1994)

9. McCabe, T.J.: A complexity measure. IEEE Trans. Softw. Eng. **4**, 308–320 (1976)

10. Moser, R., Sillitti, A., Abrahamsson, P., Succi, G.: Does refactoring improve reusability? In: Morisio, M. (ed.) ICSR 2006. LNCS, vol. 4039, pp. 287–297. Springer, Heidelberg (2006). https://doi.org/10.1007/11763864_21

11. Munaiah, N., Kroh, S., Cabrey, C., Nagappan, M.: Curating GitHub for engineered software projects. Empirical Softw. Eng. **22**(6), 3219–3253 (2017). https://doi.org/10.1007/s10664-017-9512-6

12. Murphy-Hill, E., Parnin, C., Black, A.P.: How we refactor, and how we know it. IEEE Trans. Softw. Eng. **38**(1), 5–18 (2012)

13. Opdyke, W.F.: Refactoring object-oriented frameworks (1992)

14. Pantiuchina, J., Lanza, M., Bavota, G.: Improving code: the (mis) perception of quality metrics. In: 2018 IEEE International Conference on Software Maintenance and Evolution (ICSME), pp. 80–91. IEEE (2018)

15. Peruma, A., Mkaouer, M.W., Decker, M.J., Newman, C.D.: Contextualizing rename decisions using refactorings, commit messages, and data types. J. Syst. Softw. **169**, 110704 (2020)

16. Peruma, A., Newman, C.D., Mkaouer, M.W., Ouni, A., Palomba, F.: An exploratory study on the refactoring of unit test files in android applications. In: Conference on Software Engineering Workshops, ICSEW 2020 (2020)

17. Sharma, A., Kumar, R., Grover, P.: A critical survey of reusability aspects for component-based systems. World Acad. Sci. Eng. Technol. **19**, 411–415 (2007)

18. Stroggylos, K., Spinellis, D.: Refactoring-does it improve software quality? In: Fifth International Workshop on Software Quality (WoSQ 2007: ICSE Workshops 2007), p. 10. IEEE (2007)

19. Tsantalis, N., Mansouri, M., Eshkevari, L.M., Mazinanian, D., Dig, D.: Accurate and efficient refactoring detection in commit history. In: Proceedings of the 40th International Conference on Software Engineering, pp. 483–494. ACM (2018)

20. Wilcoxon, F.: Individual comparisons by ranking methods. Biom. Bull. **1**(6), 80–83 (1945)

# Short Papers

# Analyzing the Impact of Refactoring Variants on Feature Location

Amine Benmerzoug[1]([✉]) [ID], Lamia Yessad[1] [ID], and Tewfik Ziadi[2] [ID]

[1] Ecole Nationale Supérieure d'Informatique, LCSI, Algiers, Algeria
{a_benmerzoug,l_yessad}@esi.dz
[2] Sorbonne Université, LIP6, Paris, France
tewfik.ziadi@lip6.fr

**Abstract.** Due to the increasing importance of feature location process, several studies evaluate the performance of different techniques based on IR strategies and a set of software variants as input artifacts. The proposed techniques attempt to improve the results obtained but it is often a difficult task. None of the existing feature location techniques considers the changing nature of the input artifacts, which may undergo series of refactoring changes. In this paper, we investigate the impact of refactoring variants on the feature location techniques. We first evaluate the performance of two techniques through the ArgoUML SPL benchmark when the variants are refactored. We then discuss the degraded results and the possibility of restoring them. Finally, we outline a process of variant alignment that aims to preserve the performance of the feature location.

**Keywords:** Software Product Line · Feature location · Refactoring

## 1 Introduction

Software Product Lines (SPL) represent one of the most exciting paradigm shift in software development in the last two decades [14]. The main idea is to implement at the same time a family of similar applications rather than implementing a single system. The SPL engineering framework introduces into the general process of software development new activities related to software variability management and product derivation based mainly on the concept of *features* [1]. A feature refers to a specific functionality or characteristic of a software [10]. During these decades, many concrete approaches have been proposed (ex. Sven et al. [1]). However, adopting an SPL approach and designing SPL variability is still a major challenge and represents a risk for a company [12]. Berger et al. [3] showed, in a survey with industrial companies, which participated in industrial SPLE, that around 50% of them cannot adopt SPL proactively [3]. Indeed, instead of adopting an SPL, these companies clone an existing product and modify it to fit customer requirements. This approach, called *clone-and-own*, is widely used because it is faster and more efficient to start with an already developed and tested set of variants. Thereby, the extractive approach for SPL adoption or SPL Reengineering is

© Springer Nature Switzerland AG 2020
S. Ben Sassi et al. (Eds.): ICSR 2020, LNCS 12541, pp. 279–291, 2020.
https://doi.org/10.1007/978-3-030-64694-3_17

gaining ground. It consists in migrating, automatically or semi-automatically, the existing variants into an SPL. One of the main steps in the extractive approach is what is referred to as Feature Location (FL). FL is a traceability recovery task for identifying the implementation elements associated to each feature among the family variants that are created using clone-and-own [16].

However, all FL techniques are built on the same assumption that the input variants only differ in term of features and do not consider the situation where some changes are applied on some variants, without a complete propagation to all variants. This kind of evolution is only introduced to improve the quality of the source code without introducing any variation in terms of features. *Code Refactoring* [9] is an example of such evolution.

This paper presents a study to investigate the impact of the evolution related to code refactoring of the variants on the process of feature location and perform experiments to quantify the impacts introduced by refactorings. We particularly consider the following Research Questions:

- (RQ1): Does refactoring affect feature location results?
- (RQ2): How to cover the negative impact of refactoring on feature location techniques?
- (RQ3): What is the new vision to implement for preserving the performance of a feature location technique?

To answer these questions, we have conducted a study on two feature location techniques through the ArgoUML SPL benchmark [15]. The study consists of forty-two experiments:

- The rst twenty-two experiments aim to observe and analyze if the two location techniques performed are impacted by refactorings (RQ1). Two hundred fifty refactorings are applied to analyse this impact.
- The rest of experiments aims to confirm the possibility of restoring performance of the same techniques when propagating the changes to all variants (RQ2 and RQ3). It means that unchanged variants must be modified according to the existing refactorings.

The contributions of this paper can be summarized as follows:

- We use the ArgoUML SPL benchmark to do further experiments measuring the negative impact of refactoring variants on feature location techniques.
- We identify that the negative impact represented by the distance we called *Degraded Degree* evolves linearly based on the number of the applied refactorings.
- We outline a preliminary process that aims to align the variants, i.e. propagate refactorings to all variants before performing the feature location.

The rest of the paper is organized as follows. Section 2 presents the feature location (FL) and refactoring techniques as well as the problem statement. Section 3 describes our study design and Sect. 4 discusses the results. This section also outlines the main activities towards an alignment process. Finally, Sect. 5 presents related work before concluding the paper in Sect. 6.

## 2    Background and Problem Statement

### 2.1    Feature Location for Software Product Line Reengineering

As shown by Martinez et al. [16], feature location in the extractive approach of SPLE can be illustrated by the Fig. 1. It takes as input a set of variants created using clone-and-own. For each of the variants, there are implementation elements (represented as a set diamonds in Fig. 1) and the information of which features are implemented. For example, Variant 1 implements features F1, F2 and F3 whereas Variant 2 implements F1 and F3. In this context of feature-based variants, a specific FL technique takes as inputs the information of all the variants (features and implementation elements) and finds, for each feature, which are the associated implementation elements as shown at the bottom of Fig. 1.

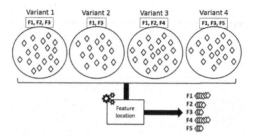

**Fig. 1.** Feature location in feature-based variants [16].

Rubin and Chechik [20] and Assunçã et al. [2] conducted surveys about the state-of-the-art in FL domain with a large variety of approaches. For instance, many approaches use techniques from the field of Information Retrieval (IR) such as Formal Concept Analysis (FCA) [25], Document Vectors (DVs) [13] and Latent Semantic Indexing (LSI) [8].

### 2.2    Problem Statement

As mentioned above, feature location techniques for feature-based variants are built on the same assumption that the input variants are very similar, and they only differ in terms of features. However, the variants created using clone-and-own can evolve independently. Many evolutions that are not related to features can be applied without a complete propagation to all variants. An example of such evolutions is related to code refactoring that can be introduced to improve the quality of the source code of a specific variant without adding or removing features [9]. Fowler [9] proposed a refactoring catalog[1] that contains from a

---

[1] Refactoring.com [online]. [date of reference: July 3rd of 2019]. Available at: https://refactoring.com/catalog/.

simple *Rename field* to more complex operations such as *Extract method* or *Move method*.

To illustrate the impact of refactoring applied on variants created using clone-and-own, let us consider the example of the banking system [26]. Figure 2 shows the source code of the *Account* class of two variants denoted Product1Bank and Product2Bank. Product1Bank implements the *Base* and *Limit* features whereas Product2Bank implements the *Base*, *Limit* and *CurrencyExchange* features. The *Base* feature represents the mandatory part in all possible variants and the *Limit* feature is mainly implemented with the limit property and its associated getter.

Figure 2 (a) shows a simple type of refactoring called *Rename field*, where the limit field in *Account* class in Product1Bank is changed into a more meaningful name limitOnAccount (all the updated references are highlighted in green). Another example of refactoring illustrated in Fig. 2 (b) is *Extract method*, where the condition statement in *withdraw* method in Product2Bank is extracted into the new method *isSufficient*, which returns a boolean. Thus, the condition statement is replaced with the call to the new method (both the call and the new method are highlighted in yellow).

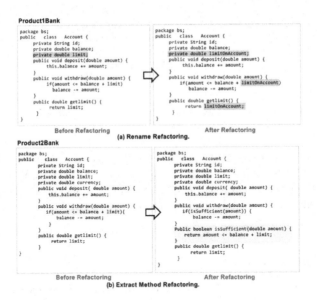

**Fig. 2.** Rename field and Extract method refactorings in the "Banking System". (Color figure online)

Applying refactoring by renaming the limit field only in Product1Bank may have an impact on FL. Indeed, the implementation of the *Limit* Feature only considers one identifier and not both. The extraction of the new method in Product2Bank may also impact the results of FL because the change is not propagated to Product1Bank.

In this simple example and even if we only applied two refactoring operations on a single class, FL results can be significantly impacted. This paper aims presenting a deeper study to evaluate systematically this impact according to the number of refactoring operations. The next sections present the design of this study using the ArgoUML SPL benchmark and highlight the results.

## 3   Study Design

### 3.1   ArgoUML SPL Benchmark for FL

To evaluate FL in feature-based variants, the ArgoUML SPL benchmark was proposed as a facto platform for evaluating FL techniques [15]. This benchmark is based on the ArgoUML SPL which is extracted as a product line from an open-source tool for UML modeling [4]. Figure 3 presents the feature model of the ArgoUML SPL where variability is mainly related to the support of the different UML diagrams. For instance, the feature *State* is the functionality related to the UML state diagrams and it is defined as optional whereas the class diagram is mandatory. The implementation of ArgoUML SPL is coded in Java using an annotative approach based on the well-known #ifdef directives.

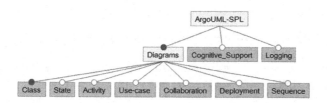

**Fig. 3.** ArgoUML SPL feature model [4].

The ArgoUML SPL benchmark was initially proposed as a challenge at System and Software Product line Conference (SPLC 2018) [15]. The idea is to propose for the research community a benchmark to implement and evaluate FL techniques. The benchmark provides scenarios, ground-truth, and metrics calculation:

- There are 15 scenarios helping to generate up to 256 different variants.
- The ground-truth contains 24 text files corresponding to each feature and its combinations. These files contain traceability information to classes, methods, and their refinements.
- The three traditional metrics *precision*, *recall*, and *F-score* are computed to evaluate the retrieval effectiveness of traceability information.

The results format of any feature location techniques that uses the benchmark should be adapted to the same format as the ground-truth where the text file name is the name of the features or their combination or feature negation.

## 3.2   Data Preparation Procedure

In this study, we used ArgoUML SPL to generate a data set of five variants using predefined Random scenario (one of the 15 scenarios). Our study is divided into three steps: Before Refactoring, After Refactoring and After Alignment.

**Data Preparation Before Refactoring.** In this step, we consider the generated five variants without modification as input artifacts of the location technique. This latter locates the source code of each feature knowing that the set of features in each variant product is already identified.

We perform the experiment #1 using the DVs location technique and the experiment #2 with the LSI technique. The results are the same obtained by Cruz et al. [5] and are taken as a point of comparison.

**Data Preparation After Refactoring.** In this step, we apply several types of refactoring on each variant. Here, it is important to consider the number of refactorings applied on variants, denoted NREFACT. For that, we perform 20 experiments (10 for each technique) starting with 25 refactorings of several types (*Rename class/method/field, Extract class/method*). Then, the number of refactorings is increased by 25 until it reaches 250 different refactorings (see Table 1).

**Table 1.** Refactorings variation

| Experiment (DVs) | #3 | #4 | #5 | #6 | #7 | #8 | #9 | #10 | #11 | #12 |
|---|---|---|---|---|---|---|---|---|---|---|
| Experiment (LSI) | #13 | #14 | #15 | #16 | #17 | #18 | #19 | #20 | #21 | #22 |
| NREFACT | 25 | 50 | 75 | 100 | 125 | 150 | 175 | 200 | 225 | 250 |

For applying the refactorings, we use two automatic refactoring tools: *Jextract*[2] [21] and *JDeodorant*[3] [17]. The *Jextract* tool is based on the similarity structure of the system to identify refactoring opportunities whereas *JDeodorant* identifies code smells in software and outputs the appropriate refactorings to resolve them. We use the two tools for extracting methods and classes. However, the rename is performed by reviewing source code and giving meaningful names to fields, methods and classes using the Eclipse rename functionality.

**Data Preparation After Alignment.** It is the third and final step of our study. It also contains 20 experiments (10 for each location technique). We keep track of all refactoring operations for each variant using Eclipse refactoring history, which provides the needed information to create refactoring scripts. So, we

---

[2] https://github.com/aserg-ufmg/jextract.
[3] https://github.com/tsantalis/JDeodorant.

use these scripts to automatically propagate the applied refactorings (in one or many variants) to all variants. For each experiment, the input artifacts still the five variants but with additional refactorings.

In the experiment #12 (see Table 1), we have a priori five refactored variants with 250 refactorings in total. Five scripts are then created where each script capitalizes the refactorings applied on one variant. Then, scripts are used to propagate the refactorings to all variants. Table 2 presents the number of refactorings applied successfully. The objective of alignment is to respond to the RQ2 and RQ3 research questions.

**Table 2.** Number of refactorings after alignment

| Experiment (DVs) | #23 | #24 | #25 | #26 | #27 | #28 | #29 | #30 | #31 | #32 |
|---|---|---|---|---|---|---|---|---|---|---|
| Experiment (LSI) | #33 | #34 | #35 | #36 | #37 | #38 | #39 | #40 | #41 | #42 |
| NREFACT | 103 | 198 | 284 | 332 | 386 | 427 | 503 | 608 | 646 | 687 |

Unfortunately, as we see in Table 2, not all refactorings can be applied because of conflicts. A conflict arises when two or more separate refactoring operations should be applied into the same code element (field, class, method, package), or when the element has been deleted.

## 3.3 Feature Location Workflows

As previously mentioned, we use two automatic IR-based feature location techniques DVs and LSI. Both extract from input artifacts (the five variants) methods and classes, then generate for each of them a document. Each variant is treated separately and have a set of characteristics such as number of features, number of LOCs (NLOCs) and number of generated documents (see Table 3). Furthermore, they give as results the code source of features in the same ground-truth's format. In that way, the ground-truth can be used to calculate the performance metrics: precision, recall and F-score.

**Table 3.** Variant characteristics

| Variant | Features | NLOCs | Documents |
|---|---|---|---|
| 1 | 05 | 305,970 | 15,563 |
| 2 | 05 | 308,821 | 15,475 |
| 3 | 05 | 295,927 | 14,881 |
| 4 | 05 | 327,311 | 16,168 |
| 5 | 05 | 337,940 | 16,730 |

## 3.4  Degradation-Based Evaluation

We define a new evaluation metric *Degradation Degree*, denoted DD to measure the performance degradation of a feature location technique. This metric is a distance between two F-score values (obtained from ArgoUML SPL benchmark). Thus, it is based on F-Score metric and defined by the following formula:

$$\text{DD (Experiment \#n)} = FScore_0 - \text{FScore (Experiment \#n)} \qquad (1)$$

Where DD refers to the Degradation Degree qualifying each experiment after alignment. $FSore_0$ denotes the F-score obtained before refactoring depending on what technique we use, and #n denotes the experiment number.

## 4  Results for Answering the Research Questions

• *RQ1:* Does refactoring affect feature location results?

To answer RQ1, we perform for each technique 10 experiments by varying the number of refactoring operations. The ArgoUML SPL benchmark provides the values of precision (P), recall (R) and F-score (F). However, DD values are calculated using the precedent formula (1). The results are shown in Table 4.

**Table 4.** Evolution of DD depending on the number of refactorings using DVs and LSI

| NREFACT | DVs | | | | LSI | | | |
|---|---|---|---|---|---|---|---|---|
| | P | R | F | DD | P | R | F | DD |
| 0 | 0.04470 | 0.04292 | 0.04379 | 0.00000 | 0.16083 | 0.19439 | 0.17602 | 0.00000 |
| 25 | 0.04309 | 0.03954 | 0.04124 | 0.00256 | 0.16020 | 0.18254 | 0.17143 | 0.00459 |
| 50 | 0.03788 | 0.03206 | 0.03473 | 0.00907 | 0.15384 | 0.16955 | 0.16131 | 0.01471 |
| 75 | 0.03109 | 0.02446 | 0.02738 | 0.01642 | 0.15084 | 0.15955 | 0.15507 | 0.02095 |
| 100 | 0.02847 | 0.02107 | 0.02422 | 0.01957 | 0.14189 | 0.12956 | 0.13544 | 0.04058 |
| 125 | 0.02147 | 0.01611 | 0.01841 | 0.02539 | 0.13124 | 0.10196 | 0.11476 | 0.06126 |
| 150 | 0.01502 | 0.01410 | 0.01454 | 0.02925 | 0.08608 | 0.07436 | 0.07979 | 0.09623 |
| 175 | 0.00645 | 0.00735 | 0.00687 | 0.03692 | 0.05908 | 0.04744 | 0.05262 | 0.12340 |
| 200 | 0.00375 | 0.00430 | 0.00400 | 0.03979 | 0.02096 | 0.02981 | 0.02461 | 0.15141 |
| 225 | 0.00170 | 0.00295 | 0.00216 | 0.04164 | 0.00811 | 0.00930 | 0.00866 | 0.16736 |
| 250 | 0.00044 | 0.00064 | 0.00052 | 0.04327 | 0.00073 | 0.00085 | 0.00153 | 0.17450 |

   In both techniques, we observe that DD increase when NREFACT increase. Furthermore, the two variables are correlated with a coefficient of correlation equal to 9.90E−01 (≈1) for DVs (resp. 9.81E−01 for LSI). Thus, we apply a linear regression, which is a technique of machine learning used to obtain a mathematical model. This latter allows developers to make predictions for (or extrapolate) the value of DD depending on the different values of NREFACT (see Fig. 4). The regression Eqs.((2) for DVs and (3) for LSI) obtained are:

$$DD = 0.000187 \times \text{NREFACT} + 0.000555 \qquad (2)$$

$$DD = 0.000798 \times \text{NREFACT} - 0.022011 \qquad (3)$$

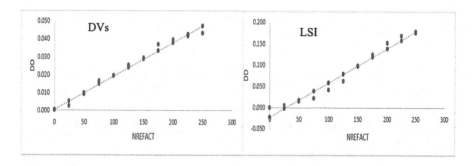

**Fig. 4.** Regression lines to predict degradation degree based on NREFACT.

For example, in our context, if the value of NREFACT is equal to 500, the expected value of the degradation degree DD will be equal to 0.094289 for DVs (resp. 0.376943 for LSI).

- **RQ2:** How to cover the negative impact of refactoring on feature location techniques?

To answer RQ2, we align the variants. As we mentioned before, we keep track of all refactoring operations in script files. Then, we perform the scripts to apply the possible refactorings on all variants. Our objective is to reduce the negative impact of refactoring variants on the feature location techniques. Figure 5 shows that the alignment allows slightly improving the precision and the recall metrics (and thus F-score). The results indicate that the alignment of variants could restore the performance for both techniques.

- **RQ3:** What is the new vision to implement for preserving the performance of a feature location technique?

Our study shows that the refactoring of variants has a negative impact on the feature location processes and the alignment of variants could deal with this problem (see Fig. 5). The alignment performed in our study is not suitable because of increasing conflictual refactorings. Therefore, we are currently working to propose a new *Alignment process*, which can include the following three activities:

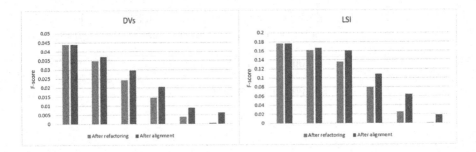

**Fig. 5.** Slightly improvement of F-score after Alignment.

1. Refactoring identification that aims to automatically identify refactoring operations by analyzing source code related to the variants to be inputted.
2. Refactoring selection that has the role of selecting the suitable set of refactorings to be propagated to all variants in a systematic way avoiding conflicts as much as possible.
3. Alignment that propagates automatically the selected refactorings to all variants.

## 5   Related Work

Existing feature location techniques can be mainly grouped into two categories: Static and Dynamic [5,7]. None of these feature location techniques consider the changes of refactorings. There are a number of benchmarks [6,15,16] that have been used to evaluate FL techniques performance [5,18,24], while we used one of them to estimate the performance of FL techniques with refactored variants. We have previously presented the ArgoUML SPL benchmark, which have been used to evaluate many FL techniques [5,18,19]. In addition, Martinez et al. [16] have proposed the use of eclipse variants to evaluate feature location techniques. This benchmark is mainly based on the assumption that eclipse features can be mapped to SPL features and proposes a generation of the ground-truth of the benchmark from a specific eclipse distribution. Many techniques have been evaluated using this benchmark. This benchmark is also useful to evaluate FL but, without considering the noises introduced by refactoring operations. As we presented in our study, our objective is to identify the impact of refactoring variants on the FL process.

Many approaches have also been proposed to identify refactorings in the source code [11,22,23]. Unfortunately, these approaches only identify refactorings from the source code of a single application. As we discussed in our Alignment Process, one interesting direction is to extend these existing approaches by first identifying refactorings from many variants and then, applying a systematic alignment process to make the refactoring activities transparent during the FL process.

# 6    Conclusion

In this paper, we have presented a study on the impact of refactorings on feature location techniques using ArgoUML SPL benchmark. We apply Document Vectors (DVs) and Latent Semantic indexing (LSI), automatic feature location approaches based on textual information retrieval techniques. We find that refactorings of a variant subset reduce the techniques performance and propagating these refactorings to all variants (alignment) slightly improves the results.

Our study provides a set of experiments to show the negative impact of refactorings on the feature location techniques by calculating the degradation degree (DD). The value of DD increases linearly based on the number of the applied refactorings. Thus, the value of DD can be extrapolated.

However, the experimental results obtained after alignment are not good because the use of an ad-hoc technique. As future work, we will implement the outlined alignment process and experiment it with other feature location techniques using different benchmarks.

# References

1. Apel, S., Batory, D.S., Kästner, C., Saake, G.: Feature-Oriented Software Product Lines - Concepts and Implementation. Springer, Heidelberg (2013). https://doi.org/10.1007/978-3-642-37521-7
2. Assunção, W.K.G., Lopez-Herrejon, R.E., Linsbauer, L., Vergilio, S.R., Egyed, A.: Reengineering legacy applications into software product lines: a systematic mapping. Empirical Softw. Eng. **22**(6), 2972–3016 (2017). https://doi.org/10.1007/s10664-017-9499-z
3. Berger, T., Rublack, R., Nair, D., Atlee, J.M., Becker, M., Czarnecki, K., Wasowski, A.: A survey of variability modeling in industrial practice. In: Proceedings of the Seventh International Workshop on Variability Modelling of Software-Intensive Systems, pp. 1–7. ACM, Pisa (2013)
4. Couto, M.V., Valente, M.T., Figueiredo, E.: Extracting software product lines: a case study using conditional compilation. In: 15th European Conference on Software Maintenance and Reengineering, pp. 191–200. IEEE Computer Society, Oldenburg (2011)
5. Cruz, D., Figueiredo, E., Martinez, J.: A literature review and comparison of three feature location techniques using ArgoUML-SPL. In: Proceedings of the 13th International Workshop on Variability Modelling of Software-Intensive Systems, pp. 1–10. ACM, Leuven (2019)
6. Dit, B., Holtzhauer, A., Poshyvanyk, D., Kagdi, H.H.: A dataset from change history to support evaluation of software maintenance tasks. In: Proceedings of the 10th Working Conference on Mining Software Repositories, pp. 131–134. IEEE Computer Society, San Francisco (2013)
7. Dit, B., Revelle, M., Gethers, M., Poshyvanyk, D.: Feature location in source code: a taxonomy and survey. J. Softw. Evol. Process. **25**, 53–95 (2013)
8. Dumais, S.T., Furnas, G.W., Landauer, T.K., Deerwester, S., Harshman, R.: Using latent semantic analysis to improve access to textual information. In: Proceedings of the SIGCHI Conference on Human Factors in Computing Systems, pp. 281–285. Association for Computing Machinery, New York (1988)

9. Fowler, M.: Refactoring Improving the Design of Existing Code. Addison-Wesley, Boston (1999)
10. Kang, K., Cohen, S., Hess, J., Novak, W., Peterson, A.S.: Feature-oriented domain analysis (FODA) feasibility study. Software Engineering Institute. Universitas Carnegie Mellon, Pittsburgh, Pennsylvania (1990)
11. Kim, M., Gee, M., Loh, A., Rachatasumrit, N.: Ref-finder: a refactoring reconstruction tool based on logic query templates. In: Proceedings of the 18th ACM SIGSOFT International Symposium on Foundations of Software Engineering, pp. 371–372. ACM, Santa Fe (2010)
12. Krueger, C.W.: Variation management for software production lines. In: Chastek, G.J. (ed.) SPLC 2002. LNCS, vol. 2379, pp. 37–48. Springer, Heidelberg (2002). https://doi.org/10.1007/3-540-45652-X_3
13. Le, Q.V., Mikolov, T.: Distributed representations of sentences and documents. In: Proceedings of the 31th International Conference on Machine Learning, pp. 1188–1196. JMLR.org, Beijing (2014)
14. van der Linden, F.J., Schmid, K., Rommes, E.: Software Product Lines in Action: The Best Industrial Practice in Product Line Engineering. Springer, Heidelberg (2007). https://doi.org/10.1007/978-3-540-71437-8
15. Martinez, J., et al.: Feature location benchmark with ArgoUML SPL. In: Proceedings of the 22nd International Systems and Software Product Line Conference, vol. 1, pp. 257–263. ACM, Gothenburg (2018)
16. Martinez, J., Ziadi, T., Papadakis, M., Bissyandé, T.F., Klein, J., Traon, Y.L.: Feature location benchmark for extractive software product line adoption research using realistic and synthetic eclipse variants. Inf. Softw. Technol. **104**, 46–59 (2018)
17. Mazinanian, D., Tsantalis, N., Stein, R., Valenta, Z.: JDeodorant: clone refactoring. In: Proceedings of the 38th International Conference on Software Engineering, pp. 613–616. ACM, Austin (2016)
18. Michelon, G.K., Linsbauer, L., Assunção, W.K.G., Egyed, A.: Comparison-based feature location in ArgoUML variants. In: Proceedings of the 23rd International Systems and Software Product Line Conference, pp. 1–5. ACM, Paris (2019)
19. Müller, R., Eisenecker, U.: A graph-based feature location approach using set theory. In: Proceedings of the 23rd International Systems and Software Product Line Conference, pp. 88–92. Association for Computing Machinery, New York (2019)
20. Rubin, J., Chechik, M.: A survey of feature location techniques. In: Reinhartz-Berger, I., Sturm, A., Clark, T., Cohen, S., Bettin, J. (eds) Domain Engineering, pp. 29–58. Springer, Heidelberg (2013). https://doi.org/10.1007/978-3-642-36654-3_2
21. Silva, D., Terra, R., Valente, M.T.: JExtract: an eclipse plug-in for recommending automated extract method refactorings, pp. 1–8. CoRR (2015)
22. Silva, D., Valente, M.T.: RefDiff: detecting refactorings in version histories. In: Proceedings of the 14th International Conference on Mining Software Repositories, pp. 269–279. IEEE Computer Society, Buenos Aires (2017)
23. Tan, L., Bockisch, C.: A survey of refactoring detection tools. In: 6th Collaborative Workshop on Evolution and Maintenance of Long Living Systems, pp. 100–105. CEUR-WS.org, Stuttgart (2019)
24. Thüm, T., Kästner, C., Benduhn, F., Meinicke, J., Saake, G., Leich, T.: FeatureIDE: an extensible framework for feature-oriented software development. Sci. Comput. Program. **79**, 70–85 (2014)

25. Wille, R.: Formal concept analysis as mathematical theory of concepts and concept hierarchies. In: Ganter, B., Stumme, G., Wille, R. (eds.) Formal Concept Analysis. LNCS (LNAI), vol. 3626, pp. 1–33. Springer, Heidelberg (2005). https://doi.org/10.1007/11528784_1
26. Ziadi, T., Henard, C., Papadakis, M., Ziane, M., Traon, Y.L.: Towards a language-independent approach for reverse-engineering of software product lines. In: Symposium on Applied Computing, SAC 2014, Gyeongju, Republic of Korea, 24–28 March 2014, pp. 1064–1071. ACM (2014)

# An Exploratory Study on How Software Reuse is Discussed in Stack Overflow

Eman Abdullah AlOmar[1]([⊠]) , Diego Barinas[1], Jiaqian Liu[2],
Mohamed Wiem Mkaouer[1] , Ali Ouni[3] , and Christian Newman[1]

[1] Rochester Institute of Technology, Rochester, NY, USA
{eaa6167,dh7445,mwmvse,cdnvse}@rit.edu
[2] University at Buffalo, Buffalo, NY, USA
jliu275@buffalo.edu
[3] ETS Montreal, University of Quebec, Montreal, QC, Canada
ali.ouni@etsmtl.ca

**Abstract.** Software reuse is an important and crucial quality attribute
in modern software engineering, where almost all software projects, open
source or commercial, no matter small or ultra-large, source code reuse
in one way or another. Although software reuse has experienced an
increased adoption throughout the years with the exponentially growing number of available third-party libraries, frameworks and APIs, little knowledge exists to investigate what aspects of code reuse developers discuss. In this study, we look into bridging this gap by examining Stack Overflow to understand the challenges developers encounter
when trying to reuse code. Using the Stack Overflow tags "code-reuse"
and "reusability", we extracted and analyzed 1,409 posts, composed of
questions and answers. Our findings indicate that despite being popular, reuse questions take relatively longer than typical other questions
to receive an accepted answer. From these posts, we identified 9 categories that group the different ways developers discuss software reuse.
We found Java and ASP.NET MVC to be the most discussed programming language and framework, respectively. Based on the programming
languages and frameworks mentioned in the posts, we noted that Web
software development is the most frequently targeted environment. This
study can be utilized to further analyze aspects about software reuse and
develop guidelines to be practiced in industry and taught when forming
new developers.

**Keywords:** Reusability · Software reuse · Stack overflow

## 1 Introduction

When dealing with unexpected coding or design problems, developers typically
refer to online forums and ask questions. One of the most used sites where
developers converge to ask and answer questions of a multitude of topics related

S. Ben Sassi et al. (Eds.): ICSR 2020, LNCS 12541, pp. 292–303, 2020.
https://doi.org/10.1007/978-3-030-64694-3_18

to programming, software engineering and related areas is Stack Overflow[1] (SO). Since its conception in 2008, SO has seen a yearly increase of its user base with over 10 million users as of 2019. Because of the growing importance of *SO* as a community of developers, a wide number of studies have been performed to understand the ways developers discuss different topics, and about aspects of *SO* and the community themselves.

In this study, we utilize *SO* to understand what are the challenges that drive developers to ask and discuss software reuse. We extract what aspects of this topic are discussed and what technologies are involved in these discussions. To do this, we mined from *SO*, all the questions that are tagged as *software reuse*. We found nine high-level categories that encompass the type of discussions that take place in *SO*, namely *Development, Third-party Software, Design Principles, Refactoring, Legacy System Wrapping, Application Product Lines, Program Generators, Configurable Vertical Applications*, and *General*. We also found that software reuse questions take longer to receive an accepted answer when compared to Web questions Among the discussed technologies, we identified Java as the most used programming language, ASP.NET MVC as the most discussed framework, and Web as the target environment for most of the questions. We provide the software reuse community with a set of well structured and classified questions and answers, for the purpose of analysis, replication and extension[2].

## 2   Study Methodology

The main goal of this work is to obtain and share insights to the Software Engineering community regarding how software reuse is discussed in practice by analyzing Stack Overflow (SO) posts. Figure 1 depicts an overview of our methodology.

### 2.1   Data Extraction

To conduct our study, we plan on extracting our data from Stack Overflow. The data should capture all the necessary information needed for our study, starting with questions, answers, discussions, and all their corresponding metadata (publication date, authors, TAGs, source code attached, etc.). We start the mining process through the Data Explorer web interface[3], which releases a regularly updated data dump of the SO network's content. We considered all questions, since SO creation, from August 2008, all the way to December 2019.

To distinguish reuse related questions, we started with using the tags *"reuse"* and *"reusability"* as they are intuitive. We have avoided using any extra tags mainly because it has been shown that developers misuse tags as an attempt to increase views, and the large number of tags tend to cause confusion among posters [4]. Additionally, in order to mitigate tag misuse issues, the relevancy of

---

[1]  https://www.stackoverflow.com.

[2]  https://smilevo.github.io/self-affirmed-refactoring/.

[3]  https://data.stackexchange.com/stackoverflow/queries.

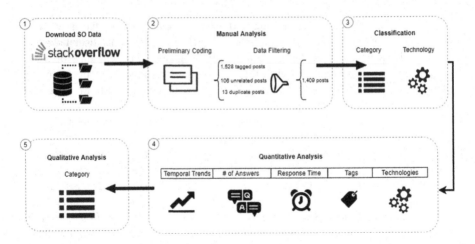

**Fig. 1.** Overview of the our study methodology.

the posts and tags were verified during the manual analysis described in Sect. 2.3, so that we only keep posts related to software reuse.

## 2.2 Manual Analysis

*Posts Filtering.* We included all posts that referred to reuse of code, and reuse of different resources that are relevant to any of the stages of the Software Development Life-Cycle. In addition, we also included questions that were related to general aspects of software reusability. We excluded all questions that were not related to the aforementioned aspects. Two authors have performed the manual verification of the questions. This process consisted of manually reading the title and question description for each post to assess its relevancy. When the description is ambiguous or short, we refer to any additional comments made to the question, and then we refer to the proposed answers, which may provide a clearer description of the problem. For instance, we found multiple posts where the question was vague, but the answers were clearer based on assuming what the question poster meant, and these assumptions were validated by the poster through either choosing one as a correct answer or by adding comments to further clarify their question.

*Duplicate Posts Removal.* During the manual validation, we found one duplicate post, 10 posts that were removed (upon looking for them in Stack Overflow), and 2 posts when accessing them redirected to unrelated questions.

To summarize, our data extraction process initially mined 1,528 reuse tagged posts, from which 106 were unrelated to reuse, and 13 were duplicate. After the filtering process, we retained 1,409 posts, created between August 2008 and December 2019.

## 2.3   Manual Classification

The classification process consists of reading *title, questions, answers* and *comments* to classify them based on various aspects, including the technology used, programming language, and category of reuse. The reuse categories were extracted from the systematic literature review, performed by Ahmaro et al. [1], on papers published from 1977 to 2013 on the different concepts surrounding Software Reusability. In this work, Ahmaro et al. [1] identified the following categories: *design patterns, component-based development, application frameworks, legacy system wrapping, service-oriented systems, application product lines, commercial off-the-shelf integration, program libraries, program generators, aspect-oriented software development and configurable vertical applications.* This set of categories was also supported by Younoussi et al. [5] whose work consisted of a another systematic literature review on *All about Software Reusability.* During the classification process, we combined questions related to *components, services,* and *aspects* into *Development,* we also combined *program libraries, application frameworks,* and *commercial off-the-shelf integration* into *Third Party Systems.* We also noticed the existence of questions that do not fit into the existing categories, so we have added two categories, namely *Refactoring,* which can be similar to design patterns, except that developers discuss refactoring opportunities without explicitly mentioning any patterns. The second added category was *General,* where questions were open-ended and their answers can belong to various categories. Table 1, enumerates each category, its related categories, its description, and an example from the classified questions.

Our categorization is not mutually exclusive, meaning that one post can be associated with more than one category at the same time. We also classified the posts regarding the technologies involved in the question. We looked into what programming language, framework and operating systems. Although most of the times these technologies were identified by the posters using the Stack Overflow provided tags, we still focus on the content of the question as the source for this classification due to previously identified issues involving tags usage. When looking at the content of the question, we not only referred to explicit mentions of the technologies, but also at implicit ones. Questions that we were not able to associate to specific technologies, were assigned with N/A (Not Available) but still considered for the categories classification.

## 3   Results and Discussion

### $RQ_1$: How challenging are reuse questions to answer?

*Approach.* Similar to previous studies that analyze *SO* [2,4], we take as indicators to measure the difficulty of the questions: 1) the percentage of questions without answers, 2) the percentage of questions without accepted answers, and 3) the average response time taken to receive an accepted answer. We present the average response times using both the mean and the median, which reduces the impact of outliers, as we noticed that some of the questions took more than

**Table 1.** Description of categories for software reuse.

| Category | Description |
|---|---|
| Development | **Related Categories.** *Aspect-oriented software development, Component-based development, Service-oriented systems*<br>**Description.** Questions related to all types of programming, namely component-based, service or aspect-oriented. Questions in this categories are typically related to programming paradigms<br>**Example.** In C++, there isn't a de-facto standard logging tool [...] This creates a bit of a problem, however, when trying to create reusable software components. If everything in your system depends on the logging component, this makes the software less reusable [...] (QuestionID 39304) |
| Third-party Software | **Related Categories:** *Program libraries, Application frameworks, Commercial off-the-shelf integration*<br>**Description.** Question related to creating and consuming APIs and third party libraries, and reusing existing frameworks<br>**Example.** I am deploying a mod-wsgi application on top of Apache, and have a client program that uses Curl. [...] What do I need to do on the Apache/Mod-wsgi side to enable connection re-use?. (QuestionID: 1056643) |
| Design Patterns | **Description.** Question related to implementing/gaining knowledge about design principles/patterns. Since the goal of applying design patterns is to achieve quality attributes, this category also includes questions that actively discuss these attributes<br>**Example.** This class is immutable and I want to make it a singleton for every distinct set of values, using the static factory pattern. [...] I am looking for the best way to cache and reuse previous instances of this class. [...] (QuestionID: 3557620) |
| Refactoring | **Description.** Questions that actively discuss how to refactor code or the usage of tools to accomplish refactoring<br>**Example.** I was wondering if there is a tool that will take a bunch of source code and find similar blocks of code so that they could be identified for possible refactoring. [...] (QuestionID: 1104543) |
| Legacy System Wrapping | **Description.** Questions related to using the features of an already developed system to avoid rewriting the functionality again or creating such type of systems. In a nutshell, reusing a system that does not provide APIs<br>**Example.** I would like to ask, has anyone successfully reused Audacity's source code in their own program? [...] I am thinking of a few concepts: 1. Compile the whole Audacity as a dll and call it in my C# program (is it possible?) 2. Extract out the functions of playing, recording and displaying waveform and compile them into dll [...] (QuestionID: 5360249) |
| Application Product Lines | **Description.** Questions discussing the continuous integration of various products, following a given line. Questions are typically around version controlling and repositories organization for better software reuse<br>**Example.** [...] I have a body of Java code, it used to be for one project. Then a second project, code was based on the first project. So a copy of the first one with many changes.[...] Now there is a third project, something like the first and the second one mixed together. How do I structure the code to have one code base/ git repo that contains all three projects code? [...] (QuestionID: 17202211) |
| Program Generators | **Description.** Questions regarding the use of code generators to avoid writing the code manually. These programs usually generate code following commonly known algorithms and patterns. Few instances of these questions were found mainly because of the existence of a "code-generation" tag on Stack Overflow which was out of scope for our research<br>**Example.** When building ASP.NET projects there is a certain amount of boilerplate, or plumbing that needs to be done, which is often identical across projects. [...] I would like to know what approach you find best for 'reusing' this plumbing across projects? [...] Code generation tools, such as T4? [...] (QuestionID: 2551849) |
| Configurable Vertical Applications | **Description.** Questions that discuss the creation of systems that can be configured to meet the requirements of different users. In other words, one system that can be adapted to different business needs, this way avoiding the creation of multiple similar systems sharing almost identical code<br>**Example.** I developed a rails app for a school alumni site. Now another school wants me to develop a similar site for them. I want to reuse the app. Data structure will be same but the actual data will be different. Design layout will be similar but design itself will be different. [...] Do you have any experience with such a case? If so, can you share it with me? [...] (QuestionID: 1329824) |
| General | **Description.** Questions that discuss aspects of software reuse from a high-level point of view and cannot be placed individually in any of the other categories<br>**Example.** [...] How do you make code reusable? What are the requirements for code being reusable? What are the things that reusable code should definitely have and what things are optional? (QuestionID: 268258) |

five years to receive an accepted answer. Using these three indicators, we use Web Development (Web) questions as a baseline to compare our SO questions with, because Web questions are found to be the most popular questions in SO [4]. We randomly selected 1,409 posts from web development questions, in the same period that we selected our reuse questions in, and using the same other tags that were also found in our reuse questions. The purpose of choosing the baseline questions, in the same period, and using similar tags, is to design a comparison sample that is as close as possible to our reuse sample, in terms of language and framework, to reduce any related bias.

**Table 2.** Percentages of questions without answers, and questions without accepted answers.

|  | Reuse questions | Web questions |
|---|---|---|
| Without answers | 16.21% | 14.90% |
| Without accepted answer | 58.97% | 46.61% |

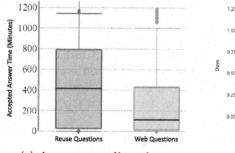

(a) **Average median time.**

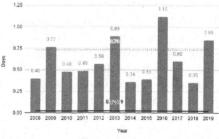

(b) **Average response time.**

**Fig. 2.** (a) Average median time to receive an accepted answer for Reuse questions vs Web questions. (b) Average response time for accepted answers.

*Results.* Table 2 shows the percentage of questions without answers, and without accepted answers, for both Reuse and Web questions. Results indicate that most of the software reuse questions (83.79%) received at least one answer, reflecting that the Reuse community is highly active, and close enough to the highest active community, *i.e.,* Web, whose percentage of unanswered questions is 85.10%. Furthermore, Asaduzzaman et al. [3] analyzed around 1.3 million *SO* questions and found that 7% of the total corpus of questions was unanswered. This shows that the percentage of unanswered Reuse questions (*i.e.,* 16.21 %) is high.

Although most of the questions received an answer, 58.97% of the questions were not marked with an accepted answer. It is important to note that the percentage Reuse questions with no accepted answer is significantly higher than the percentage of Web questions with no accepted answer (46.61%). This hypothesizes that Reuse questions are relatively harder to answer, in comparison with the Web questions. Such hypothesis itself is insufficient to affirm that Reuse questions are more challenging to answer, because $SO$ users are not always available to mark a good answer as accepted. Therefore, to further investigate this finding, we refer to the third indicator, namely the average response time taken to receive an accepted answer.

Figure 2a presents the distribution of time to receive an accepted answer for Reuse questions for Web questions. We observe that the time needed to mark an answer as accepted, for Web questions is typically below 400 min, in contrast with Reuse questions, which have a much wider spread that goes up to 800 min. Moreover, the median time for a Reuse question to mark an answer as accepted, is 410 min, while the median accepted answer's time for a Web question is 230 min. To verify the statistical significance of the difference, we use the Mann-Whitney U test, a non-parametric test that checks continuous or ordinal data for a significant difference between two independent groups. The Mann-Whitney test accepted the alternate hypothesis, and the difference between the two groups is found to be statistically significant (*i.e.*, $p < 0.05$). This shows that Reuse questions require more time for users to find the appropriate answer.

Figure 2b shows the average response days for the accepted answers. From the graph, we can see that the year where the responses took longer to be posted was 2016 with an average of 1.12 days, this was followed by 2013 with 0.89 days. Given the time when the data was collected (December 2019), 2019 might have the most unanswered questions and thus this average might be affected. The red dotted line represents the mean response time for the accepted answers of all years having a value of 0.73 days (17.52 h).

### $RQ_2$: What are the most popular technologies discussed?

*Approach.* When performing manual classification, we noted that a lot of the times posters did not tag their questions with all the used technologies or they tagged questions with technologies that had nothing to do with the content of the question. As the tags did not really represent accurate technologies, we manually classified the technologies used in terms of programming language, framework and environment. We also note that because of the nature of software development, one post could have been tagged with multiple target programming languages, frameworks or environments.

*Results.* Figure 3a shows the top 10 programming languages used when discussing software reuse in $SO$. We can see that Java was the most used one with 159 posts, followed by JavaScript and C# with 141 and 121 posts respectively. This findings suggest a similar list to the ones we can find on different programming languages ranking indexes such as Tiobe[4] and PYPL[5] where the leading positions tend to be occupied by Java, Python and C in recent years. Although our results do not show C as one of the highest used languages, it is understandable as it is not an object-oriented language where software reuse is often encouraged and one of the goals of using such type of languages. In our list, SQL stands with 33 associated posts this was formed by grouping together all found SQL dialects such as: MySQL, PLSQL, PostgreSQL and TSQL. We would also like to reflect on the number of questions that were not tagged with any programming language, this category accounted for 475 posts (around 34% of classified data). However, not all of these posts were really left without a programming language as, at times, we were simply not able to identify the used language. The list of programming languages with the highest amount of posts with no accepted answers highly resembles the list at the top 10 used programming languages. The list indicates Java and JavaScript with 67 and 61 posts respectively, as the most challenging languages, although this might be highly influenced by the number of posts related to these languages.

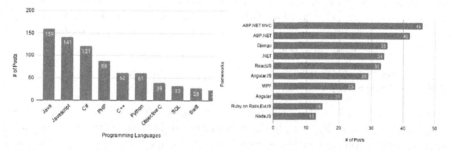

(a) **Top 10 most used programming languages.**     (b) **Top 10 most used frameworks.**

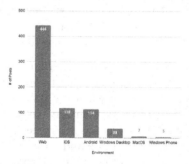

(c) **Most targeted environments.**

**Fig. 3.** Most popular technologies discussed alongside software reuse.

---

[4] https://www.tiobe.com/tiobe-index/.
[5] http://pypl.github.io/PYPL.html.

Figure 3b presents the most used frameworks when discussing software reuse in *SO*. As can be seen on the graph, the .NET family of framework stands as the most mentioned ones with ASP.NET MVC at the top of the list with 46 associated posts, followed by ASP.NET with 42 posts. Django, with 35 posts, is third on the list being the most used framework for the Python programming language. The JavaScript programming language stands as the language with the most related frameworks on this list, having ReactJS, AngularJS, NodeJS and ExtJS, which when added together would be placed 2nd only behind the .NET family.

Figure 3c displays the most targeted environments. It shows a great difference between the first and second place, having Web with 442 posts followed by IOS with 118. Although when looking at the data on a higher level (Web, Mobile and Desktop), the difference between the first and second place would be reduced. When combined, the Mobile environment stands with a total of 243 posts. The desktop environments are distributed between the Windows platform and the MacOS being the target of 38 and 7 posts respectively. This result indicates how relevant the development of mobile application has been in recent years, with an overwhelming difference when compared to the desktop environments. Moreover, the posts that target Web environments, due to their nature, might have had an underlying intention of being utilized exclusively in mobile devices which would increase their count.

### $RQ_3$: What is the trend of software reuse questions since the creation of Stack Overflow?

*Approach.* In order to obtain the temporal trends of the overall number of posts for each year, we queried our obtained dataset and plotted the results in a graph. To assess the evolution of the technologies, we considered the top three most used programming languages according to our previous findings. For the frameworks, we grouped together the different families of frameworks belonging to the programming languages associated with the most used frameworks, resulting in .NET family, JavaScript Frameworks and Python Frameworks. Similarly, for the environments, we created the following groupings: Web, Mobile and Desktop.

*Results.* Figure 4 shows the temporal trends regarding the number of posts for each year. As can be seen, there is an increasing trend from 2008 to its peak in 2012. From there until December 2019 when the data was collected there has been a decrease in the number of posts with the exception of 2016 which had more posts than the previous year. This trend suggests that due to the wide adoption of code reuse and how it is more and more taught as a fundamental programming practice, developers don't need much help to achieve software reuse as compared with other aspects of software engineering. It is hard to determine the reason for the peak in 2012, because as our *complete dataset* shows, almost all technologies presented an increase in their numbers for this year. However, when looking at the original tags that the posters tagged their questions with, IOS showed an increase from 7 posts in 2011 to 25 in 2012. Furthermore, when querying the complete *SO* data dumps to search for the temporal trends of the

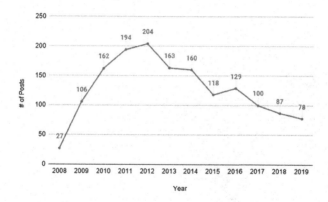

**Fig. 4.** Temporal trend of software reuse posts.

**Table 3.** Temporal trend of the most used technologies

| Technologies | Total | 2008 | 2009 | 2010 | 2011 | 2012 | 2013 | 2014 | 2015 | 2016 | 2017 | 2018 | 2019 |
|---|---|---|---|---|---|---|---|---|---|---|---|---|---|
| Java | 159 | 0 | 5 | 14 | 24 | 25 | 17 | 18 | 16 | 8 | 14 | 14 | 4 |
| Javascript | 141 | 0 | 3 | 8 | 11 | 11 | 20 | 13 | 13 | 19 | 20 | 7 | 16 |
| C# | 121 | 0 | 10 | 19 | 13 | 18 | 15 | 18 | 9 | 8 | 5 | 3 | 3 |
| Total | 421 | 0 | 18 | 41 | 48 | 54 | 52 | 49 | 38 | 35 | 39 | 24 | 23 |
| ASP.NET Family | 95 | 4 | 13 | 12 | 21 | 12 | 9 | 3 | 4 | 7 | 6 | 4 | 0 |
| Python Frameworks | 43 | 0 | 2 | 13 | 5 | 4 | 3 | 6 | 3 | 1 | 3 | 2 | 1 |
| JS Frameworks | 125 | 0 | 1 | 3 | 6 | 11 | 17 | 12 | 10 | 17 | 17 | 12 | 19 |
| Total | 263 | 4 | 16 | 28 | 32 | 27 | 29 | 21 | 17 | 25 | 26 | 18 | 20 |
| Web | 444 | 5 | 30 | 49 | 62 | 46 | 52 | 38 | 27 | 39 | 41 | 32 | 23 |
| Mobile | 243 | 0 | 4 | 22 | 42 | 40 | 34 | 32 | 27 | 14 | 11 | 11 | 6 |
| Desktop | 56 | 2 | 9 | 12 | 4 | 6 | 6 | 2 | 4 | 6 | 5 | 0 | 0 |
| Total | 743 | 7 | 43 | 83 | 108 | 92 | 92 | 72 | 58 | 59 | 57 | 43 | 29 |

usage of the *"ios"* tag, we can see that the number of posts from 2011 to 2012 almost doubled (from 41,139 to 80,276), an increase that was not seen for any other two consecutive years. This might be in relation to new features released by Apple regarding their development kit in the early months of 2012 or during 2011 (as some technologies might take some time to be fully adopted by the developers).

As seen on Table 3, almost all of the technologies had the less amount of occurrences in 2008, this is clearly due to 2008 being the year with the less amount of posts (27). The JavaScript programming language, as well as the JS Frameworks and the Web environment (where other two technologies are almost always used), presented the highest number of posts for 2019 showing how relevant these technologies are nowadays.

$RQ_4$: **What categories emerge when discussing software reuse?**

*Approach.* We showcase the results of our manual classification, performed in Sect. 2.3.

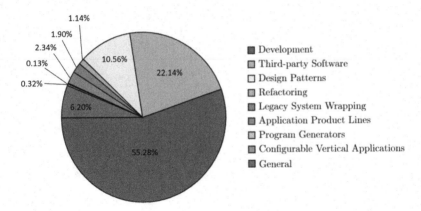

**Fig. 5.** Number of posts per category.

*Results.* Figure 5 shows the number of posts associated with each category. As can be seen, Development is the most discussed category in our dataset with 874 posts. This suggests that achieving software reuse is relevant within a single project or application. When analyzing the posts, we noted that a lot of times, in order to better receive answers from the community, posters extract away most of the aspects of their projects, thus leaving a precise and concise problem that falls under this category but that if completely described might have completely fallen under a different one.

Reusability is one of the quality attributes that speeds up the development process, because of this, it is not surprising that the second category with the most posts (350) is about reusing between projects or systems, as one of the goals in the industry is always to achieve fast releases of their products. Moreover, we expected the Third-party Software category to be one of the most discussed as it includes posts regarding the usage of program libraries and APIs which are widely used nowadays in software development.

Design Principles or Patterns are created to provide general solutions to common problems, which is why we expected this category to be among the most discussed ones, it consisted of 167 posts. We noted that a lot of the questions under this category were pertaining to the Inheritance design principle which, in simple terms, focuses on grouping coming functionality in a super class, resulting in avoiding to have the same pieces of code in multiple child classes. For the classification process, we did not take into consideration the DRY ("Don't Repeat Yourself") principle as basically all posts belonging to software reuse are about achieving this principle.

Although Refactoring is widely implemented to reduce code duplication (some IDEs even provide automatic ways of achieving this) we did not find many posts (18) that actively discussed this topic. When looking at the tags used by the posters, we found 28 occurrences of the refactoring one, but only 9 of those posts were classified as belonging to this category.

The Legacy System Wrapping and Application Product Lines category had a moderate amount of posts associated with them with 30 and 37 respectively. Because of how specific the Configurable Vertical Applications category can be, there were not many posts (only 5) belonging to this category. The category with the least amount of posts (2) was the one regarding the creation of code through code generation tools.

The General category contained 98 posts. It was interesting to see that many posts in this category, although we can not say that we were not expecting them to exist. Some of the questions in this category were related to people asking about how to achieve software reuse for personal knowledge and interestingly enough, others were asking about how to implement code reuse practices or achieving reusability in a company wide scheme.

## 4    Conclusion

In this paper, we presented insights regarding how developers discuss software reuse by analyzing Stack Overflow. These findings can be used to guide future research and to assess the relevancy of software reuse nowadays. Our findings show that software reuse is a decreasing trend in Stack Overflow which might indicate that developers have widely adopted this practice and thus few questions regarding it emerge as it is well grasped by the community. On the other hand, they might indicate that, since software reuse is so deeply embedded in achieving good quality software and is often taught as an essential quality attribute, that it has spread to a wide variety of topics and thus the questions are not posted solely as reusability or code reuse issues. Our study opens the door for software reuse researchers to further understand the software reuse challenges.

**Acknowledgements.** This material is based on work supported by the National Science Foundation under Grant No. 1757680.

## References

1. Ahmaro, I., Abualkishik, A., Yusof, M.: Taxonomy, definition, approaches, benefits, reusability levels, factors and adaption of software reusability: a review of the research literature. J. Appl. Sci. **14**, 2396 (2014)
2. Alshangiti, M., Sapkota, H., Murukannaiah, P., Liu, X., Yu, Q.: Why is developing machine learning applications challenging? A study on stack overflow posts. In: International Symposium on Empirical Software Engineering and Measurement, pp. 1–11, September 2019
3. Asaduzzaman, M., Mashiyat, A.S., Roy, C.K., Schneider, K.A.: Answering questions about unanswered questions of stack overflow. In: 10th Working Conference on Mining Software Repositories, pp. 97–100 (2013)
4. Barua, A., Thomas, S.W., Hassan, A.E.: What are developers talking about? An analysis of topics and trends in stack overflow. Empirical Softw. Eng. **19**(3), 619–654 (2014)
5. Younoussi, S., Roudies, O.: All about software reusability: a systematic literature review. J. Theor. Appl. Inf. Technol. **76**, 64–75 (2015)

# Author Index

Abbas, Muhammad 173
Abderrahmane, Seriai 152
Abdul Basit, Hamid 135
Adepoju, Benjamin 261
AlOmar, Eman Abdullah 245, 261, 292
Alrubaye, Hussein 245
Alshoaibi, Deema 245
Andonoff, Eric 35
Anquetil, Nicolas 119, 152

Babur, Önder 135
Barinas, Diego 292
Belfadel, Abdelhadi 3
Ben Said, Imen 35
Benmerzoug, Amine 279
Benzarti, Imen 100
Bonner Cherifi, Chantal 3
Bouassida, Nadia 229
Bouaziz, Rafik 35
Bowman, Jordan 261
Bragagnolo, Santiago 152
Brand, Mark van den 135

Chaâbane, Mohamed Amine 35
Chen, Yuting 190
Chouchen, Moataz 208
Costiou, Steven 87

Derras, Mustapha 119, 152
Diltz, Christopher 19
Djareddir, Fatiha 119
Ducasse, Stéphane 119, 152

Enoiu, Eduard 173
Etien, Anne 119

Graiet, Mohamed 69

Hamel, Lazhar 69
Hamid, Brahim 52
Hammad, Muhammad 135
Houekpetodji, Mahugnon H. 119

Jaskolka, Jason 52
Johnson, Logan 19

Laborde, Pierre 87
Lahouij, Aida 69
Laval, Jannik 3
Le Pors, Éric 87
Leshob, Abderrahmane 100
Lindskog, Claes 173
Liu, Jiaqian 292
Lopez, Kevin 261

Mili, Hafedh 100
Mkaouer, Mohamed Wiem 208, 245, 261, 292
Moalla, Nejib 3

Newman, Christian 261, 292
Niu, Nan 19

Oukharijane, Jamila 35
Ouni, Ali 208, 245, 261, 292

Plantec, Alain 87

Rodriguez, Philip T. 261
Rouland, Quentin 52

Saadatmand, Mehrdad 173
Sakhrawi, Zaineb 229
Sellami, Asma 229
Shen, Beijun 190
Sudich, Jerôme 119

Sundamark, Daniel    173

Toullec, Clotilde    119

Verhaeghe, Benoit    119

Wang, Tianjia    261
Wu, Qinyue    190

Yessad, Lamia    279

Ziadi, Tewfik    279

Printed in the United States
By Bookmasters